A CONCISE DICTIONARY OF CONSTRUCTION

Frederic H. Jones, Ph.D.

CRISP PUBLICATIONS, INC.
Los Altos, California

A CONCISE DICTIONARY OF CONSTRUCTION

Frederic H. Jones, Ph.D.

CREDITS

Editor in Chief: **Frederic H. Jones, Ph.D.**
Associate Editor: **Regina Sandoval**
Contributing Editors: **Linda Sandoval**
                      Judith Jones
                      William J. Fielder

Library of Congress Catalog Card Number
Jones, Frederic H., Ph.D.
A Concise Dictionary of Construction
ISBN 1-56052-068-X

INTRODUCTION

Concise Dictionary of Construction

This project has truly been a labor of love. Words have been a fascination for me all my life. I have collections of dictionaries, glossaries, word lists, etc. in many languages and on many subjects. I suppose it was just a matter of time before I was compelled to undertake a word list project of my own. I hope you find it both interesting and useful.

Many of the words and definitions included here were provided by historic dictionaries of architecture and design including the late 19th century edition by Russell Sturgis. Many of the illustrations have also been derived from these sources. In all cases the language and definitions were updated when necessary. Another primary source of words and their definitions were various associations and trade organizations. They include: The Illumination Engineering Society, Carpet and Rug Institute, Western Institute of Cabinetmakers, and many others. I wish to acknowledge their invaluable assistance and hasten to add that errors, no doubt, derive from my translation rather than from their creation.

My hope is that this and the other dictionaries in the series serve as introductory aids to students of design and architecture. The need to know both the meaning of obscure words and the obscure meanings of familiar words is one that a student of any profession encounters early in their studies. In fact the very "putting on of the mantle" of the language of the profession is the very essence of engaging the profession. We find ourselves sounding and thinking like designers and eventually we become the thing we emulate. This list of words will serve as an incomplete but helpful map on this journey.

I, in the process of editing this dictionary, encountered many words and illustrations that would extend beyond the scope of any single dictionary. I have also been very involved in the contemporary process of automating the very word management and drawing management tools essential to design practice. I speak of the computer of course. I therefore have combined the extensive database of words and images and the computer and am making available an electronic "encyclopedia" of architecture and design. If you are interested in this product please contact me at 39315 Zacate Avenue, Fremont, CA 94538.

Frederic H. Jones, Ph.D.

A

Abandonment: When a contractor stops work on a job before it is completed and removes all equipment and material.

Abated: In stone cutting, hammered metal work, and the like, cut away or beaten down, lowered in any way, as the background of a piece of ornament, to show a pattern or figure in relief.

Abatement: See asbestos abatement.

Abrasion resistance: A material's ability to resist rubbing and scraping without wearing away.

Abrasion-finished surface: A surface that results from sanding with disks coated with abrasives of different grain sizes.

ABS: Abbreviation for acrylonitrile-butadiene-styrene.

Absenteeism: Prolonged or chronic absence from duty or work.

Absolute coordinates: Coordinates based on points measured from a fixed origin in x, y, or z axes.

Absolute pressure: The total pressure measured from absolute vacuum. It equals the sum of gauge pressure and atmospheric pressure corresponding to the barometer (expressed in pounds per square inch) (kilo Pascals).

Absolute temperature: Temperature measured from absolute zero. A point of tem-perature theoretically equal to -459.73° F (-273.18° C). The hypothetical point at which a substance would have no molecular motion and no heat.

Absolute zero: Zero point on the absolute temperature scale. A point of total absence of heat, equivalent to -459.73° F (-273.18° C).

Absorbents: Sound-absorbing materials.

Absorption: (A) Capillary, osmotic, or chemical action by which fibers, yarns, or fabrics become intermixed with liquids or gases. (B) The dissipation of light within a surface or medium.

Absorption: The immersion in a fluid for a definite period of time, usually expressed as a percent of the weight of the dry pipe. The property of a material that allows it to take up liquids and to assimilate them.

Abstract of bids: A summary of prices prepared by an owner for a given job, based on bids received from contractors to select the contractor to be awarded the job and of informing all bidders.

Abuse coverings and finishes: Jackets or mastics used to protect insulation from mechanical abuse.

Abut: To touch or join by its end, as in a timber where the end grain is planted against another member of a structure, but without framing; or where an arch bears upon a pier, course of stone, skew back, or the like.

Abutment: A surface of a structure on which a body abuts or presses. Specifically, (A) That which takes the weight and thrust of an arch, vault, or truss; usually that part of the wall or pier that may be supposed to be the special support of the construction above. In the case of a series of arches or trusses, the term usually applies to the comparatively heavy piers at the ends and not to the intermediate supports, unless very large. Hence, by extension but incorrectly, the masonry or rock to which the cables of a suspension bridge are anchored. (B) In carpentry, the joining of two pieces so that their grain is perpendicular.

Abuttal: A piece of ground that bounds on one side of the lot or plot under consideration. Thus, the owner has to be careful not to encroach upon his abuttals by walls or substructures except by party wall agreement, or the like.

Acatia: A dense wood, resembling rosewood, used in making furniture with turned parts and handles. It is yellowish-red to reddish-brown in color and native primarily to Australia.

Acceleration: When a contractor is required to complete work at an earlier date than originally scheduled. See constructively accelerated.

Accent lighting: Directional lighting to emphasize a particular object or draw attention to a part of the field of view.

Acceptance inspection: An inspection that must be performed before the acceptance of a project or any part thereof for payment.

Acceptance periods: Intermediate milestones for partial completion established in a contract, with provisions for owner's inspection and acceptance of work completed up to that point before continuation of other work.

Acceptance: The essential elements of an acceptance are: (A) The offeree (recipient) must know of the offer; (B) The offeree must show an intention to accept; (C) The acceptance must be unconditional; and (D) The acceptance must be made according to the terms of the offer.

Accelerator: Any material added to gypsum plaster that speeds up the natural set.

Access door: Hinged panel mounted in a frame with a lock, normally mounted in a wall or ceiling, to provide access to concealed valves or equipment that requires frequent attention.

Access unit, Hand hole, or Junction box: An opening with a removable cover to provide access to the header and distribution ducts or cells.

Access: (A) Freedom or ability to enter, communicate with, or pass to and from; (B) An approach to premises.

Accessible (handicapped): Site, building, facility, or portion thereof that can be approached, entered or used by physically handicapped people.

Accessories: Linear formed metal, meal and paper, or plastic members fabricated to form corners, edges, control joints, or decorative effects in conjunction with gypsum board and plaster assemblies.

Accident: A sudden, unexpected event identifiable as to time and place.

Accommodation: The process by which the eye changes focus from one distance to another.

Accordion door: A door constructed with joined portions of wood that will fold together.

Account code structure: The system used to assign summary numbers to elements of the work breakdown and charge (account) numbers to individual work packages.

Account number: A numeric identification of work package (also known as shop order number, charge number, or work order number). An account number may be assigned to one or more activities.

Accumulator: A container in which fluid or gas is stored under pressure as a source of power.

Acid vent: A pipe venting an acid waste system.

Acid Waste: A pipe that conveys liquid waste matter containing a pH of less than 7.0.

Acknowledgement: A formal notice of acceptance of an order that usually states delivery date.

Acme thread: A screw thread, the section of which is between the square and V threads, used extensively for feed screws. The included angle of space is 29% as compared to 60% of the National Coarse of U.S. Thread.

Acoustic: Used with a basic sound property.

Acoustical plaster: A finishing plaster designed to correct sound reverberations or reduce noise integrity.

Acoustical tile: Tiles or sheets that are acoustical absorbents.

Acoustical: Used in the control of sound.

Acoustics: The science of the control and transmission of sound. The unit of measure of sound is the decibel. Zero decibels is no sound. Normal conversation is 45-60 decibels. Hearing injury can occur at more than 100 decibels.

Acrylic coating cured with radiation process: A coating over particleboard that meets the requirements of the Woodwork Institute of California. The coating meets the requirements of NEMA LQ 1-77, Light Duty, and shall be as manufactured by Willamette Industries product known as KorTron/EB.

3

Acrylonitrile-butadiene-styrene (ABS): A high-impact plastic. A thermoplastic compound from which fittings, pipe and tubing are made.

Active sludge: Sewage sediment, rich in destructive bacteria, that can be used to break down fresh sewage more quickly.

Activity description: A condensed explanation of the nature of the work to be performed, which easily identifies an activity to any recipient of the schedule.

Activity duration: The length of time from start to finish of an activity, estimated or actual, in working or calendar time units.

Activity splitting: Breaking down a big activity into smaller parts to allocate resources or technology better on the project.

Activity times: Time information generated through the CPM calculation that identifies the start and finish times for each activity in the network.

Activity total slack: The latest allowable end time minus earliest allowable end time. The activity slack is always greater than or equal to the slack of the activity ending event.

Activity: Any definable and time-consuming task, operation, or function to be executed in a project.

Actual completion date (Actual finish date) (TA): The calendar date on which an activity was completed. This date should be no later than the report date.

Actual costs: Program or project expenditures.

Actual start date: The calendar date on which the activity began. It must be prior to or equal to the data date.

Adaptation: The process by which the visual system becomes accustomed to more or less light than it was exposed to during an immediately preceding period. It results in a change in the sensitivity of the eye to light.

Adapter fitting: (A) Any fittings designed to mate, or fit, to other two pipes or fittings that are different in design, when connecting the two together would otherwise not be possible. (B) A fitting that serves to connect two different tubes or pipes to each other, such as copper tube to iron pipe.

Addendum: Written or graphic instrument issued before the receipt of bids that modifies or interprets the bidding documents, including drawings and specifications, by additions, deletions, clarifications, or corrections (will become part of the contract documents).

Addition (to contract sum): An amount added to the contract sum by a change order to reimburse the contractor for extra work or for unanticipated additional costs or damages for performing the work in the original contract, occasioned by delays or interference not the fault of the contractor. See extra or change order.

Addition (to the structure): A construction project physically connected to an existing structure, as distinct from alterations within an existing structure.

Additive alternate: An alternate bid resulting in an addition to the same bidder's base bid. See alternate bid.

Additive: An admixture added to a product at the mill during manufacture. See admixture.

Addressable system smoke detector: System of smoke detectors that in addition to providing alarm and trouble indication to a control unit, communicate a unique identification (address).

Adhesion: The property of a material that allows it to bond to the surface to which it is applied.

Adhesive, type I, fully waterproof: Forms a bond that will withstand full weather exposure and be unaffected by microorganisms; bond shall be of such quality that specimens will withstand shear and cyclic boil tests specified in PS 51-71.

Adhesive, type II, water-resistant: Forms a bond that will retain practically all of its strength when occasionally subjected to thorough wetting and drying; bond shall

be of such quality that specimens will withstand the coat soak test specified in PS 51-71.

Adhesive: A substance capable of bonding materials by surface attachment. It is a general term and includes all cements and glues.

Administrative authority: The individual official, board, department, or agency established and authorized by a state, county, city, or other political subdivision created by law to administer and enforce the provisions of the plumbing code.

Admixture: A substance, a chemical or color, added to a mixture of concrete or plaster, usually water repellent.

Adobe: Sundried mud bricks used for construction in Latin America, Spain, and the American Southwest.

Advertisement for bids: Published public notice soliciting bids for a construction project. Often used to conform to legal requirements pertaining to public projects and usually published in newspapers of general circulation in the geographic area from which the public funds are derived.

Aeration: An artificial method in which water and air are brought into direct contact with each other. One purpose is to release certain dissolved gases that often cause water to have obnoxious odors or disagreeable tastes. Also used to furnish oxygen to waters that are oxygen deficient.

The process may be accomplished by spraying the liquid in the air, bubbling air through the liquid, or by agitation of the liquid to promote surface absorption of the air.

Aerobic: Bacteria living or active only in the presence of free oxygen.

Affidavit of noncollusion: A sworn statement by bidders that their proposal prices were arrived at independently without consultation among them.

Agency: (A) Relationship between agent and principal. (B) Organization acting as agent. (C) Administrative subdivision of an organization, particularly in government.

Agent: A person authorized to act on behalf of another person.

Aggregate: Foreign material such as rocks or pebbles mixed with cement to form concrete. Exposed aggregate is concrete that contains decorative aggregate processed to expose to surface view. The word used in connection with plastering usually means sand, vermiculite, or perlite.

Agreement form: A printed contract describing the general provisions of an agreement, with spaces provided for insertion of specific data relating to the project.

Agreement: (A) A meeting of mind, (B) A legally enforceable promise or promises between two or more persons. (C) A construction project document which states the essential terms of the construction contract that incorporates by reference the other contract documents. (D) The document setting forth the terms of the contract between two parties, such as the architect and owner, the architect and a consultant, etc. See agreement form and contract.

Air, compressed: Air at any pressure greater than atmospheric pressure.

Air, free: Air that is not contained and subject only to atmospheric conditions.

Air, standard: Air having a temperature of 70° F (21.1° C), a standard density of 0.0075 lbs/ft (0.11 kg/m) and under pressure of 14.70 p.s.i.a. (101.4 kPa). The gas industry usually considers 60° F (15.6° C) as the temperature of standard air.

Air ambient: The air that surrounds an object.

Air break: A physical separation in which a drain from a fixture, appliance, or device indirectly discharges into a fixture, receptacle, or interceptor at a point below the flood level rim of the receptacle, to prevent backflow or backsiphonage.

Air chamber: A continuation of the water piping beyond the branch to fixtures, finished with a cap designed to eliminate shock or vibration of the piping when the faucet is closed suddenly.

Air changes: The amount of air exchanged in space volumes. This explains the amount of air moving in and out of a building.

Air circulation: The movement of air.

Air cleaner: A device that filters and washes the impurities from the air.

Air conditioned space: Building area supplied directly with conditioned air.

Air conditioning, central: A conditioning system that will manage the temperature and dehumidify and purify the air.

Air cooling: Reducing air temperature by reducing heat.

Air diffuser: An outlet that discharges air-conditioned air.

Air drain: A flue arranged to provide a supply of air to a fireplace, or the like.

Air-dried: Wood that has been naturally dried by the atmosphere.

Air entrainment: Intentionally introducing into Portland cement plaster in its plastic state a controlled number of minute disconnected air bubbles well distributed throughout the mass to improve flow and workability or to improve other desired characteristics in the mortar.

Air fitting (air bonnet, air hood, air saddle, air box): A fitting mounted to an air-handling luminaire which connects to the primary air duct by flexible ducting. It normally contains one or two volume controls.

Air gap: The unobstructed vertical distance through the free atmosphere between the lowest opening from any pipe or faucet conveying water or waste to a tank, plumbing fixture receptor, or other device and the flood level rim of the receptacle. Usually required to be twice the diameter of the inlet.

Air sampling-type detector: A sampling-type of detector consists of piping or tubing distribution from the detector unit to the areas to be protected. An air pump draws air from the protected area back to the detector through the air sampling ports and piping or tubing. At the detector, the air is analyzed for fire products.

Air shaft: A vertical or nearly vertical space reserved for the free passage of air. It can be small, like an air drain, air duct, or air flue, or large enough to form a small courtyard among high buildings.

Air test: A test applied to the completed plumbing system before the building is plastered.

Air-dried lumber: Lumber that has been piled in yards or sheds for any length of time. For the United States as a whole, the minimum moisture content of thoroughly air-dried lumber is 12% to 15% and the average is somewhat higher. In the south, air-dried lumber may have a moisture content no lower that 19%.

Airway: A space between roof insulation and roof boards for movement of air.

Alarm (signal) indicating appliance: An electromechanical appliance that converts energy into audible or visible signal for perception as an alarm signal.

Alarm check valve: A check valve, equipped with a signaling device, which will annunciate a remote alarm, when sprinkler heads are discharging.

Alarm signal: A signal indicating an emergency requiring immediate action, as an alarm for fire from a manual box, a water flow alarm, an alarm from an automatic fire alarm system, or other emergency signal.

Alarm verification feature: A feature of automatic fire detection and alarm systems to reduce unwanted alarms wherein automatic fire detectors must report alarm conditions for a minimum period of time or confirm alarm conditions within a given time period after being reset to be accepted as a valid alarm initiation signal.

Alarm: Any audible or visible signal indicating existence of a fire or emergency requiring response and emergency action by the fire fighting service. The alarm device or devices by which fire and emergency signals are received.

Alder: A hardwood that is light-brown in color, finishes nicely, and will not absorb water very well.

Alkalinity: The tendency of a material to have a basic alkaline reaction. The tendency is measured on the scale, with all readings above 7.0 alkaline and below 7.0 acidic.

Alkyds: Plastics that are resistant to acids and oils and can withstand high temperatures. They are used for lacquer and enamel as a liquid and light switches, motor insulation, and fuses as a solid. These plastics are very strong.

All-purpose compound: A joint treatment compound that can be used as a bedding compound for tape, a finishing compound, and a laminating adhesive or texturing product.

All-service jacket (ASJ): A jacket of white, chemically treated kraft paper reinforced with fiberglass yarn mesh and laminated to aluminum foil. Used as a vapor barrier on insulation.

Alley: A narrow passageway (A) Between two houses, like a very narrow street. (B) In or under a house, as affording passage directly to the inner court or yard without entering the rooms of the house. (C) A walk in a garden; (D) An aisle, as in a church (obsolete). (E) An aisle in the modern sense, that is a passage between the pews, more accurate in this sense than aisle. (F) A long and narrow building.

Alligator cracks: See check cracks.

Alligatoring: Coarse checking pattern characterized by a slipping of the new paint coating over the old coating to the extent that the old coating can be seen through the fissures.

Allowance (cash allowance): An amount established in the contract documents for inclusion in the contract sum to cover the cost of prescribed items not specified in detail, with provision that variations between such amount and the finally determined cost of the prescribed items will adjust the contract sum.

Allowance: An agreed-upon reduction of length, width, or thickness of a block or length and width of a slab. The allowance is the measure of the entire block or slab.

Alloy pipe: A steel pipe with one or more elements other than carbon that give it greater resistance to corrosion and more strength than carbon steel pipe.

Alloy: A substance composed of two or more metals or a metal and nonmetal, usually fused and dissolving in each other when molten.

Alpha (alfa): Designates alphabetical characters rather numerical (number) characters.

Alpha gypsum: Denotes a class of specially processed calcined gypsum having properties of low consistency and high strength.

Alterations: (A) A construction project comprising revisions within or to an existing structure, as distinct from additions to an existing structure. (B) Remodeling or retrofit.

Alternate bid: Amount stated in the bid to be added to or deducted from the amount of the base bid if the corresponding change in project scope or alternate materials or methods of construction is accepted.

Alternate route: A secondary communications path used to reach a destination if the primary path is unavailable.

Alternate: A different approach or design and generally requiring a separate bid.

Alternating current (AC): Flow of electricity that cycles or alternates direction many times per second. The number of cycles per second is referred to as frequency. Most common frequency used in this country is 60 Hertz (cycles per second).

Aluminum: A metal combined chiefly with bauxite. It is extremely light and resists moisture and corrosion.

Amaranth: A hardwood, purplish-red in color, used chiefly for marquetry and veneering.

Ambient lighting: General lighting or lighting of the surrounding (rather than task lighting or the lighting of the object one is looking at). It can be produced by direct lighting from recessed surface or stem-mounted luminaries, or by indirect lighting, which is wall or stem mounted, built into furniture, or free standing.

Ambient temperature: The prevailing temperature in the immediate vicinity or the temperature of the medium surrounding an object.

Ambient: Surrounding. Generally applied to temperature of the medium, usually air, surrounding the object under consideration.

Ambulant disabled: Physically disabled people who can walk.

American standard pipe thread: A type of screw thread commonly used on pipe and fittings.

Ampacity: The current a conductor can carry continuously without exceeding its temperature rating. Ampacity is a function of cable size, insulation type, and the conditions of use.

Ampere rating: The continuous current carrying capability of a fuse under defined laboratory conditions. The ampere rating is marked on each fuse. Class L fuses and E-rated fuses may be loaded to 100% of their ampere rating. For all other fuses, continuous load current should not exceed 80% of fuse ampere rating.

Amperes (amps or A): The unit of measurement of electric current.

Anaerobic: Bacteria living or active in the absence of free oxygen.

Anathyrosis: A smooth dressing of the outer contact band of a masonry joint.

Anchor bolts: Bolts to secure a wooden sill plate to concrete or masonry floor or wall.

Anchor: A device used to secure pipes to the building or structure. A piece of metal that joins building parts such as plates or joists.

Anchorage: The means by which slabs or any stone product is attached to a self supporting structure.

Andirons: Metal frames or platforms used to hold firewood above the floor of a fireplace and thereby provide air circulation for combustion.

Angle iron: A 90°-angled iron bar used as lintel support. Metal section sometimes used as main runners in lieu of channels.

Angle of bend: In a pipe, the angle between radial lines from the beginning and end of the bend to the center.

Angle valve: A device, usually of the globe type, in which the inlet and outlet are at right angles.

Angle of incidence: An angle perpendicular to the surface upon which a lighted ray falls.

Anhydrite: The mineral consisting primarily of anhydrous calcium sulfate, $CaSO_4$.

Annealing: A process that strengthens flintglass by heating it and then allowing it to cool off.

Annunciation: A visible or audible indication.

Anti-abrasive coating: Material applied to prevent wearing away of insulation at its joints or at contact with pipe or equipment.

Anticlastic: A surface with curvatures both concave and convex through any point. A hyperbolic parabolic roof is an example.

Antisweat: Any application that prevents condensation.

Antisyphon trap: A trap designed to prevent the syphonage of its water seal by increasing the diameter of the trap outlet leg so that it contains enough water to prevent syphoning.

Apex stone: The top stone in a gable end. Also called a saddle stone.

Apparatus closet: A suitable enclosure large enough to contain key telephone system apparatus power equipment, terminating facilities for key telephone system

and services, and central office and PBX lines. Apparatus closets may also serve as equipment closets, zone closets, or riser closets, according to the design of the underfloor raceway or riser system.

Apparent intent: The accepted purpose in carrying out a particular act.

Appearance covering: A material or materials used over insulation to provide desired color or texture.

Applewood: A light-colored wood more important for its fruit than the small pieces of furniture it produces.

Appliance: Equipment such as electrical fans and toasters that consume currents.

Application for payment: Contractor's written request for payment of amount due for completed portions of the work and, if the contract so provides, materials delivered and suitably stored pending their incorporation into the work.

Application temperature limits: Temperature for safe application of finishes, adhesives, and sealants.

Appraisal: Professional evaluation of the market value or worth of land, facilities, or property.

Apprentice: A person learning a skilled trade, usually four years of formal training.

Approval, engineer's or architect's: Written or imprinted acknowledgement that materials, equipment, or methods of construction are acceptable for use in the work, or that a contractor's request or claim is valid.

Approved equal: Material, equipment, or method approved by the architect or engineer for use in the work as being acceptable as an equivalent in essential attributes to the material, equipment or method specified in the contract documents.

Approved testing agency: An organization established to test approved standards and acceptable by the administrative authority.

Approved: Acceptable under an applicable standard cited for the proposed use under procedures and authority of the administrative authority.

Apron: A raised panel below a window sill. An addition or extension to the front of a stage platform.

Arbitration: Method of settling disputes between parties to a contract. The arbitrator is selected for their specialized knowledge in the field, to hear the evidence and render a binding decision.

Arc tube: An enclosure usually found on fluorescent, mercury, quartz, or high-pressured sodium lamps, made of glass or ceramic.

Arch, abutment: That arch of a series that comes next to the outer abutment, as the land arch of a bridge.

Arch, back: An arch carrying the back or inner part of a wall, where the exterior face of the wall is carried in a different way; as above a window opening, which has a stone lintel for the outer part of the wall and a concealed arch carrying the inner part.

Arch, basket handle: A three-centered arch of the more usual kind. The term might equally well be applied to a five-centered or seven-centered arch having the same general form.

Arch, bell: An arch resting upon two corbels with curved face or edge, so that the resulting compound curve has a distant resemblance to the outlines of a bell.

Arch braces: A pair of curved braces forming an arch.

Arch, built: One composed of material other then masonry and put together with rivets, spikes, or the like; therefore not depending upon the mutual support of *voussoirs* nor a solid ring of masonry. The simplest form is the laminated arch. The elaborate forms are more usually called arched truss or arch truss. Instances of this latter class can be seen in New York City at the Grand Central railway station and the Washington Bridge.

Arch, camber: Same as flat arch; so called because it is usual to give to the intrados, and sometimes to the extrados, a very slight camber. This arch has a scarcely perceptible segmental curve.

Arch, catenarian: An arch whose intrados or central line is a catenary curve. Extremely rare in architecture, though not uncommon in engineering.

Arch, contrasted: An ogee arch, or one with a reverse curve.

Arch, cusp: One that has cusps or foliations worked on the intrados. Also called foiled or lobed arch.

Arch, cycloidal: One whose intrados or center line is a cycloid; a form thought to have been recognized in the architecture of India.

Arch, diaphragm: A transverse arch across the nave of a church.

Arch, diminished: An arch having less rise or height than a semicircle, whether segmental, multicentered, or elliptical. The term is not in common use.

Arch, discharging: Built over a lintel or similar closure or opening in a wall and intended as an appliance for throwing the load above an opening to the piers on both sides, thus relieving the lintel or flat arch from the danger of fracture or dislocation. In an arched doorway, where there is a tympanum under the arch or a lintel with a glazed light above it, the arch is considered the principal thing, and the lintel, or transom, an accessory. Here the term discharging arch would hardly be used. In some cases the discharging piece of whatever nature is concealed.

Arch, drop: (A) A pointed arch in which the two centers are nearer together than the width of the arch, so that the radii are less than the span. (B) One in which the centers or some of the centers are below the springing line, as in basket handle arch. Also called depressed arch.

Arch, equilateral pointed: See pointed arch.

Arch, extradosed: One that has the extrados clearly marked, as a curve exactly or nearly parallel to the intrados. This differs from an arch whose *voussoirs* are cut with horizontal returns so as to pass into the masonry of the wall. The extradosed arch has then a well-marked archivolt.

Arch, flat: One having a horizontal or nearly horizontal intrados and, in most cases, a horizontal extrados as well. A flat arch with slightly concave intrados is called a camber arch. When built of brick, the radiation of the *voussoirs* is effected in cheap work by the thickening of the joints outward; in finer work, by cutting or rubbing the brick to the required taper or using specially molded bricks. Such arches are for square-headed openings and in fireproof flooring between steel or iron beams.

Their transverse weakness and great thrust make them undesirable for heavy structural work, and in walls they are consequently often relieved by discharging arches. Fireproof floor arches are built of specially designed hollow *voussoirs* burned very hard that can sustain a heavy load up to seven or eight feet span. Also called straight arch.

Arch, foiled: Same as cusped arch.

Arch, hand: One turned without centering, usually by the aid of a board whose edge is cut to the required curve, and serving as a template.

Arch, hanse (haunch arch; haunched arch): Arch whose crown has a different curve from the haunches, which are thus strongly marked. Usually a basket handle or three-centered or four-centered arch.

Arch, horseshoe: Arch whose curves are carried below the springing line so that the opening at the bottom of the arch is less than its greatest span. Also called moorish arch.

Arch, inverted: One whose springing lines are above the intrados and the intrados above the extrados. Such arches are used in foundations where very narrow piers have to be given a wider bearing upon the soil. The conditions are almost precisely similar to those of arches resting upon piers and with a superincumbent mass. In lofty modern buildings inverted arches are not common, since engineers prefer to give to each pier an unyielding and inelastic support. Also called inflected arch.

Arch, jack: Same as flat arch; also any arch doing rough work, or slightly or roughly built.

Arch, laminated: One built of thin pieces of material, such as boards, which are successively bent to the curve, each around the one below, and finally bolted or spiked together. Such pieces are laid so as to break joints and may be used 10 or 20 thick in a single laminated arch.

Arch, lancet: A pointed arch whose centers are farther apart than the width or span of the arch.

Arch, land: In a bridge or viaduct crossing a stream or valley, one of the two arches that come next to the bank and that spring from the exterior abutment.

Arch, metal: A sheet steel formed arch for use as base (lath) or corner reinforcement at arched openings in partitions.

Arch, oblique: Same as skew arch. The term is also applied improperly, to a rampant arch.

Arch, ogee: One having a reverse curve at the point. The name is most often applied to an arch that has only two centers on the springing line (in this, like an ordinary pointed arch) and two centers for the reversed curve but many ogee arches have four centers for the arch proper and two for the reverse curve.

Arch, ogival: A pointed arch of the type most common in Gothic architecture.

Arch, pointed: One in which two curves meet at the crown at an angle, more or less acute. Ordinary two-centered pointed arches are called lancet or acute, equilateral, and blunt.

Arch, rampant: One in which the impost on one side is higher than that on the other. Thus, in a stone balustrade for a staircase, the small arches supporting the hand rail spring upward from the top of one baluster to the top of another. The curve may be of any shape which allows imposts to be placed continually higher from one end to the other of the arcade. Also called raking arch.

Arch, rear: An arch spanning a window opening or doorway inside a wall.

Arch, rollock or row-lock: One in which the bricks or other very small pieces of solid material are arranged in separate concentric rings. Such arches are common in simple brick masonry.

Arch, round: One of semicircular curve, usually limited to one that is very slightly stilted, if at all, so that its appearance is of a semicircle and no more above the imposts.

Arch, safety: A discharging arch; an arch thrown over a lintel to relieve it or under a bearing to distribute it over a larger surface of wall.

Arch, scheme: Same as diminished arch. The term seems to be derived from the Italian *scemo* (diminished or lowered).

Arch, segment arch (segmental arch): Arch that has concentric segments of circles for the curve of its intrados and extrados and whose center, therefore, is a certain distance below the angle made by the impost with the inner face of the abutment, such as the jamb of a door or window.

Arch, skew: One in which the archivolt on either side is in a plane not at right angles with the face of the abutment. Thus, if a doorway is carried through a thick wall in a direction not at right angles with the face of that wall, the arched head of that doorway would be called a skew arch, being really a barrel vault whose axis is at an oblique angle with the face of the wall.

Arch, splayed: An arch opening that has a larger radius at one side than at the other. Like the skew arch, this is a vault rather than an arch proper. An accurate term for it would be conical vault.

Arch, stilted: One in which the architectural impost, with its moldings, abacus or, string-course, is notably lower than the springing line, so that the intrados passes into the vertical jamb of the opening. This is continued downward as if a part of the

15

intrados. The whole archivolt follows this form.

Arch, straining: An arch used as a strut, as in a flying buttress.

Arch, surbased: A depressed arch; an arch of which the rise is less than half the span.

Arch, surmounted: A stilted semicircular arch; a semicircular arch of which the center is above the impost.

Arch, three-lobed: One of which each haunch is developed into a cusplike form so that the archivolt itself, if there is one plainly distinguished, or the intrados alone assumes the form of a trefoil.

Arch, transverse: The arched construction built across a hall, the nave of a church, or the like, as part of the vaulting, or to support or stiffen the roof in some other way, or to furnish a solid substructure for the centering.

Arch, triangular: (A) The corbel arch of the Maya. (B) A structure composed of two stones that support one another and span an opening.

Arch, trimmer: An arch, usually of brickwork and very low rise, built between the trimmers where a floor is framed around a chimney breast. Its thrust is taken up usually by the stiffness of the header on one side and the brickwork of the chimney breast on the other. It supports the hearth of the fireplace in the story above.

Arch, Tudor: A four-centered pointed arch so called because common in the architecture of the Tudor style in England.

Arch corner bead: A corner bead so designed that it can be job-shaped for use on arches.

Arch: (A) A structural member rounded vertically to span an opening or recess. In this original sense the term is used either for a decorative or memorial building, of which an upward curving member forms the principal feature and spans a gate or passage below, or for the member itself, considered as a firm and resistant curved bar capable of bearing weight and pressure. (B) A mechanical means of spanning an opening by heavy wedge-shaped solids that keep one another in place, and which transform the vertical pressure of the superincumbent load into two lateral components transmitted to the abutments. The shape is immaterial, although arches are generally curved. The width or thickness horizontally is also immaterial, although an arch that acts as a roof and covers much horizontal space is called a vault.

Mechanically, an arch may be considered as any piece or assemblage of pieces so arranged over an opening that the vertical pressure of the supported load is transformed into two lateral inclined pressures on the abutments.

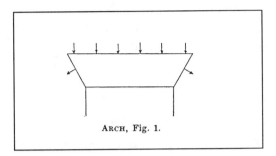

ARCH, Fig. 1.

Considered in this light, then, the stone window head shown in Fig. 1 is truly an arch. The stone is wedge-shaped, the load on it has a tendency to force this wedge down into the window opening by pushing the adjoining masonry away to the right and left, as shown by the arrows.

An arch slightly more elaborate is the primitive arch shown in Fig. 2. Here two wedge-shaped stones lean against each other, each transmits pressures similar to those just described, and the pressures at the respective upper ends counteracting each other. This form of arch may be compared to a pair of rafters whose tie beam has been removed and its function fulfilled by a weight at the feet of the rafters.

ARCH, FIG. 3.

To go a step farther, we have an arch made of three stones, as shown in Fig. 3. Each stone acts as an independent wedge tending to force its way inward, thereby exerting a lateral pressure at each of its oblique ends. The combination of all six pressures results in a lateral push on each abutment, as shown by the arrows. This lateral push (Figs. 2 and 3) is similar to that in Fig. 1, from which it differs in direction, owing to the inclination of the end pieces. Were these more steeply inclined they would evidently exert a push more nearly vertical. Hence, the higher the arch in proportion to its span, the less lateral push it will exert. These considerations apply equally well to all of the arches shown in Fig. 2 or to any other similar construction of wedge-

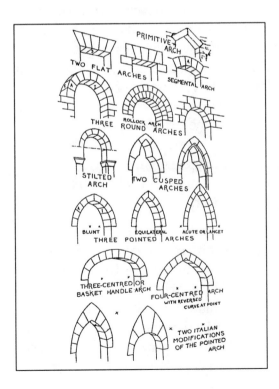

shaped pieces. It will also be observed that, in the case of two or more such wedges, each one is acted upon by the adjoining pieces, which tend to force it outward; this tendency is overcome only by proper and more or less uniform distribution of the loads to be carried. Lateral pressure on the abutment is known as thrust. Resistance to this force was the subject of constant experiment in church buildings of the Middle Ages, resulting in the elaborate systems of engaged and flying buttresses. Arches may be divided according to their form into the following classes: (1) the flat arch; (2) arch with one center: (a) semicircular or round arch; (b) segmental arch; (c) horseshoe arch; (3) arch with two centers: (a) equilateral pointed arch; (b) lancet arch; (c) drop arch or blunt pointed arch; (d) pointed horseshoe arch; (e) drop arch in the second sense. These five varieties are called pointed arches; the first three are used in many styles. (4) arches with three centers: (a) basket handle arch; (b) round arch with reversed curve at crown; (5) arches with four centers: (a) pointed arch in which two of the centers are on the springing line and two below; (b) two-centered arch that is prolonged at top with a reversed curve (see ogee arch). A six-centered arch might be composed by giving to the form (6) a reversed curve as in the other instances, and such subdivisions may be continued indefinitely. Thus a five-centered arch might be developed out of the basket handle arch, and so on. An arch is divisible into the haunches, or reins, and the crown. An arch is made up of *voussoirs*, of which there may be one in the middle occupying the center of the crown and called a keystone. The inner side of the arch ring is called the intrados. The outer side of the arch ring is called the extrados, or back. When an arch is laid down on paper, the horizontal line that passes through the center in the plane of the arch (if there is but one) or that connects two centers and (except in one- or two-centered segmental arches) marks the place where the curve of the arch joins the vertical line of the abutment is called the springing line. The height from the springing line to the intrados (or to the line which in a drawing represents the intrados) is the height or rise, sometimes called the versed line. The width between these two points of juncture is the span. The section of an arch that forms a part of the face of the wall is called the face of the arch, or archivolt. Parts of the construction immediately dependent upon or connected with an arch are the abutment, impost, skew back, spandrel, and springer.

Architect-engineer (A/E): (A) An individual or firm offering professional services as both architect and engineer. (B) The design team including the architect and consulting engineers of various disciplines retained by the architect as subcontractors. (C) The person or firm designated by the owner as its agent to be responsible for design and other designated professional services, who may be either a licensed architect or professional engineer, depending on the type of construction involved.

Architect: Designation reserved, usually by law, for a person or organization professionally qualified and duly licensed to perform architectural services, which can include analysis of project requirements, creation and development of the project design preparation of drawings, specifications and bidding requirements, and general administration of the construction contract.

Architectural terra cotta: Clay that is burned and used in building units.

Architectural: (A) Pertaining to architecture; as, an architectural publication or drawing. (B) Having the character of a work of architecture; as, an architectural composition. (C) Composed or treated in accordance with the principles of architecture; as, an architectural decoration.

Area drain: A receptacle designed to collect surface or rain water from a determined or calculated open area.

Area method (of estimating cost): Estimating probable total construction cost by multiplying the adjusted gross for area by a predetermined cost per unit of area.

Area: The plane surface within certain boundaries.

Areaway: An open subsurface space adjacent to a building used to admit light or air or as a means of access to a basement.

Armed services procurement regulation (ASPR): Formerly the primary procurement regulation of the Department of Defense and military services. These were replaced by the Defense Acquisition Regulations and, in April 1984, by the Federal Acquisition Regulations.

Arris: A sharp edge, forming an external corner at the junction of two surfaces.

Arrow diagraming method (ADM): A method of constructing a logical network of activities using arrows to represent the activities and connecting them head to tail.

Arrow: The graphic representation of an activity in the CPM network. One arrow represents one activity. The arrow is not a vector quantity and is not drawn to scale, uniquely defined by two event codes.

Arterial vent: A vent serving the building drain and the public sewer.

Article: (A) A subdivision of a document. (B) In project specifications, the primary subdivision of the section, often further subdivided into paragraphs, subparagraphs, and clauses. (C) An item of equipment or material.

As-built drawings: Drawings prepared by a contractor after completion of a job indicating variations from the original design drawings, particularly in regard to concealed locations of mechanical and electrical work, to permit maintenance thereof and to preclude damage from future alterations.

As-built schedule: The final project schedule that depicts the start and completion date, duration, costs, and consumed resources for each activity.

Asbestos abatement: Procedures to control fiber release from asbestos-containing building materials. Includes encapsulation, enclosure, and removal.

Asbestos: A mineral so fibrous that it can be woven into a naturally incombustible textile fabric; it also conducts heat slowly. Its chief use in building has been for steam pipes and floor coverings. Asbestos has been declared a health hazard and is now banned from use in most building material.

ASC standard form of agreement: A prime contract document form developed by ASC for use between the owner and a specialty contractor.

Ash: A hard, flexible, straw-colored wood similar to oak in grain.

Ashlar, bastard: Thin blocks or slabs of stone used to face walls of brick or rubble and treated to resemble solid blocks of stone. This material is often set edgeways, or with natural bed nearly vertical.

Ashlar, broken: Stones of different sizes and shapes, though always rectangular on the face.

Ashlar, coursed: Stones arranged according to height, so as to form regular courses in the face of the wall.

Ashlar, random coursed: Formed by squared stones of irregular sizes, but laid to form high courses, each of which is laid as a band of broken ashlar.

Ashlar, random range: Same as broken ashlar.

Ashlar, rough: Rough stone, little or not at all dressed after quarrying.

Ashlar masonry: Rectangular units of burned clay used in masonry.

Ashlar pece: A roof element consisting of a short vertical timber connecting an inner wall plate to a rafter above.

Ashlar (ashler): Masonry blocks hewn with even faces and square edges and laid in horizontal courses with vertical joints. This is in contrast to rubble or unhewn stone. (A) Squared and finished building stone; in recent times, especially, such stone when used for the face of a wall whose substance is made of inferior material. The term has usually a general signification, and a single piece would be called a block of ashlar; rarely, an ashlar. An attempt has been made to limit the term to stone which is set on its edge, that is to say, not on the quarry bed, and in this way to serve as a translation of the French adjectival phrase *en delit*; but there seems to be no authority for this limitation. (B) Attributively, and in combination, having the appearance of, or to be used in the place of, ashlar, as a veneer. (C) A vertical stud between the sloping roof and flooring in a garret or roof story, by a series of which vertical walls are provided for the sides of rooms, and the angular space near the eaves partitioned off either as waste space or as low closets.

Aspect ratio: The ration of CRT display width to display height.

Asphalt cut-back: Petroleum asphalt in mineral solvents. This is a vapor-barrier mastic.

Asphalt emulsion: Petroleum asphalt in water. This is a breather mastic.

Asphalt: (A) Natural mineral pitch or bitumen, as from the great Pitch Lake in the island of Trinidad. (B) An artificial compound, as of coal tar, sand, and lime; or of natural asphalt or some other form of bitumen with vegetable pitch, sand, and other ingredients. Either of these preparations is used for street paving and making walls and vaults watertight.

Aspirator: A fitting or device supplied with water or other fluid under positive pressure that passes through an integral orifice or constriction causing a vacuum.

Assembly: A group of combined functional parts that make cabinets and doors, etc.

Assigned subcontractor: A subcontractor selected by the owner as a result of negotiation or competitive bidding who is assigned to the prime contractor to function thereafter as a subcontractor. Called nominated subcontractor in other countries.

Associate (associated) architect: An architect who has a temporary partnership, joint venture, or employment agreement with another architect to collaborate in the performance of services for a specific project or series of projects.

Astragal: A molding attached to one of a pair of swinging doors, against which the other door strikes.

Atmospheric vacuum breaker: A mechanical device consisting of a check valve opening to the atmosphere when the pressure in the piping drops to atmospheric.

Atomizer: Device by which air is introduced into material at the nozzle to regulate the texture of machine-applied plaster.

Attenuation, sound: To reduce sound by absorption or diminishing sound energy.

Attic ventilators: Screened openings that ventilate an attic space. They are located in the soffit area as inlet ventilators and in the gable end or along the ridge as outlet ventilators. They can also consist of power-driven fans used as an exhaust system see louver.

Attorney in fact: A person authorized to act in behalf of another person or organization to the extent prescribed in a written instrument known as a power of attorney.

Audio: Frequencies audible by the human ear (usually between 15 Hz and 20 Hz).

Audit: To examine with intent to verify.

Authority having jurisdiction: The organization, office, or individual responsible for approving equipment, installation, or procedure.

Authorize: To give final approval.

Autoclaved lime: See lime.

Automatic fire alarm system: A system of controls, initiating devices, and alarm signals in which initiating circuits are activated by automatic devices, such as fire detectors.

Available fault current: The maximum short circuit current that can flow in an unprotected circuit.

Avodire: An African wood, light yellow in color with a clear grain, used primarily for furniture making.

Award: A communication from an owner accepting a bid or negotiated proposal which creates legal obligations between the parties.

Axe: In French, the axis, the central or determining line, *(en axe)* or placed upon the axis, as of something else, or symmetrically disposed about the axis.

Axial plan: A building planned along an axis or longitudinally.

Axial: (A) Pertaining to an axis, as in the expression, an axial line. (B) Situated on an axis, as any member of a building, either existing or shown in a drawing. The term is not common in architectural writing, but occurs sometimes as a substitute for *en axe* and to avoid circumlocution.

Axis: (A) In architectural drawing, a central line, not necessarily intended to form a part of the finished drawing, but laid down as a guiding line from which may be measured figure dimensions of rooms, the widths of openings, etc. A primary axis may pass through the middle of the ground plan. There may be as many subsidiary axes as the different rooms, wings, pavilions, or other primary parts of the building may require. (B) An imaginary line to which is referred the parts of an existing building or the relations of several buildings to one another. (C) One of three perpendicular lines intersecting at a common point in space.

B

Back charges: Charges for claimed services rendered or materials furnished by a contractor to a subcontractor without prior approval, usually deducted from progress or final payments made to the subcontractor.

Back order: An order that is to be shipped sometime in the future.

Back painting: A procedure in which a glass pane is made transparent by gluing on print and painting or tinting the back.

Back priming: A coat of paint applied to the backside and edges of woodwork or exterior siding to prevent excessive absorption of moisture.

Back putty: After the glass has been face puttied, it is turned over, and putty is run into any voids that may exist between the glass and the wood parts.

Back vent: See individual vent.

Back-siphonage: The flowing back of used, contaminated, or polluted water from a plumbing fixture or vessel into the potable water supply pipe due to a negative pressure in such pipe see backflow.

Back-up: (A) A condition where the waste water may flow back into another fixture or compartment but not backflow into the potable water system. (B) The portion of a wall that is behind the exterior facing.

Back: (A) To provide with a proper back; to finish the back of; especially, to trim or adjust the back or top of a rafter, joist, or the like to the proper level of the whole tier. (B) The further side of any part of a building, or what may have seemed more remote to the designer. (C) The rear of a building, where both of the longer faces of a large building are treated with nearly equal architectural effect, that face which has not the principal entrance will be the back. (D) The upper surface of a member, as the back of a hand rail; the back of an arch, meaning the extrados. (E) In composition, the reverse or inner side; a lining or the like.

Backband: A simple molding sometimes used around the outer edge of plain rectangular casing as a decorative feature.

Backfill: Material used to cover piping laid in an earthen trench. The replacement of excavated earth into a trench around and against a basement foundation.

Backflow connection: A condition in any arrangement whereby backflow can occur.

Backflow preventer: A device or means to prevent back-flow into the potable water system.

Backflow: The flow of water or other liquids, mixtures, or substances into the distributing pipes of a potable water supply from any source or sources other than its intended source see back-siphonage.

Backing out: Wide, shallow groove machined in back surface of members.

Backing ring: A metal strip used to prevent melted metal, formed in welding, from entering a pipe when making a butt-welded join.

Backward pass-calculation: Calculation of the late finish time, late start time for all uncompleted network activities or late time for events in ADM method.

Backwater valve: Permits drainage in one direction but has a check valve that closes against back pressure. Sometimes used conjunctively with gate valves designed for sewage.

Baffle plate: A tray or partition placed in process equipment to direct or change the direction of flow.

Baffle: An opaque or translucent element that shields a light source from direct view at certain angles or absorbs unwanted light.

Bag trap: A water seal trap with a shape resembling an inflated bag.

Balancing species: A species, of similar density, to achieve balance by equalizing the rate of moisture absorption or emission.

Balcony: A platform projecting from a wall, door, or window sill and enclosed with a railing. It may be cantilevered or supported by brackets or columns.

Ball check valve: Stops the flow of media in one direction while allowing flow in an opposite direction. The closure member used is spherical.

Ball cock: A faucet valve that is opened and closed by the fall or rise of a ball floating on the surface of a water container. The water's elevation is controlled wholly or in part by the faucet valve.

Ball valve: A spherical-shaped gate valve providing very tight shut-off.

Ballast: An auxiliary device consisting of induction windings wound around a metal core that sometimes includes a capacitor for power correction. It is used with fluorescent and HID lamps to provide the necessary starting voltage and to limit the current during operation.

Balloon framing: In the United States, a system of framing wooden buildings in which the corner posts and studs are continuous in one piece from sill to roof plate, the intermediate joists being carried by girts spiked to, or let into, the studs, the pieces being secured only by nailing, without the use of mortises and tenons, or the like.

Balusters: Usually small vertical members in a railing used between a top rail and the stair treads or a bottom rail.

Balustrade: A railing made up of balusters, top rail, and sometimes bottom rail, used on the edge of stairs, balconies, and porches.

Band puller: A device, usually handmade, consisting of light-gauge wire through a short length of tubing. Used by insulators to tighten applied jacket bands.

Band: A flat molding. An aesthetic element that limits the usable dimensions of a slab surface.

Banding tool: A device to tighten bands on insulation.

Banding: A piece of wood used for decoration on furniture of a different color or grain. Metal or plastic strapping to secure bundles of gypsum products together in a shipping unit.

Bank the job: A slang expression generally used in a negative sense when referring to an obligation of a contractor to make payments to subcontractors for work performed when the owner has not paid this money to the contractor. The term is also used negatively by subcontractors as an expression of what the general contractor expects them to do when the general contractor refuses to pay until paid.

Bar chart (GANTT chart): The most common form of scheduling used for construction work. It shows total length of time, the categories of work, and the time each is expected to take. It does not show the interrelation between the activities.

Bargeboards: Boards placed against the incline of a building or gable to hide the horizontal rafters or beams.

Barrier free: See accessible, handicapped.

Barriers: Obstructions that interfere with the intended use of a space.

Basalt: A volcanic rock lava, usually highly vesicular consisting essentially of augite and a soda lime feldspar, usually with olivine. Usually of a dark gray, sometimes almost black, color, and highly vesicular.

Base bead: See screeds.

Base bid specifications: The specifications describing only those materials, equipment, and methods of construction upon which the base bid must be predicated, exclusive of any alternate bids.

Base bid: Amount of money stated in the bid as the sum for which the bidder offers to perform the work required by the project documents. Does not include that work for which alternate bids are submitted.

Base block: A block of any material, generally with little or no ornament, forming the lowest member of a base, or itself fulfilling the functions of a base; specifically, a member sometimes applied to the foot of a door or window trim.

Base coat floating: The act of spreading, compacting, and smoothing plaster to a reasonably true plane on exterior and interior surfaces.

Base coat: The plaster coat or combination of coats applied before the finish coat.

Base line: (A) In architectural drawings, the lowest horizontal line, the line that marks the base or bottom of the design; especially, in perspective, the trace of the picture plane on the ground plane. (B) In engineering and surveying, the first line determined upon, located, and measured as a base from which other lines, angles and distances are laid out or computed in surveying or plotting a piece of ground for a map or plan.

Base or baseboard: A board placed against the wall around a room next to the floor to finish properly between floor and plaster.

Base screed: See screeds.

Base-shoe: Molding applied to a wall where it meets the floor to prevent damage.

Base: The lowest part or the lowest main division of anything, as of a column, pier, the front of a building or of a pavilion, tower, or the like. The term is used independently in the following senses: (A) The lowest of the three principal parts of a column, when the column is so divided. (B) A member of any material applied as a finish or protection at the foot of a wall, or the like, especially in interior finish, as a baseboard forming part of the wooden trim of a

room. The lowest portion or lowest point of a stack of vertical pipe.

Baseboard: A board skirting the lower edge of a wall.

Basement: (A) The lower part of the wall or walls of any building, especially when divided from the upper portions in an architectural way, as by a different material, a different and perhaps more solid architectural treatment, smaller and fewer windows, or the like. The basement may occupy only a small part of the whole height of the structure, or it may be even more than half of that height, as in some palaces of the Italian Renaissance, especially in north Italy. Frequently there is a double basement, the basement proper, serving as a foil and a support to the more elaborate story or stories above, has itself a still more massive basement, probably without openings. (B) The story that comes, behind the piece of wall above described; in this sense, an abbreviation of the term basement story. Originally, this story would have its floor almost exactly on a level with the street or courtyard. In some buildings it is raised several steps above the street, in others its floor is some distance below the street, as in city dwelling houses.

Basin: A hollow in a windowsill.

Basket strainer: A kitchen sink drain fitting, consisting of a strainer body attached to the drain opening at the bottom of the sink compartment and a removeable basket (also called a crumb cup). The strainer body has a strainer across the drain outlet. Also called a duostrainer.

Bat: A broken piece of brick.

Bathroom: A room equipped with a toilet, shower, bathtub and a sink.

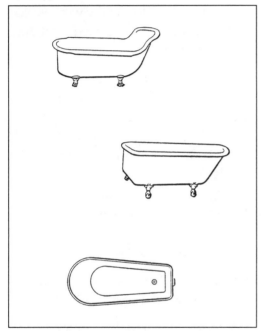

Bathtub: A water receptacle shaped to fit a human body and used for bathing.

Batt: A piece of flexible insulation cut into easily handled sizes, square or rectangular in shape, usually 24" or 48" long with a vapor barrier on one side and possibly a container sheet on the other side.

Batten plates: Tie plates at the ends of compression members or used at intervals to connect the channel beams of Z beams,

which form the column or strut, replacing, for instance, the latticing on the open side of a built strut or column.

Batten: A piece of wood that covers the connecting parts of boards or panels or furring strips for flooring or plastering. In English usage, a plank of 7" x 2-1/2" or 7" x 3", which may be cut into three boards or deals. In American usage, any thin and narrow strip of wood such as may be used for nailing over the joints between the boards of the siding of framed houses.

Battening: The affixing of battens to a wall or frame or the whole system of battens so affixed. In English usage, the application of furring strips to a wall or roof frame for plastering or to joists to receive the flooring. This is usually called furring in the United States.

Batter board: One of a pair of horizontal boards nailed to posts set at the corners of an excavation. Indicates the desired level or used as a fastening for stretched strings to indicate outlines of foundation walls.

Battery of fixtures: Any group of similar adjacent fixtures that discharge into a common horizontal waste or soil branch.

Batwing distribution: Candle-power distribution that serves to reduce glare and ceiling reflections by having its maximum output 30°-60° from the vertical and with a candlepower at nadir (0°) being 65% or less than maximum candlepower. The shape is similar to a bat's wing. In fluorescent luminaries the batwing distribution is generally found only in the plane perpendicular to the lamps.

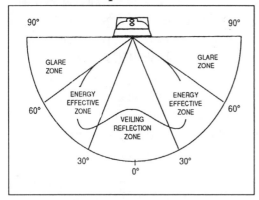

Bay window: Originally, a large window, often of many parts, and related to the modern Italian term, *balcone.* Bay means a recess or opening or one of many subdivisions of a long building. These definitions seem to have suggested its use for an enclosed structure that would form a recess, or opening, and, by means of its projection from the exterior wall, seem to constitute one subdivision, or bay, as seen from the exterior. This structure was then called bay window, and the term has no closer or more exact signification than is here explained. In some cases, the bay window is separated from the room it adjoins by a decided break in the ceiling, as by an arch or transom. The ceiling of the bay window may be lower than that of the room, or it may be continuous, and the bay window is really a prolongation, or widening, of the room.

Bay: (A) An opening, as of a window, door, or between two columns or piers. In this sense, the French *baie* should be consulted, as it is commonly used for a window. The term in England seems to include the supports, imposts, jambs and the like, on both sides of the opening. (B) In plastering, that piece of the work which is included between two screeds and done at one operation.

Bead, angle: A bead applied as a finish to an angle or corner. Specifically, a strip used in place of an angle staff as a protection to the salient angle of a plastered wall, to which it is secured under the plaster, the only visible portion being a projecting molding forming a bead at the corner. By extension, a metal contrivance for the same purpose but having no bead and arranged so as to be quite concealed by the plaster.

Bead, center: A flush bead molded at about the center of a board, or the like.

Bead, cock: A bead molded or applied so as to project beyond a surface. It is return-cocked if it occurs on the angle or arris and quirked if flanked by a groove on each side.

Bead, corner: Same as angle bead, especially in the specific sense as used in plastering.

Bead, double: Two beads side by side, there being no other surface or molding between them.

Bead, flush: One worked in material so that its rounded outside is flush with the general surface.

Bead, nosing: A molding, generally semi-cylindrical, on the edge of a board and occupying its entire thickness. Generally placed to project beyond an adjoining face, as at the juncture of a tread and riser of a staircase, where the molded projection of the tread beyond the riser is the nosing.

Bead, parting: Same as parting strip, especially when small, and having in part the form of bead.

Bead, ploughed: Same as flush bead.

Bead, quirked: A bead separated from an adjoining surface by a quirk or narrow groove along one or both sides, as is common in the case of a flush bead.

Bead, rail: A cock bead when on a uniform, continuous surface, and not at an angle, reveal, or the like.

Bead, rebate: A bead in the reentrant angle of a rebate.

Bead, return: A bead at the edge of a return, as along the edge of the salient corner of a wall.

Bead, staff: An angle staff of which the greater part forms a bead at the corner.

Bead molding: Cylindrical molding with ornament resembling a string of beads.

Bead: (A) A convex rounded molding, commonly of semicircular section. (B) A slender piece or member of wood or metal, having generally, wholly, or in part the section of a bead in sense A. (C) A sealant or compound applied in a round or ribbon extrusion.

Beaded molding: A cast plaster string of beads planted in a molding or cornice.

Beak or bird's beak molding: A continuous, slight, rounded projection manufactured onto the end of a slab or other stone product.

Beam, arched: Any beam or similar member formed with an upward curve, whether of one piece bent or cut to the required curve or made up of several parts secured together. A common form is the laminated arch which, however, acts by direct downward pressure upon its points of support and with little or no outward thrust.

Beam, bending: A beam that bends upward or downward when an extra load is applied to it.

Beam, binding: In floor framing, the beam that supports the bridging beams (or floor beams) above and the ceiling beams below.

Beam, bowstring: In British usage, a simple form of the bowstring truss.

Beam, box: An iron or steel beam, in shape like a long box with open ends, formed by two webs connected by top and bottom plates, or latticing. The webs may be either I beams, channel beams, or built beams of plates and angles. Larger or more important ones are box girders.

Beam, bridging: A floor beam carried by girders or binding beams as distinguished from one that spans the whole space between bearing walls.

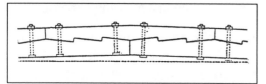

Beam, built: Any beam built of several parts, as a plate beam or a box beam. Also called compound beam.

Beam, bulb: An iron beam having a flange at one edge of the web and a nearly cylindrical rib or bar along the other edge. Its name comes from the appearance of a section of the beam showing a cross piece at one end and a rounded expansion at the other.

Beam, camber: A beam to which has been given a slight camber or upward crowning in the center to counteract any possible sagging. In England, a beam whose upper surface is cut to a slight slope from the middle toward each end, as for nearly flat roofs.

Beam, ceiling: A light joint or beam set to receive the lathing for a plastered ceiling. In English practice the ceiling joists are mortised into the binding beams or

notched into their under edges and spiked. In American practice ceiling joists are seldom used except for false ceilings under fireproof floors, the ceiling laths being usually nailed either directly to the under edges of the floor joists or to furring strips crossing the joists to whose under edges they are nailed. Their use has the advantage that heavy pressure or sudden blows upon the floor above will be less apt to injure the ceiling. Such ceilings are less apt to transmit sound.

Beam, cellular: The cellular beam or tubular bridge once popular for large bridges. It was a box beam large enough for trains to pass inside of the tube. The top, the compression member, and in a less degree the bottom, were made of cells formed by thin longitudinal partitions between their upper and lower plates. By this form of construction great stiffness and resistance to compression were obtained with a small quantity of metal. These bridges were, however, expensive to construct, difficult to repair, and remained in vogue only a short time.

Beam, channel: A beam of iron or steel of such section that it resembles a gutter or channel. It consists of a vertical web with a flange at top and bottom on one side only. Those of the smaller dimensions are commonly known as channel bars or channel irons.

Beam, collar: A tie beam in a roof truss connecting two opposite principal rafters at a level above the wall plate or foot of the truss; as, for example, in buildings whose upper story extends into the roof, the ceiling being carried by the collar beam. The collar beam is thus usually a tie taking the place of the more common tie beam. It might, however, become a strut if the horizontal thrusts of the rafters were otherwise overcome, as in some forms of truss. Also called top beam.

Beam, common: A beam to which the flooring is nailed, as distinguished from a binding joist or ceiling joist. Common joists in American practice are 2" to 3" thick and 8" to 12" deep, according to the length or span. They are ordinarily set 16" on centers or 12" for heavy or very strong floors

Beam, deck: Any beam to support a deck; specifically, same as bulb beam.

Beam, hammer: In some kinds of framing, especially for steep roofs, a short beam securing the foot of the principal rafter to the brace, strut, or tie, and in a sense replacing the tie beam. The hammer beam is usually horizontal and forms part of at least two of the triangles of construction, namely, one above connected with the principal rafter, and the other below and connected with a wall piece. The object sought in replacing the tie beam by hammer beams is usually interior decorative effect.

Beam, heading: Same as header.

Beam, I: A beam that resembles the capital letter I in the Roman alphabet, having a web that connects the upper and lower flanges at their center lines. Those of the smaller dimensions are commonly called I bars.

Beam, laced: More often lattice beam.

Beam, lattice: A beam having its top and bottom flanges connected by diagonal members forming a lattice in place of a solid web; forming, in fact, a simple truss. The term is extended to include such members when constructed with what is more specifically known as lacing.

Beam, plate: A beam or girder built with plates of rolled iron. It is used instead of standard rolled iron or steel I beams in cases where the local or structural conditions would make the latter unavailable or insufficient for the service. Such beams are built with vertical plates called webs with angle bars riveted to them on both sides at top and bottom, forming flanges, and are further strengthened where necessary by one or more horizontal plates of the total width of the flanges at top and bottom. When, for greater strength or to provide a width of top flange sufficient to build a wall or impose other superincumbent weight conveniently, two or three of such plate beams are used together, they are said to form a box beam or girder. Such girders are seldom made of greater span than 60' or of greater height than 5'.

Beam, straining: In a truss, a horizontal strut above the tie beam or above a line joining the feet of the rafters; especially, in a queen post truss, the strut between the upper ends of the two queen-posts.

Beam, strut: In a trussed structure, a horizontal member acting as a strut; a straining beam or a collar beam.

Beam, T: A beam that resembles the capital letter T in the Roman alphabet.

Beam, tie: See tie.

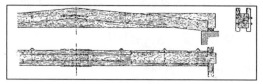

Beam, truss: Any beam built up of members, as a truss. The term is, however, usually restricted to mean a simple beam that is strengthened by the addition of two or more subordinate members by means of a bent tension rod secured to the two ends of the beam and connecting one or more vertical struts beneath its under side.

Beam, Z: A beam that resembles the letter Z of the Roman alphabet, having a web perpendicular to two flanges which it connects by their opposite edges. Those of the smaller dimension are commonly called Z bars.

Beam clip: A formed wire section used to attach lath to flanges of steel beams.

Beam hanger: A contrivance serving the purpose of a stirrup, but more elaborate and of better finish.

Beam spread: The angle enclosed by two lines that intersect the candlepower distribution curve at the points where the candlepower is equal to 10% of its maximum.

Beam: (A) A transverse horizontal timber used in roof construction. Horizontal timbers supporting floor or ceiling joists. A piece or member of which the transverse dimensions are small relative to its length; intended generally to be supported at two or more points to resist forces acting in a direction normal to its axis, but sometimes secured at one end only and sometimes acting as a member of a truss, in which case its purpose may be that of a strut but always occupying a more or less horizontal position. However, the term is still used to designate any piece of a form intended primarily for the purpose described although put to another use: thus, a steel column may be constructed of channel beams, which would then be set on end. Beams of wood or stone are usually rectangular in cross section, or nearly so. Those of iron or steel have different cross sections but are generally composed of a top and a bottom flange connected by a thin vertical web. The most common forms are the I beam, the channel beam, the Z beam, and the deck or bulb beam. Iron and steel beams are now rolled in one piece up to a depth of 2 feet. The larger sizes are made up of several pieces, and known as built beams and box beams. A large beam is frequently known as a Girder, irrespective of its use. (B) Large, horizontal cylinders or spools. Warp yarns are wound on beams and located on line in back of the weaving operation.

Bearer: Any small subordinate horizontal member, generally one of a series, to support another member or structure, as one of several small beams to carry a gutter.

Bearing partition: A partition that supports any vertical load in addition to its own weight.

Bearing plates: In pin-connected framing, reinforcing plates riveted to the web of a beam or a chord at a joint, to thicken the web and give greater bearing surface to the pin that connects the post or brace to the beam or chord.

Bearing wall: A wall that supports any vertical load in addition to its own weight.

Bearing: (A) That part of a lintel, beam, or similar horizontal weight-carrying member that rests upon a column, pier, or wall. Thus, it may be required that a beam of a certain size and span should have at each end an 8" bearing. (B) The whole length or span of a lintel, girder, or similar structure between the two points of support, that is the whole distance between the two bearings in sense A. Definition B is the one most often seen in nontechnical writing,

but in specifications the word is more commonly limited to definition A, and the word span is used for the distance between the two points. (C) Supporting, sustaining. Said chiefly of a wall or partition that supports floors or the like rather than merely encloses.

Bed mold or Bed: A flat area in a cornice, designed to have enrichment planted later. Molding that occurs between the corona and the frieze of an entablature.

Bed: (A) To give a bed to, as a stone. (B) To lay or set on a bed, as when a stone is said to be well bedded, i.e., fixed solidly upon the substructure. (C) The prepared soil or layer of cement or mortar on, or in, which a piece of material is laid, especially in masonry. (D) That face, more or less horizontal, of a stone, brick, or the like, which is in contact with a bed in the sense A or prepared for that purpose, whether beneath or on top. Such faces are known respectively as the upper and lower bed. By extension, and where no mortar is used, the upper or under flat surface of a stone prepared for building. Also the under surface of a shingle, tile, or similar piece of roofing material.

Bedding coat: That coat of plaster to receive aggregate or other decorative material of any size, impinged or embedded into its surface, before it sets.

Bedding compound: A plastic material (mastic) used to imbed insulation. Acts as a cushion, anti-abrasive, and adhesive.

Bedding in putty: Glazing whereby a thin layer of putty or bedding compound is placed in the glass rabbet, the glass inserted, and pressed onto the bed.

Beech: A hard wood, whitish to red-brown in color, that has a fine grain and is extremely dense. Beech is mainly used for flooring.

Beginning event: An event that signifies the beginning of an activity. Synonym: predecessor event.

Beginning network event: The event that signifies the beginning of a network.

Bell and spigot joint: The commonly used joint in cast iron soil pipe. Each piece is made with an enlarged diameter or bell at one end into which the plain or spigot end of another piece is inserted. The joint is then made tight by cement, oakum, lead, or rubber caulked into the bell around the spigot.

Bell: That portion of a pipe that for a short distance is sufficiently enlarged to receive the end of another pipe of the same diameter for the purpose of making a joint.

Bell trap: A trap with an inverted bell and a water seal.

Bench mark: A fixed reference mark from which heights and levels are reckoned in surveying or in laying out grounds and buildings. It is usually indicated by a notch or mark on a stone or stake firmly set at a given point of the plan.

Bending beam: A beam that bends upward or downward when an extra load is applied to it.

Bends (tube turns): Pipe, factory, or field formed, to a predetermined radii.

Beneficial clauses: The clause in a document that provides something useful or profitable.

Beneficial occupancy: Use of a project or portion thereof for the purpose intended. This generally triggers substantial completion and the transfer to the owner of certain responsibilities previously held by the contractor.

Beneficial use: (A) The right to use and enjoy property according to one's own liking or to derive a profit or benefit from it. (B) Use by an owner of mechanical or electrical equipment for its intended purpose before substantial completion of the contract as a whole. Such use under some contracts results in the declaration of the used equipment as having been substantially completed, with warranties commencing at that time and a shift of some responsibilities from contract to owner.

Benefits, mandatory & customary: Personnel benefits required: (A) By law, such as social security, worker compensation, and disability insurance. (B) Custom, such as sick leave, holidays, and vacation. (C) Those which are optional with the respective firm (such as life insurance, hospitalization programs, pension plans, and similar benefits).

Berea grit: Berea sandstone; a fine-grained, light-colored sandstone from the Berea grit (Waverly) formations in Ohio. Frequently used for building.

Berm: A level area separating a ditch from a bank.

Bevel cut: A cut on a 45% slant on any kind of object, such as glass or fabric.

Bevel: (A) The inclination of one face to another; the divergence of one part or face from the plane of another, or from a perpendicular to that plane. Thus, if a strut is to be inclined to the plate on which it is to stand, its lower end must be beveled to have an even, uniform bearing; door saddles usually have their edges beveled; parts of masonry may be beveled to form a splay about a window opening. (B) A face making a bevel in sense A. (C) An instrument consisting of two flat straight-edged legs (one or both being usually slotted) and a clamping screw by which they are set at any desired angle. Used chiefly to lay off or measure a bevel.

Bevelled edge: A slant or angled edge manufactured onto the edge of a slab; used at visible corners and joints, among other places.

Bid bond: A form of bid security executed by the bidder as principal and by a surety. See bid guarantee and surety.

Bid date: The date established (usually by the owner or the architect) for the receipt of bids for a project.

Bid errors and adjustments: Errors or omissions in a bid submitted by a contractor and adjustments made in the bid after the bid opening to compensate for such errors. This term is usually used in conjunction with laws, regulations, or policies of owners determining the circumstances under which such adjustments will be permitted.

Bid form: A form furnished to a bidder with blanks to be filled out, signed, and submitted as the bid for a project.

Bid guarantee (bid security): Deposit of cash, certified check, cashier's check, bank draft, money order, or bid bond submitted with a bid which guarantees to the owner that the bidder, if awarded the contract, will execute it in accordance with the bidding requirements and the contract documents.

Bid opening: The time, place, and date set for receiving and opening the bids for a specific project. Openings can be public or private.

Bid peddling: The practice by a subcontract bidder or supplier of offering to perform work or supply materials at a specified or nonspecified amount below the price of the preceding bidder. Also sometimes used as a synonym for bid shopping, particularly before general contractors' bids are submitted. See bid shopper.

Bid price: The sum stated in the bid for which the bidder offers to perform the work.

Bid security: See bid guarantee.

Bid shopper: Buyer who plays one proposed supplier or subcontractor against another to reduce the purchase price.

Bid time: The date and hour established by an owner, engineer, architect, or contractor for the receipt of bids. See bid date.

Bid: A complete and properly signed proposal to do all or part of the work for the sums stipulated therein; supported by data called for by the bidding requirements.

Bidder, selected: See selected bidder.

Bidder: One who submits a bid for a prime contract with the owner, as distinct from a subbidder who submits a bid to a prime bidder. A bidder is not a contractor until a contract exists between him and the owner.

Bidders, invited: See invited bidders.

Bidding and negotiation phase: A phase of the architect's services during which competitive bids or negotiated proposals

are sought as the basis for awarding a contract.

Bidding documents: Advertisement or invitation to bid. Instructions to the bidders, the bid form, and the proposed contract documents including any addenda issued before receipt of bids.

Bidding period: The calendar period beginning at the time of issuance of bidding requirements and contract documents, and ending at the prescribed bid time. See bid time.

Bidding requirements: Documents providing information and establishing procedures and conditions for the submission of bids. They consist of the notice to bidders or advertisement for bids, instructions to bidders, invitation to bid, and sample forms. See bidding documents.

Bidet: Bathroom fixture that provides quick bathing of perineal areas after using the toilet.

Bill of lading: A receipt for shipped goods to a certain destination.

Bill of materials: A list of parts represented in a drawing. In CAD this ability is usually automated. Quantity survey; a detailed listing of all items of material required for construction of a project. See quantity survey.

Billet: A large block of insulation from which pipe covering can be fabricated.

Molding made up of several bands of raised cylinders or square pieces at regular intervals. Common in Romanesque architecture.

Binder: Material or a member used to bind. (A) A binding beam or binding joist; a girder to support floor joists. (B) Loose material used to bind other pieces or materials; thus, sand or earth may be used as a binder for the crushed stone in road building. (C) In masonry, a header; a bond stone. (D) An oil or resin that forms a film. (E) Substance contained in insulation material that stabilizes the fibers.

Binding clauses: Document clauses that are obligatory to the document signers.

Birch: A hardwood used primarily for expensive furniture. Although it does not have much color, it has an extremely nice finish and can imitate walnut or mahogany.

Bird's-eye maple: A maple wood light brownish-yellow in color, decorated with dark brown circles.

Birdseye: A small central spot with wood fibers arranged around it that gives the appearance of an eye.

Bit, center: A bit used for boring across grain. It comes in sizes from 1/8" to 2".

Bit, nose: A bit for boring across or along the grain.

Bit, screw-driver: Bits made in the form of screwdrivers.

Bit, spoon: A bit for boring across grain, producing holes from 1/8" to 1/2".

Bitumen: Hydrocarbon material of natural or pyrogenous origin that may be liquid, semisolid, or solid and is completely soluble in carbon disulfide.

Black cat (slang): Any black mastic. Most commonly refers to asphalt cut-back mastic.

Black pipe: Steel pipe that has not been galvanized.

Blank flange: A solid plate flange used to seal off flow in a pipe.

Blanket, turbine: Insulation material and high temperature fabric made into an insulation unit installed on turbines and other irregular surfaces.

Blanket: Flexible insulation in sheets or rolls which may be fibrous glass, mineral wool, or ceramic fiber.

Bleeding: The diffusion of coloring through a coating from its base or substrate, such as bleeding of asphalt mastic through a paint top coat.

Blind, rolling: (A) Any blind of partially flexible structure, as of small strips of bamboo or the like, arranged to roll up, usually at the top of a window. (B) Sometimes, by extension from rolling slat or slats, one in which the slats are not fixed but free to rotate each on its own axis, the whole set being held together by a strip secured to each by a loop of wire.

Blind, venetian: A blind whose slats are made to open and close; especially, a hanging blind, of which the slats are held together by strips of webbing and controlled by cords so that they may be opened or closed at will and drawn together and packed closely above the window.

Blind stop: A rectangular molding, usually 3/4" x 1-3/8" or more in width, used in window frame assembly. Serves as a stop for storm and screen or combination windows and to resist infiltration.

Blind-nailing: Nailing in such a way that the nailheads are not visible on the face of the work, usually at the tongue of matched boards.

Blind: Having no windows; said of a building or part of a building which usually has them. Thus, a blind clerestory or a blind nave is one where the aisles rise so high on either side as to prevent the opening of windows above the aisle roofs.

Blister: A defect in the form of a slight projection of a surface detached from the body of the material. Caused in manufacturing or by weather or other agencies, as the protuberance sometimes formed on the face of a casting, due to the presence of an air bubble just below the surface; or the loose, slightly raised portions of a coat of paint which have become detached from the material to which the paint has been applied, due to defective workmanship or other causes. Protuberances on the finish coat of plaster caused by application over too damp a base coat, or troweling too soon.

Block activity: Aggregate or summary activity. A series or group of activities which span the same events are condensed as one summary activity and reported at the higher summary management level.

Block, hollow: A terra cotta slab or large brick made with an opening or several openings in its body; usually for ventilation, lightness, or economy where great strength is not needed. Those used for ventilation have two general sorts—those that when put together form a continuous tube for the passage of a current of air, and those which are intended merely to provide an air space to prevent the passage of moisture from the outside to the inside of a wall, or as a means of insulation in fireproofing. The term block is commonly used instead of brick to describe such building material made of baked clay and considerably larger than the usual bricks.

Block, concrete: Hollow or solid concrete blocks used in the construction of buildings hollow or solid.

Block printing: A block of wood with engraving of picture of patterns. Also can be done with fabrics or wallpaper.

Block-cut-finished surface: The surface that results from cutting with a diamond-disk machine. The finish is identical to that of a honed surface.

Block: (A) A piece of stone or terra cotta prepared, or partly prepared, for building. (B) A mass projecting from a larger piece of stone, as in some unfinished masonry of the Greeks. (C) In carpentry or joiner's work, any small, more or less symmetrical piece of wood, used for whatever purpose, as behind a wainscot or other work that to stand out from a wall; under any horizontal member to give it a proper level; in the angle between the sides of a box; the top and front rail of a chest of drawers or cabinet, or the like; a traditional means of giving stiffness or support where there is no room for braced framing. (D) A row or mass of buildings closely connected together, or a single structure, perhaps divided by party walls, containing shops, dwellings, or small apartment houses above them. (In this sense, peculiarly American.) (E) In a city where streets are near together, the whole space within and enclosed by three or four streets so as to present a front of houses upon each of those streets. (F) To set or provide with a block or blocks in sense of C; to secure or place in position by means of such blocks; to perform the operation of blocking. Commonly used with the adverb, as block up, block out. (G) Rigid or semirigid insulation formed into rectangular or curved shapes.

Blocking course: A projecting stone cornice at the base of a building. In classical architecture, a plain stone course with a cornice at the top of a building.

Blow molding: Thermoplastic materials formed by stretching and hardening plastic to a mold. Molten thermoplastic is shaped and put into a mold, air blown, cooled, and removed from the mold.

Blow: The distance traveled by air through an outlet.

Blue stain: A bluish or graying discoloration of the sapwood caused by the growth of certain moldlike fungi on the surface and in the interior of a piece, made possible by the same conditions that favor the growth of other fungi.

Board measure: The standard system for the measurement of lumber. A board foot is a square foot 1" thick, and hence the equivalent of 144 cubic inches. A 3" x 4" stud measures one board foot per foot of length; a 6" x 12" beam measures 6 board feet per foot of length. No allowance is made for loss by sawing, planing, or other dressing; 7/8" planed boards are reckoned as 1" thick. Lumber is sold by the board feet. The board foot, the hundred, and the M or thousand are the only units in common use.

Board: (A) A piece of lumber before gluing for width or thickness. (B) A slab of wood cut to a more or less uniform shape, and thin as compared to its width and length. Specifically, such a piece of lumber not more than about 1-1/4" inches thick. (C) To cover or sheath with boards. In housebuilding in the United States, a frame structure is said to be boarded when the frame has been covered in with the sheathing boards, previous to the addition of clapboards or shingles. (D) Rigid or semi-rigid self-supporting insulation formed into rectangular or curved shapes.

Boarding: (A) Boards in general, or a quantity of boards taken together. (B) The act of covering a surface with boards, usually by nailing to a frame of wood. (C) The covering or thickness of boards applied, as in B.

Boast: To shape stone roughly in preparation for subsequent finer dressing.

Boasted work: Rough blocked stonework prior to carving. Masonry finished with a boaster chisel.

Bodied linseed oil: Linseed oil that has been thickened by processing with heat or chemicals. Bodied oils are obtainable in a great range in viscosity from a little greater than that of raw oil to just short of a jellied condition.

Body color: A color or paint having body i.e., rendered heavy and opaque. Especially in water color work, a paint mixed with white.

Body: (A) The larger or more central mass of a building having varied parts, as a church. (B) The shaft or plain upright part of a pillar or pier. (C) Solidity, mass, or thickness, taken in the abstract; thus, it may be said that a paint lacks body. (D) The solid, firm, or full feel of a fabric. (E) The consistency of thickness of a mastic or coating.

Boiled linseed oil: Linseed oil in which enough lead, manganese, or cobalt salts have been incorporated to make the oil harden more rapidly when spread in thin coating.

Boiler blow-off tank: A vessel designed to receive the discharge from a boiler blow-off outlet to cool the discharge to a temperature that permits its safe discharge to the drainage system.

Boiler blow-off: An outlet on a boiler to permit emptying or discharge of sediment.

Boiling point: Temperature at which a liquid turns into vapor (212° F for water).

Bollard: A solid post on a quay or pier intended to receive the loops of hawsers or in other ways to serve for mooring vessels. The term is generally confined to stone posts or others of enduring materials.

Bolster: A long cylindrical bed or couch pillow. A short horizontal timber or steel beam on top of a column to support and decrease the span of beams or girders.

Bolt, barb: A bolt in which the shaft is provided with barbs pointed toward the head of the bolt, thus permitting ready insertion and, when driven, resisting an outward pull.

Bolt, barrel: A cylindrical bolt made to slide in a case which is secured to the face of a door or sash by flanges. When shot, the end enters a corresponding case or a socket.

Bolt, carriage: A small bolt having a domical or somewhat conical head, the other end being threaded for a nut.

Bolt, chain: A contrivance to secure a door when ajar. It consists of a short chain permanently secured to the frame, its outer end being attached at will in a slot on the door and arranged that the chain cannot be detached from the outside by access through the opening.

Bolt, clevis: Same as lewis bolt.

Bolt, dead: A simple form of lock consisting of a bolt shot or withdrawn by turning a knob, as distinguished from the commoner form of lock in that the bolt works by a spring.

Bolt, double ended: Having a thread and nut at each end.

Bolt, drift: A round or square bolt about 1" thick, to secure together the successive layers of timers in a grillage.

Bolt, expansion: Screw into a shell divided longitudinally into two parts that spread laterally when the bolt is screwed into it, thus making a very close connection with the sides of the hole provided for it.

Bolt, eye: A bolt whose head is a fixed ring.

Bolt, fish: Any bolt to secure a fish or fishes.

Bolt, flush: Sinks into the face of a door or sash so that the face of its case is flush with the surface.

Bolt, fox: A bolt secured by a foxtail wedge, which is forced into its inner end.

Bolt, hook: One whose head forms a hook.

Bolt, lewis: Having a dovetail shank or shaft flaring at its inner end, to be inserted in a hold of similar shape in stone or metal and secured by lead calking. Sometimes forming part of a lewis.

Bolt, mortise: Sinks in a mortise in the edge of a door or sash, so that the face of its case is flush with the surface of the edge.

Bolt, prig: Same as barb bolt.

Bolt, rag: Same as barb bolt.

Bolt, ring: An eye bolt having a loose ring held by the eye.

Bolt, screw: A bolt with a tapering point, having a screw thread, differing only by its larger size from a screw in the ordinary sense.

Bolt, spring: A bolt that is shot and retained in that position by a spring, which must be compressed, as by a knob, to allow the bolt to be withdrawn.

Bolt, stud: A bolt with a screw thread at each end one for screwing into any fixed surface, the other having a stud or nut.

Bolt-in-fuse: A fuse intended to be bolted directly to bus bars, contact pads, or fuse blocks.

Bolt: A pin or rod used to secure two or more parts or members permanently together. It can be movable, as for a temporary fastening, or fixed, to afford a more or less temporary support or means of attachment. More specifically, (A) A pin or bar, generally of wrought iron or steel, to secure parts or members together, having a head worked on one end and a screw thread and nut at the other, or sometimes nuts at both ends. Distinguished from a rod by connecting two or more members in immediate contact and as being shorter. (B) A pin, hook, or large screw driven or let into a wall, or the like, as a means generally temporary of support or suspension. Similar to a spike or screw except larger or more elaborate. (C) A length of rolled wallcovering that contains an area specified by the manufacturer. (D) An anchor, usually a metal rod or pin with a head at

one end and a screw thread at the other, that is secured with a nut.

Bolting: Threaded bolts used to hold steel together.

Bona fide bid: Bid submitted in good faith, complete, and in prescribed form, which meets the conditions of the bidding requirements and is properly signed by someone legally authorized to sign it.

Bond, American: In brickwork, a course of headers to every five or six courses of stretchers.

Bond, block and cross: In brickwork, that which leaves the wall with one face in block bond and the other in cross bond.

Bond, block: Same as Flemish bond.

Bond, block in course: In an arch built of otherwise unbonded concentric rings (as of rowlocks) a bond formed through the full depth of the archivolt of a block of bonded brick or by a voussoir inserted at intervals.

Bond, chain: Formed by building in the wall, longitudinally, a bar, strap of metal, or a timber.

Bond, clip: In brickwork, a bond formed by clipping off the inside corners of face bricks laid as stretchers so as to form notches for the insertion of diagonal headers; used the same as split bond, where it is desired to have the face composed entirely of stretchers.

Bond, common: In the United States, same as American.

Bond, cross: (A) Courses of Flemish bond alternating with courses of stretchers whose joints come opposite the centers of the stretchers in the second course above and below. (B) A modified English bond, the successive stretching courses breaking joints with each other. (C) In roofing, the amount by which one slate, tile, or shingle overlaps the second course below or sometimes the distance from the nail of one to the lower edge of the course above. In bonding masonry, the following names are given to the pieces of stone or brick, binder, header, one laid lengthwise across a wall, generally perpendicular with the face. Perpend, in stonework, a binder extending entirely through, from face to face (French *parpaing*). Stretcher, one laid lengthwise parallel with the face. Through, same as perpend.

Bond, diagonal: Raking bond, in which diagonal headers form continuous rows across the wall and bar therefore commonly joined to the face bricks by clip bond.

Bond, English: Alternate courses of headers and stretchers.

Bond, English cross: Same as cross bond (B).

Bond, Flemish: Headers and stretchers alternating horizontally and vertically, each header centered with the stretchers above and below.

Bond, flying: Formed by occasional headers at considerable intervals in a wall formed mainly of stretchers.

Bond, garden or garden wall: Same as flying bond; so called because commonly used in thin boundary walls 8" or 9" thick.

Bond, heading: Formed by a course of headers, as in American or English.

Bond, heart: The bond formed where two headers meet at the center of a wall, the joint being covered by a header above and below.

Bond, herring bone: Raking bond in which the rows of diagonal headers are laid at right angles, forming in plan a series of zigzags.

Bond, hoop iron: Chain bond formed by strap or hoop iron.

Bond, in-and-out: Formed by headers and stretchers alternating vertically, especially when formed at a corner, as by quoins.

Bond, plumb: Same as diagonal bond.

Bond, raking: Formed by diagonal headers.

Bond, ranging: Chain bond formed by small strips of wood at the face of the wall, commonly laid in the joints, and projecting slightly to afford nailing for battens, furring, and the like.

Bond, running: Formed by two overlapping stretchers. American and English bond are also frequently called running bond.

Bond, split: The face composed entirely of stretchers which are split lengthwise so that headers behind may lap the stretchers above and below, used in every fifth or sixth course to secure the face bricks; accomplishing the same result as a clip bond.

Bond, timber: Formed by a heavy timber, generally forming a chain bond.

Bond, yorkshire: Same as a flying bond.

Bond agent (Bonding agent): An independent agent, representing bonding or surety companies, who acts as the liaison between the contractor and the surety company.

Bond cource: Joints that overlap the ones below them.

Bond plaster: See gypsum.

Bond stone: See parapen.

Bond strength: The force in tension, compression, impact, or cleavage required to break an adhesive assembly.

Bond: The connection of two or more parts or members that overlap and are made to adhere more or less closely; hence,

a piece or pieces used for that purpose. Specifically, (A) In carpentry, the securing or framing of timbers by means of a third crossing them; and the timbers, placed in or on the walls, which stiffen and bind the parts of a building, as wall plates, templates. (B) In masonry, the tie or binding of the pieces made by laying one piece across two or more pieces. A piece of material used for that purpose; hence, the entire system of bonding or breaking joints as used in a masonry structure; for example, a wall may be said to be built in English bond. Incorrectly, the securing or holding together the parts of a masonry structure by the mortar or similar adhesive material.

Bonding time: Time period after application of adhesive during which the adherents may be combined.

Bonnet: That part of a valve which connects the valve actuator to the valve body; may also contain the stem packing.

Bonus clause: A provision in the construction contract for additional payment to the contractor as a reward for completing the work before a stipulated date.

Book match: A pattern used for floors and veneers, so named because the two halves of the patter are joined like pages in a book.

Border stone: A linear element obtained with a multidisk block cutter.

Boring: In building preparations a process of examining the soils or rocks beneath the surface where a building is to be erected. Boring is properly limited to the softer materials alone, such as sand, gravel, clay, and the like; but when a rock is struck it is drilled, and this is included in the general term. Different augers are used, even a common pump auger turned by a long bar screwed to its head and slowly moved by several workers; but for a proper examination of the materials beneath the surface it is customary to use an auger working through a pipe that retains a core of the excavated materials in their original relative positions. If careful note is taken of the exact depth to which the pipes had been sunk when each sample of the soil was collected, a fair notion of the soils beneath can be obtained. When a larger and smaller pipe used together, the smaller one is put within the larger, and water is forced into the space between the two pipes; the materials below, if divisible and not too firmly indurated, are then washed up through the inner pipe and may be collected at the surface.

Boss: (A) A projecting mass of stone, usually not large and commonly intended to be cut away after the completion of the work. (B) A mass projecting, as in A, but intended as a permanent feature; thus, in Gothic architecture, the molded sill course of a window, or a row of windows, is often terminated by sculptured projections of the sort. Where the different ribs meet at the top of the vault, such a piece of stone

(called by the French *def*) is an almost essential feature, and this, if treated in a decorative way, is the boss.

Boston ridge: A method of applying asphalt or wood shingles at the ridge or hips of a roof as a finish.

Bottom: The soil or other natural resisting material on which a building is founded, as at the bottom of an excavation or on which piles may bear.

Boulevard: A wide street with plants or trees down the middle.

Boundary survey: A mathematically closed diagram of the complete peripheral boundary of site, reflecting dimensions, compass bearings and angles. It should bear a licensed land surveyor's signed certification, and may include a metes and bounds or other written description.

Box trench: Built-up enclosure either in a shallow trench or buried underground.

Box-frame: Concrete construction in which the load is carried by cross walls.

Brace, angle: A brace set across the corner of a more or less rectangular structure, as at the corner of a frame house.

Brace, batter: The inclined braces at the end of a truss, as of a pratt truss.

Brace, counter: In a truss an extra or supplementary brace crossing the main brace. It is introduced in those panels that are exposed to change of shape in two directions.

Brace, portal: In ironwork, a brace approaching the form of a knee inserted in the angle between a vertical and a horizontal member to resist lateral pressure. Being commonly bent approximately to a quarter-circle, a pair of them, placed so as to face each other, will produce the effect of an arched portal.

Brace, principal, principal sway brace: A brace to stiffen a principal rafter or its supporting structure; as, especially, in the angle between a tie beam and its end-support.

Brace, purlin: In carpentry, a brace from a roof truss to relieve or stiffen a purlin between its bearings upon the principals.

Brace, sway: A brace inserted to prevent sideways motion, as under the influence of wind; therefore, usually horizontal or in the plane of the main structure. This term, common in bridge building, is rare in architecture.

Brace, wind: A sway brace designed primarily to resist the lateral action of wind.

Brace and bits: The brace is merely the handle or stock for various bits or cutters, which are places in it, and revolved continuously, with high speed; at the same time great pressure can be brought on them by resting the head of the brace against the breast.

Brace: A piece or member, generally long as compared to its lateral dimensions, used to stiffen or steady another member or structure. Specifically, bar introduced into a framework to prevent distortion, usually a diagonal in a quadrilateral. It may act either by tension or compression. The quadrilateral *abcd* may change its shape by the rotation of its sides about the joints. If the rigid diagonal brace *bd* is introduced and firmly attached, deformation is rendered impossible except by rupture of the parts. If the rectangle is exposed to deforming forces in two directions i.e., to the right or to the left in the diagram, a single rigid brace firmly attached to the frame will prevent change of shape. It is customary in such cases to introduce two diagonals, both ties or both struts as the case may be, which facilitates construction. If the four sides of the quadrilateral are rigid members, the diagonals will be ties. If two of the opposite sides are tension members, the braces will be struts.

Bracing: Strengthening a framed or other structure by means of braces; or any system or aggregation of braces. Bracing depends for its efficiency or the principal of the triangle, whose shape cannot be changed without breaking, bending, or altering the length of one or more of its sides.

Bracket: A member prepared for carrying a weight that overhangs or projects, as a projecting story of a building or a shelf. Although a bracket would not be applied often to a cantilever, corbel, cul-de-lampe, or modillion except carelessly, it covers all varieties which have no specific names of their own. The action of the bracket is two-fold: it pulls outward along the line of the horizontal top bar or edge and presses inward more solidly at the foot. If, therefore, a bracket is secured to a wall along the whole height of its vertical member, the more the horizontal member above is loaded, as with a balcony, bay window, or the like, the more of a pull is exercised upon the wall immediately below this projecting member. This may even become dangerous; and it is, therefore, customary to make the bracket a part of a floor or other horizontal member that can resist a strong outward tendency. The term is applied also to small movable objects that project from walls to resemble distantly the architectural bracket. Thus, a gas fixture for a wall opening and, equally, a support for a bust or vase hung upon a hook, received the name.

Bradawl: The simplest consists of a steel bar tanged at one end to fix in the handle and ground to a double-wedge edge at the other. It should taper slightly from the cutting edge to the haft; if the taper is reversed the wood will split in boring. It can be driven either by the hammer, or by hand pressure accompanied by a twisting motion.

Branch circuit: An electrical circuit running from a service panel having its own overload protection device.

Branch interval: A length of soil or waste stack corresponding in general to a story height, but in no case less than 8' (2.4m), within which the horizontal branches from one floor of a building are connected to the stack.

Branch tee: A tee having one side branch.

Branch vent: A vent connecting one or more individual vents with a vent stack or stack vent.

Branch: (A) A part of a system or structure that diverges from the main portion; especially in heating, ventilation, plumbing, and the like; a smaller or subordinate duct or pipe extending from the main line for whatever purpose. (B) A piece of piping having two or more arms by which a branch is connected with another or with the main line.

Brass: A metal alloy consisting of copper and zinc.

Brazing ends: The ends of a valve or fitting which are prepared for silver brazing.

Breach of contract: Failure to carry out terms of a legal contract.

Break: An interruption in the continuity of a plastered wall or cornice.

Breakdown, contractor's: See schedule of values.

Breaking load: That load, concentrated in the middle of a span, which will just break a measured sample of insulation under test.

Breakout schedule (look ahead schedule): Job-site-oriented schedule is used to communicate the day-to-day activities to all working levels on the project.

Breast: (A) The projecting portion of a chimney, especially when projecting into a room or other apartment. (B) The under side of a hand rail, beam, rafter, or the like. (C) That portion of a wall between a window sill and the floor.

Breather mastic: A mastic that permits vapor to pass through to the low pressure side.

Bressumer: Horizontal timber carrying a wall.

Brick, air: A hollow and pierced brick or piece of hard material, about the size of a brick, built into a wall with ordinary bricks to allow the passage of air.

Brick, angle: A brick shaped to any oblique angle; especially one made to fit an oblique, salient corner, as in a polygonal building.

Brick, arch: (A) Generally, a wedge-shaped brick for a voussoir of an arch. (Also called compass brick.) (B) A brick from

the arch of a brick kiln, usually more thoroughly burned and harder, and therefore regarded as more valuable for certain kinds of work.

Brick, ashlar: Brick made especially for the facing of walls in expensive and decorative work and intended to resemble ashlar. A common form has a very rough finish, so as to resemble rock-faced stone.

Brick, brick: One of a superior quality used for the face of a wall.

Brick, clinker: A very hard-burned brick, so called from its metalic sound when struck. Hardly to be distinguished from arch brick or flemish brick.

Brick, Dutch: A hard, light-colored brick originally made in Holland and used in England for pavements; hence, a similar brick made in England.

Brick, fire: One made of a refractory clay that resists great heat, used for the lining of flues, furnaces, and the like.

Brick, Flemish: Similar to Dutch brick.

Brick, floating: A brick so light that it will float on water. This brick is remarkable as a non-conductor of heat, and for its fire-resisting qualities.

Brick, furring: A hollow brick for furring or lining the inside face of a wall. Usually of the size of an ordinary brick, so as to bond readily, and grooved on the face to afford a key for plastering.

Brick, gauged: Any brick, ground or otherwise, prepared to fit accurately a given curve; specifically, same as arch brick (A).

Brick, hollow: A brick having one or more perforations forming more or less continuous ducts or channels when laid up. Used extensively for noncombustible floors and partitions, because of its lightness and fire-resisting qualities.

Brick, pilaster: A brick for constructing pilasters or slightly projecting piers, the end of which is so notched or rebated that it bonds more readily with the backing; and this increases the stiffening of the wall.

Brick, pressed: One that has been pressed, before drying, in a mold by hydraulic or other means, to become very hard, compact, and uniformly shaped.

Brick, red: In Great Britain, a brick of a more or less pronounced red color used in better classes of construction, so called to distinguish it from the common kinds, which are browner.

Brick, salmon: A soft, imperfectly burned brick; so called from its pale, salmon-like color. Also called place brick.

Brick, stone: A hard brick made in Wales and valuable as a fire brick.

Brick, ventilating: A hollow brick used as an inside lining, or in the body of a wall, so as to form continuous air ducts.

Brick, washed: A brick rendered inferior by exposure to rain before burning.

Brick, water struck: A brick in which water was used instead of sand to prevent the adhesion of the clay to the mold. This process was in use in New England before 1840, and the bricks made in this way can be recognized by peculiarities of surface.

Brick veneer: A facing of brick laid against and fastened to sheathing of a frame wall or tile wall construction.

Brick: (A) A regularly shaped piece of clay hardened in the sun or by the heat of a kiln and intended for building; commonly one of very many pieces of uniform size. The term is usually limited to pieces of clay not very thin and flat, which are called tiles; ordinary bricks are, as in parts of the United States, about 2-1/2" x 4" x 8", or, as in parts of Europe, about 2-5/8" x 4 /8" x 9". Bricks made for facework, that is, the smoother and more elegant facing of the exterior of a wall, are made of many shapes and colors and commonly laid with mortar joints much smaller than those between the common bricks in the same wall. Molded bricks are made in many patterns, and so arranged as to form, when laid up in the wall, continuous lines of molding, curves of an arch, or patterns in relief, even to the extent of having a raised leafage or the like upon their faces. (B) Baked clay in small pieces in a general sense.

Bricklaying: The art and practice of laying bricks in masonry. Because the purpose of bricklaying, when simple and confined to ordinary walls, is merely to produce a solid, almost homogeneous mass of small pieces of baked clay held together by strong mortar, the chief training given to a bricklayer is to lay bricks rapidly with fair accuracy and tolerable neatness. Face bricks are laid by men especially trained for that purpose or who have become especially skillful. The more difficult parts of bricklaying are the laying up of flues, where no lining, as of earthenware pipe, is to be used; the building of the throats of chimneys, upon the accurate adjustment of which much depends; and the doing of corbelled-out work with chimney tops and the like, all of which may be considered, together with the laying of molded brick, as unusual and ornamental parts of the trade.

Brickwork, closer: A half header often used to finish every other course of a wall or and opening.

Brickwork, English bond: Bricks laid so that alternate courses on the face of the wall are composed of headers or stretchers only.

Brickwork, English garden wall bond: Bricks laid so that three courses of stretchers alternate with one course of headers on the face of the wall.

Brickwork, Flemish bond: Bricks laid so that alternate headers and stretchers appear in each course on the face of the wall.

Brickwork, header: Brick laid so that the end shows only on the face of the wall.

Brickwork, heading bond: Courses composed only of headers.

Brickwork, nogging: Brickwork used to fill spaces between timbers in timber-frame construction.

Brickwork, stretcher: A brick laid so that the side only appears on the face of the wall.

Bridge: A structure spanning a river, ravine, etc., with space below to allow passage underneath.

Bridging ability: The capability of an insulation material or coating to span a gap over which it is applied.

Bridging: (A) A piece, or pieces, of scantling or heavier timber placed transversely between other timbers to stiffen them and distribute the weight of a load more evenly on them. (B) The setting of bridging pieces or any pieces which are to serve as struts or stiffeners between parallel beams. When the bridging between the floor joists forms a series of *x's*, it is often called cross bracing and cross bridging, in the United States.

Brightness (luminance): The degree of apparent lightness of a surface, brilliancy, concentration of candlepower. Brightness is produced by a self-luminous object, light energy transmitted through objects or reflection. Unit of measurement of brightness is the footlambert (fl).

Bringing forward: The operation of so priming or painting old work and new, when juxtaposed, that the whole shall be uniform in color and finish.

British thermal unit (BTU): Originally the amount of heat necessary to raise one pound of water one degree Fahrenheit at standard atmospheric pressure. Now established at 778.26 ft. lbs. by international agreement.

Brittle: A nonmalleable material such as glass.

Broach: A straight, slender, and pointed object. Especially (A) In ancient English usage, any spire. In local modern English usage, a spire that springs directly from the tower beneath, without any parapet or similar feature at the base. (B) In a lock, the pin over which the barrel of a key fits. (C) A pointed tool for roughly dressing stone.

Broadcast: Sending information to several stations simultaneously.

Bronze trim or bronze mounted: An indication that certain internal parts of the valves known as trim materials (stem, disc, seat rings, etc.) are made of copper alloy.

Bronze: An alloy of copper and tin usually in the proportions of about nine parts of copper to one of tin; but the proportions vary, and the metal may still be called bronze if a small amount of lead or zinc enters into it. The term is used also in combination to give names to many modern alloys in which some other metal takes the place of tin.

Brown coat: Cost of plaster directly beneath the finish coat. In two-coat work, brown coat refers to the basecoat plaster applied over the lath. In three-coat work, the brown coat refers to the second coat applied over a scratch coat. Brown coats are applied with a fairly rough surface to receive the finish coat.

Brown out: To complete application of basecoat plastering.

Bubble tight: The condition of a valve seat that, when closed, prohibits the leakage of visible bubbles.

Bubble: An internal void of air or other gas.

Buck: Often used in reference to rough frame opening members. Door bucks used in reference to metal door frame.

Buckle: To bulge or curve under excessive strain; to deviate from the normal. Describes walls and other members that suffer deflection under extreme load; of metal plates; of boards, and the like, that warp or twist because too thin or light.

Buckled plate: A metal plate, generally square, stamped, or wrought with a slight domical convexity, leaving a flat rim with straight edges. Laid on iron beams, they are commonly used because of their stiffness as a foundation for fireproof floors.

Buckled: In a special sense, corrugated; said of thin metal plates. The term was originally applied to corrugations of a peculiar form, connected with a patent.

Buckles: Raised or ruptured spots that eventually crack, exposing the lath beneath. Most common cause for buckling is application of plaster over dry, broken, or incorrectly applied wood lath.

Budget, construction: (A) The sum established by the owner as available for construction of the project. (B) The stipulated highest acceptable bid price or, in the case of a project involving multiple construction contracts, the stipulated aggregate total of the highest acceptable bid prices.

Budget, project: The sum established by the owner as available for the entire project, including the construction budget, land costs, equipment costs, financing costs, compensation for professional services, contingency allowance, and other similar established or estimated costs.

Budget: A planned allocation of resources. The planned cost of needed materials is usually subdivided into quantity required and unit cost. The planned cost of labor is usually subdivided into the hours required and the wage rate.

Builder's risk insurance: A specialized form of property insurance to cover work in the course of construction. See property insurance.

Building (house) drain-combined: A building (house) drain that conveys both sewage and storm water or other drainage.

Building (house) drain-sanitary: A building (house) drain which conveys sewage only.

Building (house) drain-storm: A building (house) drain that conveys storm water or other drainage but no sewage.

Building (house) -drain: The lowest piping of drainage system that receives the discharge from soil, waste, and other drainage pipes inside the walls of the building (house) and conveys it to the building (house) sewer which begins outside the building (house) walls.

Building (house) sewer-sanitary: A building (house) sewer that conveys sewage only.

Building (house) sewer-storm: A building (house) sewer that conveys storm water or other drainage but no sewage.

Building (house) sewer: The horizontal piping of a drainage system that extends from the end of the building (house) drain and that receives the discharge of the building (house) drain and conveys it to a public sewer, private sewer, individual sewage-disposal system, or other approved point of disposal.

Building (house) subdrain: That portion of a drainage system which cannot drain by gravity in the building (house) sewer.

Building (house) trap: A device, fitting, or assembly of fittings installed in the building (house) drain to prevent circulation of air between the drainage of the building (house) and the building (house) sewer. It is usually installed as a running trap.

Building (house): A structure built, erected, and framed of component structural parts designed for the housing, shelter, enclosure, or support of persons, animals, or property of any kind.

Building entrance cable: The cable that crosses the property line and terminates within a building. Building entrance cables (feeder cable) is the link between the telephone company's distribution facilities and the in-building cable system.

Building inspector: A representative of a government authority employed to inspect construction for compliance with applicable codes, regulations and ordinances.

Building paper: Paper used in immediate connection with building, usually either to provide warmth or deafen sound. Many patent papers are in the market they are usually of heavy and soft material, as thick-

ness is needed while strength would be unimportant. The use in the United States of paper applied between the first sheathing and the outer clapboards in all kinds of frame buildings has proved most useful to the comfort of the houses so protected.

Building permit: A permit issued by appropriate governmental authority allowing construction of a project in accordance with approved drawings and specifications.

Building supply pipe: The first section, after the water meter, of building water supply piping.

Building system: Means plans, specifications, and documentation a system of manufactured buildings or for a type or system of building components, which may include structural, electrical, mechanical, plumbing, and fire protection systems and other building systems affecting life safety.

Built-ins: Furniture such as bookcases, cabinets, bars, or window seats built into closets or niches.

Built-up level: A floor level elevation change of one or more risers not exceeding four vertical feet.

Built-up roof: A roof composed of layers of felt mopped with hot asphalt and usually topped with gravel.

Built-up: Assembled at the construction site.

Bull head tee: A tee, the branch of which is larger than the run.

Bull nose trowel: A rounded end tool for applying cement or mastic.

Bull nose: External angle that is rounded to eliminate a sharp corner. Used largely at window return and door frames. Advantages are ease of cleaning and durability. Can be made by running with plaster or obtaining a bull nose corner bead with the proper radius.

Burl: In softwoods, a distortion of the grain due to injury of the tree. In hardwoods, a whirl or twist of the grain near a knot but does not contain a knot. It must have a sound center. The measurement of the burl is the average of the maximum and minimum dimensions of the burl. (A) Very small burl does not exceed 1/2" in diameter. (B) Small burl-does not exceed 3/4" in diameter. (C) Medium burl-does not exceed 1" in diameter.

Burst pressure: That pressure which can be slowly applied to a valve at room temperature for 30 seconds without causing rupture.

Bush-hammering: A process of rough texturing concrete after it is set. A bush-hammer with a grooved head is used to texture the surface.

Bushing: A pipe fitting for connecting a pipe with a female fitting of larger size. It is a hollow plug with internal and external threads.

Busways (busbar, busduct): Copper or aluminum conductors.

Busy hour: That time during a business day when the largest volume of communication is handled.

Butt joints: On pipe insulation, any joints that join two similar materials. The junction where the ends of two timbers or other members meet in a square cut joint.

Butt strips: Strips of jacket applied around pipe insulation end joints.

Butt weld joint: A welded pipe joint made with the ends of the two pipes butting each other, the weld being around the periphery.

Butt weld pipe: Pipe welded along a seam butted edge to edge and not scarfed or lapped.

Butt: The end or back of a member or piece; especially, such part when prepared for another member to butt, or abut against it. Specifically, the larger of the two ends of a log; the back edge of a door; the squared end of a timber prepared for framing and the like. To join squarely, as when two girders meet end to end, forming a butt joint.

Butterflies: Color imperfections on a lime putty finish wall. Large varieties that smear out under pressure of the trowel.

Caused by lime lumps not put through a screen; insufficient mixing of the gauging.

Butterfly reinforcement: Strips of metal reinforcement.

Butterfly valve: A device deriving its name from the wing-like action of the disc that operates at right angles to the flow. The disc impinges against the resilient liner with low operating torque.

Butterfly wedge: A piece of wood used to hold together joined boards.

Buttress, angle: Two buttresses that meet at 90° angles of a building.

Buttress, clasping: A buttress that encases an angle.

Buttress, diagonal: A buttress at a right angle formed by two walls.

Buttress, flying: A half-arch or arch that transmits the thrust of a vault or roof to an outer buttress.

Buttress, lateral: A buttress standing on axis with one wall at the corner of a building.

Buttress, pier: (A) A pier that serves as a buttress while having another purpose, as when a pier dividing openings in an outer wall receives also the thrust of a vault within and is, therefore, shaped so as to resist that thrust.

Buttress, setback: A buttress set back from the angle.

Buttress tower: A towerlike structure that acts or seems to act as a buttress, as on either side of a great archway of an entrance.

Buttress: Brickwork or masonry projecting from a wall for structural lateral reinforcement. Used in Gothic architecture to distribute lateral loads from arches, vaults, and roofs.

BX cable: A cable comprised of a flexible metallic covering inside of which are two or more insulated wires for carrying electricity.

By-pass valve: A device used to divert the flow to go past the part of the system through which it normally passes.

By-pass: An auxiliary loop in a pipeline, intended for diverting flow around a valve or other pieces of equipment.

C

C value (thermal conductance): Indicates the rate of heat flow for the thickness of a material. Significant when the smallest thickness of material is required to achieve a certain insulation value.

Cabinet finish: Interior finish in hard woods, framed, paneled, molded, and varnished or polished like cabinetwork in distinction to finish in soft woods nailed together and commonly painted.

Cabinetmaking: The art and trade of making fine woodwork, whether for furniture (to which the term was formerly confined) or the interior finish of houses, ships, and offices. It is distinguished from rougher carpentry work by careful and accurate fitting and high finish, the lightness and relatively small scale of its productions, and by its predominant use of fine and hard woods. In carpentry the pieces used are relatively large, and secured by nailing in most cases, while the exterior finish is commonly painted. In cabinetmaking the pieces are small, glue enters largely into the joining of parts, and fine varnishing and polishing are required for the finish.

Cable, coaxial: A cable with at least one transmission line consisting of two conductors concentric with and insulated from each other.

Cable: Assembly of conductors within a common protective sheath that permits the use of conductors separately or in groups. The number of fine gauge conductors in a single telephone cable may run into many thousands.

Calcium gypsum: A dry powder, primarily calcium sulfate hemihydrate, resulting from calcination of gypsum. Cementitious base for production of most gypsum plaster. Also called plaster of Paris or stucco.

Caen stone: A soft, fine-grained, light-colored, Jurassic limestone from near Caen in Normandy. One of the most noted limestones of modern history.

Caisson: (A) As used for building upon pile foundations or other firm bottoms under water, a water-tight box in which the masonry is built and then lowered into its place. The floor is made strong enough to carry the weight of the masonry, the sides are detachable and taken off when the caisson rests upon the bottom. The caisson is sometimes made large enough to be buoyant with its load of masonry and sunk by letting in water, is sometimes lowered by chains from a fixed platform, but usually is floated into position and sinks as the masonry is built in it. (B) Generally with the qualifying term pneumatic or compressed air, a device for sinking foundations under water or in soil containing much water or too soft to be supported by other means. It is an air-tight box the size of the pier to be built upon it; the bottom is open, the top is strongly floored to carry the weight of the masonry. It is sometimes framed of wood, but for architectural building it is generally made of steel plates and beams. Entrance and exit are by means of an air lock; materials are generally supplied through a separate air lock. In use, the caisson is loaded sufficiently to overcome the friction of the earth on its sides and the lifting power of the compressed air within it. This loading is usually the masonry it is to support. The air is introduced under a pressure sufficient to exclude or expel the water or fluid earth entering under the lower edge. The earth in the center and under the edges is excavated by laborers working in the compressed air and is lifted out in buckets through an air lock or blown out through special pipes by compressed air or by a water jet. As weight is added above and the supporting earth beneath is removed by excavation aided at times by reducing the air pressure, the caisson gradually sinks until the lower or cutting edge rests upon the rock or other surface upon which it is to remain. It is then filled solid with concrete, and the air locks are removed for use elsewhere. The masonry upon it has meantime been carried above water, so as to be accessible when the caisson has come to rest. The air pressure is generally taken at half a pound to the square inch for every foot in depth of water, although this is in excess of their actual relation. (C) A sunken panel in a ceiling.

Calcine, calcining: To make powdery or to oxidize by removing chemically combined water by action of controlled heat.

Calcium silicate: A pipe covering or block insulation manufactured from a granular compound containing silicon, oxygen, and a metallic or organic radical.

Calcium sulfate: The chemical compound $CaSO_4$.

Calendar range (calendar span): The maximum number of time units included in any given or defined calendar. The calendar start date is unit number one. The calendar range is expressed in years.

Calendar start date: The date assigned to the first unit of the defined calendar.

Calendar unit (time unit): The smallest time unit of the calendar, used in estimating activity duration. This unit is generally in hours, shift, day, or week.

Calendar(s): Used in scheduling the project activities identifies working days, holidays, and the length of the working day in time units.

Calibration: A reduction in thickness in the manufacture of a stone product to a preset value with nearly no tolerance.

Callipers: A tool used for ascertaining the dimensions of curved solids that cannot easily be measured with the rule.

Calorie: The heat needed to increase the temperature of one gram of water 1° C.

Cam loom: A loom in which the shedding is performed by means of cams. Also called velvet loom.

Camber piece; slip: A piece of wood having its upper surface slightly curved upward; used as a centering in building flat arches to give the intrados a slight camber; sometimes a mere board with one edge cut to a convex arc of a very long radius, or a barrel stave.

Camber: A slight rise or upward curve of an otherwise horizontal, or apparently horizontal, piece or structure. In a steel truss having apparently parallel, horizontal chords, the pieces composing the upper chord are usually made slightly longer between joints than the corresponding parts below; the result a slight invisible camber, by which the tendency to sag is overcome. A so-called flat arch is usually built with an intrados having a camber.

Camp-on: A method of holding a call for a busy line and automatically establishing the connection when the line becomes free.

Can pump: A vertical shaft turbine-type pump in a can (suction vessel) for installation in a pipeline to raise water pressure.

Candela: The unit of measurement of luminous intensity of a light source in a given direction.

Candelabra: Several candles branched out and supported by one stem.

Candlepower distribution curve: A graphic presentation of the distribution of light intensity in a given plane of a lamp or luminaire. It is determined by photometric tests. The curve is generally polar, representing the variation of luminous intensity of a lamp or luminaire in a plane through the light center.

Candlepower: Luminous intensity expressed in candelas.

Cant: (A) The angle of inclination of a piece or member to the general surface, especially to the horizontal. (B) A portion or surface that makes an oblique angle with adjoining parts, especially a slope of considerable relative extent.

Cantilever: A member intended to support an overhanging weight, like a bracket; but generally large and having a projection much greater than its height; especially, a projecting beam-one that is fixed in a wall or other support at one end and unsupported at the other ends. Applied to a bridge or a beam, it means an end projecting beyond the support.

Canting: (A) Sloping or tipping, especially from the horizontal. (B) The cutting away of the corner of a rectangular beam or sill to form a beveled or oblique plane intermediate between the original faces.

Canvas: A light, plain weave cotton fabric used for jacketing.

Cap: The crowning or terminal feature of a vertical member of any structure, either fitting closely upon it or extending somewhat beyond it in horizontal dimensions; thus distinguished from a finial.

Capacitor: An electric energy storage device which when built into or wired to a ballast, changes it from low to high power factor.

Capacity: The maximum or minimum flows obtainable under given conditions of media, temperature, pressure, velocity, etc. Also, the volume of media which may be stored in a container or receptacle.

Capillary: The action by which the surface of a liquid, where it is in contact with a solid, is elevated or depressed depending upon the relative attraction of the molecules of the liquid for each other and for those of the solid.

Capital or gap: The ornamental head of a column or pilaster.

Care, custody and control: The term used to describe a standard exclusion in liability insurance policies. Under this exclusion, the liability insurance does not apply to damage to property in the care or custody of the insured, or to damage to property over which the insured is for any purpose exercising physical control.

Carnauba: A wax used in furniture polish. It is made from a Brazilian palm and is very hard.

Carpenter: A worker in wood; especially one who does the larger and rougher work, as of building construction, and as distinguished from a joiner and cabinetmaker.

Carpentry: The work of a carpenter. Also, the result of such work; building in wood, or woodwork in general. Carpentry is sometimes distinguished from framing as referring rather to the smaller members of a building, as window frames, stairs, if not highly finished, flooring, and the like; it is distinguished from joinery and cabinetmaking as being rougher and building the essential parts of a structure rather than the more decorative parts without which the building might still exist.

Carriage: (A) An inclined beam or stringpiece for supporting a stair. (B) In a lumber mill, the movable framework that carries the log or plank and feeds it to the saw or plane.

Carrying channels: See channels, carrying.

Case door: A frame or case consisting of jamb pieces and lintel or head framed or nailed together, in which the door is hung on one side and closes on the other. The face of the frame has a rebate so that the door when closed into it shall be flush with the wall or in a plane parallel with the face of the wall. In thin walls and partitions the case is as thick as the partition, and finished with a trim on either side of the latter. In thick walls the case finishes with a trim on one side and a bead or molding against the masonry or plastered jam on the other.

Case mold: Plaster shell used to hold various parts of a plaster mold in correct position. Also used with gelatin and wax molds to prevent distortions during pouring.

Case: (A) A box, enclosure, or hollow receptacle, as the space in which a stairway is built: a staircase. (B) Same as casing. (C) The carcass of structural framework of a house or other building. (Rare in United States.)

Casement, French: A casement having two meeting, hinged leaves opening inward, secured usually when closed by an *espagnolette*.

Casement: (A) A window having hinged or pivoted sash, opening either outward or inward. (B) One leaf or swinging frame forming part of such a window and thus, in British usage, distinguished from a sash. In the United States, usually called casement sash. (C) In medieval architecture, a deep, hollow molding similar to the Scotia of classic architecture.

Casing bead: Sometimes called a plaster stop, this bead is used where plaster is discontinued, around openings, thus providing a ground; where the plaster adjoins another material; and to form the perimeter of a plaster membrane or panel.

Casing clip: A formed metal section that puts pressure on a casing bead to assure rigid positioning.

Casing: In general, the exterior covering of a structure or member of a structure; a shell or boxing of some superior material, as the mahogany casing of a ceiling beam. Specifically, in the United States, the boxing or frame about an opening; that portion which is parallel to the surrounding surface and therefore usually at right angles to the jambs. It may be structural, as those parts that form the inside and outside of a cased frame, or decorative, as the trim or architrave of a door. A door or window set into a wall.

Cast in place: Concrete casts made on the construction site.

Cast iron: Iron shaped by being run into a mold while melted, as described under casting. In ordinary commercial usage, a compound of iron and carbon; the material that runs directly in liquid form from the blast furnace and that hardens in the mold. From cast iron are made the steel and purer iron which is used for working with the hammer. Cast iron is brittle and hard and cannot be welded; that is, two parts cannot be united when hammered together while hot, the property that makes iron important as a material for decoration.

Caster: A wheel placed on the bottom of furniture enabling it to be rolled rather than carried.

Casting plaster: A fast-setting gypsum plaster.

Casting: A method of turning thermoplastics into sheeting, film, and rigid sheets. The material is heated into a fluid, poured into a mold, cured, and then removed from the mold.

Casts: Finished product from a mold. Sometimes referred to as staff. Used generally as enrichments and stuck in place.

Catch: A contrivance for automatically securing a door, shutter, or a similar movable leaf by the action of gravity or a spring. In some of its more elaborate forms hardly to be distinguished from a latch or spring lock.

Catface: Flaw in the finish coat comparable to a pock mark. In some regions basecoat knobs showing through the finish coat are referred to as catfaces.

Cathodic protection: (A) The control of the electrolytic corrosion of an underground or underwater metallic structure by the application of an electric current in such a way that the structure is made to act as the cathode instead of a node of an electrolytic cell. (B) The use of materials and liquid to cause electricity to flow to avoid corrosion.

Caulk (sound or finish caulking): To seal small openings such as windows and doors in wall or ceiling systems to prevent leakage of sound or to effect a finished appearance and seal between dissimilar materials. To make watertight.

Caulking: (A) To secure the end of a timber, such as a girder or tie beam, to another on which it rests at right angles (as the wall plate or sill) by means of a cog hold. (B) To render a joint tight, as against water or gas, by driving into its interstices with a chisel or other tool some plastic or elastic substance, such as oakum and tar, in the decks of ships, lead in the hubs of soil pipes, etc. (C) In boiler and hydraulic work, a process for making a joint steam or watertight by upsetting the edges of the steel or iron plates. Also called calking, caulking, cocking, cogging.

Cavetto molding: Hollow molding with a quarter circle-section.

Cavitation: A localized gaseous condition found within a liquid stream.

Cavity iron: A small iron anchor for tying together the parts of the masonry on opposite sides of a cavity wall.

Cavity ratio: A number indicating cavity proportions calculated from length, width, and height.

Cavity wall: A masonry wall that provides air space.

Cedar: A red wood with a fragrance that protects clothing from moths.

Ceiling, barrel: A rounded or semi-circular ceiling.

Ceiling beam: A ceiling, generally of wood, made in imitation of exposed floor beams with the flooring showing between. Hence, sometimes, the under side of a floor, showing the actual beams, and finished to form a ceiling.

Ceiling cavity ratio: A numerical relationship of the vertical distance between luminaire mounting height and ceiling height to room width and length. It is used with the zonal cavity method of calculating average illumination levels.

Ceiling outlet: An air diffuser mounted in the ceiling.

Ceiling track (ceiling runner track or ceiling runner): A formed metal section, anchored to the ceiling, into which metal studs for hollow or solid partitions are set; a formed metal section to which lath is attached for studless partitions; a metal channel or angle used for anchoring the partition to the ceiling.

Ceiling: (A) The covering of a wall surface, especially on the interior; or of the under side of a floor; the material used being always supposed to be a simple and ordinary one. Thus, ceiling is of thin boards or of lath and plaster, but never of tile, nor is the term applied to the surface afforded by the solid material of a wall or floor; except as under B. (B) By extension from A, the under side of a floor which provides the roofing or enclosure at top of a room or other space below. In this case, it is the surface alone which is designated without reference to material.

Ceilings: Contact, furred, and suspended. (A) Contact, as applied to ceiling construction, means that the laths attached in direct contact with construction above, without use of runner channels or furring. (B) Furred ceiling construction means that the furring members are suspended below the structural members of the building. (C) Suspended ceiling means that the furring members are suspended below the structural members of the building. (D) Cross furring means the furring members are attached at right angles to the underside of main runners or other structural supports. (E) The term main runners denotes the metal channels that are attached to or suspended from the structure above for the support of cross furring.

Cellar, earth: A cellar excavated in the face of a steep slope of ground and at its foot, so as to have a floor at about the level of the ground in front. Such a chamber will be nearly enclosed on three sides by the natural soil. The roof is usually boarded, but perhaps of earth supported from below. A common means in the United States of obtaining a cool storage place.

Cellar, sub: In a building having more than one cellar, the lower of the underground stories. The great height of the skyscrapers of the United States has made it desirable in many cases to extend the foundations to solid rock, as in New York City. The foundations will then reach a depth of perhaps 30' or 40', allowing the construction of three or more stories below the street level. The uppermost story will then usually be known as the cellar, and lower ones as subcellars.

Cellar: (A) The space below the ground story or the basement story of a building, enclosed by the foundation walls, and therefore entirely or almost entirely, below the surface of the surrounding ground. The distinction between cellar and basement story is not absolute and, in some cases, may depend on the use to which such a space is put as much as its relative situation. (B) Any underground or partly underground place of deposit for wine, provisions, fuel, or the like. In cities there is often a special chute for coal, kindling wood, or other fuel and the cellars of stores and warehouses have elevators or lifts, often outside the walls of the building.

Cellular carrying capacity: The capacity for wire is determined by the safest operating temperature.

Cellular glass: Glass insulation produced in a closed-cell by expanding the material into a foam by thermal or chemical means.

Cellular insulation: See insulation, cellular.

Cellular plastic: Plastic expanded by thermal or chemical means and containing open and closed cells throughout.

Cellulosics: Plastics that can withstand below freezing temperatures and moderate heat. They are the strongest plastics. They are good insulators and are used for recording tape, pipe, tubbing, and tool handles.

Celsius (C): A metric system for measuring temperature in which the freezing point of water is 0° and the boiling point is 100° at sea level atmospheric pressure.

Cement, calcareous: A cement consisting largely of lime and clay, which gives it hydraulic ability (see hydraulic cement). It may be either a natural cement; that is, prepared directly from one of many natural forms of impure limestone as is the common Rosendale cement extensively used in the eastern United States, or artificial; that is, prepared by mixing limestone or chalk in certain proportions with clay and perhaps other ingredients, such as Portland cement. Such elements are supplied in the form of a fine powder and require only to be mixed with water and sand for use as mortar, although a certain proportion of common lime is frequently introduced, usually for reasons of economy.

Cement, hydraulic: A calcareous cement which has the property of setting under water without exposure to the air, which is therefore valuable for subaqueous and similar masonry work. The hydraulic cements used in building are derived from the impure limestones, containing different proportions of clay and silica, or are artificial combinations of those materials with common lime, calcined and ground. The name Roman cement is applied in Europe to all the light, natural cements, the materials for which are found in great variety, and widely distributed. The stone generally contains about 60% lime and magnesia to about 40% clay (silica and alumina), generally with a little iron and potash. The stone is burned in kilns until completely calcined, but care is taken that it is not over-burned, which would render it inert. The Rosendale cements, among the best of those found in the United States, are of this class. They contain carbonate of magnesia in much greater proportion than the Roman cements of England and France. Others of this class are found in many parts of the United States in the valleys of the Potomac and James rivers, along the Erie Canal, and in Ohio and Kentucky. With slight differences in composition, they possess nearly the same practical value. The Rosendales, from the valley of the Hudson and Louisville, Kentucky, are perhaps the best.

Cement, Keene's: A white finish plaster that produces an extremely durable wall. Because of its density, it excels for use in bathrooms and kitchens and is also used extensively for the finish coat in auditoriums, public buildings, and other places where walls may be subjected to unusually hard wear or abuse.

Cement, insulating: A mixture of various insulating fibers and binders with water to form an insulation material for irregular surfaces.

Cement, Maya: One composed of lime and zaccab.

Cement, Portland: An artificial calcareous cement composed primarily of limestone and clay. So called because of its resemblance, when finished with a smooth surface, as on the face of a wall, to the well-known Portland stone of England, where such cement was first manufactured. The Portland cements differ from the Roman cements in the relative proportions of lime and clay which they contain. The best proportions are 20-22 parts of clay and 70-80 parts of lime. The clay should contain about 1-1/2 or 2 parts of silica, forming a silicate of calcium by the reaction of silica and lime in the presence of fusible combinations of iron and alumina. There is produced in Portland cements a fusible silica-aluminate identical with that which forms the essential element of blast-furnace slag, in which sesquioxide or iron partially replaces the alumina. Its only useful purpose is to serve as a flux to favor, during the burning, the combination of silica and lime. When blast-furnace slags are precipitated as liquid into cold water, they combine with hydrated lime in setting and produce silicate and aluminates of lime identical with those formed by entirely different reactions during the setting of Portland cement. These are the slag cements. The various Portlands are made by mixing and grinding the generally wet material, drying it, breaking it into pieces, and burning to incipient calcination. The weight of good Portland cement should be not less than 112 pounds to the bushel; that of the Roman and Rosendale cements is about 75 lbs.

Cement, Roman: See cement, hydraulic.

Cement, slate: (A) A hydraulic cement manufactured from argillaceous slate. (B) A plastic roofing material made of broken slate mixed with tar, asphalt, or some similar material.

Cement, water: Same as hydraulic cement.

Cement joint: The union of two fittings by insertion of material. Sometimes this joint is accomplished mechanically, sometimes chemically.

Cement plaster: See gypsum plaster and Portland cement plaster.

Cement: (A) To secure together by means of cement. (B) A plastic roofing material made of broken slate mixed with tar, asphalt, or some similar material. (C) Any material used to adhere substances. In this sense, glue is the cement most used in carpentry work; gum tragacanth, gum Arabic, and various mixtures are used under the general term mucilage for minor operations of the sort; shellac is much used in making small repairs in cut stone. Especially, in building, same as calcareous cement; also mortar made with a large share of that material.

Cementitious material: Material binding aggregate particles together into a heterogeneous mass.

Center drawer guide: Wooden tracking placed under a drawer to allow it to open easily.

Center mold: A thin piece of board or the like, the edge of which is shaped to a given profile, and which, when rotated about a pivot at one end, will cut corresponding circular moldings in soft plaster.

Centering: A timber framework or mold, upon which the masonry of an arch or vault is supported until the key is placed which renders it self-supporting. The centering for a stone arch is composed of parallel frames or longitudinal ribs regularly spaced, which follow the form of the intrados of the arch; upon them the transverse laggings are placed which support the stones of the arch. In small arches the laggings are planks forming a close surface; in larger works, each course of arch stones is supported by a single light timber. The ribs are formed sometimes of beams of convenient length, dressed on the outside to the curve of the arch and supported at their ends, or junctions. For small arches they are formed of several thicknesses of boards cut to the proper curve and nailed together, breaking joints. The framing, or supports of the ribs, vary according to the conditions and skill of the designer. They may be divided into two general classes: those which are supported from the ground or floor under the arch by means of radial or normal struts or by vertical posts; and those carried by the piers or abutments at the ends of the arch span, being either trussed or supported by arch braces transmitting the weight to the ends. The former method is much preferred when points of direct support can be obtained. The centering must be not only strong enough to carry the weight of the arch, but also so arranged that it will not change its shape as the successive weights are placed upon it. To facilitate this purpose in long spans, the masonry is sometimes placed on the arch in blocks, so that nothing is keyed or closed until the whole weight is on the center, and there is no risk of its changing its shape.

Centigrade: A scale of measuring the temperature of water. The freezing point is $0°$ and the boiling point is $100° C.$

Central air conditioning: See air conditioning, central.

Central office: The place where customers' communications lines are terminated and where the equipment which interconnects those lines is located.

Central vacuuming: A system of centralized vacuum cleaning where the air pumps are connected to piping installed in building walls. The cleaning attachments are connected to inlets in individual rooms.

Centrally planned: A building planned to radiate from a central point in contrast to axial plan.

Centrex: A communications service that offers a flexible mix of phone services especially selected to meet the needs of the high-volume and relatively sophisticated customer. Each station may have its own phone number, so each may be dialed directly and dial its own calls without the intervention of an attendant. Typical centrex services include direct outward and inward dialing; direct inside dialing for intraorganizational communications; automatic call transfer; automatic identification of outward dialing for accounting and cost-control purposes; station hunting, which automatically routes calls to another line when a called line is busy; and other services.

Centrifugal pump: A pump in which the pressure is developed principally by the action of centrifugal force.

Ceramic fibers: Fibers used to make certain high temperature (up to 3200° F) insulation materials.

Ceramics: (A) The art and industry of making objects of baked clay. (B) Objects made of baked clay taken collectively. The arts of baked clay applicable to architecture are of two sorts: in one the clay surface, whether flat or modelled, is left without glaze or polish of any kind; in the other, which forms the subject of the present article, the processes of the potter are employed. The most common forms of earthenware in use in architecture are floor, roof, and wall tiling, the last having for its primary object the protection of buildings by an indestructible surface, capable of resisting the effects of weather and changes of temperature. The glazed or enamelled face that offers most opportunity for the characteristic colors of pottery in decoration is less durable under friction than bodies of a semivitreous fracture (such as porcelain or stoneware) and consequently less adapted for floor tiling than for walls or roofs. When an ordinary earthenware body is used for this purpose, the floor is slippery as long as the glaze retains its freshness; as soon as it is worn down by use, the soft substratum offers little resistance, and its decoration is quickly destroyed.

Certificate for payment: A statement from the architect to the owner confirming the amount of money due contractor for work accomplished or materials and equipment suitably stored, or both.

Certificate of insurance: A memorandum issued by an authorized representative of an insurance company stating the types, amounts, and effective dates of insurance in force for a designated insured.

Certificate of occupancy: Document issued by a governmental authority certifying that all or a designated portion of a building complies with the provisions of applicable codes, statutes, and/or regulations, and permitting occupancy for its designated use.

Certified payments: Payments or partial payment authorized to a contractor or subcontractor by an architect or engineer on a certificate of payment form, which is sent to the owner or his agent for payment of funds.

Cesspool: A sunk pit, generally covered, intended for the reception of solid and liquid waste matters, as from inhabited buildings. There are two kinds of cesspools, leaching and tight cesspools. The former is built of stones laid dry, with open sides and bottom, permitting the liquid sewage to escape or leach away into the subsoil; the latter is built of stone or brickwork, laid in hydraulic cement mortar, and made watertight in the same manner as cisterns.

Chain course: A bond course of stone headers fastened together continuously by metal cramps. A noted example is the triple chain course in the choir of Notre Dame, Paris (1195).

Chain: An inclusion with irregular veining consisting of material with an appearance or structure different from that of the rock. A chain may be considered a decorative defect. It is a defect when it compromises the physical and mechanical stability of the rock.

Chainwheel operated valve: A device operated by a chain driven wheel which opens and closes the valve seats.

Chairbound: A person who is confined to or needs to use a wheelchair during the working day.

Chalkboard: A surface that can be written on, usually with chalk.

Chalk line: A straight working line made by snapping a chalked cord between two points.

Chalk: A limestone composed mainly of the calcareous tests of foraminifera, though also, containing, shells of larger mollusks. When much indurated, as in the valley of the Seine, it is used as a building material.

Chalking: Powdering of the paint film on the film surface. Mild chalking can be desirable, however, heavy chalking should be removed prior to repainting.

Chamfer: The bevel or oblique surface produced by the cutting away of a corner or arris. When the chamfer does not extend the whole length of the arris, it is called a stopped chamfer. When instead of a bevel a concave surface replaces the arris, it is called a concave chamfer. A beaded chamfer is one in which a convex bead is left projecting from the bevel of the chamfer. A beaded chamfer is one in which a convex bead is left projecting from the bevel of the chamfer. Chamfers occur principally in woodwork and occasionally in stone cutting.

Change in direction: A term describing a turn or reverse run of drainage pipe.

Change order: A written order to the contractor signed by the owner and engineer or architect, issued after the execution of the contract, authorizing a change in the work or an adjustment in the contract sum or contract time. A change order may be signed by the architect or engineer, providing they have written authority from the owner and that a copy of such written authority is furnished to the contractor upon request. A change order also may be signed by the general contractor if he agrees to the adjustment in the contract sum or the contract time of the subcontract. The contract sum and the contract time may be changed only by change order.

Changes in the work: Changes ordered by the owner consisting of additions, deletions, or other revisions within the general scope of the contract; the contract sum and the contract time adjusts accordingly. All changes in the work, except minor ones not involving adjustment to the contract sum or the contract time, should be authorized by change order.

Channel iron: An iron or steel member shaped as a channel, especially one having the form of a small channel beam (see beam).

Channel type: Cold-rolled channels of 3/4", 1-1/2" and 2" widths. Hot-rolled channels of 3/4", 1", 1-1/2" and 2" (not always available).

Channel: Any furrow or groove, whether for carrying off water or for any other purpose.

Channelling: Breaking up a surface by channels or grooves, usually near together and parallel; channels collectively.

Channels, carrying: The heaviest integral supporting member in a suspended ceiling. Carrying channels, or main runners, are supported by hangers attached to the building structure and in turn support various grid systems or furring channels or rods to which lath is fastened.

Channels, furring: The smaller horizontal member of a suspended ceiling, applied at right angles to the underside of carrying channels and to which lath is attached; the smaller horizontal member in a furred ceiling; in general, the separate members used

to space lath from any surface member over which it is applied.

Channels: Hot or cold-rolled steel used for furring, studs, and in suspended ceilings. Sizes vary according to requirements.

Chase wall: A partition to enclose mechanical and plumbing systems.

Chase: A groove or channel formed in a structure, as in the face of a wall, to receive some accessory such as flues, wires, sliding weights, or the like. A chase may be left in a wall so that an abutting wall can be built onto it later. A chase differs from a groove mainly because it is relatively large and does not ordinarily call for accurate fitting to whatever it is to receive.

Check cracks: Cracks in plaster caused by shrinkage, but still bonded to its base.

Check valve: A device designed to allow a fluid to pass through in one direction only.

Check: (A) In masonry, a rabbet-shaped cutting along an edge of a stone by which it is made to fit another stone adjoining. Commonly used in uncoursed and random-coursed masonry to reduce the height of a stone at one end to correspond with an adjoining stone of less height, so that the next stone above or below will overlap the two, breaking joints. (B) A crack or split caused by the uneven shrinkage of wood while seasoning or drying. It is to guard against checks that lumber is quarter sawed and large sticks, especially posts, have their hearts bored out.

Checking: A defect in a coated surface characterized by the appearance of fine cracks in all directions.

Checkrails: Meeting rails sufficiently thicker than a window to fill the opening between the top and bottom sash made by the parting stop in the frame of double-hung windows. They are usually beveled.

Cheek: A narrow upright face forming the end or side of an architectural or structural member. Usually, one of two corresponding opposite faces, whether forming the sides of an opening, as the jambs of a doorway, or forming the two side faces of a projection, as a buttress or chimney breast. The term is often extended to mean an upright member or piece forming such a face, and this definition is accepted by the dictionaries.

Chemical bond: A term, used to describe adherence of one plaster to another or to the base, which implies formation of interlocking crystals or fusion between the coats or to the base.

Chemical reaction: The property of a material to combine or react with other materials to which it may come into contact.

Chemical resistance: Capability of a material to withstand exposure to acids, alkalies, salts, and their solutions.

Chemical waste system: Piping that conveys corrosive or harmful industrial, chemical, or processed wastes to the drainage system.

Cherry: A wood that is pale brown in color but darkens with age. It carves well and has a fine grain.

Chestnut: A hard wood reddish-brown in color, often used for inlay.

Chicago window: A window that takes up the full width of a bay and is divided into a large fixed sash bound by movable sash windows.

Chicken wire needle: A crooked-end tool similar to a screw driver used to lace poultry mesh.

Chicken wire: Hexagonal steel wire netting (poultry mesh) used as reinforcement in plastic and mastic.

Chimney bar: A bar or beam that supports the masonry above a fireplace. It is either straight or curved, according to the form of the chimney arch, and is usually set a few inches back from the face of the arches.

Chimney-breast: The masonry structure that projects into the room and houses the flue.

Chimney-piece: See mantelpiece.

Chimney-stack: Masonry containing one or more flues and projection above the room.

Chimney: That part of a building which contains a flue or flues for conveying smoke or the like to the outer air and often encloses the fireplace, if there is one; specifically, that portion which rises above the roof.

Chink: A hairline crack, often barely visible, oriented in any direction. A blind chink is so small that it can be seen only when the material is wet; an embedded chink, only when the block has been sawed.

Chinking: The process of filling small openings, or chinks, especially the interstices between the timbers of a log building, with chips, moss, clay, and the like. This operation is commonly followed by daubing, the entire process being known as chinking and daubing.

Chip cracks: Similar to check cracks, except the bond has been partially destroyed, causing eggshelling. Sometimes referred to as fire cracks, map cracks, crazing and fire checks, and hair cracks.

Chisel, drawer lock: A steel chisel used to cut mortises in confined spaces such as drawer openings. It has a cutting edge at each end, the edges lying in transverse directions.

Chisel, firmer: Chisel of firmer or stiffer substance than the paring chisel. It is a general utility tool, used for short paring work or light mortising, and it is handled in a manner to be suitable either for steady pressure or the percussions of the mallet. It may be had with several forms of handles, but the round-swell shape is best. These chisels are made in the same width as the paring, length from 4" to 8".

Chisel, mortise: A chisel made abnormally thick to prevent bending when levering the core out of mortises. It is solely used for producing mortises. Width from 1/8" to 5/8", advancing by 1/8".

Chisel, paring: The typical chisel tool. It is used for shaping and preparing relatively long plane surfaces, especially in the direction of the grain of the wood, and as it is invariably manipulated by steady and sustained pressure, as distinguished from the intermittent force used with other chisels, its handle is shaped to enable the hand to exercise great control over its movements. The better forms have beveled edges, which reduce the friction when propelling the tool in a groove or trench. They are made from 1/4" to 2" in width, advancing by 1/8" to 1", thereafter by 1/4", their lengths vary from 9" to 21".

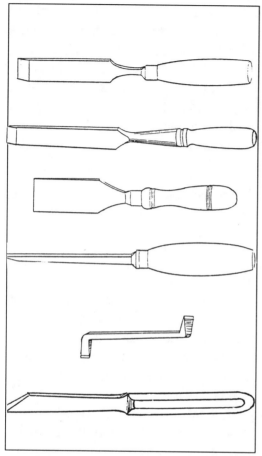

Chisel, plugging: A bar of low-tempered steel forged into an octagon-shaped handle at one end and drawn out to a flat obtuse-angled point at the other. This part should be parallel on the front edge and not more than 5/16" thick and be slightly thinner at the back. It should also be wider at the point than at the hilt. It is used for cutting mortises in the joints of brickwork to receive wood plugs.

Chisel, pocket: A wide, short, and very thin chisel made entirely of steel, used for cutting the ends of pocket pieces in pulley stiles of common sash frames. They advance in width by 1/4" from 1-1/2" to 2-1/2".

Chisel, sash: A lighter form of mortise chisel with a nearly parallel stem, used chiefly for the narrow mortises required in sash bars.

Chisel, swan's neck (lock-mortise chisel): Used for cutting across the grain at the bottom of a deep mortise. It is only make in three sizes, 3/8", 7/16" and 5/8".

Chisel, toothed: A chisel whose cutting edge is indented. Used to roughen regularly, give texture to, or dress a surface of masonry.

Chiseling: Surface processing done manually with a chisel.

Chrome: A bright metallic coating applied to steel and other metals to protect it from oxidation.

Circuit vent: A branch vent that serves two or more traps and extends from in front of the last fixture connection of a horizontal branch to the vent stack.

Circuit: The directed route taken by a flow of media from one point to another.

CISPI: Abbreviation for Cast Iron Soil Pipe Institute.

Cistern, supply: A reservoir or cistern that supplies a house with water. It is generally excavated in the earth, lined with brick, stone, or cement, domed over at the top, and furnished with a chain pump for aerating purposes.

Cistern: An underground structure for the reception and storage of water. It is built of brick, stone, or wooden staves; one differently built is usually called a tank. Cisterns are built round, except those of unusually large sizes, which are made square or rectangular. The size of a cistern is determined by the amount of rain water to be stored, the area of the roof, and the rainfall. To prevent contamination, cisterns are built watertight; the inside, when of masonry, is plastered with Portland cement. The overflow pipe from a cistern must never connect with a house or street sewer and is best carried into an open ditch or road gutter, the outfall being protected by a flap-valve, grating, or bar strainer. The cistern top is arched over and covered with iron or stone cover, and the surface graded away. Cisterns should be well ventilated to prevent the water from becoming stagnant.

Cladding: The external skin of a structure applied for both aesthetics and protection.

Claim denial: See payment claim denial.

Claim: (A) All the facts that make up one party's case in a disputer or lawsuit. (B) An application for relief.

Clamp gate valve: A gate valve whose body and bonnet are held together by a U bolt clamp.

Clamp: An instrument for securing or holding, which is applied to the surface of the parts and does not pass through the material, although perhaps enters a short distance. It may be a member to unite parts of a structure permanently together, as a cleat or strap, or a tool to hold temporarily material in process of being prepared or finished, as a carpenter's screw clamp.

Clapboard: (A) A board for the outside covering of the walls of a wooden building, intended to be applied horizontally, each board overlapping the one below. Clapboards are usually 6" to 8" wide, about 5/8" thick at the lower edge, diminishing nearly to a feather edge at the top. They are made of clear pine, cedar, or cypress, and are laid with about 4" or 4-1/2" to the weather. An attempt has been made to limit the term specifically to a particular kind of such boards made in New England. These are made in lengths of 4' by cuts radiating from the center of the log, so that each board is quarter sawed, and hence superior to those as usually worked. According to this distinction, all other such boards would be merely bevelled siding. (B) In English usage, one of a certain variety of imported oak boards for wainscoting. The term formerly signified as unfinished stave or shook.

Clarification drawings: A graphic interpretation of the drawings or other contract documents issued by the architect or engineer as part of an addendum, modification, change order or field order.

Class P ballast: Contains a thermal protective device which deactivates the ballast when the case reaches a certain critical temperature. The device resets automatically when the case temperature drops to a lower temperature.

Class A circuit (loop): An arrangement of supervised initiating device, signaling line, or indicating appliance circuits that prevents a single open or ground on the installation wiring of these circuits from causing loss of the system's intended function.

Class B circuit (loop) (see class A circuit): An arrangement of supervised initiating device, signaling line, or indicating appliance circuits, which does not prevent a single open or ground on the installation wiring of these circuits from causing loss of the system's intended function.

Clause: In the AIA documents, a subdivision of a subparagraph, identified by four numerals; e.g., 2.2.10.1.

Cleanout: A plug or cover joined to an opening in a pipe, which can be removed clean or examine the interior of the pipe.

Clear finish: A transparent coating or paint.

Clear water waste: Cooling water and condensate drainage from refrigeration and air conditioning equipment, cooled condensate from steam heating systems, cooled boiler blowdown water, waste water drainage from equipment rooms and other areas where water is used without an appreciable addition of oil, gasoline, solvent, acid, etc., and treated effluent in which impurities have been reduced below a minimum concentration considered harmful.

Clear: (A) Open, free of obstruction. (B) Clean, without impurities or defects; without admixture. Thus, clear cement is cement unmixed with sand or lime. (C) In connection with lumber, free from knots, shakes, sap, and the like. (D) Unobstructed space; opening considered as between the inside limits of two opposite parts. Chiefly used in the adjectival phase, in the clear, i.e., taken or measured at the narrowest part of an opening. In general, the shortest or perpendicular distance so taken.

Clearance: Adequate space allowed for installation of insulation materials.

Clearing I2t: The total I2t passed by a fuse as the fuse clears a fault, with it being equal to the time elapsed from the initiation of the fault to the instant the fault has been cleared.

Cleat: (A) A strip of wood nailed, screwed, or otherwise fastened across a number of boards to hold them together or to stiffen or otherwise strengthen them; or secured to a wall or other upright as a support for a shelf, or the like. The cleat differs from the batten generally in being smaller and having only the significance of a piece used to secure together planks or boards laid edge to edge, or of stiffening a very wide piece of plank or board. The common term batten door would be better described as cleat door, for the transverse piece is short and need not be nearby; it may be thought, however, that the battens referred to in this term are the longitudinal or principal pieces. (B) A device for temporarily attaching a cord, as of an awning; usually of metal and consisting of a shank or short leg from which two arms extend in opposite directions. The cleat being secured in place by the shank, the cord may be wound about the arms.

Cleavage: The natural tendency of certain materials, especially of stones and crystals, to fracture or split in certain definite directions determined by the molecular or physical structure of the material; also, the direction or manner in which such materials tend to divide. Thus, stones which have a stratified structure are commonly capable of being readily divided in the direction of the layers.

Cleft slab: A slab that has been naturally split along the grain.

Clerestory: That part of a building which rises above roofs of other parts and has windows in its walls. The term is especially used for medieval churches, whose division into a central nave and side aisles of less width and height made the opening up of the wider central nave a natural and obvious arrangement.

Clerk of the works: Obsolete; use project representative.

Clinch: To bend over and hammer down the protruding point of a nail so that it cannot be withdrawn; to secure or fasten a nailed structure by so doing. That which clinches; a clinched fastening; the turned-over point of a clinched nail.

Clincher: A wrought-iron nail used in clinching, have usually a broad head. Called also clinching nail and clinch nail.

Clip for control of movement: A flexible, resilient metal section separating the plaster membrane from supports to reduce sound transmission and plaster cracking due to structural movement.

Clip: To make notches or grooves during manufacturing.

Clips: Special, sometimes patented, devices used to attach lath to steel supports.

Close nipple: A nipple with a length twice the length of a standard pipe thread.

Closed construction: That condition when any building, component, assembly, subassembly, or system is manufactured in such a manner that all portions cannot be readily inspected at the installation site without disassembly or destruction thereof.

Closed joint: A barely visible or invisible junction between adjacent slabs.

Closed list of bidders: See invited bidders.

Closed specifications: Specification stipulating the use of specific products or processes without provision for substitution.

Closed system: A system made up of components and subsections that are related in dimension.

Closed-cell plastic: A cellular plastic with a large predominance on noninterconnecting cells.

Closet: (A) Originally, a private room; the sitting room or chamber of a person of some distinction. (B) In modern usage, a place for storage, distinguished from a cupboard only as being larger, perhaps large enough for a person to enter. By extension, the term covers such a small room when fitted with conveniences, such as a wash closet, a dressing closet.

Closure: A wall, balustrade, or arcade serving as a screen; but where standing at the edge of a roof, gallery, or the like, serving as a parapet. The term is especially used for a short length of such wall, etc., which is set between two columns, having usually no connection with the columns, but standing free.

Coat: A layer of paint, plaster, mortar, or the like as applied to a wall or floor. The term is restricted to a liquid or semiliquid substance.

Coating adhesion: A measure of the strength of the bond between the surface coating and the substratum or backing of a wallcovering.

Coating system: Coating materials and their method or means of application to an appropriately prepared surface.

Coating: A layer of finish material that may be sprayed or hand applied to a surface to decorate, preserve, protect, seal the substrate, or to bridge cracks.

Coaxial cable: A central cable which is surrounded by and insulated from a larger cable.

Cobwebbing: The formation of web-like threads, along with droplets leaving the nozzle of a spray gun during application of some adhesives.

Cock, bibb: A fitting for the discharge of water into fixtures, usually with a bent down nozzle. Sometimes abbreviated bibb.

Cock: A mechanical device for controlling the flow of water or other liquid, either at any point in the line of pipe (stop cock) or at an outlet end of a pipe line, in combination with a nozzle or discharge spout at a plumbing fixture (bibb cock, faucet). Cocks are designated by the fixture for which they are intended (as a basin or bath cock); by the service which they are intended to render; by their mechanical construction (ball cock, compression cock, three-way cock, ground key cock, self-closing cock); or by the fluid flowing through them (water, gas, steam cock).

Code, building: A set of construction and materials standards.

Code of accounts/chart of accounts: A systematic method of identifying (numbering, coding) categories of costs incurred in the progress of a job.

Codes: Regulations, ordinances, or statutory requirements of a governmental unit relating to building construction and occupancy, adopted and administered for the protection of the public health, safety, and welfare.

Coefficient of expansion: The increase in unit length, area of volume for 1° rise in temperature.

Coefficient of utilization (CU): A ratio representing the portion of light emitted by a luminaire that gets down to the work plane. The coefficient of utilization thus indicates the combined efficiency of the luminaire, room proportions, and room finish reflectances. The ratio of the luminous flux (lumens) from a luminaire is calculated as received on the work-plane to the luminous flux emitted by the lamps alone.

Coffer, coffering: A ceiling decoration of sunken square or polygonal ornamental panels.

Coffer dam: A temporary dam made to exclude the water from a place upon which it is desired to build. In the usual form it is composed of an outer and an inner row of piles with waling pieces, or stringers, to guide and support the sheet piling that is driven between the piles of each row, forming a double enclosure. The space between the rows is then cleaned of all material not watertight and filled in with puddled clay and gravel to make the enclosure watertight. It is sometimes made of large timber piles driven close together, jointed and caulked, and tied together with waling pieces. A bank of earth is sometimes sufficient in shallow water. The water is pumped out, and the construction proceeds.

Coffered ceilings: Ornamental ceilings made up of sunken or recessed panels.

Coil: A pipe heating and cooling element.

Cold cathode lamp: An electric-discharge lamp whose mode of operation is that of a glow discharge.

Coliform group of bacteria: All organisms considered in the group as set forth by the American Water Works Association.

Collar beam: A horizontal transverse timber connecting a pair of rafters between the apex and the wall plate.

Color and sample boards: Presentation aids used in interior design to show samples.

Color rendering index (CRI): Measure of the degree of color shift objects undergo when illuminated by the light source as compared with the color of those same objects when illuminated by a reference source of comparable color temperature.

Color temperature: The absolute temperature of a blackbody radiator having a chromaticity equal to that of the light source.

Column, clustered: Same as clustered pier; the term column in this sense is not accurate.

Column, coupled: Set in a pair or in pairs. These may be in a continuous colonnade, as a peristyle or portico, and the disposition is then called araeostyle.

Column, demi: A column sunken halfway into a wall, although not a pilaster.

Column, engaged: A round pilaster-like member, generally ornamental, and most commonly built with the wall, or as part of the wall whose courses of stone are continued through the shaft. Even where the engaged column is a piece of costly and beautiful material and therefore not continuous with the structure of the wall, it is

to be considered as a pilaster with a rounded horizontal section, rather than as a column. Also called attached column.

Column, knotted: A column, the shaft of which is shaped to appear as if tied in a knot, or as if composed of two ropelike parts interlacing.

Column, lally: A column made of steel and filled with concrete and used on commercial and residential furniture.

Column, memorial: A structure having approximately the form of a column, with capital, shaft, and base complete, but having no heavy superstructure and erected independently as a memorial.

Column, midwall: A column or the like that carries a part of a wall much thicker than its own diameter and which, therefore, stands about halfway between the face and the back of the wall, its axis being about the same as the axis of the wall. In some medieval styles, slender columns are seen carrying very thick walls that rest upon them, and this disposition greatly affects the general design.

Column, unbending: A column whose diameter is of such proportion to its height that, under vertical pressure, it cannot be fractured transversely by any tendency to lateral bending. This proportion of safety varies according to the material used: a column of iron or steel much more slender for a given service than one of stone or marble, which finds its idea of stability in the proportions of the Greek orders.

Column, wreathed: A column so shaped as to present a twisted or spiral form.

Column: (A) A pillar or post; a pier rather slender than thick and especially one that carries a weight and acts as an upright supporting member. In this general sense, the word has been applied to the supporting parts of iron frames of all sorts, so that where the uprights of a piece of carpentry work would commonly be called posts, the cast-iron or wrought-iron uprights are called columns. (B) In special architectural sense, a supporting member of stone or some material used in close imitation of stone and composed of three parts, capital, shaft, and base. The shaft, moreover, is either cylindrical or approximately so; that is, a many-sided prism or a reeded or fluted body whose general shape is cylindrical. In this sense a column need not carry a weight at all large in proportion to its mass; thus the decorative use of columns for memorial purposes involves the placing of a statue, bust, globe, vase, or similar object slight in proportion to the column itself as the only weight superimposed upon the capital. The term is still employed where some one of the above characteristics does not exist; thus, in the earliest columnar architecture, that of the Egyptians, there is no base, and the earliest columnar structures of the Greeks, namely those of the Doric order, were also without bases. Capitals

are, however, universal and mainly decorative in character.

Columna rostrata: An ornamental column decorated with ships' prows. From Roman architecture.

Comb-back chair: A chair that has spindles on the back which resemble a comb.

Combination doors or windows: Combination doors or windows used over regular openings. They provide winter insulation and summer protection and often have self-storing or removable glass and screen inserts. This eliminates the need for handling a different unit each season.

Combination fixture: A fixture that combines one sink and tray or a two- or three-compartment sink or tray in one unit.

Combination sewer: Conveys both storm water and sewage.

Combination: Refers to yarns or fabrics. (A) A combination yarn is composed of two or more yarns having the same or different fibers or twists; e.g., one yarn may have a high twist; the other, little or no twist. (B) A combination fabric is one which uses the above yarns.

Combined waste and vent system: A specially designed system of waste piping, embodying the horizontal wet venting of one or more floor sinks or floor drains by means of a common waste and vent pipe, adequately sized to provide free movement of air above the flow line of the drain.

Combined water: The water chemically held as water of crystallization by calcium sulfate dihydrate, or hemihydrate crystal.

Combustibility: A measure of the tendency of a material to burn.

Combustible: Capable of burning.

Common brick: Ordinary bricks used for walls.

Common seal trap: A P-trap with a 2" to 4" water seal depth.

Common vent: A vent that connects at the junction of two fixture drains and serves as a vent for both fixtures. Also called dual vent.

Compaction resistance: That property of a fibrous or loose fill material which resists compaction under load or vibratory conditions.

Companion flange: A pipe flange to connect with another flange or a flanged valve or fitting. It is attached to the pipe by threads, welding, or other method and differs from a flange, which is an integral part of a pipe or fitting.

Compatible for color and grain: In Millwork, that members shall be selected so that lighter-than-average color members will not be adjacent to darker than average color members, and there will be no sharp color contrast between the adjacent members. Two adjacent members shall not be widely dissimilar in grain, character, and figure.

Compatible materials: Substances that can be mixed or used together without separating, reacting, or affecting the materials adversely.

Compensation: (A) Payment for services rendered or products or materials furnished or delivered. (B) Payment in satisfaction of claims for damages suffered.

Completed activity: An activity with an actual finish date.

Completed operations insurance: Liability insurance coverage for injuries to persons or damage to property occurring after an operation is completed but attributed to that operation. An operation is completed (A) When all operations under the contract have been completed or abandoned; (B) When all operations at one project site are completed; (C) When the portion of the work out of which the injury or damage arises has been put to its intended use by the person or organization for whom that portion of the work was done. Completed operations insurance does not apply to damage to the completed work itself.

Completion, substantial: See date of substantial completion.

Completion date: The date established in the contract documents for substantial completion of the work. See date of substantial completion; time of completion.

Completion list: See inspection list.

Component: (A) A constituent part, ingredient. (B) In codes, any assembly, subassembly, or combination of elements for use as a part of a building which may include structural, electrical, mechanical, plumbing and fire protection systems, and other building systems affecting life safety. (C) In mechanics, one of two or more forces that make up the force with which the constructor is concerned, or into which that force may be considered as being divided. Thus, in estimating the force of wind against a sloping roof, that force may be considered as resolved into two components; one acting normal to the roof and producing a transverse stress on the rafters, the other acting in the direction of the slope and tending to overturn the roof.

Comprehensive general liability insurance: A broad form of liability insurance covering claims for bodily injury and property damage that combines under one policy coverage for all liability exposures (except those specifically excluded) and automatically covers new and unknown hazards that may develop. Comprehensive liability insurance automatically includes contractual liability coverage for certain types of contract. Products liability, completed operations liability and broader contractual liability, coverages are available

on an optional basis. This policy may also be written to include automobile insurance.

Comprehensive services: Professional services performed by the architect in addition to the basic services, in such related areas as project analysis, programming, land use studies, feasibility investigations, financing, construction management, and special consulting services.

Compression faucet: A faucet where the flow of water is shut off by a washer that is compressed or forced down onto its seat.

Compression joint: A multipiece joint with cup-shaped threaded nuts which, when tightened, compress tapered sleeves so that they form a tight joint on the periphery of the tubing they connect.

Compression member (piece): In a framework, truss, or the like, a brace, post, or strut, which are the more specific terms for pieces calculated to resist strains of compression in the direction of their length. The term is not usually understood as applying to a piece of material that merely sustains a weight through its resistance to crushing, as a template.

Compression molding: Heat is applied to thermosetting materials and squeezed into desired shape. This process is not usually done on thermoplastic.

Compression stop: A nonrated glove valve.

Compression: Stress given to a body causing it to become shorter or smaller.

Compressive strength: Significant where insulation must support a load or withstand mechanical abuse without crushing.. When cushioning or filling in space is needed (i.e., expansion/contraction joints), low compressive materials are specified. That property of a material which resists any change in dimensions when acted upon by a compaction force.

Compressor: A mechanical device for increasing the pressure of air or gas.

Concave: A curved or vaulted surface; the opposite of convex.

Concealed damages: Injury to property not immediately apparent from the outside of the object or packaging with superficial inspection.

Concealed picture mold: See screeds.

Concealed spaces: Spaces not generally visible after the project is completed such as furred spaces, pipe spaces, pipe and duct shafts, spaces above ceilings, unfinished spaces, crawl spaces, attics, ,and tunnels.

Conceptual schedule (proposal schedule): A condensed schedule used primarily to give the client a general idea of the project scope containing a few number of activities.

Concrete blocks: Hollow or solid blocks of concrete used in building.

Concrete plain: Concrete either without reinforcement or reinforced only for shrinkage or temperature changes.

Concrete: A building material made by mixing small fragments of hard material with mortar to form an artificial stone. There are different ways of mixing and applying it; thus, in good work, granite, trap rock, or other hard stone is broken into pieces with a given size limit as when it is specified that every fragment shall pass through a 2" diameter ring. This precaution is often very improperly dispensed with. So in putting the concrete into place, it is sometimes mixed on the spot, shovelled into place, rammed, and left to harden.

Concrete may be made in solid blocks by ramming it in a mold. These may be used to build with even in the form of lintels, because, if made of good materials, it can endure a considerable transverse strain. It is most commonly used for foundations by filling up trenches in the ground and so forming a level and permanent bed for the mason work above. Even in foundations laid upon solid rock, great use is made of concrete, because the irregular broken surface left from blasting or the pickaxe can be smoothed to a perfectly uniform bed capable of receiving the most carefully laid walling.

Modern concrete is made of broken stone or gravel, usually not more than 2-1/2" in any dimension. Mortar composition varies with the purpose of the work. If natural light-burned cements are used in concrete for foundations above water and the backing or hearting of heavy walls, 2 parts of sand to 1 part of cement and 5 parts of broken stone and gravel is sufficient. For subaqueous work, foundations, and walls much exposed to the weather, Portland cement only should be used, which will bear more sand and consequently more of the hard material, two and a half to three parts of sand may be mixed with one part of cement and five or six parts of broken stone and gravel. They are mixed preferably by machinery; if mixed by hand, the mortar is spread upon a solid bed, the stone or gravel placed upon it, and the whole turned over until each stone is coated with mortar. It is then transported to its place in the work, leveled in layers of 6" to 8" and rammed until the fluid mortar appears upon the surface. The finer kinds of concrete, made with very small materials carefully mixed and molded, may be classed as artificial stone.

Condensate barrier: A coating or laminate on the inner surface of metal jacketing.

Condensate drain: Piping carrying condensed water from air conditioning or refrigeration drip pans to a point to discharge.

Condensate: The liquid formed by condensation of vapor. In steam heating it is water condensed from steam. In air conditioning it is the water extracted from the air by cooling.

Condensation: The act of water vapor turning into liquid water upon contact with a cold surface.

Condition of the bid: Conditions set forth in the instructions to bidders, the notice to bidders or advertisement for bids, the invitation to bidders or other similar documents prescribing the conditions under which bids are to be prepared, executed, submitted, received, and accepted.

Condition precedent: (A) A condition that must exist or an event that must occur before the execution of a contract document or an agreement. (B) Under explicit terms of an agreement, a condition that must exist or an event that must occur before an obligation under the agreement becomes mandatory.

Conditional payment clause: A clause in some subcontracts making receipt of payment by the prime contractor from the owner a condition precedent to payment of the subcontractor for work the subcontractor has performed.

Conditioned air: Air treated to control simultaneously its temperature, humidity, and cleanliness to meet the requirements of a conditioned space. May be chilled and/or heated and should be clearly defined.

Conditioned space: See air conditioning space.

Conditions of the contract: Those portions of the contract documents that define, set forth, or relate to contract terminology, the rights and responsibilities of the contracting parties and others involved in the work, requirements for safety and compliance with laws and regulations, general procedures for the orderly prosecution and management of the work, payments to the contractor, and similar general, nontechnical provisions. The conditions of the contract include general, supplementary, and other conditions.

Conductance (C): A measure of the rate of heat flow for the actual thickness of a material (either more or less than 1"), 1 square foot in area, at a temperature difference of 1° F. If the K of a material is known, the C can be determined by dividing the K by the thickness. The lower the C, the higher the insulation value.

Conduction: The transfer of heat energy within a body or between two bodies in physical contact.

Conductivity, thermal (K): Based on 1" thickness, necessary for heat loss calculations.

Conductivity (K): The amount of heat that passes through a homogeneous material 1" thick and 1 square foot in area in an hour's time with a temperature difference of 1%

between the two surfaces. Values of K are expressed in Btu's per hour (Btuh). The lower the K, the higher the insulating value.

Conductor, plumbing: The piping from the roof to the building storm drain, combined building sewer, or other approved means of disposal located inside of the building.

Conduit, electrical: A pipe, usually metal, in which wire is installed.

Conduit metal (flexible): Flexible tubing.

Conduit: (A) A channel or pipe for conveying water or other fluids. (B) A passage, underground or otherwise concealed, for secret communication. (C) A tube for protecting electric wires.

Cone of vision: The angle that encompasses the view of the observer, usually 45°-60°. The important elements of the drawing should be within this cone of vision.

Cone reflector: Parabolic reflector that directs light downward thereby eliminating brightness at high angles.

Confluent vent: A vent serving more than one fixture vent or stack vent.

Consent of surety: Written consent of the surety on a performance bond or labor and material bond to contract changes, such as change orders or reductions in the contractor's retainage, final payment, or to waiving notification of contract changes. The term is also used with respect to an extension of time in a bid bond.

Consequential damage: Loss or injury that does not follow directly from an act but only from its results.

Consideration: Something of value requested by the offer or in exchange for a promise to the offeree. It is an inducement to get a person to perform their part of the bargain, or contract, such as by paying money. A valid contract requires consideration by both parties. Consideration may be in the form of a forbearance, which is refraining from suing or from doing something that one is legally entitled to do.

Consistency (normal): The number of millitres of water per 100 g of gypsum plaster or gypsum concrete required to produce a mortar or slurry of specified fluidity.

Consolidation and joinder: The act of uniting lawsuits or arbitration cases and parties into one trial or arbitration proceeding when they involve substantially the same subject matter, issues, and defenses.

Constant dollars: The number of dollars required in a specified base year to produce the same business result in some future or past year.

Constraint (restraint): An externally or internally imposed factor affecting the start or completion of a project.

Construction, frame: Construction in which the structural parts are wood or depend upon a wood frame for support. In codes, if masonry veneer is applied to the exterior walls, the classification of this type of construction is usually unchanged.

Construction, general: (A) The manner in which anything is composed or put together. (B) The act and the art of putting parts together to produce a whole. (C) A completed piece of work of a somewhat elaborate kind; especially a building in the ordinary sense.

Construction change: A change in the nature, cost, or time required for a construction project created by conditions or the acts or failures to act of the owner or representative rather than by a written change order, but for which an adjustment in compensation or time under change provisions is explicitly or implicitly permitted by the contract documents or legal precedents, in lieu of a breach of contraction.

Construction coordinating conferences: A meeting of the principal parties involved with the planning and execution of a construction project to establish coordination and job requirements understanding.

Construction cost: The cost of all of the construction portions of a project, generally based upon the sum of the construction contracts) and other direct construction costs. Construction cost does not include the compensation paid to the architect and consultants, the cost of the land, rights-of-way, or other costs defined in the contract documents as the responsibility of the owner.

Construction document phase: The third phase of the architect's basic services. In this phase the architect prepared from the approved design development documents for approval of the owner, the working drawings and specifications and the necessary bidding information. In this phase the architect also assists the owner in the preparation of bidding forms, the conditions of the contract, and the form of agreement between the owner and the contractor.

Construction documents: Working drawings and specifications.

Construction dry-wall: A type of construction in which the interior wall finish is applied in a dry condition, generally in the form of sheet materials or wood paneling rather than plaster.

Construction inspector: See project representative.

Construction management: Special management services performed by the archi-

tect or others during the construction phase of the project under separate or special agreement with the owner. This is not part of the architect's basic services but is an additional service sometimes included in comprehensive services.

Construction manager: A firm that represents the owner in taking bids of trade contractors, coordinating the actions of trade contractors, and administering all of the construction contracts for a fee or a guaranteed minimum price.

Construction phase: Administration of the construction contract; the fifth and final phase of the architect's basic services.

Construction progress delays: Delays in construction projects caused by events not anticipated when the schedules were completed.

Construction representative: A civil service employee or the Officer in charge of construction (OICC) or resident officer in charge of construction (ROICC) staff whose primary function is to inspect or supervise on construction projects for the federal government.

Constructively accelerated: When an owner refuses to grant an extension of time to complete work to which the contractor is entitled and it may entitle the contractor to additional compensation.

Consultant: An individual or organization engaged by the owner or architect to render professional consulting services complementing or supplementing the architect's services.

Contact adhesive: An adhesive which when dry to the touch will adhere to itself instantaneously on contact.

Contact: The application of fire-resistive material directly to structural members to protect them from fire damage.

Contacts: The external live parts of the fuse that provide continuity between the fuse and the balance of the circuit. Also referred to as ferrules, blades, or terminals.

Contaminator: A media or condition that spoils the nature or quality of another media.

Contingency agreement: An agreement, generally between an owner and architect, in which some portion of the architect's compensation is contingent upon the owner's obtaining funds for the project (such as by successful referendum, sale of bonds, or securing of other financing), or some other specially prescribed condition.

Contingency allowance: A sum designated to cover unpredictable or unforeseen items of work or changes subsequently required by the owner.

Contingent clauses: Clauses in the contract that depend on future events or actions that might happen.

Contingent payment clause: See conditional payment clause.

Continuous vent: A vent that is a continuation of the drain to which it connects.

Continuous waste: A drain from two or three fixtures connected to a single trap.

Contract administration: The duties and responsibilities of the architect during the construction phase.

Contract date (scheduled dates, plug dates): Any date specified in the contract or imposed on any project activity or event that affects activity/project schedule.

Contract documents: The owner-contractor (or contractor-subcontractor) agreement, conditions of the contract (general, supplementary, and other conditions), drawings, specifications, all addenda issued before execution of the contract, all modifications thereto, and any other items specifically stipulated as being included in the contract documents.

Contract limit: A limit or perimeter line established on the drawings or elsewhere in the contract documents designing the boundaries of the site available to the contractor for construction.

Contract lines: The survey lines on the construction drawing within which the contractor has the responsibility under the contract. Work outside the contract lines such as sewer or street mains will be the responsibility of the owner or developer.

Contract number: The numeric designation, or a representative code, for the contract included in each report.

Contract sum: The price stated in the owner-contractor (or contractor-subcontractor) agreement, which is the total amount payable by the owner to the contractor for the performance of the work under the contract documents. The contract sum can be adjusted only by change orders.

Contract time: The period of time established in the contract documents within which the work must be completed. The contract time can be adjusted only by change order.

Contract: A legally enforceable promise or agreement. Also see agreement.

Contracting officer: Person designated as an official representative of the owner with specific authority to act in his behalf in connection with a project.

Contractor quality control plan: A plan prepared by the contractor and approved by the owner or agent that outlines the procedure, instructions, reports, and personnel the contractor intends to use in the implementation of the CQC program.

Contractor quality control representative (CQC Rep): An employee of the contractor, appointed in writing and approved by the owner or agent who administer and implements CQC at the job site.

Contractor's affidavit: A certified statement of the contractor, properly notarized, relating to payment of debts and claims, release of liens, or similar matters requiring specific evidence for the protection of the owner. See noncollusion affidavit.

Contractor's liability insurance: Insurance that protects the contractor from the specified claims that may result from the operations under the contract, whether they be by the contractor, any subcontractor or anyone directly or indirectly employed by any of them, or by anyone for whose acts any of them may be liable.

Contractor's option: Provision of the contract documents under which the contractor may select certain specified materials, methods, or systems at his own option, without change in the contract sum.

Contractor: (A) One who contracts. (B) The person or organization responsible for performing the work and identified as such in the owner-contractor agreement.

Contractual liability: Liability assumed by a party under a contract. An indemnification of hold harmless clause is an example of contractual liability.

Contractual obligations: A binding promise or obligation that arises out of the contract documents or an agreement.

Contractual relationship: The mutually benefitting and obliging conditions under which the two parties to a contract work together in fulfilling the terms of the contract.

Contrast rendition factor (CRF): The ratio of visual task contrast with a given lighting environment to the contrast with sphere illumination. Contrast measured under sphere illumination is defined as 1.00.

Contrast: The difference in brightness (luminance) of an object and its background.

Control joint (expansion): A formed metal section limiting the areas of unbroken plaster surfaces to minimize possible cracking due to expansion, contraction, and initial shrinkage in Portland cement plaster.

Controller: The cabinet containing motor starter(s), circuit breaker(s), disconnect switch(s), and other control devices for the control of electric motors and internal combustion engine driven fire pumps.

Conurbation: A city planning term denoting a group of towns geographically or functionally linked together.

Convection: Heat transferred through movement of fluid or air.

Convector: A device that produces convection.

Convex: A protruding rounded surface.

Coordination: The use of main, feeder, and branch circuit overcurrent protective devices that will isolate only that portion of an electrical system which has been overloaded or faulted. See selectivity.

Cope: To overhang with a downward slope, as the soffit of a corona. Generally, cope over.

Coped joint: See scribing.

Coped: To cut the end of one member to match the profile of another molded member.

Coping: Material or member used to form a capping or finish at the top of a wall, pier, or the like to protect it by throwing off the water on one or both sides. In some cases a level coping suffices, if of stones or tiles wider than the walls; usually it is formed with a pitch one way or from the center both ways.

Coping, parallel: A coping that is not sloped on top to shed the water, but flat; it should consequently only be used on inclined surfaces, such as gables, or in places not exposed to the rain.

Corbel course: A projecting course of stones supporting horizontal members.

Corbel out: To build out one or more courses of brick or stone from the face of a wall to form a support for timbers.

Corbel table: A set of corbels below the eaves. Common in Norman architecture.

Corbel: A bracket of that form which is best fitted to ordinary conditions of cut stone or other masonry. In French, the corresponding term *corbeau* is limited to a bracket having, particularly, two opposite vertical sides, as distinguished from the *cul de lampe*, which has a generally pyramidal or conical shape. In this limited sense a modillion is a corbel; but the term corbel is used more commonly for medieval and outlying styles of architecture. In English books the term has a special application to those wall brackets of many forms which in Gothic architecture serve as starting places for vaulting ribs. Sometimes these are simple *culs de lampe*; but sometimes they are dwarf vaulting shafts with caps and bases.

Corbelling: Masonry course progressively extending out beyond the course below.

Core cock: A valve through which the water flow is controlled by a plug or circular core closely fitted in a machined seat. The core is partly bored through to serve as a waterway. A plug valve.

Core: The gypsum structure between the face and back papers of gypsum board.

Cored tile or block: See gypsum tile or block.

Cork: The outer bark of a Mediterranean oak tree used for wall coverings and insulation.

Corner bead clip: A metal section used, where necessary, to provide an extension for attachment of corner beads.

Corner bead: Fabricated metal with flanges and bead at junction of flanges; used to protect arrises.

Corner boards: Used as trim for the external corners of a house or other frame structure against which the ends of the siding are finished.

Corner braces: Diagonal braces at the corners of a frame structure to stiffen and strengthen the wall.

Corner reinforcement, exterior: A metal section, usually shaped of wire, for the reinforcement of exterior plaster arrises.

Corner reinforcement, interior: Flat or shaped reinforcing units of metal or plastic mesh. See cornerite.

Corner: The section of a facade where two edges meet at an angle.

Cornerite: Corner reinforcement for interior plastering where the plaster base is not continuous around an internal corner or angle.

Cornerstone: A carefully prepared and dressed stone which is put in place with certain ceremonies on a fixed day soon after the beginning of an important building. It is usual to select a prominent part of the building, such as one of its corners, and also to carry up the foundation walls to a little distance above the ground level of the site, in order that the stone, once laid by the officiant, may remain in place permanently. It is also common to prepare a small cavity in the stone to receive certain documents, such as a description of the undertaking, a list of its promoters, a few newspapers of the day, and some current coins. Anciently, a stone of the actual foundation was treated in this way, and the term foundation stone (A.P.S.) was used to describe it.

Cornice or cove lighting: Lighting fixtures hidden in a wall or ceiling by a cornice.

Cornice return: That portion of the cornice that returns on the gable end of a house.

Cornice: The crowning member of a wall or part of a wall, such as a coping or water table treated architecturally. It has several special meanings. (A) In the classical entablature, the uppermost of its three principal members. It may crown a colonnade, a dado or basement wall, porch, or even a purely ornamental feature, such as the casing of window. In buildings of classical design having more than one story, a cornice crowns the whole wall and is proportioned rather to the height of that wall than to the height of the uppermost order if the building is of columnar architecture. In this sense the wall cornice has been said to have been borrowed from the order. (B) A piece of light woodwork, embossed metal, or the like, set horizontally at the top of a window

casing within, either to conceal the rod and rings that carry the curtains to form a lambrequin as part of the upholstery, or to give emphasis to the height of the window.

Cornice, block: In neoclassic architecture, a wall cornice produced by a simplification of the classic entablature. Modillions of some sort, usually very plain, carry a cornice proper of slight projection and rest upon a simple bed mold. The term is used loosely for any very plain wall cornice.

Corporation cock: A stopcock screwed into the street water main to supply the house service connection.

Corridor rest stops: Wheelchair parking and seating provided at intervals in a corridor.

Corrosion: Gradual decomposition by chemical action, as by the action of water on iron, producing rust. Differing from disintegration, which is the result of mechanical action. In practice, the term is generally used only in the case of metals; decay is the usual term in the case of stone or wood.

Corrugate: To form into alternate ridges and furrows (corrugations), as in preparing certain forms of sheet metal, wire lathing, etc., for use in building.

Corrugated metal: Thin plates of metal that have been drawn or rolled into parallel ridges and furrows. The object of the corrugation is to give greater strength to the plates of metal to resist bending in the direction of the furrows, or perpendicular to the general plane of the sheet, also to permit expansion and contraction laterally. Corrugated iron is used largely to cover roofs of buildings of a certain class, machine shops, car houses, barns, etc. The sides and ends of such buildings of the cheaper class are sometimes covered with it. The sheets of corrugated metal are supported on purlins, to which they are attached by long hooks, or on sheathing, where they are secured with long, soft nails driven through and bent on the under side. All holes for nails, rivets, or clamps are made in the top part of a corrugation.

Cost breakdown: See schedule of values.

Cost category: The name and number of a functional, hardware, or other significant cost category for which costs are to be summarized.

Cost control: Utilizes data on planned and actual expenditures by activity, provides reports on status of expenditures compared with those planned; predicts ultimate cost of project compared with planned cost, summarizes data by accounting periods.

Cost optimization: Utilizes normal and crash cost estimated for each activity to make time-out trade-cost trade-off computations, provides list of alternative project duration and associated costs.

Cost-plus-fee agreement: An agreement under which the contractor (or subcontractor or architect) is reimbursed for all direct and indirect costs and in is paid a fee for all services. This fee usually is stated as a stipulated sum or percentage of cost. Also referred to as a cost reimbursement agreement.

Cost-plus-fee change orders: A change order agreement under which the contractor (or subcontractor or architect) is reimbursed for his direct and indirect costs and, in addition, is paid a fee for his services. This fee is usually stated as a stipulated sum or percentage of cost.

Counter ceiling: A secondary ceiling interposed between the floor and ceiling of a room to exclude sounds originating in the room above. A layer of sound-obstructing material or deafening, either mineral wool, sawdust, or the like, is sometimes spread over the upper surface of the counter ceiling to assist in opposing the transmission of sound.

Counter sinks: Bits for dishing holes in iron, brass, and wood.

Counterflashing: A flashing usually used on chimneys at the roofline to cover shingle flashing and to prevent moisture entry.

Counterpoise: A weight that tends to balance the action of another weight; in architecture, especially, a weight considerably greater than another which prevents any injurious action by the latter. A corbel, for instance, acts by means of the heavy counterpoise which holds in place its longer and heavier member, generally built into the wall; and prevents the dislocation of the building by the weight acting upon the projecting part of the corbel.

Countersink: (A) To form a depression or hole for the reception of a piece that is not to project beyond the general surface. The cutting may be made to fit the object accurately, as in setting a hinge flush with the surrounding woodwork, or it may be a recess larger than the member, as a hole made to receive the head of a bolt. (B) To let into a surface by means of a recess as above described.

Couple, main: A pair of principals; one of several couples that support other subordinate rafters.

Couple: (A) A pair of forces equal, parallel, and acting in opposite directions, but not in the same straight line. They tend to make the body acted upon rotate about an axis upon which they exert no pressure. (B) A pair of rafters with their tie beam, collar beam, or other pieces which go to make up the simplest form of truss. (C) To arrange, set, or unite in pairs.

Coupling: A pipe fitting with female threads only, used to connect two pipes in a straight line.

Course, blocking: A parapet, usually a very plain wall like a range of stone blocks, used to replace a pierced parapet, a balustrade, or the like. In some cases the blocking course is not a true parapet, because it is too low to serve in that capacity or because the roof has been raised to the top of it. In this case it is a mere flat band above the wall cornice.

Course: (A) Generally one of many horizontal or less frequently inclined, rows of relatively small pieces, uniformly disposed and more or less connected, bonded, or united in one structure or member, as of bricks when laid in a wall, slates on a roof, and the like. (B) To lay in courses, as masonry; to lay evenly and more or less regularly, approximating uniform and regular courses. (C) To build in courses of masonry, as a wall or pier.

Cove ceiling: The upper side of a room which is so designed that coves, large in proportion to the extent of the ceiling, join the vertical wall with the flat part of the ceiling. In interiors of the eighteenth century the cove is often very large and without strong horizontal markings either on the wall side or the ceiling. It is richly adorned with paintings and carved panels which are, therefore, displayed in a position relative to the eye of a person sitting or standing below, which makes them easy to see and enjoy.

Cove molding: A molding with a concave face used as trim or to finish interior corners.

Cove: (A) A surface of concave, more or less cylindrical, form, whether of a small molding or a large structure, as a vault or cornice. (B) To construct with a cove or coves; to give the form of a cove to.

Cover fillet: A molding used to cover a paneling joint.

Cover: To place insulation or finish materials on, over, or around a surface to insulate, protect, or seal.

Coverage: The rate in square feet per gallon (coatings), or gallons per hundred square feet (mastics), at which products must be applied to obtain satisfactory performance.

Coving: (A) That part of a structure which forms a coved projection beyond the parts below, as a concave, curved surface under the overhang of a projecting upper story; a cove or series of coves. (B) The curved or splayed jambs of a fireplace which narrows toward the back.

Cowl: A cap, hood, or like contrivance for covering and protecting the open top of a pipe, shaft, or other duct while permitting the free passage of air. It may be merely a bent-over portion of the pipe or a more elaborate device, such as a contrivance for improving the draught of a chimney; usually a metal tube or pipe nearly as large as the flue and arranged at the top with a curve bring the smoke out in a nearly horizontal direction. It is customary to make the curved tube separate, free to rotate, and fitted with a wind vane, so that it will turn easily and always present the convex or closed part of the curve to the force of the wind. The term is also applied to a similar contrivance at the top of a ventilating shaft.

Crawl space: A shallow space below the living quarters of a basementless house, normally enclosed by the foundation wall.

Craze cracks: See check cracks.

Creasing: A course, or several courses, of tiles or bricks laid upon the top of a wall or chimney with a projection of an inch or two for each course over the one below to throw off water. The coping, if there is one, comes above the creasing. A layer of slates or metal over a projecting string course or window cap, serving as a flashing to prevent the infiltration of moisture, is also called a creasing. The term is little used in the United States.

Cricket: A piece of sloped roofing laid in an otherwise horizontal valley to produce one or more sloping valleys to throw off water that would otherwise be retained. Thus, if a sloping roof is interrupted by a chimney standing squarely across the slope, a horizontal valley would naturally result along the upper side. It is therefore usual to construct there a small piece of roofing sloping laterally in one or both directions, so as to produce one or two diagonal valleys at its meeting with the main roof.

Critical activity: Any activity on a critical path.

Critical level: The point on a backflow prevention device or vacuum breaker conforming to approved standards and established by the recognized (approved) testing laboratory (usually stamped or marked CL or C/L on the device by the manufacturer) which determines the minimum elevation above the flood level rim of the fixture or receptacle served at which the device may be installed. When a backflow prevention device does not bear critical level marking, the bottom of the vacuum breaker, combination valve, or any such approved device shall constitute the critical level.

Critical path method: A charting of all events and operations to be encountered in completing a given process, showing the relative significance of each event, and establishing the optimum sequence and duration of operations. A scheduling technique using arrow or precedence diagrams to determine the length of a project and identify the activities and constraints that are on the critical path.

Critical path: That particular sequence of activities in a path that has the greatest negative or least positive slack; therefore, the longest path through the network. The sequence of operations charted under the critical path method that must be completed by the dates specified to prevent delays in the project.

Cross bracing: (A) Any system of bracing with crossed struts or ties, as in many bridge trusses. (B) In house carpentry, continuous lines of crossed braces or struts between the floor joists, which are put in at intervals of 6' or 8' to stiffen the floors by distributing over several joists any shock or strain upon one. Generally called bridging, cross bridging, or herringbone bridging.

Cross bridging: A kind of bridging consisting of a series of small diagonal braces set in rows transversely to the timbers. The braces are generally of light scantling, about 2" x 3", or somewhat less and, in floors, extend from the top of one beam to the bottom of the next, crossing each other at the middle. The term, as also herringbone bridging, is usual in the United States; drumming, twanging, strutting, and herringbone strutting being applied in different parts of Great Britain. The continuous rows of such crossing braces are generally put in about 5' or 6' apart.

Cross connection: Any physical connection between two otherwise separated piping systems, one of which contains potable water and the other water or other substance of unknown or questionable safety, whereby flow may occur from one system to the other, the direction of flow depending on the pressure differential between the two systems see backflow and back-siphonage.

Cross cut: To cut transversely or against the grain of a slab. In ornamental rocks, a distinction is made between smooth-cut and cross-cut slabs, which usually look different.

Cross furring: The smaller horizontal members attached at right angles to the underside of main runners or other structural supports. See channels and furring.

Cross rail: A primary horizontal member of a timber-form wall.

Cross scratching: Scratching in two directions of the plaster scratch coat, to provide mechanical bond for the brown coat. See scoring.

Cross section: A view of an object that cuts through at its longest axis from a right angle.

Cross valve: A valve fitted on a transverse pipe so as to open communication between two parallel pipes.

Cross-bridging: Diagonal bracing between adjacent floor joists, placed near the center of the joist span to prevent joists from twisting.

Cross-over: A pipe fitting with a double offset or shaped like the letter U with the ends turned out, used to pass the flow of one pipe past another when the pipes are in the same plane.

Cross: A pipe fitting with four branches in pairs, each pair on one axis, and the axis at right angles.

Crossgrained: Having the grain transverse or oblique to the length, said particularly of boards in which, owing to the crookedness of the log from which they are cut, the grain lies diagonally or crooked in the plane or width of the board, such stuff being liable to chip under the plane, and difficult to work.

Crown molding: A molding used on a cornice or wherever an interior angle is to be covered.

Crown of a trap: The part of a trap in which the direction of flow changes from upward to downward.

Crown vent: A vent pipe connected at the topmost point in the crown of a trap.

Crown weir: The highest part of the bottom inside surface of the crown of a trap.

Crown-post: A vertical timber standing centrally on a tie-beam and supporting a collar purlin.

Crown: (A) The head of anything, especially of an arch or vault. Like haunch, the term is applied to a part of an arch which cannot be limited exactly. By extension, used attributively, as crown cornice, crown molding, and the like. (B) That part of the trap in which the direction of flow is changed from upward to horizontal.

Cryogenic insulation: See insulation.

Cubage: The architectural volume of building; the sum of the products of (A) the areas and (B) height from the underside of the lowest floor construction system to the average height of the surface of the finished roof above, for the parts of the building.

Cubic foot: Measuring unit. Water is measured by gallons and cement is measured by pounds.

Cup: A deviation in the face of a piece from a straight line drawn from edge to edge of a piece. It is measured at the point of greatest distance from the straight line.

Cupola: A bowl-shaped vault, and the imitation of such a vault in lighter materials.

Curb box: A device at the curb that contains a valve that is turned to shut off a supply line, usually of gas or water.

Curb cock or curb stop: A valve placed on the water service nearest the curb line.

Curb: A piece or series of pieces along the edge of a structure to protect, strengthen, or retain other parts or materials, especially when rising above an adjoining level. Specifically: (A) A dwarf wall or similar structure, acting more or less as a retaining wall, as the upper part of the wall surrounding a well and which projects above the ground: a well curb. (B) A line of vertical stones along the edge of a sidewalk, often called

curbstone or, collectively, curbstones. (C) A retaining number or belt, forming a ring at the base of a dome, as an iron framework, or connected stones of a course. (D) A similar horizontal member set between two successive slopes of a roof, retaining the feet of the upper ties of timbers; a coaming. (E) A stone block used for border or edging, having a variable length.

Cure (Portland cement plaster or stucco): (A) To provide conditions conductive to the hydration of Portland cement, plaster, or stucco. (B) To maintain proper temperature and sufficient quantity of water within the plaster to ensure cement hydration.

Cure: To change the properties of a plastic or resin by chemical reaction, usually accomplished by the action of either heat or a catalyst.

Curf: An incision, groove, or cut made by a saw or other cutting tool, especially one across the width of a board or molding, usually for the purpose of facilitating its being bent to a curve. Chimneys and piers that have leaned from the vertical are sometimes restored to verticality by cutting a curf in the side from which they lean. In shaping a square timber from the log by hewing, it is common first to cut along one side of the log a series of curfs; that is, notches, the depth of which is regulated so as to form a gauge for the subsequent cutting away of the wood between. Written also kerf.

Curing gent: An additive incorporated in a coating or adhesive resulting in an increase or decrease in the rate of cure.

Current dollars: Dollars received or spent in any year.

Current-limiting fuse: A fuse that will limit both the magnitude and duration of current flow under short circuit conditions.

Current-limiting range: The available fault currents a fuse will clear in less than 1/2 cycle, thus limiting the magnitude of current flow.

Curtail step: The lowest step in a flight of stairs.

Curtail: In stair building, the outward curving portion of the hand rail and the outer end of the lower step or steps of a flight; possibly an abbreviation of curved tail. An ample curtail to the lowest two or three steps not only enhances their appearance, but offers an easier start to persons approaching from the side. A plain semi-circular curtail to the lowest step is called a bull nose.

Curtain wall: A portion of wall contained between two advancing structures, such as wings, pavilions, bastions, or turrets. The term indicates position, and not character or function. A curtain wall may be a mere screen, as to a court or yard, or a part of a facade; it may be solid or fenestrated, either higher or lower than its flanking structures, or of the same height. In modern construc-

tion, most often a thin subordinate wall between two piers or other supporting members; the curtain being primarily a filling and having little or no share in the support of other portions of the structure. Thus, in skeleton construction, curtain walls are built between each two encased columns and usually on a girder at each floor level or thereabouts.

Custom or one-of-a-kind building: Any building manufactured to individual system specifications and not intended for duplication or repetitive manufacture.

Cut end: The end of the gypsum lath with the exposed core.

Cut Stone: Stone accurately shaped for the place it is to occupy in the wall, vault, or other construction, having carefully cut beds and joints and a face more or less smoothed to the general surface of the wall.

Cut-in brace: Nominal 2" thick members, usually 2 by 4's, cut in between each stud diagonally.

Cut-off angle: (of a luminaire) The angle from the vertical at which a reflector, louver, or other shielding device cuts off direct visibility of a light source. It is the complementary angle of the shielding angle. In the case of reflector-type lightshields, it is also important to ascertain the cut-off angle to the reflected image of the light since as this is often almost as bright as the source itself.

Cutoff luminaries: Outdoor luminaries that restrict all light output to below 85° from vertical.

Cypress: A soft wood that smells similarly to cedar.

D

Dado, blind or stopped: A dado that is not visible when the joint is completed.

Dado: (A) In Italian, a tessera or die; hence the flat face of a pedestal between the base and cap. In English it denotes a continuous pedestal or wainscot, including the base and cap molding or sometimes only the plane surface between the baseboard and cap molding of such a continuous pedestal. A panelled wooden dado is generally called a wainscot; the words are often used erroneously as if synonymous. Dado is not usually used of an external pedestal course. (B) A groove formed by dadoing. (C) To cut or form with a groove or grooves of a rectangular section, as in making the upright sides of a bookcase which are so grooved to receive the ends of shelves. (D) To insert in such a groove or grooves; to perform the whole operation of connecting parts in such a manner. Thus, it may be said of a bookcase that the shelves are to be dadoed in. The term is usually applied only to such a method of connection when the groove is made to receive the full thickness of the inserted piece.

Damages: Costs incurred due to the actions or failure to act of another from whom the injured entity seeks compensation. Damages may result from a breach of contract or from damages to persons or property caused by noncontracting parties.

Damp course: A course or layer of impervious material in a wall or floor to prevent the ingress of moisture from the ground or lower courses. It extends entirely through the wall and perhaps upward on the outer face or in the thickness of the wall. It may be of lead, asphalt, or compact and nonporous stone.

Dampen: To check or reduce; to deaden vibration.

Damper: A valve or diaphragm to check or control the draft in a flue or duct. In open fireplace flues, the damper is often a cast-iron or soapstone flap in the throat, lying back, when open, upon a ledge at the back above the throat and tilted forward when it is desired to close the throat against downdrafts. In smoke pipes and furnace flues, it is commonly a metal diaphragm pivoted transversely. An air volume device that regulates air that moves through an outlet.

Darby: A flat wooden tool with handles, about 4" wide and 42" long; used to smooth or float the brown coat; also used on finish coat to give a preliminary true and even surface.

Dash coat: See finish coat.

Dash-bond coat: A thick slurry of Portland cement, sand, and water dashed (thrown or blown) on concrete or masonry surfaces by hand or machine to provide a mechanical bond for the succeeding plaster coat.

Data date (DD): The calendar date that separates historical data from scheduled data or the date when the project has been updated and the network revised.

Date of agreement: The date stated on the face of the agreement. If no date is stated, it could be the date on which the agreement is signed, if this is recorded, or it may be the date established by the award. Also sometimes referred to as the contract date.

Date of commencement of the work: The date established in a notice to proceed or, in the absence of such notice, the date of the agreement or such other date as may be established therein or by the parties thereto.

Date of substantial completion: The date certified by the architect when the work or a designated portion thereof is sufficiently complete, in accordance with the contract documents, so the owner may occupy it. Warranties and responsibilities of ownership commence on this date. See beneficial occupancy and beneficial use.

Daub: A glob of adhesive. To cover or smear roughly, as in building, with coarse plaster or clay; especially when done without any attempt to produce a uniform and regular coat, as in covering wattle work or filling the chinks of a log construction.

Dead burned: Removal of all water content during calcining of gypsum.

Dead end: A branch leading from a soil, waste or vent pipe, building (house) drain or building (house) sewer which is terminated at a developed distance of 2" (0.6m) or more by means of a plug or other closed fitting.

Dead load: A more or less permanent and stationary load, as distinguished from the load of persons, movable furniture, and the like. Especially the load caused by the weight of a structure as distinguished from the load it may be intended to support. Thus, in designing a truss or calculating the size of timbers to carry a floor, the weight of the flooring, ceiling, and other portions of the structure are considered as dead load.

Dead shore: A vertical shoring timber introduced into a wall for repairs or underpinning and left there after the completion of the work. The masonry or brickwork is built up to it on either side or even around it on all sides.

Deafen: Properly, to render or construct to be impervious to sound, as by the introduction of felt or other nonconducting material between the two thicknesses of a double floor or by plaster filling between beams or studs. In this sense, same as deaden. By extension, to fill in or construct in a manner similar to the operations described above, whether primarily to prevent the passage of sound or not; as in making a floor fireproof by filling the spaces between the beams with noncombustible materials.

Deal: In English usage, a piece of pine or fir lumber cut to the dimensions commonly required in joiner work and the lighter branches of carpentry; and hence, without the article, such lumber collectively. The standard deals average 12" x 3" x 9"; these are sawed into whole deals of 1-1/4" thick; slip deals of 5/8" thickness (three cuts), and five-cut stuff when the thickness is 1/2" or less. Pieces less than 7" wide are called battens; if less than 6' long deal ends. This whole system of cutting and naming sawed lumber is unknown in the United States.

Decay: Disintegration of wood due to the action of wood-destroying fungi. Doze, rot, and unsound wood mean the same as decay.

Decibel (DB): A logarithmic measure of the ratio of like power quantities, as used in describing levels of sound pressure or sound power.

Deck paint: An enamel with a high degree of resistance to mechanical wear, designed for use on such surfaces a porch floors.

Decomposition: The separating or breaking down of a substance into its component parts or basic elements.

Deduction (from contract sum): Amount deducted from the contract sum by change order.

Deductive alternate: An alternate bid resulting in a deduction from the same bidder's base bid. See alternate bid.

Deed: A legal document stating rights to a building or land.

Deep seal trap: A P-trap with a water seal more than 4" deep.

Defect: Fault that detracts from the quality, appearance, or utility of the piece. Handling marks or raised grain due to moisture shall not be considered a defect.

Defective language: Language in a contract or agreement that lacks something to be legal or binding.

Deficiencies: See defective work.

Deflection: Turning aside from the normal form or direction; especially, the bending of a horizontal or other member, as a beam or post under a load, by the force of pressure, heat, or the like. Deflection may be temporary or permanent. Every member has a limit of safe deflection, which varies greatly according to the material. Thus, a stone lintel cannot be said to receive any perceptible deflection without rupture; but an iron or wooden beam may be deflected very considerably from the normal and yet be able to recover itself perfectly if case the load is removed, or it may carry that load with safety for a length of time. The displacement that occurs when a load is applied to a member or assembly.

Deformation: The change in shape of a body brought about by the application of a force. Deformation is proportional to the force within the elastic limits of the material. Deformation can entail shortening, which is caused by compression; deflection, which is caused by bending; and elongation, which is tensile deformation.

Dehumidify: The removal of water from a space.

Delamination: The separation of layers in an assembly because of failure of the adhesive, either in the adhesive itself or at the interface between the adhesive and the lamination. For plywood, if separation between the plies is greater than 2" in continuous length, more than 1/4" in depth at any part, and .003" in width, it shall be considered delamination. For solid stock, if the separation between the members is greater than 1/4" deep, more than .00" in width, and the total length of all such delamination is more than 5% of the total length of the glue line, it shall be considered delaminated. If more than one delamination occurs in a single glue line, the total length of all such delamination shall determine whether or not it is considered to be delaminated.

Delays: Anything that delays the completion of the job. It may not be the fault of any party and hence, result only in the extension of time to finish the job. If, however, the delay is the fault of any party, damages may be assessed against him; e.g., a subcontractor who fails to install his work on time may be liable to the general contractor and the other trades for their added expenses caused by his holding up the job. He may be backcharged by the general contractor and sued by the other subcontractors. An owner who fails to deliver the site on time may be liable to the general contractor for the added expenses caused the general contractor by the late start.

Delinquent payment: Monies due from certified payments to contractor (or subcontractor) not paid after expiration of authorized time period.

Demolition: Taking down a building by the gradual and systematic removal of its materials, as distinguished from destruction by fire, explosion, or the like. Demolition of old buildings requires care and system, and in cities must be carried on under special precautions against accident and public annoyance from dust, dirt, and falling materials.

Density: The mass of substance in a unit volume. When expressed in the metric system, it is numerically equal to the specific gravity of the same substance.

Dentil: A small rectangular block, forming one of a series closely set in a row, generally between two moldings, and intended for ornamental effect by alternation of light, shade, and shadow.

Department having jurisdiction: The administrative authority, including any other law enforcement agency affected by any provision of a code, whether such agency is specifically named or not.

Deposit for bidding documents: Monetary deposit required to obtain a set of construction documents and bidding requirements, customarily refunded to bona fide bidders on return of the documents in good condition within a specified time.

Design development phase: The second phase of the architect's basic services, where the architect prepares from the approved schematic design studies for approval by the owner, the design development documents, consisting of drawings, other documents, and such other essentials as may be appropriate, including probable construction costs.

Detailed schedule: This schedule displays the lowest level of detail necessary to manage and control the project through job completion.

Detector, smoke: Listed device for sensing visible or invisible products of combustion.

Detector coverage: The recommended maximum distance between adjacent detectors or the area that a detector is designated to protect.

Detrimental reliance: Liability created by the difference between the low bid and second bid when contractor (subcontractor) withdraws low bid.

Developed length: The length along the center line of the pipe and fittings.

Dewpoint: The temperature of a gas or liquid at which condensation or evaporation occurs.

Diameter: An imaginary line through the center of a circle or sphere, terminating in the perimeter or surface; a similar line in a circular cylinder.

Diamond work: A kind of mason work in which the pieces are set to form diamonds on the face of the wall.

Diamond-edge disk: A rotating cutting tool having a steel body and an abrasive, segmented blade coated with diamond dust; often used for mass-produced products.

Diaphragm control valve: A control valve having a spring-diaphragm actuator.

Diaphragm: A flexible disc used to separate the control medium from the controlled medium and which actuates the valve stem.

Dielectric fitting: A fitting having insulating parts or material that prohibits flow of electric current.

Differential: The variance between two target values, which are the high and low value of conditions.

Diffusivity: The time rate of temperature change within a body or between two of its surfaces.

Digestion: That portion of the sewage treatment process where biochemical decomposition of organic matter takes place, resulting in the formation of simple organic matter.

Dimension: See lumber dimension.

Dimensional stability: That property of a material which enables it to hold its original size, shape, and dimensions.

Dimensioning: Measurement and placement of dimensional information during drawing.

Dimming ballast: Special fluorescent lamp ballast, which when used with a dimmer control, permits varying light output.

Dining room: The room in which the family and guests, if any, come together and dine formally.

Dip of a trap: The lowest part of the top inside surface of the channel through a trap.

Direct cost: Costs charged directly to an activity or work package in the contract.

Direct current (DC): Flow of electricity continuously in one direction from positive to negative.

Direct expense: All items of expense directly incurred by or attributable to a specific project, assignment, or task.

Direct glare: Glare resulting from high luminances or insufficiently shielded light sources in the field of view. It usually is associated with bright areas, such as luminaries, ceilings, and windows that are outside the visual task or region being viewed.

Direct nailing: To nail perpendicular to the initial surface or the junction of the pieces joined. Also called face nailing.

Direct personnel expense: Salaries and wages of principals and employees engaged on a project, assignment, or task, including mandatory and customary benefits.

Direct stress: Stress that is evenly distributed.

Disbursement agreement: An agreement, usually involving a third party, setting forth responsibilities and procedures under which construction funds will be disbursed to contractors whose payments have been certified.

Disc: That part of a valve which actually closes off the flow.

Discharge lamp: A lamp in which light (or radiant energy near the visible spectrum) is produced by the passage of an electric current through a vapor or a gas.

Discomfort glare: Glare producing discomfort. It does not necessarily interfere with visual performance or visibility.

Dishwasher: An appliance for washing dishes, glassware, flatware, and some utensils.

Disintegration: The destruction of the cohesion of the particles of which a body is composed; especially as applied to stone. It is generally due to the destruction of the cementing substance by the action of frost, water, etc., because water that has been absorbed into the pores of the stone, in freezing expands and throws off grains and even scales from the surface.

Dispersion: Distributing or scattering sound in space.

Displacement: The volume or weight of a fluid, such as water, displaced by a floating body.

Disposer: An appliance, motor driven, for reducing food and other waste by grinding, so that it can flow through the drainage system.

Distress writer: A surety company that specializes in writing bonds for principals who do not qualify for bonding by more conservative surety companies. Such companies may rely more heavily on security posted by the principal or on collateral in-

demnities rather than the traditional three C's of surety underwriters: character, competence, and credit.

Distribution duct or cell: A raceway of various cross-section, placed within or just below the floor and from which the wires and cables serve a specific floor area.

Distribution panel: Box containing circuit breakers or fuses where power is distributed to branch circuits.

Dividers, bisecting: Dividers so adjusted that the distances between two pairs of points have a constant ratio of one-half.

Division (of the specifications): One of the 16 basic organizational subdivisions used in the Uniform System for Construction Specifications, Data Filing, and Cost Accounting.

Document Deposit: See deposit for bidding documents.

Documentary: A document from the eighteenth century that has been printed on wallpaper or cloth.

Dolomite: A stone resembling limestone but consisting of the carbonates of lime and magnesia.

Dome: (A) A building, generally one of importance, and a public building rather than a dwelling. The use, in Italian, of the word *duomo*, and the corresponding German word *dom*, applied to a cathedral church, seems to have had no influence in

England. (B) A cupola; more commonly used for a large one covering in a good part of a building. In this sense also it is loose and inaccurate, and it would be far better if the word cupola were used exclusively for a roof of this kind. (C) An evenly curved vault on a circular base.

Domestic sewage: The liquid and water-borne wastes derived from ordinary living, free from industrial wastes, and of such character as to permit satisfactory disposal, without special treatment, into the public sewer or by means of a private sewage disposal system.

Door, batten: The body of the door is made of boards or planks having battens nailed across them to keep all in place; common in very rough work, barracks, sheds, outbuildings, etc.

Door, blind: In the United States, a door having the character of, and serving as, a blind; i.e., having fixed or movable slats.

Door, crapaudine: A door turning upon a pivot at top and bottom, the pivots being let into sockets in the lintel and threshold.

Door, double: Door divided into two folds, hung on each side of a doorway; the two folds, or valves, meeting in or near the middle and close the opening; commonly known as a folding door.

Door, double framed: Door with an outside framed structure, complete with stiles and rails, which encloses and holds a sec-

ondary framed structure of stiles, rails, and panels, the latter forming a panel to the outside frame.

Door, double margin: A door made to appear as though consisting of two leaves, as in imitation of a folding door. It has a stile at the center twice as wide as the side stiles and is center beaded or otherwise finished to resemble two stiles, therefore showing a double margin.

Door, Dutch: In the United States, a door divided horizontally into two pieces, so that the lower half can be kept shut while the upper half remains open for the admission of air.

Door, flap: (A) A door placed horizontally or on an incline, and opening up, as is common, over steps leading to a cellar from the street. (B) A small door or shutter in a vertical opening but hinged at the bottom so as to open downwards. Also called falling door.

Door, folding: A door divided into two or more folds, or valves, which are hinged to the frame or to one another. A few doors exist in which each half is again halved, much on the principle of the folding inside shutters of a window. Of similar character are the doors arranged in schoolhouses, church lecture rooms, and the like, which, by means of a series of valves hinged one to another, may divide a large room as if by a partition, and open it up again into one room by folding against the wall the valves forming the partition. Something similar is to be found in connection with certain park gates which are closed by night and opened by day. In such cases, it is essential that the valves should be supported by means of little wheels running on arcs of metal set in the floor or the road. The above are properly folding doors, or gates; the word is applied also to double doors.

Door, half: (A) Properly, one half of a dutch door; the term is also applied to the Dutch door complete, as when it is said that the outer doorways of a frame house are hung with half doors. (B) In the United States, a door less in height than the doorway, so as to leave a considerable opening above and below.

Door, jib: A door hinged to be flush with the wall on either side and, if carefully adjusted, almost indistinguishable when shut. The object of it is usually not secrecy but the preservation of perfect symmetry in a room where other doors correspond each to each, and no such feature is desired at the place where the jib door is put.

Door, ledged: Door constructed with the use of ledges, as in a batten door.

Door, overhung: Door hinged at the top and swinging upward, requiring to be held open by a hook.

Door, revolving: A weather door devised in the United States, which, when in opera-

tion, consists of four equal flaps hung at right angles to a pivot at the axis of a cylindrical structure within which the doors revolve. The outer edges of the doors are finished with rubber strips maintaining close contact with the inside face of the cylindrical shell, which is pierced with two opposite doorways so disposed that the direct passage between them is at all times closed by the doors, in whatever position. Pedestrians pass by pushing any one flap, as in a turnstile. When not in operation, the doors may be folded together to allow direct passage at either side or bolted across the passage for security.

Door, rolling: A rolling shutter applied to a doorway.

Door, sash: Door whose upper half, or thereabouts, is constructed as a sash to hold glass; generally as one piece, but sometimes having a movable sash.

Door, sham: A door finished only on one side and set in a wall or partition to appear like a practicable door.

Door, sliding: A door arranged to slide sideways. In stables, freight houses, etc., it slides in the open against the back face of the wall; in dwelling houses it slides into a pocket in the wall or partition. It may be either single or double.

Door, swing: Door that has no striking piece and swings past the door post at the side opposite the hinges. Such doors are commonly hung with double action spring hinges, but it is easy to arrange one with two pairs of single action hinges by using a strip of wood as thick as the door, hinged to the doorpost on one side and to the door on the other, the hinges being naturally turned in the opposite ways.

Door, trap: Door that is fitted to an opening in a horizontal, or nearly horizontal, surface, as a floor or roof. A person ascends head first through it and descends feet first. The cellar door, as described above, is a variety of trap door.

Door, window, and room finish schedules: Charts of blueprints that give information about doors, windows, etc.

Door, Venetian: A doorway divided into three parts by two mullions, or shafts. The central and wider part is occupied by the door, and the narrow side openings are windows. The central opening generally has a glazed arch over the door.

Door hanger: A hanger for the support of a sliding door, especially such a door when hung from above. The meaning of the term is usually extended to mean the entire apparatus for such purpose, including the track or rails from which the door may be supported.

Door: The filling, usually solid, of a doorway, so secured as to be easily opened and shut. It is much more common to support a door by hinges secured to the doorpost or frame at the side; but a door may turn on pivots at top and bottom, as frequently in antiquity, or may slide or roll up horizontally or vertically. Where the solid filling is hung by hinges at the top of the doorway, or where it slides vertically, in the manner of a portcullis, it is rarely called a door.

Doorjamb, interior: The surrounding case into which and out of which a door closes and opens. It consists of two upright pieces, called side jambs, and a horizontal head jamb.

Doors, French: Two doors that are joined together, open in the middle, and have glass panes.

Doors, weather: A door or pair of doors planned to shut quickly behind persons passing through the outer doors of a lobby and so prevent much ingress of cold air. These are commonly extra doors fixed outside of the usual entrance in cold weather, and the term is often used to include the light and sometimes temporary vestibule or porch which includes the door.

Doorstep: (A) The sill of a doorway; that upon which one steps in passing from a lower level through the doorway. (B) By extension, the platform with two or three steps outside of an outer door.

Doorway: An opening for entrance and exit from a building or part of a building;

such an opening, together with its immediate surroundings.

Dope: Term used by plasterers for additives made to any type of mortar to either accelerate or retard its set.

Dormer: An opening in a sloping roof, the framing of which projects out to form a vertical wall suitable for windows or other openings.

Dosing tank: A watertight tank in a septic system placed between the septic tank and the distribution box and equipped with a pump or automatic siphon designed to discharge sewage intermittently to a disposal field. This is done so that rest periods may be provided between discharges.

Dot: A small projection of basecoat plaster placed on a surface and faced out between grounds to assist the plasterer in obtaining the proper plaster thickness and surface plane; occasionally pieces of metal or wood applied to plaster base at intervals as spot grounds to gauge plaster thickness. See screeds, plaster.

Double disc: A two-piece disc used in the gate valve. Upon contact with the seating faces in the valve, the wedges between the disc faces force them against the body seats to shut off the flow.

Double hung: (A) Furnished with, or made up of, two sashes one above the other, arranged to slide vertically past each other; said of a window. Old houses, both in America and in England, often have only one of the two sashes hung with weights; the other being fixed, or, if movable, held in place by means of a button or prop; such may be said to be single hung. (B) Hung on both sides with cord and pulley; said only of vertical sliding sash. In some cases, where windows are narrow or divided by mullions into narrow lights, a window box with cord, pulley, and weight is furnished on one side only, the other side of the sash being sometimes fitted with rollers to facilitate its movement. Such sash may be said to be single hung.

Double offset: Two changes of direction installed in succession or series in continuous pipe.

Double payment: A duplication of payment to a subcontractor or supplier by an owner to avoid liens when the owner has previously paid for the same work to a contractor or higher tier subcontractor who has failed to pass the payment through to the party who earned it.

Double ported valve: A valve having two ports to overcome line pressure imbalance.

Double sweep tee: A tee made with easy (long radius) curves between body and branch.

Double wedge: A device used in gate valves, similar to double disc in that the last downward turn of the stem spreads the split wedges and each seals independently.

Double-hung sash window: A window that slides vertically and has two portions.

Double-up: When plaster is applied in successive operations without a setting and drying interval between coats.

Dovetail, lap: A dovetail for joining two boards, as at a corner, in which part of the thickness of one board overlaps the end of the other. Thus, the dovetail of the overlapping board is formed in the angle of a rebate that receives the end of the other board. It is frequently formed as a secret dovetail.

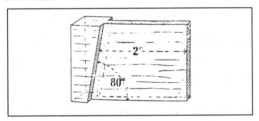

Dovetail: (A) Any piece or member having two flaring sides or edges, giving more or less a wedge shape, similar to that of the spread tail of a pigeon; especially a member, tenon, tongue, or the like, having such a form and intended to fit a corresponding mortise or recess. This form of framing is especially adapted to unite parts subject to a tensile strain, the tongue being made to flare in the direction opposite to the applied force, as to unite the front and sides of a box or drawer to prevent their separation under the influence of a pull applied to the front. (B) In masonry, the device is limited to cut stone as used in some elaborate con-structions, such as fortress walls or sea walls.

Dowel plate: A tempered steel plate with several holes, the exact size of corresponding twist bits drilled square through it to produce dowels of true cylindric shape filling the bit holes accurately. The plate is preferably mounted in a block of hardwood about 3" thick, with holes bored through it slightly larger than those in the plate. These act as guides to the pins, keeping them perpendicular to the plate. A slight burr, or projection, should exist at one side of each hole in the plate to score a groove in the dowel and to provide an escape for excess glue, which would otherwise burst the sides of the socket when the dowel was driven. Dowels should be cleft with the chisel, not sawn, to ensure perfectly straight grain, but they must be roughly rounded with the chisel before driving through the plate to finish.

Dowel: (A) A pin or similar projecting member that connects two parts. It may be formed on one of the two parts to be united and fitted to an aperture in the other; or, more commonly, a separate member, as a short rod, or the like, inserted part way into each piece. (B) Wood peg or metal screw used to strengthen a wood joint. See cramp.

Dowel: To secure or fasten together by means of one or more dowels.

Doweled: A joint using dowels (doweled construction); also doweled edge joint.

Down: Piping running through the floor to a lower level.

Downlight: Surfacemounted or suspended direct lighting.

Downspout: The rainleader from the roof to the building storm drain, combined building, sewer, or other means of disposal, located outside of the building.

Downstream: Location in the direction of flow after passing a referenced point.

Drain, barrel: A drain of circular section of brick or stone masonry.

Drain, box: An underground drain of masonry, rectangular in section, commonly covered with flat stones.

Drain, catch: A drain to receive and carry away the overflow of a canal or other open water conduit or open drain.

Drain field: The area of a piping system arranged in troughs to dispose unwanted liquid waste.

Drain: An open or covered (underground) channel or pipe for the conveyance or removal of water or sewage. Drains are usually circular and made of earthenware, porous or unglazed, as well as glazed or vitrified. That part of the main horizontal drain and its branches inside the walls of the building and connecting with the (out-side) house sewer. Any pipe that carries waste water or waterborne wastes in a building drainage system.

Drainage fitting: A type of fitting used for draining fluid from pipes. The fitting makes possible a smooth and continuous interior surface for the piping system.

Drainage system: The drainage piping within public or private premises, which conveys sewage, rain water, or other liquid wastes to an approved point of disposal but does not include the mains of a public sewer system or a private or public sewage-treatment or disposal plant.

Draw knife: A double-handed paring chisel of considerable width. They vary in width or length form 4" to 12".

Drawing chisel: A chisel-like instrument having a broad blade with a very sharp oblique end. It is used for trimming the ends of tenons and for cutting or marking deep incisions across the grain of the wood, guided by a square or rule.

Drawings: The portion of the contract documents showing in graphic or pictorial form the design, location, and dimensions of the elements of a project.

Dress: To prepare, shape, or finish by cutting or rubbing one or more faces of stone, brick, or lumber; to face. (A) Brick is commonly dressed by roughly chipping to the required form and then rubbing on a smooth surface with sand and water.

When required to be more elaborately shaped or molded, the dressing is done by chisels and similar cutting tools in the same manner as stone. These processes are being largely superseded by bricks that are manufactured in a great variety of stock patterns and by machinery that readily and cheaply cuts or grinds, bricks of the usual type as for *voussoirs*. Where only a few elaborately shaped bricks are needed, they may be had cheaper by dressing than by molding. (B) Lumber is said to be dressed when planed on one or more faces and is described or specified according to the number of sides so finished. Such dressing is almost always done by machinery in planing mills, hand working being resorted to for small quantities or to give a more perfect and true finish in parts left somewhat inaccurate and irregular by mill planing. Planing, whether by hand or machinery, commonly includes not merely the dressing of lumber so as to form true and smooth faces and arrises, but also molding, either for decoration or constructive reasons; such molding is produced in one operation with simple planing. Thus, floor boards are commonly manufactured as a stock article, planed on one side, and the edges tongued and grooved; while sheathing and ceiling is to be had finished in a similar manner, beaded on one or both edges of the face, or ever more elaborately molded.

Dressed and matched (tongue and grooved): Boards or planks machined in such a manner that there is a groove on one edge and a corresponding tongue on the other.

Dressing: (A) In general, any one of the decorative furnishings, such as moldings, keystones, groins, and the like, projecting from the general surface of a building. (B) In a more restricted sense, the molded finish or framework around openings; as, for example, the architraves of doors and windows.

Drier paint: Usually oil-soluble soaps of such metals as lead, manganese, or cobalt, which, in small proportions, hasten the oxidation and hardening (drying) of the drying oils in paints.

Drift: The sustained deviation in a corresponding controller, resulting from the predetermined relation between values and the controlled variable and positions of the final control element. Also called wander.

Drill, electric: A power woodworking tool used to drill holes in material. Drills can be hand-held or mounted on a press or stand for more accurate boring or drilling.

Drill: A punch or boring instrument operated mechanically to drive holes through any hard material such as rock or metal.

Drip cap: A molding placed on the exterior top side of a door or window frame to cause water to drip beyond the outside of the frame.

Drip groove: A milled dado extending lengthwise on the underside of an overhang that is exposed to rainfall, which prevents water from creeping up the bottom of the overhang. Enhanced or highlighted joint: a decorative treatment of open or closed joints that calls attention to them, usually achieved by beveling or using colored fillers.

Drip: Any projecting piece of material, member, or part of a member, shaped or placed to throw off water and prevent its running or trickling back to the wall or other surface or part.

Droop: The amount by which the controlled variable pressure, temperature, liquid level, or differential pressure deviates from the set value at minimum controllable flow to the rated capacity.

Drop elbow: A small elbow having wings cast on each side; the wings having countersunk holes so that they may be fastened by wood screws to a ceiling, wall, or framing timbers.

Drop shipment: Any shipment that does not go directly to the interior designer but to the client or another address.

Drop tee: A tee having the wings of the same type as the drop elbow.

Drop: Term referring to piping running to a lower elevation within the same floor level. The lower projecting end of a newel.

Dross: (A) The solid scum that forms on the surface of a metal, such as lead or antimony, when molten or melting, largely as a result of oxidation but sometimes because of the rising of dirt and impurities to the surface. (B) Waste or foreign matter mixed with a substance or left as a residue after that substance has been used or processed.

Drum trap: A cylindrical trap with its axis vertical. The cylinder is as large in diameter as the inlet or outlet pipe.

Dry bulb temperature: The temperature of air as measured by an ordinary thermometer.

Dry cleaning powder: A dust sprinkled on the tracing as the drafter works. It keeps the tracing clean of graphite smudges. It is best not to rub it on the paper. The material is similar to eraser dust and absorbs the loose graphite dust that can smudge drafting paper.

Dry out: Soft, chalky plaster caused by water evaporating before setting.

Dry rot: (A) A condition caused by attack by microorganisms on fibers, textiles, carpets, or other materials, characterized by loss of strength and integrity. Attack on carpet backings permits carpet to break and tear easily. Cellulosics such as jute are susceptible, whereas polypropylene and most other synthetics are virtually immune. (B) Decay in wood due primarily to dampness and, especially, lack of ventilation. If the end of a timber is built up too closely in a wall or enclosed in an iron shoe, it will be attacked by this decay, even if well seasoned.

Dry well: See leaching well.

Dry weather flow: Sewage collected during the summer that contains little or no ground water by infiltration and no storm water at the time.

Dry-pipe valve: A valve used with a dry-pipe sprinkler system, where water is on one side of the valve and air is on the other side. When a sprinkler head's fusible-link melts, releasing air from the system, this valve opens, allowing water to flow to the sprinkler head.

Dry: (A) In masonry, built without the use of mortar or any cementing material. (B) To change the physical state of a substance by the loss of solvent constituents by evaporation, absorption, oxidation, or a combination of these factors.

Drywall: See gypsum wallboard.

Dual element fuse: Often confused with time delay, dual element is a manufacturer's term describing fuse element construction.

Dual temperature: Systems or equipment that operate as both cold and hot systems.

Dual vent: See common vent.

Dubbing out: Leveling or smoothing a wall of masonry by filling up the hollows before the final coat of cement of stucco is applied.

Duct flange (stiffener): A perpendicular projection exterior to a duct wall composed of structural shapes such as pocket type transverse joints or reinforcement angles.

Duct: A conduit, tube, or pipe that allows fluid or air to be conveyed or conducted.

Due care: A legal term indicating the requirement for a professional to exercise reasonable care, skill, ability, and judgement in the performance of duties and services consistent with the level of such services provided by reputable professionals in the same geographical area and at the same period of time.

Dummy activity: A zero time activity placed in the network merely to show a dependent relationship (logical restraint). Usually these dummy activities in arrow diagramming representation are shown as a dashed directional line headed by an arrow.

Dummy start activity: An activity entered into the network for the sole purpose of creating a start for the network.

Duo strainer: See basket strainer.

Duration: See activity duration.

Durham system: A term used to describe soil or waste systems where all piping is of threaded pipe, tubing, or other such rigid construction, using recessed draining fittings to correspond to the type of piping.

Durion: A high silicon alloy that is resistant to practically all corrosive wastes. The silicon content is approximately 14.5% and the acid resistance is in the entire thickness of the metal.

Dust: Solid particles in the air.

Dutchman: A piece of wood or other material used to cover an opening or defect on another piece of wood or material.

Dwelling: A one-family unit with or without accessory buildings.

DWV: Abbreviation for drainage, waste and vent. A name for copper or plastic tubing used for drain, waste or venting pipe.

E

Earliest expected date (TE): The earliest calendar date on which the completion of an activity work package or summary item occurs.

Early event time: The earliest time at which an event may occur.

Early finish (early finish date) EF: The earliest time at which an activity can be completed.

Early start: The earliest time at which an activity can be started.

Eaves: The lower portion of a sloping projection beyond the walls and forming an overhanging drip for water.

Ebony: A hard wood, black in color, and used for furniture and piano keys. It is a tropical wood and polishes well.

Eccentric fittings: Fittings whose openings are offset, allowing liquid to flow freely.

Echo: Sound reflection loud enough to be heard as distinct as the source.

Edge (of gypsum board): The paper-bound edge as manufactured.

Edge band, concealed: Not more than 1/16" of the edge band shall show on the face of the plywood or particleboard.

Edging: The operation of trimming the edges; that is, the narrow, upper, or lower faces of rafters, joists, or ribs to a required

plane or surface, whether by cutting down or furring out. Also called ranging.

Effective opening: The minimum cross-sectional area at the point of water-supply discharge, measured or expressed in terms of (A) diameter of a circle, (B) if the opening is not circular, the diameter of a circle or equivalent cross-sectional area. This is applicable to air gap.

Efficacy: See lamp efficacy.

Efficiency: See luminaire efficiency.

Efflorescence: A whitish powder, formed by slow chemical process, on the surface of substances. The white alkaline efflorescence upon brickwork, and to a less extent on stone, laid up with the natural hydraulic cements, not only produces an unsightly appearance but promotes the disintegration of the surface. The material is in some cases a nitrate or carbonate of potash, more frequently a carbonate or sulphate of soda.

Effluent: Sewage, treated or partially treated, flowing out of sewage treatment equipment.

Eggshelling: Chip-cracked plaster, either base or finish coat. The form taken is concave to the surface and the bond is partially destroyed.

Elastic limit: The limit of stress up to which the material takes no permanent deformation or from which, being stretched or bent, it returns to its original form when the stress is removed.

Elasticity: (A) The power possessed by solid bodies for regaining their form after deformation which has not been so great as to overpass their limit of elasticity. When an ivory ball rebounds after falling on a hard surface it is because the ball seeks to regain its perfectly spherical shape, and the surface, as of a billiard table, also seeks to return from the compression it has undergone under the blow. Ivory has much elasticity, marble somewhat less. Many stones are very elastic, and the harder they are the more elastic they are, as a general rule. Wood is of limited elasticity, and a bar of it is rather easily bent in such a way that it will remain bent, different woods differing greatly in this respect. However, notable instances of wood's elasticity may be named. Thus, two heavy beams of hard pine supported a floor of artificial stone and, when the flooring was still wet, yielded under its weight nearly 2-3\4" in the middle. Still, the beams returned to an apparently perfect level as the floor dried, thus lifting the whole weight of this floor by their elasticity. Iron beams have much elasticity, as is evident from the peculiar vibration which a floor composed of them so frequently undergoes. (B) By extension, and inaccurately, flexibility or the power of adapting itself to irregular pressures and strains, said of a building or part of a building.

Elastomer: Any macromolecular material (such as rubber or a synthetic material having similar properties) that returns rapidly to approximately the initial dimensions and shape after substantial deformation by a weak stress and release of stress.

Elastomeric: A foamed plastic insulation containing elastomers which lend it the property of high elasticity.

Elbow: In general, any relatively small piece or part of a structure bent or formed to an angle, as a pipe; an angle formed by two surfaces, or the like. Specifically: (A) In English usage, (a) a short return or sharp angular change of direction for a short distance in a wall, as for a recess; (b) in joinery, that portion of the jamb of a recessed window between the floor and bottom of the shutter boxing. (B) A piece of pipe formed either by a curve or a mitre joint to connect two sections of pipe at an angle. (C) The ear or projecting portion of a crossette to a door or window architrave.

Electrical closet: A small room that holds electrical equipment.

Electrolysis: The process of producing chemical changes by passage of an electric current through an electrolyte (as in a cell), the ions present carrying the current by migrating to the electrodes where they may form new substances (as in the deposition of metals or the liberation of gases).

Element: A fuse element is a calibrated conductor that melts when subjected to excessive current. The element is enclosed by the fuse body and may be surrounded by an arc-quenching medium such as silica sand. The element is sometimes referred to as a link.

Elevation: (A) A two-dimensional graphic representation of the design, location, and certain dimensions of the project, or parts thereof, seen in a vertical plane viewed from a given direction. (B) Distance above or below a prescribed datum or reference point.

Elevator, screw: One of the earliest forms of elevator, in which the cage is raised or depressed by the direct action of a screw. In later elevators the principle of the screw is more scientifically applied in the form of a worm gearing acting on the drum of the elevator machine.

Elevator: (A) A car or platform to convey persons or articles up or down to the floors of a building. It may be raised and lowered by hand, steam, hydraulic, pneumatic, or electrical power, or by the force of gravity acting on weights. An elevator generally moves vertically, but may be arranged to run on an incline. Small elevators for conveying dishes and other small household articles are commonly known as dumb-waiters, and these are usually operated by hand. Large hand elevators are commonly known as hoists or hand hoists.

(B) An apparatus for raising merchandise of any kind, such as grain in bulk; and, by extension and more commonly, a building containing many grain lifters and large bins for the storage of the grain.

Elutriation: Sludge conditioning in which certain constituents are removed by successive decontaminations with fresh water or plant effluent, thereby reducing the demand for conditioning chemicals.

Embankment: A banking or building of a dyke, pier, causeway, or similar solid mass; hence, by extension, the result of such work, especially in the form of a waterside street. The term is used to translate foreign words, such as the Italian and Venetian *riva*, *fondamenta*, and *molo*; also, for the French *quai*, for which the English quay is not always an adequate translation.

Emissivity: The ability of a surface to radiate energy as compared to that emitted by an ideal black body at the same temperature.

Employer's liability insurance: Insurance protection for the employer against claims by employees for damages that arise out of injuries or diseases sustained in the course of their work and are based on common law negligence rather than liability under worker's compensation acts.

Emulsion: A colloidal suspension of one liquid in another, usually a waterbased material.

End clip: A metal section used to secure ends and edges of gypsum lath.

End connection: Method of connecting the parts of a piping system, i.e., threaded, flanged, butt weld, socket weld, etc.

End network event: The event that signifies the end of a network.

End (of gypsum board): The end perpendicular to the paper-bound edge. The gypsum core is always exposed.

End of line device: A device such as a resistor or diode placed at the end of a Class B wire loop to maintain supervision.

End of line relay: Device used to supervise power (usually for four-wire smoke detectors) and installed within or near the last device on the loop.

End suction pump: A single suction pump having its suction nozzle on the opposite side of the casing from the stuffing box and having the face of the suction nozzle perpendicular to the longitudinal axis of the shaft.

Ending event: The event that signifies the completion of an activity. Also called successor event.

Engineer: See professional engineer.

Engineered plumbing system: Plumbing system designed by use of scientific engineering design criteria other than design criteria normally given in plumbing codes.

Engineering officer: A person designated (usually by a military component or a corporation) as having authoritative charge over certain specific engineering operations and duties.

Enrichments: Any cast ornament that cannot be executed by a running mold.

Entitlement: The legal right to receive something.

Entrance: The place in which a building may be entered.

Environmental design professions: The professions collectively responsible for the design of a physical environment, including architecture, urban planning, and similar environment-related professions.

Epoxy: A plastic that is flexible and resistant to corrosion and weather. It is used for surface protective coverings and bonding agent for metal, wood, ceramics, and rubber.

Equilibrium: The state of repose of a body under the application of forces that mutually counteract each other.

Equipment room: A room designed to accommodate PBX (private branch exchange) equipment. On occasion it may also include key telephone system apparatus and terminating facilities.

Equipment: All equipment, materials, appliances, devices, fixtures, fittings, or accessories installed in or used in a building.

Equivalent sphere illumination: (ESI) The level of sphere illumination which would produce task visibility equivalent to that produced by a specific lighting environment. Suppose a task at a given location and direction of view within a specific lighting system has 100 fc of illumination. Suppose this same task is now viewed under sphere lighting and the sphere lighting level is adjusted so that the task visibility is the same under the sphere lighting as it was under the lighting system. Suppose the lighting level at the task from the sphere lighting is 50 fc for equal visibility. Then the equivalent sphere illumination of the task under the lighting system would be 50 ESI fc.

Elliptical reflector (ER): Lamp whose reflector focuses the light about 2" ahead of the bulb, reducing light loss when used in deep baffle downlights.

Erosion: The gradual destruction of metal or other material by the abrasive action of liquids, gases, solids, or mixtures of these materials.

Errors and omissions insurance: See professional liability insurance.

ESS: Electronic switching systems.

Estimate (contractor's): (A) A forecast of construction cost, rather than a firm proposal prepared by a contractor for a project or a portion thereof. (B) A term sometimes used to denote a contractor's application or request for a progress payment. See application for payment.

Estimate of construction cost, detailed: A forecast of construction cost prepared on the basis of detailed analysis of materials and labor for all items of work, as contrasted with an estimate based on area, volume, or similar unit costs.

Estimate to complete: The estimated hours, costs, and time required to complete a work package or summary item (includes applicable overhead unless only direct costs are specified).

Evapotranspiration: Loss of water from the soil by evaporation and transpiration from the plants growing thereon.

Event name: An alphanumeric description of an event.

Event number: A numerical description of an event. for computation and identification purposes.

Event slack: The difference between the latest allowable date and the earliest date for an event.

Event times: Time information generated through the CPM calculation that identifies the start and finish times for each event in the network.

Event: A point in time representing the intersection of two or more arrows. Events do not consume time or resources.

Exception: A term indicating an acceptable alternative to a standard or code.

Excess pressure pump: UL listed or FM approved, lowflow high head pump for sprinkler systems not supplied from a fire pump. Pump pressurizes sprinkler system so that loss of water supply pressure will not cause a false alarm.

Exculpatory clauses: Clauses in contracts relieving one party of liability for damages resulting from the party's actions or failures to act which otherwise would carry liability under law.

Exhaust duct: A duct carrying air from a conditioned space to an outlet outside the building.

Exhaust opening: An opening used to remove air.

Existing work: A plumbing system, or any part thereof, installed before the effective date of an applicable code.

Expanded metal: Sheets of metal that are slit and drawn out to form diamond-shaped openings. This is used as a metal reinforcing for plaster and termed metal lath.

Expansion joint: A joint whose primary purpose is to absorb longitudinal thermal expansion in the pipe line due to heat.

Expansion loop: A large radius bend in a pipe line to absorb longitudinal thermal expansion in the line due to heat.

Expansion: Growing larger, especially as caused by heat. All bodies can be expanded by heat, but in different degrees.

Expected begin date (TBA): Begin date assigned to a specific activity.

Expected duration (TE): The expected duration for a particular activity . In PERT method: te = to + 4tm + tp.

Expenditure: Disbursement of funds for expense pertaining to a contract.

Expert witness: A witness in a court case, or other legal proceeding who, by virtue of experience, training, skill, and knowledge of a particular field or subject, is recognized as being especially qualified to render an informed opinion on matters relating to that field or subject.

Exposed aggregate: Concrete that contains decorative aggregate that has been processed to expose the aggregate to surface view.

Exposed face: The surface of a stone product that is visible after installation.

Exposed spaces: Those spaces not referred to as concealed or defined by the specifier.

Exposed surfaces: Surfaces visible after installation, except for exposed portions of casework.

Express condition: A condition intended and created by the parties of a contract document which is incorporated in definite terms.

Extended coverage insurance: See property insurance. See steam boiler and machinery insurance.

Extended length: The length of pile yarn in one running inch of one tuft row in tufted carpet. Sometimes called take-up.

Extended life lamps: Incandescent lamps that have an average rated life of 2,500 or more hours and reduced light output compared to standard general service lamps of the same wattage.

Extended overhead: Additional overhead costs incurred beyond those estimated when bidding because of completion delays and an extended work schedule.

Extension of time: A change order granting a contractor or subcontractor additional time to complete a project or portion thereof without liquidated or other damages for late completion as a result of delays generally not the fault of the contractor.

Extra heavy: Description of piping material, usually cast iron, indicating piping thicker than standard pipe.

Extra: An item of work involving additional cost for which a change order is issued. See addition to contract sum.

Extraction: Counting and measuring graphic data, to isolate numeric values for use in determining the real contents of a drawing. Extraction typically passes symbol counts and layer line lengths as numeric values to estimate programs. Other attributes (such as color) may also be involved in the extraction process.

Extrude: To shape by forcing through a die.

F

F.O.B. (Free On Board) : Point from which a purchaser pays freight when purchasing a product.

Fabric : A material used for reinforcing or finishing surfaces of insulation materials.

Fabricating: Thermoplastics and thermo-settings are turned into tubes, sheets, rods, and films. There are three categories of fabricating. (A) Machining, in which materials are ground, reamed, milled, and drilled. This process is done to tubes, rods, and rigid sheets. (B) Cutting-sewing-sealing of film and sheets, in which films and sheets are cut into patterns and made into raincoats, luggage, toys, etc. (C) Forming, in which thermoplastic sheets are cut into the approximate shape and folded into final form. The sheets are turned into shapes by a vacuum or by molding.

Facade: The architectural front of a building, not necessarily the principal front, but any face or presentation of a structure nearly in one plane and treated as a single vertical wall with but minor modifications. Thus, if a large building presents toward one street a front consisting of the ends of two projecting wings with a low wall between them enclosing a courtyard, that would be hardly a facade, but rather two facades of the two pavilions. The facade refers to street architecture and buildings that have but one front considered of sufficient importance to receive architectural treatment.

Face brick: A brick used on the exposed surface because of a special quality in texture or color.

Face to face dimensions: The dimensions from the face of the inlet port to the face of the outlet port of a valve or fitting.

Face: The surface designed to be left exposed to view.

Facia or fascia: A flat board, band, or face, used sometimes by itself but usually in combination with moldings, often located at the outer face of the cornice.

Facilities: Equipment, hardware, or space provided to house communications systems to operate tenant services.

Facing: A thin layer or laminate, usually factory applied, on the surface of an insulating material. Finish applied to the exterior of a building. Materials such as wood, glass, or stone that are put onto the outer surface of a building.

Factory inspection: Product inspection performed at the point of manufacture.

Fahrenheit (F): A temperature scale with the freezing point at 32% and the boiling point at 212%, sea level, atmospheric pressure.

Faience: (French) Terra cotta. Pottery of coarse or dark colored body covered by an opaque coating, such as enamel, which may be elaborately painted. This is the proper signification, and it covers all the beautiful decorative wares of Italy from the fifteenth to the eighteenth centuries, including the richest varieties of majolica and the potteries of France of slightly later epoch, such as those of Rouen, Nevers, Moustiers, and many more. These wares are often very soft, both enamel and body, but when used for external decoration such as wall tiles and the like, the same effects of color and brilliancy are possible with an extremely hard and enduring substance. The greatest epochs have been marked by the production of cresting tiles, ridge tiles, finials for painted roofs, and the like, which are perfectly durable.

False bearing: In English usage, a bearing or point of support that is not vertically over the supporting structure below, as is afforded by a projecting corbel or cantilever.

Fan-shaped step: A step having a trapezoidal or circular section.

Fan: A mechanical air-moving device.

Fanlight: A semicircular window over a door, common in Georgian and Regency architecture.

Fascia: A nailed board under the eaves of a building, used for facing. A plain horizontal band in an architrave.

Fast track: A method of design and construction management under which sequential contracts for specialized trade work are awarded as plans and specifications are ready while design is continuing on other work. The objective is to shorten the total time between the beginning of design and the completion of construction.

Fastener: A device used to secure.

Fat: Material accumulated on the trowel during the finishing operation used to fill in small imperfections. Also describes working characteristics of any mortar.

Faucet: A tube or hollow plug to facilitate the discharge or passage of water or other fluid and fitted with some contrivance by which the flow is controlled. More specifically, in plumbing, a contrivance for allowing the outward flow of water and stopping it at will, this being usually a fixture at the end of a supply pipe for hot or cold water. Waterspouts so small as to be evidently intended for faucets and wrought into very beautiful representations of lions' and, dogs' heads, and the like, are found among Roman remains. These are usually of bronze.

Fault current: The current flowing in a faulted circuit.

Fault: An accidental condition in which a current path becomes available which bypasses the connected load.

Feasibility study: A detailed investigation and analysis conducted to determine the financial, economic, technical, or other advisability of a proposed project.

Feather edge: A beveled edge wooden tool, varying in length, used to straighten angles in the finish coat.

Featured edge: An edge configuration of the paperbound edge of gypsum board that provides special design or performance.

Federal acquisition regulations (FAR): A single set of regulations adopted April 1, 1984, to replace and consolidate the separate Defense Acquisition Regulation (DAR), Federal Procurement Regulation (FPR), and NASA Procurement Regulation. FAR constitutes the procurement regulations binding on all federal agencies, some of which also publish supplementary regulations pertaining to their specific procurement.

Fee: (A) A term used to denote payment for professional ability, capability, and availability of organization, excluding compensation for direct, indirect or reimbursable expenses, as an agreement based on a professional fee plus expenses. (B) The amount paid to a contractor for profit and sometimes for overhead as compensation for management services rendered on a cost reimbursable contract. (C) Compensation of any kind for services rendered.

Felt: An insulation material composed of interlocked fibers that have been compacted under pressure.

Female thread: Internal thread in pipe fittings, valves, etc., for making screwed connections.

Fence: Term used in cast shops describing a wall of plaster or clay placed around model before pouring material to make the mold.

Fenestration: The arrangement of windows in a building.

Fiber glass: A composite material consisting of glass fibers with a resin binder.

Fiber: (A) Sisal or glass mill additives to gypsum plaster. (B) Mill-added grained or shredded nonstaining wood fiber aggregates in gypsum plaster. Provides fire-rated and dense hard gypsum plaster. (C) Long-length sisal fiber used to affix and reinforce cast ornamental plaster.

Fidelity: Reproduction of the source of sound.

Field engineer: Term used by architectural, engineering, and contracting firms and some governmental agencies to designate their representative at the project site. See project representative.

Field order: A written order effecting a minor change in the work not involving an adjustment in the contract sum or an extension of the contract time, issued by the architect to the contractor during the construction phase.

Field representative: See project representative.

Fielded panel: A panel with a plain raised central area.

Fieldstone: Rubble. Also, rough or unshaped stones used in construction, as in fireplaces.

Fill Insulation: See insulation.

Fill: Coloring, shading, or pattern of line segments applied to an entity or object in a drawing.

Filler (wood): A heavily pigmented preparation used for filling and leveling off the pores in open-pored woods.

Fillet: A flat, narrow, raised band coursing down a shaft of a column.

Filling: To plug the hollow spaces or fissures of a slab before finishing. Filling may be done with hot or cold, colored or transparent mastic or cement. This operation is commonly done on brecciated or naturally defective materials.

Film (wet): The applied layer of mastic or coating before curing or drying.

Filter element or media: A porous device that filtrates..

Filter: A device through which fluid is passed to separate contaminants from it.

Final acceptance: The owner's acceptance of the project from the contractor upon certification by the architect that it is complete and in accordance with the contract requirement. Final acceptance is confirmed by the making of final payment unless otherwise stipulated at the time of making such payment.

Final completion: Term denoting that the work is complete and all contract requirements have been fulfilled by the contractor.

Final inspection: (A) Final review of the project by the architect before the issuance of the final certificate for payment. (B) That inspection performed at the request of the contractor to insure that the entire project has been completed in accordance with the plans and specifications and, as a result, the project is accepted by the owner.

Final payment: Payment made by the owner to the contractor, upon issuance by the architect of the final certificate for payment, of the entire unpaid balance of the contract sum as adjusted by change orders. See final acceptance.

Fine aggregate: Sand or other inorganic aggregate for use in plastering.

Fineness modulus: An empirical factor obtained by adding total percentages of a sample of aggregate retained on each of a specified series of sieves and dividing by 100. The sieve sizes used are No. 100 (150mm), No. 50 (300mm), No. 30

(600mm), No. 16 (1.18mm), No. 8 (2.36mm), No. 4 (4.75mm), 3/8", (9.5mm), 3/4", (19.0mm), 1-1/2", (38.1mm) and larger, increasing the ratio of 2 to 1.

Fines: Aggregate particles with a high percentage passing the No. 200 sieve.

Finger: A series of prongs, machined on the ends of two pieces of wood to be joined, which mesh together and are securely glued in position.

Finish coat floating: The finishing act of spreading, compacting, and smoothing the finish coat plaster or stucco to a specified surface texture.

Finish coat: The final layer of plaster over a basecoat or other substrate.

Finish: (A) Elegance or refinement in a completed piece of work, especially in the workmanship or mechanical excellence of the work as distinguished from its design or significance. However, in some kinds of work the significance itself depends upon high or elaborate finish. (B) Those parts of the fittings of a building that come after the heavy work of masonry, flooring, etc., have been done, are generally in plain sight, and are closely connected with the final appearance of the building. The term is especially applied to interior work and often in connection with some other word forming a compound term.

Finished slab: A slab with an exposed face that has been finished after sawing.

Finishing cement: A mixture of long fibers and binders with water to form an insulation material for irregular surfaces.

Finishing: Work done after roughing-in. Usually the installation of the plumbing fixtures and appliances.

Fir: A soft yet durable wood of evergreen trees used for interior parts of furniture.

Fire alarm system: A functionally related group of devices that when either automatically or manually activated will sound audio or visual warning devices on or off the protected premises, signaling a fire.

Fire and extended coverage insurance: See property insurance.

Fire blocking: Intermittent solid cross-framing to retard the spread of flame within the framing cavity.

Fire brick: A brick used to line chimneys and furnaces because it has a high fusing point.

Fire department connection: A piping connection for fire department use in supplementing water supply for standpipes and sprinkler systems. See standpipe system.

Fire door: A door with metal on one side used between a garage and another building. It retards the spread of fire for one or two hours.

Fire hazard: Anything that increases the menace of fire to a greater degree than that customarily recognized by persons regularly engaged in preventing or extinguishing fire, or that will obstruct or delay the operations of the fire department or the egress of occupants in the event of fire.

Fire hydrant valve: A valve that, when closed, drains at an underground level to prevent freezing.

Fire line: A system of pipes and equipment used exclusively to supply water for extinguishing fires.

Fire pump: UL listed or FM approved pump with driver, controls, and accessories, used for fire protection service. Fire pumps are centrifugal or turbine type, usually with electric motor or diesel engine driver.

Fire resistance: That property of a material which enables it to resist fire.

Fire retardance (FR): That property of a material which retards the spread of fire.

Fire stop: A solid, tight closure of a concealed space, placed to prevent the spread of fire and smoke through such a space. In a frame wall, this usually consists of 2 x 4 cross blocking between studs.

Fire-resistance classification: A standard rating of fire-resistance and protective characteristics of a building construction or assembly.

Fire-resistive: In the absence of a specific ruling by the authority having jurisdiction, applies to materials for construction not combustible in the temperatures of ordinary fires and that will withstand such fires without serious impairment of their usefulness for at least one hour.

Fire-retardant chemical: Chemicals used to reduce flammability or retard spread of flame.

Fire: A chemical reaction between oxygen and a combustible material in which rapid oxidation results in the release of heat, light, flame, or smoke.

Fireplace: A place where a fire can be built at the bottom of a chimney.

Firm material prices: Prices quoted by material suppliers on a guaranteed basis without possible escalation if the costs to the supplier increase before delivery.

First event number: The number of the first event in time for a work package or summary item. This event number defines the beginning of the work package or summary item in relation to the network.

Fish-mouth: A gap between layers of sheet materials caused by warping or bunching of one or both layers.

Fishplate: A wood or plywood piece used to fasten the ends of two members together at a butt joint with nails or bolts. Sometimes used at the junction of opposite rafters near the ridge line.

Fitting, compression: A fitting designed to join pipe or tubing by means of pressure or friction.

Fitting, flange: A fitting that utilizes a radially extending collar for sealing and connection.

Fitting, welded: A fitting attached by welding.

Fitting cover: The insulation for pipe fitting composed of the specified thickness of insulation material and preformed into its proper shaped before application.

Fittings: Items used to change size, direction of flow, level, or assembly of piping, except for unions, grooved couplings, flanges, valves, or strainers.

Fixed limit of construction cost: The maximum allowable cost of the construction work as established in the agreement between the owner and the architect. Also see budget construction.

Fixed-size slab: A slab cut to a predetermined shape and size. A standard fixed-size slab is mass-produced to standard dimensions. A custom fixed-size slab is cut to dimensions appropriate to the job.

Fixture, plumbing: See plumbing fixture.

Fixture branch: A pipe connecting several fixtures.

Fixture carrier fittings: Special fittings for wallmounted fixture carriers. Fittings have sanitary drainage waterway with minimum angle of <30° - 45°> so that there are no fouling areas.

Fixture carrier: A metal unit designed to support an off-the-floor plumbing fixture.

Fixture drain: The drain from the trap of a fixture to the junction of that drain with any other drain pipe.

Fixture supply: A water supply pipe connecting the fixture with the fixture branch or directly to a main water supply pipe.

Fixture unit (drainage-DFU): A measure of probable discharge into the drainage system by plumbing fixtures. The drainage fixture unit value for a particular fixture depends on its volume rate of drainage discharge, the duration of a single drainage operation, and the average time between successive operations. Laboratory tests have shown that the rate of discharge of an ordinary lavatory with a nominal 1.25" (31.8 mm) outlet, trap, and waste is about 7.5 gal./min. (0.5 L/s). This figure is so near to 1 ft.3/min. (0.5 L/s) that 1 ft.3/min. (0.5 L/s) has become the accepted flow rate of one fixture unit.

Fixture unit (supply - SFU): A measure of the probable hydraulic demand on the water supply by plumbing fixtures. The supply fixture unit value for a particular fixture depends on its volume rate of supply, the duration of a single supply operation, and the average time between successive operations.

Flag: A stone tile used for rustic pavement with a rough face and sides.

Flagstone (flagging or flags): Flat stones, from 1" to 4" thick, used for rustic walks, steps, floors and the like.

Flame cutting: Cutting done to materials that are too heavy for machines.

Flame detector: A device that detects the infrared, ultraviolet, or visible radiation produced by a fire.

Flame spread classification: A standard rating of relative surface burning characteristics of a building material as compared to a standard material.

Flame spread: The rate expressed in distance and time at which a material will propagate flame on its surface.

Flammability: That property of a material which allows continuous burning, as compared to a standard material.

Flange bonnet: A valve bonnet having a flange through which bolts connect it to a matching flange on the valve body.

Flange cover: The insulation for a pipe flange composed of the specified thickness of insulation material and preformed into its proper shape before application.

Flange ends: A valve or fitting having flanges for joining to other piping elements. Flange ends can be plain faced, raised face, large male and female, large tongue and groove, small tongue and groove and ring joint.

Flange faces: Pipe flanges that have the entire surface of the flange faced straight across, used as either a full face or ring gasket.

Flange: A rim projecting laterally on one or each side of any member, usually at right angles to the general surface, as the flat upper and lower portions of an I beam at right angles to the web. In pipe work, a ring-shaped plate on the end of a pipe at right angles to the end of the pipe and provided with holes for bolts to allow fastening the pipe to a similarly equipped adjoining pipe. The resulting joint is a flanged joint.

Flap valve: A nonreturn valve in the form of a hinged disc or flap, sometimes having leather or rubber faces.

Flash point: The temperature at which a fluid first gives off sufficient flammable vapor to ignite when approached with a flame or spark.

Flashing: Pieces of sheet metal covering the joints or angles between a roof and any vertical surface against which it abuts, such as a wall, parapet, or chimney, to prevent the leakage of rain water. Also, such pieces covering the hips and valleys of shingle or slate roofs, or the like, or covering the joints about window frames, etc., in frame buildings. Plain flashing is formed with a single strip turned up a few inches against the vertical surface to which it is tacked or otherwise secured and runs up under the slates, tiles, or shingles to a slightly higher level. For greater security, an apron, usually of lead, may be affixed to the wall above the first strip, which it overlaps. The apron is driven into the joints of the masonry protecting the joint of the flashing proper. Against a brick chimney or gable parapet the sloping joint is protected by step flashing, short pieces overlapping like slates replace the continuous strip, each turned into a different horizontal joint of the brickwork. Flashings against stonework are driven into grooves cut to receive them. In all cases the joint is cemented with common or elastic cement.

Flat paint: An interior paint that contains a high proportion of pigment and dries to a flat or lusterless finish.

Flat: A finish without gloss or luster.

Flex: A flexible metal channel used to convey electrical wiring.

Flexibility: That property of a material which allows it to be bent without loss of strength.

Flexural strength: The maximum load sustained by a standard specimen of a sheet material when subjected to a bending force.

Flight: An unbroken run of stairs.

Flitch: (A) A plank or similar thin piece, secured to the side of a beam with which it corresponds in length and depth, or nearly so, and which it serves to strengthen. One of several such pieces or beams secured together to form a larger beam or girder. (B) Same as slab. (C) A lengthwise cut in a tree from its trunk.

Float valve: A valve operated by means of a bulb or ball floating on the surface of a liquid within a tank. The rising and falling action operates a lever which opens and closes the valve.

Float: (A) A term used in connection with the critical path method or other network schedule diagramming. See free float and total float. (B) A tool shaped like a trowel with a handle braced at both ends of cork or felt attached to wood, or rubber, or formed plastic.

Flood level rim: The top edge of the receptacle or fixture from which water overflows.

Flooded: A condition when liquid rises to the flood level rim of the fixture.

Floodlighting: A system designed for lighting a scene or object to a luminance greater than its surroundings. It may be for utility, advertising, or decorative purposes.

Floor drain: A floor receptacle used to conduct water into the drainage system.

Floor plan: A sketch showing the doors, windows and interior design.

Floor slab: A concrete floor that has been reinforced 4" thick.

Floor-set: A plumbing fixture that rests on the floor.

Flooring: Materials used to lay a floor.

Flow payment: Payment of the entire contract sum, including changes, and all retained funds.

Flow pressure: The pressure in the water supply pipe near the water outlet while the faucet or water outlet is fully open and flowing.

Flow rate: The volume of water used by a plumbing fixture in a given amount of time. Usually expressed in gallons per minute (gpm).

Flue lining: Fire clay or terra-cotta pipe, round or square, usually made in all ordinary flue sizes and in 2' lengths, used for the inner lining of chimneys with brick or masonry work around the outside. Flue lining in chimneys runs from about a foot below the flue connection to the top of the chimney.

Flue: An enclosed passage, primarily vertical, for removal of gaseous products of combustion to the outer air.

Fluorescent lamp: A low-pressure mercury electric-discharge lamp in which a fluorescing coating (phosphor) transforms some of the ultraviolet energy generated by the discharge into light.

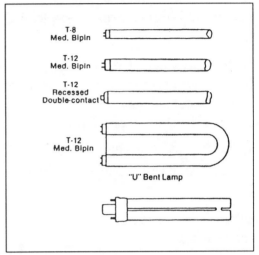

Flush: To wash out with a large amount of water.

Flush: Even with, or in the same plane with something else, whether adjacent or not, and in exact alignment with the surrounding surface. Thus, a flush panel has its surface in the same plane with the surrounding frame. Two piers having the same projection from a wall may be said to have their outer faces flush. Within 1/4" maximum protrusion from surrounding surfaces.

Flush bead molding: A convex molding with its outer surface flush with adjacent surfaces.

Flush valve: A device located at the bottom of the tank to flush water closets and similar fixtures.

Flushing type floor drain: A floor drain equipped with an integral water supply, enabling flushing of the drain receptor and trap.

Flushometer valve: A device that discharges a predetermined quantity of water to fixtures for flushing purposes and is actuated by direct water pressure.

Flushwork: Knapped flint used with dressed stone forming patterns of a tracery, etc.

Flutter: A reflection or echo between two parallel walls.

Flux: Continuous flow of luminous energy.

Fly rafters: End rafters to the gable overhang supported by roof sheathing and lookouts.

Foam plaster base (rigid type): A rigid foamed backing that acts as a plaster base.

Foamed plastic: See cellular plastic.

Foil-back gypsum wallboard: A gypsum wallboard with the back surface covered with a continuous sheet of pure bright finished aluminum foil.

Foil-backed lath: The same as plain gypsum lath except that, in addition, the back surface shall be covered with a continuous sheet of pure bright finished aluminum foil.

Foil-skrim-kraft facing (FSK): A facing of aluminum foil reinforced with fiberglass yarn mesh and laminated to chemically treated fire resistant kraft paper. Used as a vapor barrier on insulation.

Foot lambert (fl): A unit of luminance of a perfectly diffusing surface emitting or reflecting light at the rate of one lumen per square foot.

Foot valve: A check valve installed at the base of a pump suction pipe. The purpose of a foot valve is to maintain pump prime by preventing pumped liquid from draining away from the pump.

Footcandle (FC): The unit of illuminance when the foot is taken as the unit of length. It is the illuminance on a surface one square foot in area on which there is a uniformly distributed flux of one lumen.

Footing stone: Any stone intended for the construction of a footing, especially a broad, flat stone for forming the base course of a foundation.

Footing: The lowermost part of a foundation wall, especially the wide base course, or the series of stepped courses that begin with stones or concrete three or four times as wide as the superstructure, and gradually growing narrower.

Force account: Term used when work is ordered to be done without prior agreement as to lump sum or unit price cost and is to be filed for at cost of labor, materials and equipment, insurance, taxes, etc., plus an agreed percentage of overhead and profit.

Force majeure: An "Act of God," something resulting from floods, earthquakes, lightning, storms, etc. (also called force majesture).

Force: The exertion of tension or motion.

Forced entry fasteners: See power driven fastener.

Forbearance: (A) Waiting for a debt to be paid without taking action to collect the debt. (B) A delay in enforcing one's rights.

Forecast: A prediction of future conditions and events based on information and knowledge available at the time of the forecast.

Foreword pass: Network calculations that determine the earliest start/finish time at each activity based on data date (start event) through the logical flow at each activity to all ending activities.

Format (for construction specifications): Standardized arrangement for the project manual including bidding information, contract forms, conditions of the contract, and specifications subdivided into 16 divisions.

Forms: Wood or metal molds that support a concrete mixture until it is set.

Formwork: Temporary metal or wood forms into which concrete is poured.

Foundation screed: See screed.

Foundation wall: The part of a load-bearing wall that is below the beams or joists.

Foundation: The supporting portion of a structure below the first-floor construction, or below grade, including the footings.

Foyer: The entrance hall or entrance vestibule of a building.

Frame saw: A multiblade (or single-blade) cutting machine in which the blades move alternately, which produces squared blocks.

Frame-saw-finished surface: The surface that results from cutting with an alternating multiblade frame saw. The surface finish depends on the type of abrasive material used; frame-saw finish from metal grit (uneven surface), frame-saw finish from sand (slightly uneven surface), frame-saw finish by diamond dust (dressed surface).

Frame: (A) A structure of smaller parts brought together to form a whole, especially, an assemblage of slender and relatively long pieces (see framing). The carcase of a house, when of masonry, is not called the frame, but the skeleton of wood or iron-work put up for a building or part of a building is so designated.

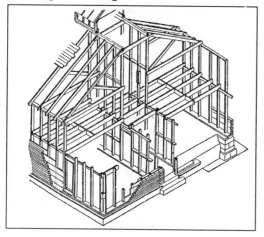

Frames may be composed of hollow parts, such as tubes or boxes. Thus, the common window frame of sliding sash windows is made of two upright boxes to contain the weights and cords, a sill below, and a head or yoke above. (B) A border prepared to enclose and isolate a picture, bas-relief, or the like. The use of the frame in strictly architectural practice is not very common, because the wainscoting, marble lining, stucco decoration, or the like, usually provides for the setting of whatever decorative panels may be inserted.

Framing, balloon: A system of framing a building in which all vertical structural elements of the bearing walls and partitions consist of single pieces extending from the top of the foundation sill plate to the roofplate and to which all floor joists are fastened.

Framing, platform: A system of framing a building in which floor joists of each story rest on the top plates of the story below or on the foundation sill for the first story, and the bearing walls and partitions rest on the subfloor of each story.

Framing: Originally and properly, the putting together of parts to produce a whole. The making of a structure of definite form and purpose out of parts especially prepared for it. The putting together of slender and comparatively long pieces, such as beams, joists, girders, posts, and the like, of timber or similar or corresponding parts of iron or both, in a skeleton, which is the essential structure of the building. The term was formerly used by carpenters exclusively for the putting together of wood by means of mortices and tenons. This distinction disappears in ironwork of all kinds and, in modern times, is rarely used in any class of work.

Fraud: The deliberate misrepresentation or concealment of an important fact of a contract to induce another person to enter into it. When there is fraud there can be no mutual assent, and because there can be no meeting of the parties' minds, a contract brought about by fraud is either void or is voidable and unenforceable. Nor will the signing of a contract obligate the signer if, by trickery, a different contract has been substituted for the one he intended to execute.

Free float (FF): The amount of time that the finish time of an activity may exceed its earliest finish time without increasing the earliest start time of any other activity.

Free water: All water contained by gypsum board or plaster in excess of that chemically held as water of crystallization.

Freestone: A stone that is easily cut in any direction, e.g., sandstone or limestone.

Freeze/thaw resistance: The property of a material that permits it to be alternately frozen and thawed through many cycles without damage.

Freight on board (FOB): The term is followed by a designated location such as factory or job site. It means that the price quoted for an item or shipment is for delivery at the point specified. Any additional shipping costs are to be paid by the consignee.

French doors: Two doors that are joined together and open in the middle and have glass panes.

French drain: A drain consisting of an underground passage made by filling a trench with loose stones and covering with earth. Also known as rubble drain.

French window: A window similar to a French door.

Frequency: The number of complete vibration cycles per second.

Fresco: An art or decorative method consisting of applying a watersoluble paint to freshly spread plaster before it dries.

Fresh air duct: Any duct used to convey outdoor air to a point within a building, terminating at a mixing plenum or duct, air handling equipment, or discharge grille.

Fresh air: Air taken from outdoors.

Fresh-air inlet: A vent line connected with the building drain just inside the house trap and extending to the outer air. It provides fresh air at the lowest point of the plumbing system and with the vent stacks provides a ventilated system. A fresh-air inlet is not required where a septic-tank system of sewage disposal is employed.

Frieze: A decorated strip along the upper section of a wall. The middle division of an entablature.

Front main cleanout: A plugged fitting located near where the building drain leaves the building. It may be located either inside or directly outside of the foundation wall.

Front-end loading: The practice of overpricing the work done at the beginning of a job and underpricing at the end so that the contractor or subcontractor can receive disproportionately large payments at the beginning of the contract.

Frontispiece: The primary facade of a building.

Frostline: The depth of frost in soil. This depth varies in different parts of the country. Footings should be placed below this depth to prevent movement.

Frostproof closet: A hopper that has no water in the bowl and has the trap and the control valve for its water supply installed below the frost line.

Fuel contribution: Flammable by-products of fire generated by and emitted from a burning object.

Fuel: Basic substance to produce heat energy.

Fulcrum: A support that allows free rotation about it.

Full bath: A bathroom with at least a water closet, lavatory, and bathtub.

Fumed oak: Oak wood that has been exposed to ammonia fumes giving it an antique appearance.

Fungi, wood: Microscopic plants that live in damp wood and cause mold, stain, and decay.

Fungicide: A substance that retards or prevents fungi growth.

Fur: To apply furring. A ceiling that is suspended some distance below the joists by means of furring is said to be furred down. A roof that is carried on furring some distance above the roof beams is said to be furred up; a wall that is furred is said to be furred *out*.

Furnace: An apparatus in which a fire may be brought to a great heat, which may then be utilized in any way desired, ordinarily, to heat a building. A furnace is distinguished from a stove in that the hot air, collected in a large chamber, passes to different parts of the building by means of pipes and flues, whereas a stove generally heats the room in which it stands by direct radiation.

Furnished by others: Materials or apparatus to be installed by the contractor but to be supplied by the owner, a different contractor, or others.

Furred ceiling: See ceilings.

Furring channels: See channels, furring.

Furring clip: A metal section for attaching cross furring to main runners.

Furring strip: Any strip, generally of wood, used for furring. Specifically, in the United States, a strip of spruce, 1" x 2" used chiefly in furring on the inner face of an outside wall to form an air space.

Furring: A light framework or simply strips, generally of wood but sometimes metal, applied to walls, beams, or similar surfaces to support sheathing, plaster, or other form of finish. Its purpose is to give a more uniform and even structure for the application of such a finish, to form an air space behind such a finish, or to give a semblance of a constructive form, as the imitation of a vault, by means of some plastic material carried on a frame of the necessary shape. By extension, hollow brick or tile used for such purposes.

Fuse: An overcurrent protective device containing a calibrated current carrying member that melts and opens a circuit under specified overcurrent conditions.

G

Gable end: In a building having a double-pitched roof, one of the end walls that terminates at top in a gable.

Gable: A more or less triangular-shaped piece of wall closing the end of a double-pitched or gable roof. The top of the wall may be bounded by the two slopes of the roof when this overhangs, or it may form a parapet following, more of less, the slopes of the roof behind. Hence, any piece of wall of the same general shape, having a more purely ornamental purpose. The French make a distinction between the *pignon*, which is properly the enclosure of the roof at either end, and the gable, which is more commonly ornamental, but in English no separate term has been introduced. It is often impossible to fix the lower boundary of a gable; but also very often a horizontal band, either of projecting moldings or of merely ornamental inlay, is carried across, usually for the artistic purpose of holding the parts firmly together in appearance.

Galvanic action: When two dissimilar metals are immersed in the same electrolytic solution and connected electrically, there is an interchange of atoms carrying an electric charge between them. The anode metal with the higher electrode potential corrodes, the cathode is protected. Thus magnesium will protect iron, iron will protect copper, etc. See electrolysis.

Galvanic corrosion: Pitting or eating away of one of the metals when two metals of different electric potential are in direct contact or electrically connected by an electrolyte.

Galvanized iron: Iron coated with zinc. The purpose of so protecting iron is to prevent rusting by keeping the moisture from its surface. It is, however, common to paint thoroughly all articles of galvanized iron as soon as they are put into place.

Galvanizing: A process where the surface of iron or steel piping or plate is covered with a layer of zinc.

Garbage disposal: An electric grinding device used with water to grind food wastes and discharge them into the drainage system.

Gate valve: A valve that controls the fluid flow moving through the valve by means of a gatelike wedge disk fitting against smoothly machined surfaces, or seats, within the valve body.

Gate: (A) A movable barrier, hung or sliding, that closes a gateway. The distinction between door and gate is not observed. The term gate carries with it (a) the idea of closing an opening in a barrier, as a fence, wall, grating, or the like, rather than an opening into a covered building; (b) the idea of iron grating or a framing of timber, rather than a solid and umpired valve or valves. This distinction is not always observed, as when a large and important pair of doors are called gates, as in city gates. Where there are solid doors closing a doorway into a public building and outside of these are doors of iron grating meant to shut at night, the latter are often, and properly, called gates. (B) A gateway; hardly accurate in this sense, although common, especially in composition and proper names.

Gauge, circular: Differs from the straight marking gauge in having the fence shaped convex on one side and concave on the other, to enable parallel lines to be drawn to curved surfaces.

Gauge, cutting: A gauge with a small adjustable knife in the place of the steel marking point of the other gauges. It is used for cutting off parallel strips of veneers and other thin stuff. The cutter is sharpened to a lancet point; the basil should be towards the stock.

Gauge, handrail: A gauge used chiefly for gauging lines on work of double curvature, such as handrail wreaths. It has a long fence to enable it to rise over the crown of the curve, and the stem is bored and slotted to receive at one end a pencil and at the other a steel point. These are adjustable in height or distance from the stem, and the stem is adjustable on the fence, so that markings can be made on any shaped surface.

Gauge, mortise: A gauge with a stem about 6" long, having two steel points, one fixed near the end and the other attached to a brass slider, adjustable by means of a screw in the end of the stem. This enables two lines to be marked at any distance apart within the range of the slider. The stock of fence slides stiffly upon the stem and is fixed by a flush set screw, the fence determining the distance of the lines from the edge of the material. The tool is chiefly used for setting out mortices and tenons. Some gauges have two movable teeth and one fixed. They are used for gauging meeting rails of sashes.

Gauge: (A) To bring to a given size or dimension, as thickness, or the like. The term properly signifies to test or measure, but it is in common use as implying the rubbing, cutting, or other process that brings the object into shape. Thus, the bricks required for the *voussoirs* of an ornamental arch especially if small in proportion to the size of the material, are commonly specified to be gauged and rubbed, that is, brought to the exact size and shape and rubbed smooth. (B) In plastering, to prepare or mix with plaster of Paris. The term originally meant to measure the quantities, then to mix such measured quantities, finally, to mix especially those ingredients that are submitted to careful measurement. (C) In roofing, the exposed portion of a slate, tile, or the like, when laid in place. (D) The closeness of the pile rows in tufted or knitted fabrics as measured across the width of the carpet. For example, 1/8" means the pile rows are 1/8" apart the entire width of the carpet. The higher the number the closer the pile tufts are to each other widthwise. (E) Tools for producing lines upon the surface of wood, parallel with the edge they are used upon. There are various forms and sizes, according to the kind of work they are required for.

Gauges, marking: Gauges used for gauging panels and other wide materials, the fence being much larger than in the common gauge. It is also rebated on the lower edge to prevent it slipping under the pressure necessary to keep it down upon its work. The gauge point should have a hardwood slip under it to prevent the stem rubbing on the surface of the work.

Gauging: The process of mixing gauging plaster or Keen's cement with lime putty or type-S hydrated lime to control setting time.

Gauging plaster: Specially ground gypsum plaster that mixes easily.

Gelatin: A product of the packing house. Gelatin can be cast into a semirigid mold and because of its flexibility, it is particularly adaptable to mold containing undercuts, etc.

General conditions (of the construction contract): That part of the contract documents which sets forth many of the rights, responsibilities, and relationships of the parties involved. See conditions of the contract.

General contract: (A) Under the single contract system, the contract between the owner and the contractor for construction of the entire work. (B) Under the separate contract system, that contract between the owner and a contractor for construction of architectural and structural work. Also known as the contract for general construction.

General provisions (GP) (construction contract): The preprinted standard form 23-A that is attached to and becomes part of a federal construction contract.

General quality controls: The inspections performed visually or with little equipment by the CQC Representative or staff to ensure the quality level required by the specifications.

General requirements: Title of Division 1 of Uniform System for Construction Specifications, Data Filing and Cost Accounting.

General service lamps: "A" or "PS" incandescent lamps.

Generally accepted standard: A document referred to in a code, covering a particular subject and accepted by the administrative authority.

German silver: An alloy known as nickel silver, composed of copper, tin, and nickel. It is corrosion resistant and malleable.

Gesso: A mix applied as a base coat for decorative painting consisting of glue and linseed oil.

Gimlets: Small boring tools driven by a revolving hand pressure. The shell gimlet has a stem ground out in part of its length to form two cutting edges at the sides, and the point is threaded to assist the tool into the wood.

Girder: Any generally horizontal member fulfilling the functions of a beam. Girders differ from beams only by being larger, more complicated, or used to support other beams. In their more elaborate framed forms, girders are not to be distinguished from certain simpler forms of trusses. A beam of concrete, steel, or timber used to support concentrated loads to various points. A large or principal beam of wood or steel used to support concentrated loads at isolated points along its length.

Glare: The sensation produced by luminance within the visual field that is sufficiently greater than the luminance to which the eyes are adapted to cause annoyance, discomfort, or loss in visual performance and visibility.

Glass, corrugated: Glass ridged on one or each face. The whole substance of the glass is bent into wavelike corrugations exactly

as in corrugated metal, the valley on one side forming the ridge on the other.

Glass, crown: Glass made by the blowing tube, which produces a bulb-shaped mass which, transferred to the pontil, is revolved rapidly until it suddenly opens out into a circular plate. Crown glass is often streaky and of unequal thickness. This peculiarity, which has caused its abandonment for ordinary window glass, has caused its use in partly opaque and richly colored glass for decorative windows, but the sheets made in this way are usually small.

Glass, flint: A composition of white sand, potash, nitre, and half as much red lead as all the other ingredients together, to which is added cullet, as in the case of plate glass. This glass is not used in strictly architectural work. It is very soft and scratches easily. It has, however, extraordinary refractive power, and thus is used for imitation jewelry of all sorts. In this way it enters into architectural decoration, not only in windows, but in the jeweled frames of altarpieces and similar decorative appliances. Flint glass with a still greater amount of red lead is called stress and is the substance commonly used under the name of "paste" for mock diamonds.

Glass, ground: Glass whose surface has been roughened by grinding, acid, sand blast, or in some similar way, to make it opaque.

Glass, iridescent: A common translucent glass, the surface of which has received by artificial means an iridescence like that of a soap bubble. Ancient glass, especially that found buried in the earth, has an iridescence that comes from slow decomposition. The sheet of glass gradually resolves itself into thin films, and the iridescence is thus a natural result, like that in a metallic ore. Iridescent glass is supposed to be made in imitation of this, but it does not resemble it very strongly.

Glass, jealous: Glass depolished or otherwise finished to let light pass while it has lost its transparency.

Glass, marbleized: Glass in which the surface is marked by small irregular veins, indicating the places where the glass has been deliberately shattered by plunging into water while hot and then remelted.

Glass, obscure: Glass that is translucent.

Glass, plate: A compound of white sand, sodium carbonate, lime, and either alumina or manganese peroxide, together with a quantity, almost equal to the mass of the above materials, of cullet, or old window glass broken up for remelting. The plate glass is then made by pouring the melted metal on a flat table of cast iron upon which a cast iron roller of the same length as the table's width moves from end to end. The movement of the roller, which rests upon ridges at the sides of the table, fixes the thickness of the plate, and bubbles or other flaws are snatched from the semiliquid mass by pincers. The perfect evenness of the surface and the high polish, upon which, after the purity of the piece, the unequalled transparency and brilliancy of plate glass depend, are obtained by careful grinding and polishing on both sides. Rough plate glass, used for parts of floors, is cast very thick, and its upper surface is left as it cools, neither face being polished.

Glass, prismatic: A glass with one smooth surface while the other is marked by ridges of prismatic section. It is distinguished from ribbed and corrugated glass by the sharp-edged character of the ridges. This glass may be so made and fixed in windows that daylight passing through it may be refracted horizontally, or nearly so, and in this way illuminate a very large internal space.

Glass, ribbed: Glass that has at least one surface ridged or ribbed. The term is usually confined to that which has only one surface so marked, to distinguish it from corrugated glass.

Glass, sheet: Glass produced by blowing into a cylinder that is constantly increased in size and then split lengthwise by a cutter. Being then heated afresh, it falls open by its own weight, the sheet so produced being generally about 3' x 4'. It is rubbed smooth with some soft material, formerly a piece of partially charred wood. When sheet glass is highly polished, it is sometimes called picture glass and sometimes, when it is deceptively clear and smooth, patent plate glass.

Glass, stained: Glass colored in its whole mass (pot metal) or by means of flashing or an applied stain. The only perfectly successful stain is that which gives a yellow color, which, coming into use toward the close of the fifteenth century, caused a sudden change in decorative windows throughout the north of Europe. The crimson of flash glass is produced by certain oxides of copper and by a mixture of gold with oxide of tin. Blue in many different shades, green, purple, etc., are produced by cobalt, though other chemicals are sometimes combined with it. Manganese gives a dark purple glass, approaching black, which can be brought to almost complete opacity of the depth of color alone, thus giving to the worker in colored glass great results in the way of gradation.

Glass, window: Glass used for ordinary windows, as in dwellings. This used to be crown glass, but this manufacture has nearly ceased. It is now more commonly sheet glass.

Glass, wire: Glass that has a continuous network of wire enclosed in the solid mass. A plate of this glass may bear a very great heat, as of a conflagration, without losing its consistency altogether, although its translucency may be destroyed, and it may crack.

Glass cloth: Closed-weave glass fiber used as a finish jacket.

Glass fabric: Open-weave glass fiber used for reinforcing a mastic or coating finish on insulating materials.

Glass fiber: See fiber glass.

Glass-cellular: See cellular glass.

Glass: A mixture of silica and some alkali resulting in a substance that is hard, usually brittle, a poor conductor of heat, and possessed of a singular luster which, as it resembles the brilliancy of no other common substance, is known by the name of vitreous or glassy luster. The most common kinds of glass are made by fusing together some ordinary form of silica, such as sand, with a sodium salt or some compound of potassium replacing the sodium either wholly or in part, and sometimes with lead. There is no formula of universal application. Moreover, some varieties of glass contain ingredients that are kept secret by the maker or are compounded in a way that is kept secret. (A) Clear glass in sheets more or less perfectly transparent and including ordinary window glass and plate glass. Under this head come the modern varieties of glass whose surface is deliberately roughened ridged, furrowed, or pressed in patterns to reduce its transparency and allow it to transmit light while shutting off the view of what may be beyond. (B) Glass in small tesserae or tiles of moderate size, usually opaque and very commonly colored. These are used for ordinary mosaic, as in flooring and the adornment of walls and vaults. The tiles are usually cast in one piece, in this resembling plate glass; and it is easy to produce very interesting bas reliefs and inlaid patterns of great beauty, which may be complete in each tile or require many tiles to complete the design. (C) Glass in sheets colored throughout its mass and used chiefly for decorative windows. (D) Glass in sheets, or flashed, that is, colored by means of a finer coating of deep colored glass on one or both sides. This device is used for colors that would be somber if the whole substance were colored, as in pot metal. The deep reds are the colors usually so treated. This also is used for decorative windows. Both the third and fourth kinds of glass are modified in many ways by the addition of an opaline tinge using arsenic or other chemicals. The opalescent quality, when applied to otherwise uncolored glass, may be described as clouded with a whitish gray opacity, which, however, shows by transmitted light a ruddy spark. (E) Glass cast in solid prisms and in prismatic and pyramidal shapes to be set in metal frames and used for vault lights. (F) Glass into which some foreign substance in introduced. This may be done with purely decorative effect, as by the artists of the Roman imperial epoch in vessels of considerable thickness and mass, and imitated by modern Venetian glassworkers. Wire glass

is made on a similar plan for purposes of safety from fire. (G) Soluble glass.

Glaze: (A) To furnish with glass, as a window sash or a door. The term glazed is used more especially to describe the use of glass in a place where it is not uniformly put, as a glazed door, the more common phrase for which in the trade is a sash door. However, the phrase glazed sash means machine-made window sash with the glass in place ready for delivery, the common way of supplying both sash and glass to a new building. It is only the large lights of plate glass, as for show windows, that are brought to the building without being first fitted to their sash. (B) To give (to anything) a polish or glassy surface. In this sense, glazed tile is commonly used in contradistinction to unglazed (i.e., mat or rough surface) tile.

Glazing: (A) condition created by the fines of a machine-dash texture plaster traveling to the surface and producing a flattened texture and shine or discoloration. This may be caused by the basecoat being too wet or the acoustical mortar being too moist. Glazing occurs in hand application when mortar being worked is excessively wet. (B) A transparent wash or stain used over a dry coat of paint.

Glitter: A reflective material such as glass, diamond dust, or small pieces of colored aluminum foil projected into the surface of

146

wet plaster or paint as a decorative treatment.

Gloss enamel: A finishing material made of varnish and sufficient pigments to provide opacity and color, but little or no pigment of low opacity. Such an enamel forms a hard coating with maximum smoothness of surface and a high gloss.

Gloss (paint or enamel): Contains a relatively low proportion of pigment and dries to a sheen or luster.

Gloss: Shine, sheen, or luster of a dried film.

Glove valve: A compression valve in which the flow of water is controlled by a circular disk forced onto or withdrawn from a ring surrounding the water flow opening.

Glow: Visible, flameless combustion of the solid phase of a material.

Glue block: A wood block, usually triangular in cross-section, securely glued to an angular joint between two members for greater glue bond area.

Glued, securely: The bonding of two members with an adhesive forming a tight joint with no visible delamination at the lines of application.

Gouges: Curved-faced chisels used and made in similar sizes to firmer and paring chisels, the resulting face of the cut being circular instead of flat. When a gouge of either type is curved in its length with a short bend near the cutting end, it is termed a bent gouge, and if curved throughout its length, a curved gouge. These are chiefly used by joiners in cutting the molded surfaces of shaped work, such as handrail wreaths and the like.

Governing codes: Codes applicable to a project, including federal and local codes.

Gradation: The particle size distribution of aggregate as determined by separation with standard screen.

Grade: The slope or fall of a line of pipe in reference to a horizontal plane. In drainage, it is expressed as the fall in a fraction of an inch or percentage slope per foot (mm/m) length of pipe.

Grain, edge (vertical): Edge-grain lumber that has been sawed parallel to the pith of the log and approximately at right angles to the growth rings, i.e., the rings form an angle of 45° or more with the surface of the piece.

Grain, flat: Flat-grain lumber that has been sawed parallel to the pith of the log and approximately tangent to the growth rings, i.e., the rings for an angle of less than 45° with the surface of the piece.

Grain, quartersawn: Another term for edge grain.

Grain character: A varying pattern produced by cutting through growth rings,

exposing various layers. It is most pronounced in veneer cut tangentially or
rotary.

Grain figure: The pattern produced in a
wood surface by annual growth rings,
rays, knots, or deviations from natural
grain, such as interlocked and wavy grain,
and irregular coloration.

Grain: (A) An embossed design impressed on a wallcovering. (B) The fibers
in wood and their direction, size, arrangement, appearance, or quality. When se-
vered, the annual growth rings become
quite pronounced and the effect is referred
to as grain. (C) The fibers of wood taken
together. The fibrous or strongly marked
longitudinal texture of wood in which the
sheaves of the sap vessels, all running one
way, cause a marked distinction between
the character of wood if cut crosswise or
lengthwise of the log. Blocks for wood engraving are cut across the grain, but in
nearly all other careful workmanship the
end grain is avoided, and a perhaps excessive care is shown by modern carpenters
and joiners never to allow this end grain
(that is the texture of the wood as shown
when cut across) to be seen. Even in wood
when cut in the direction of the grain, that
is, lengthwise, there is a difference in the
adhesiveness of the parts. Accordingly, as
a log is cut into parts in the direction or
nearly in the direction of the radii of one
section of the log considered as a circle, the
wood will be found tougher and less liable

to split. A log allowed to dry naturally will
be checked, or divided deeply by checks.
If, then, parts are taken out of a log in such
a way that the broad surfaces of these parts
go in the direction of these checks, the parts
will have little or no tendency to split. Advantage is taken of these circumstances to
saw wood quartering. Oak is often treated
in this way because of the open character of
its grain. Grain also means the pattern or
veining caused by the irregularity of the
arrangement of the sap vessels and fibers.
This, in some woods, is of great beauty,
and it often happens that a knot, part of the
root, or a wart or protuberance sometimes
found projecting from the trunk of a large
old tree, contains wood of a very beautiful
pattern. These are called burls. The finest
and most precious pieces of this kind are
commonly sawed into thin veneers, which
are then used by gluing them to thicker
pieces of inferior wood. (D) The direction
the fibers of a paper run as it is manufactured. It affects surface, directional patterns, folding, tear qualities and
dimensional stability.

Grain: To produce by painting an imitation of the natural grain of wood. This is
done by holding a cloth firmly on the end
of a stick, and wiping narrow bands in
freshly laid paint; these bands showing
light in contrast with the darker and thicker
paint left on either side. If, for instance,
paint the color of walnut is laid over a lighter priming, a skilled grainer will use the

wiping tool with greater or less pressure, as he wishes to produce broader and paler or narrower and darker stripes. These stripes, kept close together and nearly parallel, constitute graining of the simplest kind, the process in the more elaborate patterns is similar to this.

Granite: A very hard rock made up of mica, quartz, and feldspar.

Granulometry: A system to analyze the size and shape of a material's grain.

Grate: Originally and properly, a grating used to retain fuel in place while the air that supplies combustion passes freely upward from below between the bars. Especially, (A) A basket-like receptacle of bars as is used in an ordinary fireplace, sometimes hung by rings or sockets upon hooks built into the jambs, sometimes supported on feet, and in this latter case often called basket, or basket grate. Soft or bituminous coal is more commonly burned in grates of this form. (B) The bottom, or floor, of a fire room or fire box in a furnace or stove. Usually flat and placed horizontally, but often arranged to revolve, to drop at one side while remaining supported on a pivot, or even to fold upon itself. These devices were for greater convenience in dumping the fuel when it was desired to clean the grate and start a fresh fire.

Grating: A structure of bars held together by cross pieces of any sort or similar bars crossing one another in at least two direc-

tions or, finally, bars arranged in some more elaborate pattern. The term is equally applicable to a frame made of thick bars or beams of wood and to a lighter and slender structure, as of metal. Gratings of wood are used to admit air and light or to allow for vision through an obstacle while prohibiting entry or exit or, when placed horizontally, to protect an opening against persons or things falling into it accidentally. This is its most common use in building. The openwork partition across the parlor of a convent or the visitor's room in a prison is called by this name, although frequently the bars are wide apart and may even reach from floor to ceiling without cross pieces.

Grease interceptor: See interceptor.

Grease trap: See interceptor.

Green: Wet or damp plaster.

Grid: A metal frame inserted in a stone product during manufacture to increase resistance to stress.

Grillage: A framework composed of main runner channels and furring channels to support ceilings.

Grille: A grating of metal or wood used as a barrier or decoration.

Grinder pump: A special class of solids-handling pump that grinds sewage solids to a fine slurry, rather than passing through entire spherical solids.

Groin: A sharp edge resulting from the intersection of vaulting surfaces.

Groove: A narrow continuous sinking, usually of the same width and depth throughout. Grooves are worked on the edges of boards and planks to make tongued and grooved flooring and sheathing. Rectangular slot of three surfaces cut parallel with the grain of the wood.

Ground floor: Properly, that floor of a building most nearly on a level with the surrounding surface of the ground. Same as ground story.

Ground story: That story of a building that is nearly on a level with the surrounding surface of the ground. The term should be limited to such a story when its floor is not more than two or three steps above or below the sidewalk in a city or the courtyard, greensward, or the like, nearest approaching it, in the country. Thus, in the case of a house with a high stoop, as in many American cities where the principal floor is seven feet above the sidewalk and the floor of the basement story is five feet below it, there is properly no ground story.

Ground: (A) Anything used to fix a limit or regulate the thickness or projection of the more permanent of exterior finished work. Generally used in the plural. Thus, grounds in ordinary building are pieces of wood secured to the jamb of a doorway, as in a brick wall, or to the base of a stud partition to stop the plastering at the edge and to determine its thickness, and to these grounds the wooden trim may be nailed, or the grounds may be removed. Also, any strip secured to a wall and embedded in the plaster to furnish a nailing, as to secure a wooden mantel, heady trim, or the like. (B) In painting, the surface upon which ornaments and the like are relieved, corresponding nearly to background in relief sculpture, and to the French *champ*. (C) Having to do with the ground or background, thus, ground color is the color used for the ground as in definition A.

Grounded: A conductor that is in contact with or connected to the earth.

Grounding: Connection of electric components to earth for safety.

Grounds: A piece of wood or metal attached to the framing with its exposed surfaces acting as a gauge to determine the thickness of plaster to be applied. Also used by carpenters as a nailing base to support trim.

Group relamping: Relamping of a group of luminaries at one time to reduce relamping labor costs.

Grout: Concrete used as filler between voids of joists. Mortar made thin for pouring into the interstices of a masonry wall, spreading over a bed of concrete to form a smooth finish, and for other purposes where the use of stiff mortar is unpractical.

Guarantee bonds: A bond that is posted to assure the performance of the contractor's warranty obligations. See bid bond, labor and material payment bond, performance bond, surety bond.

Guarantee: Legally enforceable assurance of the duration of satisfactory performance or quality of a product or work for a stated time limit.

Guaranteed maximum cost: Amount established in an agreement between owner and contractor as the maximum cost of performing specified work on the basis of cost of labor and materials plus overhead expenses and profit.

Gum, gumwood: A wood white to greygreen in color and used on low-grade cabinet making. It often warps but finishes well.

Gusset: A wood or metal plate affixed over joints (such as truss members) to transfer stresses between members.

Gutter spout: A water spout leading from a roof gutter, either as a gargoyle or in the way of a pipe led to the ground or to another roof.

Gutter: (A) A channel, trough, or like contrivance to receive and convey away water, whether in connection with the roofs of a building, or forming part of a pavement, roadway, or the like. When used on a building it may form part of a roof-covering turned up and supported along or near the lower edge of the slope, it may be a trough of metal or wood hung from the edge of the roof, or it may be part of a masonry structure below, in which case perhaps of cut stone and forming part of the cornice or serving itself as the crowning feature. (B) A shallow channel or conduit of metal or wood set below and along the eaves of a house to catch and carry off rainwater from the roof. Also known by eave trough.

Gypsum backing board: A 1/4" to 5/8" gypsum board used as a backing for gypsum wallboard, acoustical tile, or other dry cladding.

Gypsum board: The generic name for a family of sheet products consisting of a noncombustible core primarily of gypsum with paper surfacing.

Gypsum concrete: A calcium gypsum mixed with wood chips, aggregate, or both, used primarily for poured roof decks.

Gypsum core board: A 3/4" (19.0mm) to 1" (25.4mm) gypsum board consisting of a single board or factory laminated multiple boards used as a gypsum stud or core in semisolid or solid gypsum board partitions.

Gypsum formboard: A gypsum board used as the permanent form for poured gypsum roof deck.

Gypsum gauging plaster: A plaster for mixing with lime putty to control the setting time and initial strength of the finish coat. Classified either as quickset or slow-set.

Gypsum high strength basecoat plaster: A gypsum cement for use with sand aggregate to achieve high compressive-strength plaster.

Gypsum molding plaster: A specially formulated plaster used in casting and ornamental plasterwork which may be used neat or with lime.

Gypsum neat plaster: A plaster requiring the addition of aggregate on the job. It may be unfibered or fibered (vegetable or glass fibers).

Gypsum plaster: Ground calcined gypsum combined with additives to control the set, used also to denote applied gypsum plaster mixtures.

Gypsum ready-mixed plaster: Plaster mixed at the mill with a mineral aggregate. It may contain other ingredients to control time of set and working properties. Similar terms are mill-mixed and premixed. Only the addition and mixture of water is required on the job.

Gypsum sheathing: A gypsum board used as backing for exterior surface materials. Manufactured with water-repellent paper and sometimes a water-resistant core.

Gypsum tile or block: A cast gypsum building unit.

Gypsum wallboard, type X: A gypsum wallboard specially manufactured to provide specific fire-resistant characteristics.

Gypsum wallboard: A gypsum board used primarily as an interior surfacing for building structures.

Gypsum wood-fibered plaster: A mill-mixed plaster containing a small percentage of wood fiber as an aggregate, used for fireproofing and high strength.

Gypsum: The mineral consisting primarily of fully hydrated calcium sulfate, $CaSO_4 + 2H_2O$ or calcium sulfate dihydrate (C 22).

H

Hack: To cut back and roughen a plastered or other surface.

Hangers: The vertical members that carry the steel framework of a suspended ceiling, the vertical members that support furring under concrete joist construction, or the wires used in attaching lath directly to concrete joist construction.

Half lap: A joint formed by extending (lapping) the joining part of one member over the joining part of the other member.

Half-bath: A bathroom containing only a water closet and lavatory.

Half-rip saw: A ripping saw used solely for cutting in the direction of the fibers in such operations as splitting and tenon-cutting. The length of the blade is 28", the teeth are spaced from 1/4" apart at the point of the blade to 3/8" apart at the heel. The best cutting angle for the teeth is 80°. The angle of the back needs only sufficient space for the sawdust, but is usually made at 60° with the front of the tooth. The angle of the front is sometimes made 90° or perpendicular with the line of points. This is termed "giving the tooth hook" and produces a rough cut and jars the arm of the operator in working. Spacing should be 4 teeth to the inch, depth of tooth 1/4" from point to root.

Half-timber: A wooden framework with another substance filling in the spaces.

Halon 1301 (bromtrifluoromethane CBrF3): A colorless, odorless, electrically non-conductive gas that is an effective medium for extinguishing fires.

Halon system types: There are two types of systems: total flooding systems and local application systems.

Hammer, claw: A carpenter's nail hammer with a steel head that has a face on one end for driving nails and a claw on the other for pulling nails. It can have a flat bell or checkered face and a straight or curved claw. Claw hammers with straight claws are often called ripping hammers.

Hammer, ball peen: A mechanic's hammer with a flat or bell face on one end and a rounded peen on the other. It is designed for diving pins, forming metal, and other such tasks.

Hammer, tack: A small hammer designed to drive tacks and small brads or nails.

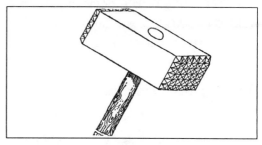

Hammer, bush: A hammer with a head forming a pick on one end and a scored face . Used to rough the face of concrete and stone.

Hammer, upholsterers: A tack hammer with a curved head. One end of the head is a flat face and the other is a magnet for picking up tacks. Designed for upholstery work.

Hammer, cross peen: A mechanic's hammer with a flat or bell face on one end and a chisel-shaped peen on the other. It is designed for diving pins, forming metal, and other such tasks.

Hammer-post: A vertical timber set on the inner end of a hammerbeam to support a purlin.

Hammerbeam: Horizontal brackets projecting at a wall plate level on opposite sides of the wall like a tie beam with the center cut away.

Handrail: The railing along side a stair or steps used to maintain balance while climbing.

Hanger (insulation): A device such as a welded pin, stud, or adhesive-secured fastener which carries the weight of insulation.

Hanger (pipe): Device that supports piping.

Hanger, wall: A formed metal section inserted in concrete members for the attachment of hangers.

Hard finish: Fine white plaster which, when used, forms the last coat of a piece of plastering.

Hard money: (A) When applied to bids and contracts, a vernacular expression for a firm, fixed price contract as contrasted to cost reimbursement or time and material contracts. (B) Metal currency, such as copper, nickel, silver, or gold, rather than paper money.

Hard: When referring to paper, describes high finish but indicates a high degree of water resistance imparted by surface sizing.

Hardboard: Panel manufactured primarily from interfleted ligno-cellulose fibers consolidated under heat and pressure in a hot press.

Hardening: The gain of strength of a plastered surface after setting. See set.

Hardwall: Basecoat plaster. Regionally the term differs; in some cases it refers to sanded plaster, while in others to neat.

Hardware: Metal products such as hinges, keyhole plates, and handles.

Hardwood: Lumber or veneer produced from broadleaved or deciduous trees in contrast to softwood, which is produced from evergreen or coniferous trees.

Hasp: A fastener for a door, lid, or the like, usually in the form of a plate or bar of metal hinged at one end and with a slot or opening to receive a staple. A padlock or wood pin or the like is passed through the staple, which holds the door fast.

Hatch: A rough door. The original signification was connected with grating or crib work, but now applies to that which is solid and uniform in surface; especially, (A) A heavy door filling the lower part of a doorway; either completed by a second heavy door above (Dutch door), or shut when the larger or more permanent door is opened, as when business of some kind is to be done across and above this lower door acting as a barrier or counter. (B) A door in a nearly horizontal position; in this sense like trap door, except that it conveys the idea of a much larger opening to be filled by the door in question. The hatches of ships are not hinged, but slide or are lifted off and put on again so as to cover the coaming. In architectural practice a hatch is usually hinged and often secured by a counterpoise, or is held in some way to avoid falling heavily when allowed to close. (C) The opening closed by a hatch. In this respect, exactly resembling the use of gate for gateway, door for doorway, and the like.

Hatching: Drawing by means of small and numerous lines laid close together. In freehand drawing, hatching may be used to produce effects of rounding and distinguish shades from shadows, and the like. In architectural drawing, it is more commonly used to distinguish the cut or sectional parts from those shown in ordinary projection. Filling of an area in a drawing with a regular pattern of lines.

Haunch: The midway part of an arch and the point of greatest lateral thrust.

Hawk: A flat wood or metal tool 10" to 14" square with a handle, used by the plasterer to carry mortar.

Head jamb: The horizontal element at the top of the frame for an opening (door or window).

Header course: A continuous course of header brick.

Header or feeder duct: A raceway of rectangular cross-section placed within or just below the floor which ties the distribution duct or cell to the terminal or equipment space.

Header: Any piece or member laid in a direction transverse to a series of other similar members which abut it. Specifically, (A) In the framing of a floor or roof, the piece that is framed into one or two trimmers and that in turn supports the tail pieces. (B) In brickwork, and more rarely in building with cut stone, a piece of material, as a brick, having its length placed across the wall and serving to a certain extent as a bond. (C) A pipe with many outlets, which are usually 90° to or parallel to the centerline of the header.

Heading course: A course of headers in a brick wall, or the like. In ordinary brick building in the United States, four or five courses of stretchers alternate with one heading course; in Great Britain, every alternate course is usually a heading course.

Heading: That which forms or serves as a head or header. A classification of related data used in the filing system (part two of the Uniform System) as the first step in subdividing each of the 16 divisions and corresponding generally to the sections used in parts one and three.

Headroom: The clear space allowed above a flight of steps, floor, platform, or the like, so that a person passing will have abundant room. The space should be sufficient to remove all sense of annoyance from the nearness of the floor or flight of stairs above. Thus, where stairs are arranged one flight above another, 7' in the clear vertically is the least space that should be allowed. As soon as a stair and its surroundings assume some architectural character, the headroom must be much greater than this, and its proper distribution is an important consideration in planning. By extension, the term is loosely applied to any space allowed vertically for a given purpose; as when an attic room is said to have 4' headroom at the low side nearest the eaves.

Hearth: A piece of floor prepared to receive a fire; whether in the middle of a room, as in primitive times, the smoke was allowed to escape through openings in the roof; or, as in later times, the floor of a fireplace. The hearth includes properly the entire floor from the back lining of the fire-

place to the outermost edge of the incombustible material. In builders' usage, however, it is customary not to include in the term the rougher flooring, as of hard brick, which is enclosed between the cheeks of the recess made in the wall or chimney breast. According to this custom, the hearth, or, as it might be called, the outer hearth, is usually a slab of slate, soapstone, marble, or other fairly resistant material, which is placed outside of the fireplace proper. The mantelpiece, fender, front feet of the basket grate, and other fittings generally rest upon it. A flooring of tile sometimes replaces the slab of stone. Whatever the material of the hearth, it is usually supported upon a flat arch of brickwork, which often is built between the trimmers of the floor below. The area in front of the fireplace.

Heartwood: The wood formed at the interior or heart of a tree. It is quite free from sap, the more so as the tree ages, and has finer and more compact and even grain and is therefore harder. It is usually considered better for general use than the outer portion of the trunk that contains the sap and is, hence, known as sapwood. Sapwood has comparatively little strength and is more liable to rapid decay.

Heat detector: A device that detects abnormally high temperature or rate-of-temperature rise.

Heat extraction: Removing heat from a luminaire by passing return air through the lamp cavity.

Heat resistance test: A sample of laminated plastic approximately 12" x 12" glued to substratum for a minimum of 21 days shall be used for this test. A hot-air gun rated at 14 amperes, 120 volts, with a nozzle temperature of 500° F or 274° C shall be directed at the surface of the test panel. A thermometer set at the panel surface shall register 356° F or 180° C for an exposure time of 5 minutes. The formation of a blister or void between the overlay and the substratum shall constitute a failure of the adhesive. A metal straightedge shall be used to determine if a blister has occurred. This determination shall be made within 30 seconds of heat removal.

Heat: The form of energy that is transferred by a temperature difference or a change of state.

Heated space: Building area supplied directly with heat.

Hertz (Hz): A measurement of sound frequency measured in cycles per second.

Hewn stone: North American word for ashlar.

Hexagonal wire mesh: Poultry netting, chicken wire, etc.

Hidden joint: An open or closed joint that is made invisible by puttying or caulking.

High density: Materials or structures that have above-average weight per unit volume.

High intensity discharge (HID) lamp: A discharge lamp in which the light-producing arc is stabilized by wall temperature, and the arc tube has a bulb wall loading in excess of three watts per square centimeter. HID lamps include lamps known as mercury, metal halide, and high pressure sodium.

High output fluorescent lamp: Operates at 800 or more milliamperes for higher light output than the standard fluorescent lamp (430MA).

High pressure condensate: That condensate directly from high pressure steam lines.

High pressure laminated plastic: Decorative laminated thermosetting sheets, consisting of layers of a fibrous sheet material, such as paper, impregnated with a thermosetting condensation resin and consolidated under heat and pressure. The top layers have a decorative color or a printed design. The resultant product has an attractive exposed surface that is durable and resistant to damage from abrasion and mild alkalies, acids, and solvents, meeting the requirements of the National Electrical Manufacturers Association (NEMA) LD 3-80.

High pressure laminating: Plastics are put into a hopper and fed through a heating chamber. The material is softened into a fluid, which is forced through a nozzle that abuts an opening into a mold. The plastic is then cooled and ejected from the press.

High pressure sodium (HPS) Lamp: High intensity discharge (HID) lamp in which light is produced by radiation from sodium vapor. Includes clear and diffuse-coated lamps.

High pressure steam: Steam gauged at 75 lbs. per square inch or greater.

High rib lath: A metal lath with a built-in rib used to provide air space under insulation applications.

High speed saws: Light columns and cut beams.

High velocity duct: An airflow duct with air flow designed at more than 2,000 feet per minute velocity with a static pressure exceeding 6 ".

Hinge, double-acting: A hinge that permits a door to swing in either direction.

Hinge: A connection used to attach and support a member or structure so that it may be movable as about a pivot, as a door, sash, table leaf, or the like. The movable member may be hung by the hinge to a fixed support as a frame, jamb, or another movable piece. In its common form, a

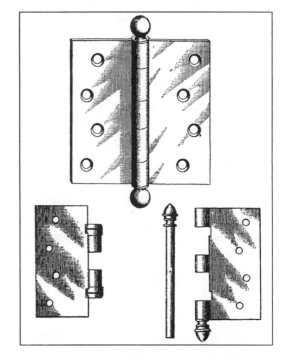

hinge consists of two flaps or leaves of metal, each of which has one edge bent about a pin, forming the knuckle. The pin thus forms a pivot about which one flap is free to turn when the other is permanently secured. The simplest form of hinge may be formed by a hook permanently fixed, as the stationary member, and a ring secured to the movable member.

Hip bevel: The angle between the two slopes of a roof which are separated by a hip, or the bevel that must be given to the end of a rafter so that it will conform to the oblique construction at a hip.

Hip: A sloping salient angle in a roof, where the slope of the roof changes direction and one plane cuts or intersects another. Thus, in a double pitch roof, where there are no gables and the ridge is shorter than either of the wall plates that run parallel to it, the roof falls back at a slope above the end walls (which would otherwise be gable walls), and at either end two hips are formed.

Hob: (A) The horizontal upper surface of the masonry filling on either side of a grate in a fireplace. The term, as well as the thing itself, is English and of the eighteenth century. Old fireplaces arranged for burning wood were readily adapted for the use of coal by building in a dwarf wall of masonry, in the middle of which was set a grate with space left below for the access of air. The two small spaces on the top of the dwarf wall were convenient for setting things that had to be kept warm, and each of these was a hob. According to the N.E.D., the term signifies the whole piece of masonry. (B) In recent English usage, the iron-plated sides of a small grate on which things may be set to warm"

Hod elevator: A contrivance for raising many loaded hods at one time. One of the forms is an endless chain resembling a flexible iron ladder; this serves the workers in ascending or, when set in motion, carrying up the hods.

Hod: A box for carrying building materials, especially mortar, usually shaped like a trough and with a pole secured to the bottom. The trough or box is set upon the laborer's shoulder, and the pole serves to steady and balance the load. Hods are now usually raised to the scaffolding by machinery of some kind.

Hog ring: A heavy galvanized wire staple applied with a pneumatic gun which clinches it in the form of a closed ring around stud, rod, pencil rod, or channel.

Hoist: An appliance for raising passengers or materials to a height, as to a scaffold or within a building to an upper floor. In its simplest form it was merely a tackle operated by a horse or by hand. In its more elaborate forms, as when operated by steam, electricity, etc., it is not to be distinguished from an elevator except, possibly, as being rougher or having simpler machinery or lower speed. The two terms are often used synonymously.

Hold harmless clause: Contract document clauses under which one party agrees to pay certain claims that might be asserted against others. See indemnification and contractual liability.

Holding time: In data communications, the length of time a communication channel is in use for each transmission. Usually this is the sum of operating time and message time.

Hole: Applies to holes from any cause. A pin hole is approximately 1/16" in diameter.

Hood-molding: Molding projecting above a doorway or window to shed rain.

Hood: A rooflike canopy over an opening, especially over a fireplace. In particular: (A) In medieval and later architecture, a structure of masonry or plaster work held by a frame of wood or the like, which is entirely secured and protected by the plaster, and projecting from a wall above a hearth. (B) A light pyramidal or conical covering, as of iron suspended over the furnace of a laboratory or the like, or even a cooking range, either hung free from the ceiling or supported on light uprights or set against the wall, as the furnace stands free or has one side engaged. The use of such a hood is mainly for ventilation, sometimes very important to prevent disagreeable or noxious smells from pervading the building. A flue and special provision for the circulation of air in the flue are therefore necessary.

Horizontal branch drain: A drain pipe extending horizontally from a building drain, or oil or waste stack with or without vertical sections or branches, which receives the discharge from one or more fixture drains on the same floor as the horizontal branch.

Horizontal pipe: Any pipe or fitting that makes an angle of less than 45° with the horizontal.

Horizontal pump: A pump with the shaft normally in a horizontal position.

Horizontal Split-Case Pump: A centrifugal pump characterized by a housing that is split parallel to the shaft.

Housing (casings): Enclosures of sheet metal or other material to house fans, coils, filters, or other components of air-handling equipment.

Housing: (A) A groove, recess, or the like, cut or formed in one piece, usually of wood, to insert the edge of another. (B) Any light, houselike structure, as for a temporary shelter.

Hub and spigot: Piping made with an enlarged diameter or hub at one end and plain or spigot at the other end. The joint is made tight by oakum and lead or by use of a neoprene gasket caulked or inserted in the hub around the spigot.

Hub: The enlarged or bell end of vitrified-clay or cast-iron pipe. See bell.

Hubless: Soil piping with plain ends. The joint is made tight with a stainless steel or cast iron clamp and neoprene gasket assembly.

Hubs: Caulking or cement connections between pipe joints.

Humidifier: A machine that adds moisture to the air.

Humidity: A measure of the amount of water vapor in the atmosphere.

Hung: Secured in place, especially, secured in such a way that the object is free to move within certain limits. Thus, a door or shutter is hung when it is secured by its hinges to the jamb or doorpost, and the sliding sash of a window is hung by means of cords that pass through a pulley and are secured to weights. See hanger and hanging.

Hydrated lime: See lime.

Hydration: In Portland cement plaster the chemical reaction between water and the cementitious binder, which may be accompanied by a volumetric change or shrinkage.

Hydraulic cement: Any cement, such as Portland cement, which will set and harden under water. Also refers to a quick-setting expansion-type cement compound used to fill cracks and to waterproof.

I

I-beam: A steel beam with a cross section resembling the letter I. It is used for long spans such as basement beams, or over wide wall openings, such as a double garage door, when wall and roof loads are imposed on the opening.

I-node: The event (node) signifying the start of the activity.

I·t (ampere squared seconds): A measure of the thermal energy associated with current flow. I·t is equal to (Irms) $2 \times t$, where t is the duration of current flow in seconds. Published I·t values for fuses are valid for clearing times of less than 1/2 cycle (.008 seconds).

Ignition temperature: The minimum temperature required to initiate combustion.

Ignition: The initiation of combustion.

Impact insulation classification (IIC): A measure of sound transmission through floor/ceiling assemblies.

Impact resistance: Capability of an insulation material or finish to withstand mechanical or physical abuse.

Impact-processed surface: A surface finished with impact tools, manual or pneumatic. The surface finish depends on the tool used: scabbled surface, with pinted chisel and mallet; hack-hammered surface, with stonecutter's chisel; bush-hammered surface, with bush hammer.

Impale: To pierce or fix by piercing on a sharp point.

Implied condition: An unstated condition that the law presumes was understood between the parties as part of their agreement, based on the nature of the transaction or conduct of the parties.

Imposed date: See contract date.

In-line pump: A centrifugal pump whose drive unit is supported by the pump having its suction and discharge flanges on approximately the same center line.

In-progress activity: An activity that has been started but not completed at the data date.

Incandescent lamp: A lamp in which light is produced by a filament heated to incandescence by an electric current.

Incised work: Work done by cutting into a surface. If the metal is cut through this is called pierced work or (in French) *A Jour* or more rarely in Italian *A Giorno.* Lettering of any sort cut into the metal is properly called inscription. The term incised work is then limited to decorative sculpture in which a flat surface is adorned with a pattern sunk beneath it or with a pattern left in relief while the background is cut away. If this pattern is rounded and modeled into sculpture, it becomes relief. If the pattern or the cut away parts which surround the pattern, are filled in with some other material, the term used is inlay or inlaid work;

but it is also said that a pattern is incised and then filled in with mastic or other soft material.

Inclination: Slope of any kind, but especially in building for decorative effect rather than batter, which is the slope of walls made thicker at the base for strength or in a fortification for defense. Any slope that is more commonly applied to a roof or ramp of a staircase. The angle that a roof, ramp, or other sloping member makes, with the horizon or a vertical plane is the angle of inclination. It is rare that this is estimated by builders in terms of degrees and minutes. More commonly it is estimated by the horizontal dimensions compared with the vertical dimensions. Thus a carpenter will say that the inclination of his roof is three (horizontal) to two (vertical).

Inclusion: The presence in a crystalline mass of an element that is structurally and chromatically different from the bulk of the material.

Indemnification clauses: Clauses in an agreement or contract to protect and secure against damage or loss.

Indemnification implied: An indemnification that is implied by law rather than arising out of a contract.

Indemnification: A contractual obligation by which one person or organization agrees to secure another against loss or damage from specified liabilities.

Indemnity bond: A bond to compensate for a loss to a person to whom an obligation has been incurred.

Indent: A stone niche carved to hold a statue or object.

Indentation: Diversifying a surface, an arris, a molding, or the like, by depressions or hollows, usually in a series.

Index of key words: Part four of the Uniform System for Construction Specifications, Data Filing, Cost Accounting.

Indirect expense: Overhead expense; expense indirectly incurred and not directly chargeable to a specific project or task.

Indirect waste pipe: A pipe that does not connect directly with the drainage system but conveys liquid waste by discharging into a plumbing fixture or receptacle which is directly connected to the drainage system.

Individual vent: A pipe installed to vent a fixture trap. It connects with the vent system above the fixture served or terminates in the open air.

Induced siphonage: Loss of liquid from a fixture trap due to pressure differential between inlet and outlet of trap, often caused by discharge of another fixture.

Industrial waste: All liquid or waterborne waste from industrial or commercial processes.

Infiltration: Air that flows through cracks in a wall, etc.

Information: The meaning assigned to data.

Initiating circuit: A circuit that transmits a manual or automatic alarm signal, such as a fire alarm box, smoke, heat, or flame-sensing device, sprinkler, waterflow alarm switch, or similar device to a control panel or other equipment which, when activated, causes an alarm to be indicated or retransmitted.

Initiating device circuit (loop): A circuit to which automatic or manual signal-initiating devices are connected where the signal received does not identify the individual device operated.

Inlay: Laying a material such as bone or pewter into metal or wood.

Inorganic: Relating to the chemistry of compounds not classified as organic. Involving neither organic life nor the products of organic life.

INR (impact noise rating): A single figure rating that provides an estimate of the impact sound-insulating performance of a floor-ceiling assembly.

Insanitary: A condition contrary to sanitary principles or injurious to health.

Insert: A circular or ellipsoid cross-section opening into the distribution duct or cell, from which the wires or cables emerge. It can be factory installed, preset, or after set when required.

Inside finish: In the United States, the fittings: doors and door trims, window trims, shutters, door-saddles and the like, dadoes or wall lining with wood, marble, or tile; sometimes also mantelpieces and even sideboards, presses, or dressers if put up permanently. The term is most commonly used for the woodwork of ordinary dwelling houses and business buildings but is extended to the most elaborate and permanent work.

Inspection list: A list of items of work to be completed or corrected by the contractor, commonly called punch list.

Inspection: (A) Examination of work completed or in progress to determine its compliance with contract requirements. (B) The examination of work by a public official to determine compliance by the contractor with codes or ordinances. (C) A critical examination of the work to determine compliance by the contractor with plans and specifications.

Inspector: See building inspector, owner's inspector, resident engineer.

Installation: The assembly of a building component on site and fixing it in position for use.

Instant start fluorescent lamp: A fluorescent lamp designed for starting by a high voltage without preheating of the electrodes.

Instructions to bidders: Instructions contained in the bidding requirements for preparing and submitting bids for a construction project. See notice to bidders.

Insulate: To cover with a material of low conductivity to reduce the passage or leakage of heat.

Insulating lath: Same as plain lath except that the back surface is covered with a continuous sheet of finished aluminum foil.

Insulation, cellular: Insulation composed of small individual cells separated from each other. The cellular material may be glass or plastic such as polystyrene (closed cell), polyurethane, and elastomeric.

Insulation, cryogenic: Insulation for extremely low temperature surfaces from -100° to -459° F (absolute zero).

Insulation, fibrous: Insulation composed of small diameter fibers that finely divide the air space. Fibers used are silica, rock wool, slag wood, or alumina silica.

Insulation, granular: Insulation composed of small nodules that contain voids or hollow spaces. The material may be calcium silicate, diatomaceous earth, expanded vermiculite, perlite, or cellulose.

Insulation, loose or fill: Insulation consisting of loose granules, fibers, beads, flakes,

etc., which must be contained and are usually placed in cavities.

Insulation, reflective: Insulation composed of closely spaced sheets of aluminum or stainless steel. The insulation obtains its insulation value from the ability of the sheets to reflect a large part of the radiant energy incident on them.

Insulation, refractory: Insulation of temperatures above 1,500° F.

Insulation, sprayed-on : Fibrous or foam insulation applied to a surface by power spray devices.

Insulation, sound: Parts of a mechanical system that are acoustically treated to reduce the vibrations from noise.

Insulation, thermal: Any material high in resistance to heat transmission that, when placed in the walls, ceiling, or floors of a structure, will reduce the rate of heat flow. Insulation applicable within the general temperature range of -150° F to 1,500° F.

Insulation, underground: Any insulation applied on piping and equipment located below grade and in direct contact with the surrounding soil.

Insulation: Those materials that retard the flow of heat.

Insulation board, rigid: A structural building board made of course wood or cane fiber in 1/2" and 25/32" thicknesses. It can be obtained in various sizes densities, and treatments.

Intelligent system smoke detector: A system smoke detector capable of communicating information about smoke conditions at its location to a control unit. This type of detector will typically communicate a unique identification (address) along with an analog signal that indicates the level of smoke at its location.

Intensity: Sound energy transmitted at a certain rate in a specific direction and through a unit area.

Interceptor: A device to separate and retain hazardous or undesirable matter from normal wastes and permit normal sewage to discharge into the disposal terminal by gravity.

Interface activity: Connects an event in one subnetwork with another event in another subnetwork, representing a logical or imposed interdependence in one direction only.

Interface node (interface event): A common node between two or more subnetworks representing a logical or imposed interdependence.

Interior, finish: Material used to cover the interior framed areas, or materials of walls and ceilings.

Interior stucco: A term (often used interchangeably with the term interior plaster)

designating a smooth or textured finish plaster for walls and ceilings. It is a mechanically blended compound of Keene's cement, lime (type S) and inert fine aggregate color pigment may be added to produce integrally colored interior stucco. See stucco.

Intern architect: One pursuing a training program under the guidance of practicing architects with the objective of qualifying for registration as an architect.

Interrupting rating (I.R.): The maximum current a fuse can safely interrupt. Some special purpose fuses may also have a minimum interrupting rating. This defines the minimum current that a fuse can safely interrupt.

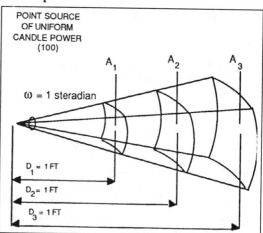

Inverse square law: The law stating that the illuminance at a point on a surface varies directly with the intensity of a point source, and inversely as the square of the distance between the source and the point.

If the surface at the point is normal to the direction of the incident light, the law is expressed by fc=cp/d².

Invert: Term referring to the lowest point on the interior of a horizontal pipe.

Invitation to bid: A portion of the bidding requirements soliciting bids for a privately financed construction project.

Invited bidders: The bidders selected by the architect and owner as the only ones from whom bids will be received.

Ionization smoke detector: Contains a small amount of radioactive material that ionizes the air in the sensing chamber, thus rendering it conductive and permitting a current to flow between two charged electrodes. This gives the sensing chamber an effective electrical conductance. When smoke particles enter the ionization area, they decrease the conductance of the air by attaching themselves to the ions, causing a reduction in mobility. When the conductance is less than a predetermined level, the detector responds.

Iron: (A) A metal which in practical use is approximately pure only in the form known as wrought iron. This is peculiarly malleable and can be welded; that is, one piece can be united to another when both are heated to a certain high temperature and then hammered together. Cast iron contains much carbon. This, in the form in which the melted metal flows from the

melting furnace, is called pig iron, the term cast iron being reserved for that which has been remelted and cast in molds for special purposes. As compared with wrought iron, this is brittle, not malleable, and cannot be welded. Steel, which has less carbon than cast iron, is to a certain degree malleable and capable of being welded; its peculiar value is, however, in its capacity for being tempered, which makes it very hard. Steel is made cheaply and easily, and its use for rolled beams, built beams, build columns, and the like, is superseding the use of wrought iron and of cast iron. (B) Any small or subordinate member of cast or wrought iron.

Ironwork: Decorative or structural elements made from wrought iron.

Isolux chart: A series of lines plotted on any appropriate set of coordinates, each line connecting all the points on a surface having the same illumination.

Isometric drawing: A form of three-dimensional projection in which all of the principal planes are drawn parallel to corresponding established axes and at true dimensions. Horizontals are usually drawn at 30° from the normal horizontal axes; vertical remain parallel to the normal vertical axis.

Isometric projection: A drawing showing an object in three dimensions. A plan is established with lines at an equal angle to the horizontal, usually 30°. Vertical lines

remain vertical. All lines are drawn to
scale. Diagonals and curves are distorted.

Item: A summary item on the work breakdown structure.

J

J-node: The node (event) signifying the finish of the activity.

Jack, builders': (A) Sometimes, same as jack. (B) A small staging or platform hung or bracketed from a window opening.

Jack, hydraulic: A modification of the hydraulic press. By means of this instrument, weights far beyond the power of the ordinary jackscrew can be moved.

Jack, hydrostatic: A variety of hydraulic jack, the term adopted by the inventor to describe his invention.

Jack, window: Same as builders' jack.

Jack rafter: A rafter that spans the distance from the wallplate to a hip or from a valley to a ridge.

Jack: (A) Inferior, secondary, Terms compounded with jack are often coined to explain the idea of smaller size or secondary position. (B) An apparatus for raising, lowering, or sustaining a part of a building; consisting, in its usual and simplest form, of a vertical screw which is raised or lowered when turned in a fixed nut, and the top of which supports the given load.

Jacket: A covering placed over insulation for various functions.

Jamb shaft: A shaft with capital and base fastened to the jamb of a door or window.

Jamb: (A) An upright finished member forming the side of an opening. The side of a door frame, doorway, or window; usually the side on which the opening for the lock is placed. (B) One of the lateral upright surfaces of an opening; hence, also, a piece forming, or intended to form, the side of an opening. In thick walls, the door jamb is often richly panelled.

Jib: A concealed flush door painted or decorated to match the wall into which it is cut.

Jig: A woodworking tool used as a pattern or guide.

Job captain: Member of the architect's staff normally responsible, on a given project, for the preparation of drawings and their coordination with other documents.

Job site security: Provisions for protection of the job site and tools and materials stored thereon from theft, vandalism, fire, or weather damage.

Job site storage: Provisions for storing the contractor's materials, tools, and equipment on the site.

Job specifications: A detailed list of all products, measures, and manufacturing needed to carry out a construction job.

Job superintendent: See superintendent.

Joggle joint: In cut stones, or the like, joint between two blocks that fit into each other by a joggle.

Joggle: A projection, as a tongue or shoulder, which unites one piece to another adjoining, either by the insertion of the joggle into a corresponding notch or recess or by its overlapping a similar projection on the adjoining piece. Hence, a separate piece, as a dowel or key, used for the same purpose by its insertion into the aperture framed by two adjoining recesses. In the latter connection the term is more commonly restricted to masonry. The term is not very definite and includes methods of joining and decorative and structural projections for which there are no more specific terms. Thus, the stiles of a window sash may extend below the rail to afford greater support for the tenons of the latter, these downward projections are called joggles. Likewise, the term is applied, to stonecutting that enables stones to hold one another in place, so that one stone cannot drop without breaking or breaking its neighbors.

Joinery: Joiners' work; the interior fittings of dwellings, dadoes, door trim, and the like. The term would be more appropriate for the entire decorative woodwork of interiors than for cabinet work, but has nearly become obsolete, at least in the United States.

Joining: point where two mixes on same surfaces meet.

Joint, abutment; abutting joint: (A) In carpentry, joint formed where the end of one piece of wood is made to abut the side of another; the grain of the respective parts is at right angles, or approximately so. The connection may be made in various ways. (B) In iron construction, the joint between two compression members whose axes are continuous, or nearly so.

Joint, bed: In masonry, one formed at the beds of two adjoining stones and, therefore, horizontal, or nearly so. Among masons, commonly known specifically as "bed," as distinguished from the "joints," which are more or less vertical.

Joint, bevel: In general, any joint in which the meeting edges are cut obliquely or with a bevel, whether the joined pieces meet at an angle or in a continuous line. Specifically, same as miter joint, but usually restricted to mean such a joint when the pieces do not meet at 90°.

Joint, blown: Joint formed in lead or other soft metal. The blowpipe, as in plumbing, between lead pipes that are not subject to much pressure.

Joint, breaking: One formed by several heading joints coming together in one continuous line; especially used in connection with the laying of floor planks.

Joint, bridle: A joint for uniting the end of a timber with the side of another. The end has a deep groove or recess cut across to leave two projecting equal tongues, like tenons. These fit into recesses or notches cut in the edges of the second timber, leaving a ridge. A common method of securing the foot of a rafter to a tie beam.

Joint, butt: Any joint formed by two butts, i.e., by pieces meeting end to end. More frequently used in carpentry than in other trades.

Joint, compass: A joint between two members, of which a part, usually circular, laps over and is closely fitted to the similar part of the other; a round pin or pivot passes through both parts. In practice, as in the making of drawing instruments, one member has two nearly circular disks separated from one another and enclosing the single disk in which the other member terminates; or one member has three disks, which enclose the two disks with which the other number terminates. If properly adjusted and smoothly planed, such a joint allows great uniformity of movement, the parts of the compass or other utensil moving one upon another freely and with equal pressure at whatsoever angle they are adjusted.

Joint, coursing: The continuous joint between two courses of brick or stone masonry; any horizontal joint as distinguished from a vertical or heading joint.

Joint, dog ear: One formed at the corners of a trough or dish-shaped receptacle made from a sheet of metal. The edges of the sheet being turned up, the triangular portion left projecting at the corner is bent back

against one of the sides and soldered or otherwise secured.

Joint, drip: In metal roofing, (A) a method of connecting two sheets to form a drip across the slope of a roof and prevent rain water from entering the joint. (B) A joint formed by overlapping the edges of adjoining sheets. The portions so joined are bent downward to form continuous channels following the slope of the roof. It has a form the reverse of a roll.

Joint, faucet: Same as spigot and faucet joint.

Joint, feather: A joint made by inserting a feather edge of one piece into a mortise or groove of another.

Joint, flange: One in which the two joined members each have a flange, which are secured by bolts or rivets. The term is especially used in connecting wrought iron pipes whose extremities have perforated flanges or collars, by which means they are bolted or riveted together, end to end.

Joint, flush or flat: Any joint in which the surfaces of the two joined pieces are flush. In masonry, specifically, a flat joint.

Joint, folding: Any joint that permits the member to be folded one upon the other, as for the flap or leaf of a Pembroke table; specifically, a rule joint arranged for this purpose or (where a narrow bearing and great stiffness are required) a compass joint.

Joint, foliated: A joint made by two over-lapping, related edges, showing a flush joint on each face. A form of joggle.

Joint, heading: One formed at the meeting of a header, or a heading, with the transverse piece or pieces.

Joint, hook and butt: A form of scarf in which part of the thickness of the timbers forms a butt joint, and the remainder being interlocked by one or more hook-shaped notches.

Joint, lap: One formed by lapping the adjoining pieces with little or no interlocking or framing. Thus, in sheet metal work, such a joint is commonly made by overlapping the edges of two sheets without bending and soldering them flat. In framing, the ends of two timbers are sometimes overlapped longitudinally and bolted together or secured by keys and straps.

Joint, match: One formed by matched boards.

Joint, miter: One formed by two pieces meeting at an angle. The meeting ends or edges are equally bevelled so that the plane of the joint bisects the angle between the pieces. The term is commonly restricted to mean a joint whose bevels are at 45°, thus making an angle of 90° between the two pieces when joined.

Joint, peen: In a stone stair, the joint between two steps that are secured by a peen check.

Joint, pig lug: Same as dog ear joint.

Joint, pin: One in which the meeting parts overlap and are pierced to receive a pin. The common joint used for connecting chords with braces in American iron trusses.

Joint, pipe: A joint connecting the lengths of pipe in which the interior is left full size and even, and the joint is secured against leakage. Common examples are the wiped joint for lead pipe and the usual connection of iron pipe by means of hubs, with or without screw threads.

Joint, plumb: In sheet-metal work, a joint made by lapping the edges and soldering them together flat.

Joint, prop: Same as rule joint.

Joint, ring: A flange joint formed at the meeting of two circular flanges, as in securing wrought-iron pipes end to end.

Joint, roll: In sheet-metal work, a joint formed by rolling the edges of adjoining sheets together and then flattening the roll.

Joint, rule: A joint between two leaves or flaps of equal thickness, which are movable about the joint. One part has a half round and fillet which fit a cove and fillet on the other; the pivot (usually formed by a hinge) is at the common center. This is the usual way of jointing a leaf of a table to the fixed top.

Joint, rust: In metal work and plumbing, an inferior joint made by a mixture of iron filings with chemicals which produces rapid oxidation of the iron so that the parts are thus rusted together.

Joint, rustic: In masonry, a joint formed in rustication.

Joint, saddle: In a weathered course of masonry, as a coping or sill, a joint formed between two adjoining stones whose ends are cut higher than the surface of the weathering between. These projections at the ends are usually sloped or rounded away from the joint and toward the weathering, so as to shed water from the mortar.

Joint, shove: In bricklaying, a mortar joint formed when putting a brick into its place by shoving it over a full bed of mortar, so that some of the mortar is forced up into the interstices between the brick and the adjoining parts of the masonry. The method is advocated as a means of obtaining well-filled joints.

Joint, slip: A joint by which two parts are more or less connected while they are free to move, one along the other. Especially, such a joint between two masonry walls which allows the heavier wall to settle without affecting the lighter one.

Joint, spigot: One formed by the insertion of the spigot end of a pipe into the mouth or hub of another.

Joint, splay: In wood-working, a joint between two surfaces which are splayed with relation to the adjoining surfaces, especially applied to the meeting rails of a vertically sliding sash. No absolute distinction can be made between this and a beveled joint.

Joint, struck: A mortar joint in facework dressed or finished with a pointer or striker. A trowel-finished joint.

Joint, tabled: In cut stonework, a bed joint formed by a broad, shallow channel in the surface of one stone, into which fits a corresponding projection of the stone above or below.

Joint, water: (A) A joint through which water will not leak, as in the framework of a water gate, the gate of a canal lock, or the junction of two pipes, etc. (B) Same as drip joint.

Joint, wiped: In connecting the ends of lead pipe, a joint made by inserting one into the other and securing the two together by a mass of solder which is wiped around the juncture, with a cloth. The joint is finally covered and concealed by a more or less spherical mass of the solder. In joining two ends of the same caliber, one is pared to a conical shape to be inserted into the other, which is reamed out to receive it.

Joint cement: A powder usually mixed with water and used for joint treatment in gypsum-wallboard finish. Often called spackle.

Joint photographing: The shadowing of the finished joint areas through the surface decoration.

Joint reinforcing metal: Strips of expanded metal, woven or welded wire mesh, used to reinforce corners and other areas of plaster and lath.

Joint reinforcing tape: A type of paper, metal, fabric glass mesh, or other material, commonly used with a cementitious compound, to reinforce the joints between adjacent gypsum boards.

Joint venture: A collaborative undertaking having the legal characteristics of a partnership, for a specific project or projects.

Joint: (A) Any horizontal or nearly horizontal beam intended primarily for the construction or support of a floor, ceiling, or the like. By extension, a sleeper as used for the support of a wooden floor over a masonry or fireproof floor. (B) In the United States, a stud or piece of scantling about 3" x 4" in size. (C) The place at which two parts meet and sometimes unite; the surfaces so brought together considered collectively; the space between two such faces, which may be filled with a cohesive material to unite the two parts; hence, the mass of cohesive material so placed. Any two pieces brought into close contact form a joint between them. A wall built of stones without the use of mortar is said to have dry joints; that is, the interstices, or spaces between the stones, are not filled with mortar. An architect's specifications may call for joints of stonework to be dressed in a certain manner, which would apply to the faces which it is intended to bring into contact. It may be required that brickwork is to be laid in certain mortar with 3/8" joints, such stipulation referring to the thickness of the mass of mortar between the bricks. Two timbers may be framed by a mortise and tenon joint, the term in such case being applied to the several contiguous surfaces, together with the parts immediately connected.

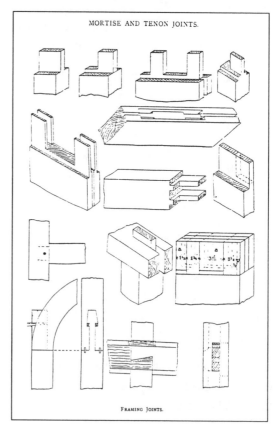

MORTISE AND TENON JOINTS.

FRAMING JOINTS.

Jointer: Any tool for jointing or finishing or embellishing a joint.

Jointing: Finishing the surface of wet mortar in brickwork rather than raking it out.

Joist: Structural member (wood, steel, other) used as floor, ceiling, or roof framing members.

Joists, exposed: Joists whose undersides are exposed to the room below. They are often molded to trim.

Journeyman plumber: A plumber who has served an apprenticeship.

Jump: An abrupt change of level in masonry, as in the base of a foundation wall or a course of stonework, which is adjusted to a slope by an occasional step.

Junction box: A metal box in which circuit wiring is spliced. It may also be used for mounting luminaries, switches, or receptacles.

K

Keene's cement: An anhydrous gypsum plaster characterized by a low mixing water requirement and special setting properties, primarily used with lime to produce hard, dense finish coats.

Keeper: A metal plate set in a door jamb for a door bolt.

Key, blank: A key before the bit or other part is finished or shaped to fit any particular lock.

Key, change: One fashioned to fit one of a set of locks, as distinguished from the master key which controls the entire series.

Key, desk: A reversible key commonly used for the locking of the top of a desk; usually small and of simple form.

Key, extension: One with a telescope shank, the shank of the bow working in the cylindrical shank of the bit. Used as a sliding door key.

Key, flat: One fashioned entirely from a flat strip of metal. A form commonly used for latch keys and the like, because convenient for carrying.

Key, folding: A key with a joint in the shank allowing the bit to fold back upon the bow.

Key, latch: A key to open a latch.

Key, master: One so fashioned that it will lock and unlock all of a set of locks, each differing slightly from the other.

Key, night: One for opening a night latch.

Key, reversible: One having two similar bits, one on each side of the shank, permitting the key to be inserted in its lock either side up, and operating the lock by a half turn of the key.

Key, skeleton: An instrument, usually a slim strip of metal, used for picking locks.

Key, sliding door: One fitted for the lock of a sliding door. The shank has a joint, or extension, which allows the bow to be turned closed to the countersunk escutcheon and clear the jamb strips of the sliding door pocket.

Key item (milestone activity): An activity considered of major significance in the project life. Sometimes is referred to as a milestone activity.

Key item schedule or milestone schedule: A schedule of key activities or events (milestones) selected as a result of close coordination between client and subcontracts or project management.

Key: (A) An instrument for fastening and unfastening a lock. The key can be inserted or withdrawn at pleasure; and when withdrawn, the lock cannot be opened or shut except by violence. The principal parts of an ordinary key are the bow, bit, and shank. The bow is the enlargement at one end of the shank whereby the key is turned by the fingers. The bit is the lug at the end of the shank that fits the lock, raises the tumbler, and turns the bolt of the lock. The bit is cut and grooved to fit the wards and levers of the lock. The shank is the shaft connecting the bow and bit. (B) A wedge, or a tapering piece or member, used singly or in pairs to draw two parts together and tightly secure them when it is forced into an aperture prepared for the purpose. A wedge that holds two members or surfaces apart; hence, a member for a similar purpose, whether so shaped or not, designed for insertion into recessed in two or more adjoining parts, and commonly secured in place by wedges or keys of the specified form. Thus a key may be used instead of a cleat for securing boards edge to edge and will be formed of a tapering board forced into a corresponding groove cut across the assembled boards. The cross section of such a key and its corresponding groove has usually a dovetail shape, flaring inward, for greater security. A common use of keys is in heavy framing, as in forming a scarf joint, or assembling the parts of a truss. For the last purpose, a key known as a cotter, is commonly of iron, and used in connection with a gib, or gibs. (C) In plastering, that part of the plastic material which enters into the interstices or clings to the rough surface of the backing or prepared support and by its adherence sustains the coat of mortar, or like material.

Thus, the first coat of plaster applied to lathing forms a key when pressed through the spaces arranged for it, this coat being scratched or roughened, enables the next coat to form a key.

Keyhole: A hole for the reception of a key; more specifically, the aperture by which a key is inserted into a lock.

Keystone: The central stone of an arch or rib vault

Kiln-dried lumber: Lumber that has been kiln dried often to a moisture content of 6% to 12%. Common varieties of softwood lumber, such as framing lumber, are dried to a somewhat higher moisture content.

Kiln: A heated room used to dry lumber or an oven used to fire ceramics.

Kiloamperes (abbreviated KA): 1,000 amperes.

Kilowatt-hour (KWH): Unit of electrical power consumed over a period of time. KWH=watts/1000 x hours used.

King-post: A vertical timber standing centrally on a tie-beam and rising to the apex of the roof where it supports a ridge.

Kiosk: A small open pavilion. A small shop in a park or on a street side. A polygonal or cylindrical sign board or information booth.

Kitchen sink: A shallow, flat-bottomed fixture used in a kitchen.

Kitchen: The room in which food is prepared and usually eaten.

Knee: (A) A curved or bent member of metal or wood used as a bracket or brace to stiffen two parts of a structure that meet at an angle. It is generally applied at the interior of the angle. There is no absolute distinction between knee and brace, except that the former extends well into the angle, commonly filling the space up to the apex. In timber work, however, a knee is properly formed of a naturally bent piece of wood, the grain following a curve which makes it peculiarly adapted to fit into a re-entrant angle, as in the construction of wooden ships. (B) A stone cut to an angle, generally a right angle, to fit a sharp return as at the corner of a label; making the angle of a merlon or the like.

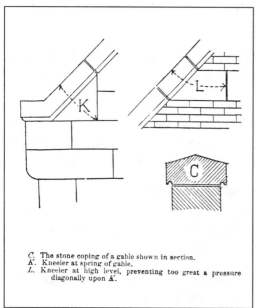

C. The stone coping of a gable shown in section.
K. Kneeler at spring of gable.
L. Kneeler at high level, preventing too great a pressure diagonally upon K.

Kneeler: A stone block set at the top of a masonry wall to finish the eaves or coping. A piece of church furniture padded and used to kneel on during prayer.

Knob: A rounded projection, sometimes a piece of utility, as when furnishing the handle to a door lock or latch, and sometimes an ornament. In this latter sense the term implied generally the termination of a slender and isolated member.

Knock-off: Copy of an original that is sold at a lower price.

Knocked down: Unassembled, as contrasted to assembled or built-up.

Knocker: A contrivance, generally of metal, attached to the outside of an outer door that enables a visitor's presence to be announced by means of a knock or light blow. Its essential part is a hammerlike, pivoted arm that is raised and allowed to fall against a plate.

Knot, sound tight: A portion of a branch or a limb whose growth rings are intergrown on the face with the growth rings of the surrounding wood. It shall not contain any decay and shall be so fixed by growth shape that it will retain its place in the piece. The average of the maximum and minimum dimensions of the knot on the exposed surface shall be used in measuring the size. For plywood: pin knot does not exceed 1/4" in diameter. For solid stock: small pin knot does not exceed 1/4" in diameter, pin knot does not exceed 1/2" in diameter, and small knot is larger than 1/2" but does not exceed 3/4".

Knot: (A) Same as knob; an ancient form. (B) In ornament, resembling the tying together of cords, whether this is in flat carving (as in interlaced or strap work) or in the carving of two or four shafts of a compound pier, these being cut out of a single block and treated as if each shaft had been flexible and so intertwined with the other or the others. (C) In lumber, the portion of a branch or limb of a tree that appears on the edge or face of the piece.

Knotty pine: Pine wood with knots that, when cut, forms a decorative pattern.

Knulling: A convex rounded molding of slight projection, consisting of a series of elaborate and fantastic members separated by indentions; intermediate between the egg and dart and the bead and reel.

L

L: (A) A piece of pipe or bar making a right angle with another (compare elbow). (B) A subordinate part of a building projecting from the main structure at right angles, giving to the whole the shape of the letter L. Hence, in local United States usage, any small extension or wing, however situated.

Labeled: Equipment bearing a label of certification of an approved listing organization.

Labor adder, labor burden, or labor direct job expenses: Accounting terms for non-wage expenses incurred through the employment of labor, including payroll taxes, workers' compensation insurance premiums when based on labor hours, supervision when not classified with productive labor, and employee benefits that have not been included as part of wage cost

Labor and material payment bond: A bond of the contractor, in which a surety guarantees to the owner that the contractor will pay for labor and materials used in the performance of the contract. The claimants under the bond are defined as those having direct contracts with the contractor or any subcontractor.

Labor only contracts: Contracts under which the contractor furnishes labor and management but the owner or higher tier contractor supplies materials.

Lacquer: Properly, a substance made of lac; that is, of the substance sold as gum-lac, stick-lac, seed-lac, shell-lac, or shellac, but by extension applied also to a varnish made in Asian countries from the sap of certain plants.

Laddering: A method of showing the logic relationship of a set of parallel activities with the arrow technique.

Lag relationship: The four basic types of lag relationships between start or finish of another activity are finish to start, finish to finish, start to start and start to finish.

Lag: To apply lagging. A single piece of lagging material.

Lag: A specified time increment between the start or completion of an activity and the start or completion of a successor activity.

Lagging-insulation: A block of any of several insulation materials for insulating tanks and boilers, usually curved or tapered.

Lagging-metal: Metal covering installed over insulation.

Laminate: A product made by bonding together two or more layers of material or materials.

Laminated: Layer construction of lumber. May be either horizontal or vertical layers securely glued together.

Lamination: The application of two or more layers of gypsum board.

Lamp efficacy: The ratio of lumens produced by a lamp to the watts consumed. Expressed as lumens per watt.

Lamp lumen depreciation (LLD): Multiplier factor in illumination calculations for reduction in the light output of a lamp over a period of time.

Lamp: An artificial source of light (also a portable luminaire equipped with a cord and plug).

Lampshades: Decorative covers for table and floor lamps and sconces which prevent direct glare from the light source.

Land survey: A survey made to determine the lengths and directions of boundary lines and the area of the tract bounded by these lines, or a survey made to establish the positions of the boundary lines on the ground. See boundary survey, survey.

Land surveyor (topographical surveyor): A person who measures land and buildings for mapping. Most structural, civil or mechanical engineers can act as surveyors since designing requires a knowledge of surveying.

Landing: (A) That portion of a floor, or a confined floor space, immediately adjoining or connected with a staircase or flight of stairs. It may be either the floor space meeting the foot or top of a flight. (B) Any structure, or at the water's edge, at which persons or goods can be embarked or disembarked. In this sense often landing place.

Landscape architecture: The design of a garden using flowers, trees, shrubs, and borders to achieve a balanced effect of color.

Lap adhesive: The adhesive used to seal the sides and laps of insulation jackets.

Laser: A low-intensity rotating, columnated, (relatively nondivergent) light beam construction tool used to establish accurate sightings, plumb and level alignments, vertical and horizontal.

Last event number: The number of the last event in time for a work package or summary item. This event number defines the end of the work package or summary item in relation to the network.

Latch: A form of door bar permanently secured to the door by a pivot at one end, the other end being free to fall into a slot or hook, out of which it must be raised to allow the door to open. There is also, generally, a projecting member near the edge of the door beneath the bar which is thus prevented from falling when the door is open. The meaning of the term is extended to include spring locks designed especially for outer doors.

Late event time (LET): The latest day an event may occur without increasing the proposed scheduled completion date.

Late finish (latest allowable date): The latest time at which an activity can be completed without lengthening the project.

Late start: The latest time at which an activity can start without lengthening the project.

Lateral sewer: A sewer that does not receive sewage from any other common sewer except house connections.

Latest revised estimate: The sum of the incurred costs plus the latest estimate-to-complete for a work package or summary item as reviewed and revised (including applicable overhead where direct costs are specified).

Lath, counter: (A) An intermediate lath or batten interposed between a pair of gauge laths. (B) One of a supplementary set, as when laths are nailed across others used as furring.

Lath, gauge: In roofing, one of several laths placed by accurate measurement to support a tile or slate at the proper points, as at the nail holes.

Lath, lead-back: Plain gypsum lath to which sheets of lead have been laminated

for shielding from X-rays and other radiation.

Lath, perforated: same as plain lath except that it has perforations not less then 3/4" in diameter, with one perforation for not more than each 16 square inches (no longer manufactured).

Lath, type X: Same as plain lath, except that the core has increased fire retardant properties to improve its fire-resistive rating.

Lath clip (generic): A metal section to secure lath to supports.

Lath-plaster: Plasterer's lath.

Lath: A strip of metal or wood, generally quite thin and narrow, but often approaching a batten or furring strip in size. Laths are intended to be secured to beams, studs, and such members to support tiles, slates, plaster, and similar finishing materials.

Lathe: A machine that shapes circular pieces of metal or wood by rotating the material.

Lathing: (A) Laths collectively, or material used as a substitute for laths. (B) The operation and the result of securing laths in place for the reception of plaster, tiling, or other finish.

Lattice: A system of small, light bars crossing each other at regular intervals. In modern country houses this is often made of laths, or light slips of wood, forming regular square or lozenge-shaped openings. The term is extended to cover glazed sash in which the sash bars form square or lozenge-shaped openings filled with pieces of glass of the same shape. Thus, an iron girder having a web composed of diagonal braces is commonly known as a lattice girder. A distinction is sometimes made in iron construction between latticing and lacing: the former applies to a double diagonal system of bars crossing each other; the latter mean a single series arranged in zigzag.

Laundry tray: A fixed tub in a laundry room, supplied with cold and hot water and a drain connection.

Lavatory: A fixture designed for washing the hands and face.

Layer: A way of managing graphic data in groups. Layers may be edited, saved, or plotted discreetly or in any combination. This data management method is similar to overlay drafting.

Leaching well: A pit or receptacle having porous walls that permit the contents to seep into the ground. Also known as dry well.

Lead glass: A lustrous, soft glass and made of a lead oxide. See flint glass.

Lead: An arrow introduced before a series of activities to schedule them at a later time.

Leaded lights: Rectangular or diamond-shaped leaded panes that form a window.

Leader: The water conductor from the roof to the building (house) storm drain. Also known as downspout.

Leak, sound: An opening that allows the transmission of sound.

Ledger strip: A strip of lumber nailed along the bottom of the side of a girder on which joists rest.

Legal precedents: Court decisions that are thought to be worthy to serve as models for future cases.

Leisure run stairs: Stairs with small rise-to-run ratio or with an unusually shallow slope.

Length of pipe: See developed length.

Lengthening bar: A bar for lengthening a leg of a compass by the insertion of one end into the standing part, and the insertion of one of the detachable points at its other end.

Lens: Used in luminaries to redirect light into useful zones.

Let-in brace: Nominal 1" thick boards applied into notched studs diagonally.

Letter agreement (letter of agreement): A letter stating the terms of an agreement between addresser and addressee, usually prepared to be signed by the addressee to indicate acceptance of those terms as legally binding.

Letter of intent: A letter signifying an intention to enter into a formal agreement, usually setting forth the general terms of such agreement.

Level, sound: Electrically determined measure of sound pressure.

Level, spirit: An instrument used in fixing operations. It consists of a small hermetically sealed glass tube nearly filled with alcohol, firmly cemented into a hardwood, aluminum, or fiberglass stock. The axial line of the tube is exactly parallel with the under surface of the stock. The tube is sunk flush and protected by a metal plate having a longitudinal opening crossed by a thin bar in the center. The tube is very slightly curved in length, the convex side being placed uppermost to assist the motion of the bubble of air confined within. When it is desired to use the instrument to test a piece of work, the bottom of the stock is laid either on the upper surface of the work or on a parallel straightedge resting on it. When it is dead level the air bubble will lie centrally under the bridge, if out of level the bubble will run to the highest end.

Level: The number of the level on the work breakdown structure at which a charge or summary number appears.

Leveller: Anything intended to bring about a level horizontal surface. Any contrivance by which the upper surface of a structure may be brought to a horizontal or nearly horizontal plane. Especially in stone masonry, a stone of the proper dimension to make up a difference in height between two adjoining stones, to produce a level bed for the next course above; also a flat stone for making a level bearing, as in a footing course.

Liability insurance: Insurance that protects the insured against liability because of injury to the person or property of another. See comprehensive general liability insurance, contractor's liability insurance, employer's liability insurance, owner's liability insurance, professional liability insurance".

Library: A collection of graphic data or symbols that may be drawn upon to create elements of a drawing without redrawing.

Licensed architect: See architect.

Licensed contractor: A person or organization certified by governmental authority, where required by law, to engage in construction contracting.

Lie: The direction of rock stratifications.

Lien enforcement: Liens may be enforced by an action to foreclose on the recorded property.

Lien waiver: See waiver of lien.

Lien: See mechanic's lien.

Light, angel: In a decorative window, a light that may be adorned by stained or painted glass representing an angel, as in some English Gothic windows, one of several smaller openings in the window head in which figures of angels are commonly inserted.

Light, borrowed: A light that is received from another room or passage, which itself is lighted directly by windows or the like.

Light, vault: A light prepared expressly for underground rooms, cellars extended under streets, and the like, often called (erroneously) vaults (see vault). The vault light is usually an arrangement of prismatic or lenticular glasses in a metal frame. In modern cities, large horizontal surfaces, such as area floors, of treads, and entrance platforms and even public sidewalks, are composed entirely of the upper surface of such vault lights.

Light loss factor: (LLF) A factor used in calculating the level of illumination, such factors as dirt accumulation on luminaire and room surfaces, lamp depreciation, maintenance procedures, and atmosphere conditions. See maintenance factor.

Light output: Amount of light produced by a light source such as a lamp. The unit most commonly used to measure light output is the lumen.

Light scattering: The action of light being reflected or refracted off particles of combustion for detection by a photoelectric smoke detector. The action of light being refracted or reflected.

Light: (A) The volume of daylight received in a room, corridor, or the like. The term is often used in composition, as in borrowed light. By extension, a similar volume of light from an artificial source as a closet may have a borrowed light from a room lighted by electricity. (B) An opening or medium through which daylight may pass, as a pane (called generally by glaziers and carpenters a light) of glass. More especially the opening between two mullions or window bars in a decorative window, the glass of which is commonly in irregular or other small pieces, hardly called lights in this case. (C) An artificial source of light; a means of providing light, as in the compound or qualified terms gas light, electric light. Thus, in arranging for the lighting of an interior, it may be stipulated that 10 lights be ranged along the cornice on either side. (D) The manner or nature of the illumination received by a picture or other work of art, or by a wall or ceiling considered as the medium for the display of such work of art. Thus, it may be said that there is no good light for pictures on the east wall. (E) Radiant energy that can excite the retina and produce a visual sensation. The visible portion of the electromagnetic spectrum extends from about 380 to 770 nm.

Lightweight aggregate: See vermiculite, perlite, pumice.

Lime plaster: An interior basecoat plaster containing lime, aggregate, and sometimes fiber. Lime basecoat plaster is slow-setting. It should not be applied to gypsum lath. See Portland cement-lime plaster.

Lime: Oxide of calcium, most frequently found combined with carbonic acid forming limestone, or with sulfuric acid forming gypsum. All calcareous cements have lime as their base. When carbonate of lime is calcined, the carbonic acid is thrown off and lime, commonly known as caustic lime, or quicklime is obtained. If it is mixed with its equivalent of water, it slakes; that is throws out great heat, swells to two or three times its original bulk, and subsequently falls to powder. Then it has become a hydrate of lime, commonly known as slaked lime. Its affinity for carbonic acid is restored, it absorbs it from the atmosphere and gradually hardens. For use as a mortar in building, sufficient water is added to make a paste, and this is mixed with two or three times its bulk of sand. The hardening of lime mortar is due almost entirely to the absorption of carbonic acid from the air.

Limiter: A special-purpose fuse intended to provide short-circuit protection only.

Line switching: The temporary connection of two lines to permit the direct exchange of information. See message switching.

Line wire: See string wire.

Line-item concept: An arrangement under which payments are made and retainage is reduced or released for individual categories of work listed in a prime contract schedule of values. Normally each line item represents the work performed by one trade subcontractor.

Linear expansion or contraction: See mechanical properties of insulation - coefficient of expansion.

Lining: (A) A cushioning material made of felted cattle hair and jute, rubber or plastic foam, or other materials, used as an underlayment of rugs and carpets. Also known as cushion or underlay. (B) Material used to cover the interior of anything; hence, a member forming the back or internal face of a structure. Seldom used except in special combinations, as jamb lining, window back lining.

Lintel: A horizontal architectural element spanning and usually bearing the load above an opening.

Liquid waste: The discharge from any fixture, appliance, or appurtenance in connection with a plumbing system that does not receive fecal matter.

Liquidated damages: (A) Clauses in a construction contract relating to sums payable for delays amounting to breach of contract. These sums can generally only be recovered from the contractor if it can be proved that they are related to the loss caused by the delay. (B) A fixed sum per day established in a construction contract as the measure of damages suffered by the owner due to failure to complete the work within a stipulated time. See penalty clause, bonus clause.

Listed: Equipment or materials included in a list published by an organization acceptable to the authority having jurisdiction and concerning a listing agency.

Listing agency: An agency accepted by the administrative authority that lists and maintains a periodic inspection program on production of listed models. It publishes its finding which included that the product has been tested, complies with generally accepted standards, and is safe for use in a specified manner.

Lites: The panes of glass between narrow strips of wood on a window.

Litigation: A lawsuit or action in a court of justice to enforce a right.

Live load: That part of the total load on structural members that is not a permanent part of the structure. It may be variable, as in the case of loads contributed by occupancy, wind, or snow loads.

Load factor: The percentage of the total connected fixture unit flow which is likely

to occur at any point in the drainage system. Load factor represents the ratio of the probable load to the potential load and is determined by the average rates of flow of the kinds of fixtures, the average frequency of use, the duration of flow during one use, and the number of fixtures installed.

Load-bearing partition: A vertical structural interior wall supporting an integral part of the construction above. Low consistency plaster. See gypsum.

Load-bearing: A wall that can bear another weight as well as its own.

Load: That which has to be carried or supported, as a column may be strong enough to carry a load of 13 tons.

Loan commitment: A commitment from a financial institution to an owner or developer to provide funds for design and construction of a facility.

Local agreement: (A) A collective bargaining agreement between a local union of a trade and a contractor's association covering work of that trade within the local union's geographic jurisdiction. (B) A standard or model agreement, such as a subcontract agreement, developed by contractor's associations within a given geographical area for voluntary use by contractors. (C) Guidelines established by contractor's and, sometimes, architect's associations in a locality for efficient division of responsibilities for providing temporary site services and utilities to expedite bidding and minimize conflicts.

Local application system: Consists of a supply of Halon 1301 arranged to discharge directly on the burning material.

Local government: Any municipality, county, district, or combination thereof comprising a governmental unit.

Local lighting: Lighting designed to illuminate a relatively small area without providing any significant general surrounding lighting.

Lock, burglar alarm: Lock connected, usually by means of electricity, with a gong or other means of sounding an alarm when the bolt is tampered with.

Lock, combination: Lock in which the bolt can be drawn only when a certain arrangement of external parts, as of three rings with letters on them, has been made. When the combination is made by bringing the rings into a certain relation to one another, the handle can be turned and the bolt withdrawn.

Lock, crossbolt: Lock in which the key shoots two bolts at the same time in opposite directions, an arrangement easy to make by means of a short lever. This is useful for doors of bookcases and similar pieces of furniture; the bolts shooting at top and bottom at the same time hold the stile of the door straight and prevent its winding or warping with heat and use.

Lock, cylinder: Lock that has a cylinder into which falls a series of tumblers, preventing the cylinder from being turned until the tumblers are pushed out by the insertion of the proper key into the cylinder. This is a flat key, or a modification, with its edge serrated or notched to fit the ends of the tumblers. The cylinder can then be turned and the bolt shot. This lock is one of the safest of keylocks, its security lying in the arrangement of the series of tumblers, of which an almost infinite number of combinations can be made.

Lock, dead: Bolt actuated by a key only, or by a key on one side and a knob on the other, thus distinguished from a knob lock, which has a bolt actuated from either side by a key and a latch or catch actuated from either side by a knob.

Lock, drawbolt: Lock in which a bolt or latch, ordinarily movable by a knob or the like, can also be held by locking with a key and can only be withdrawn when the key is used to unlock it.

Lock, extension bolt: Same as cross bolt lock, knob lock.

Lock, latch: A lock designed especially for an outer door, as of a suite of offices, a front door, or the like, and therefore taking the place of a latch. Usually a spring lock, in which the bolt is automatically shot by a spring and can only be operated from outside by a key. Such a lock usually has a device by which the bolt may be retained and the action of the spring prevented, as during the hours in which the door is in frequent use. Such a lock, when designed or adapted especially for night use, is commonly known as a night latch.

Lock, mortise: One specially arranged to be sunk in a mortise in the edge of a door or sash. It has usually an edge plate, which is set square or diagonally with the sides of the box of the lock according to the angle made by the edge of the stile in which the lock is to be entered.

Lock, rim: One in which the case is secured against the face of the stile of the door, as distinguished from a mortise lock, which is let into and concealed by the wood. The case is ordinarily secured by screws, so that the lock can be readily removed. It is therefore usual to place such locks on the inside of the apartment or closet. If on the outside, clinched nails or bolts should be used, they are passed through the door.

Lock: (A) To provide with locks and, by extension, with other builders' hardware, as when a firm contracts to lock a house. A contrivance for fastening and unfastening at will a door, casement, chest, drawer, or the like, usually one of which the essential part is a bolt shot and withdrawn by means of a removable key. Door locks have usually a latch as well as the bolt moved by the key. Locks for safes and strong rooms are sometimes of extraordi-

nary complication, and many inventions have resulted in a system of defence against burglary which amounts almost to perfect security so far as the lock is concerned. Locks of this sort sometimes shoot bolts in all four directions and are frequently operated without keys, thus avoiding the necessity of a keyhole into which an explosive may be forced. (B) Interlocking machine joint between two members.

Log construction: A building made of hewn or raw logs notched and stacked to form walls often filled with mud or mortar between the cracks.

Log mean (radius): The equivalent value of insulation thickness for pipe (curved surfaces) to produce the same resistance to heat flow as per flat areas.

Logical restraint: An arrow connection that is used as a logical connector but does not represent work items. It is usually represented by a dotted line. Sometimes called a dummy because it does not represent work. It is an indispensable part of the network.

Long life lamps: See extended life lamps.

Lookout: A short wood bracket or cantilever to support an overhang portion of a roof or the like, usually concealed from view.

Loop vent: See vent, loop.

Loop: A path in a network closed on itself passing through any node or activity more than once or a sequence of activities in the network with no start or end.

Loose and long: Run to pattern only. Not assembled, machined for assembly, cut to length. The terms material only, and mill run, mean the same as loose and long.

Loss of use insurance: Insurance protecting against financial loss during the time required to repair or replace property damaged or destroyed by an insured peril.

Loudness: Hearing the effects of sound pressures.

Louver: (A) A series of baffles used to shield a source from view at certain angles or to absorb unwanted light. The baffles usually are arranged in a geometric pattern. (B) In lighting, one or a series of parallel, overlapping boards, metal or glass strips formed at angles to exclude rain and admit air.

Low bid: Bid stating the lowest bid price, including selected alternate, and complying with all bidding requirements.

Low consistency plaster: A neat (unfibered) gypsum basecoat plaster especially processed so that less mixing water is required than in standard gypsum basecoat plaster to produce workability. This type plaster is particularly adapted to machine application.

Low pressure condensate: That condensate directly received from low pressure steam.

Low pressure decorative polyester overlay: Overlays comprised of polyester resin saturated cellulosic sheets thermobonded to the particleboard, hardboard, or plywood core. The face overlay shall contain a decorative color or printed design. The other side may have a suitable balance sheet bonded in the same manner. The resultant product has an attractive exposed surface which is durable and resistant to damage from abrasion and mild alkalies, acids, and solvents.

Low pressure laminated melamine: Melamine-saturated sheets thermal-fused to a particleboard core.

Low pressure polyester overlay cabinet liner: Overlays comprised of polyester resin saturated cellulosic sheets thermobonded to the particleboard, hardboard, or plywood core. The resultant product has a solid color exposed surface which is durable and resistant to damage from abrasion and mild alkalies, acids, and solvents.

Low pressure sodium lamp: A discharge lamp in which light is produced by radiation of sodium vapor at low pressure, producing a single wavelength of visible energy i.e., yellow.

Low velocity duct: A duct with air flow designed at over 2,000 feet per minute velocity with a static pressure not above 2".

Low voltage lamps: Incandescent lamps that operate at 6 to 12 volts.

Lower tier subcontractor: A subcontractor of a subcontract. See sub-subcontractor.

Lowest responsible bidder (lowest qualified bidder): Bidder who submits the lowest bona fide bid and is considered by the owner and architect to be fully responsible and qualified to perform the work for which the bid is submitted.

Lowest responsive bid: The lowest bid that is responsive to and complies with the bidding requirements.

Lucite: A manmade clear acrylic plastic.

Lumber, boards: Yard lumber less than 2" thick and at least 2" wide.

Lumber, dimension: Yard lumber from 2" to, but not including, 5" thick and at least 2" wide. Includes Joists, rafters, studs, planks, and small timbers.

Lumber, dressed size: The dimension of lumber after shrinking from green dimension and after machining to size or pattern.

Lumber, matched: Lumber that is dressed and shaped on one edge in a grooved pattern and on the other in a tongued pattern.

Lumber, shiplap: Lumber that is edge-dressed to make a close rabbeted or lapped joint.

Lumber, timbers: Yard lumber at least 5" in least dimension. Includes beams, stringers, posts, caps, sills, girders, and purlins.

Lumber, yard: Lumber of those grades, sizes, and patterns generally intended for ordinary construction, such as framework and rough coverage of houses.

Lumber: In the United States, wood as prepared for the building and manufacture market, whether in the log or in sawed or more elaborately dressed pieces. In Great Britain, such material is known simply as wood. As usually prepared for building, lumber intended for the rougher operations is squared from the log in sawmills according to standard dimensions, but is otherwise undressed; while the lighter material, as for sheathing, ceiling, and other finish, is commonly planed on one face and perhaps slightly molded, as with a tongue and groove, a bead, or the like. The British system of classifying wood under definite names, according to its dimensions, is quite unknown in the United States, except in a very general way. Thus, squared pieces for framing and the like are commonly all designated as scantling when not more than about 30 square inches in cross section; pieces of larger size are known as timber, with or without the article. Thus, a piece 5 " x 6 " more or less officially defined as a scantling; a piece of 6" x 6" as a dimension timber. Therefore, in the United States, it is quite common to designate lumber by the use for which any given size may be primarily designed, such as studding, furring, sheathing, veneer.

Lumen: The unit of luminous flux. It is the luminous flux emitted within a unit solid angle (one steradian) by a point source having a uniform luminous intensity of one candela.

Luminaire dirt depreciation (LDD): The multiplier to be used in illuminance calculations to relate the initial illuminance provided by clean, new luminaries to the reduced illuminance that they will provide due to dirt collection on the luminaries at the time when they will be cleaned.

Luminaire efficiency: The ratio of luminous flux (lumens) emitted by a luminaire to that emitted by the lamp or lamps used therein.

Luminaire: A complete lighting unit consisting of a lamp or lamps together with the parts designed to distribute the light, position and protect the lamps, and connect the lamps to the power supply.

Luminance: The amount of light reflected or transmitted by an object.

Lump sum agreement: See stipulated sum agreement.

Lump sum bid: A bid of a set amount to cover all labor, equipment, materials, overhead, and profit necessary for construction of an improvement to real estate.

Lump sum change order: See change order.

Lump sum proposal: A complete and properly signed proposal to do the work or designated portion thereof called for by the bidding documents for a single sum.

Lux: The metric unit of illuminance. One lux is one lumen per square meter (lm/m^2).

M

Machine direction: The direction parallel to the paper-bound edge of the gypsum board.

Machine or pump: See plastering machine.

Machine run: Not sanded after machining.

Machined, smoothly: Free of defective manufacturing, with a minimum of 16 knife marks to the inch. Torn grain should not be permitted. Handling marks or grain raising due to moisture is not considered to be a defect.

Machined and knocked down: All pieces fully machined, ready for assembly.

Magnolia: A hard wood, pale in color, used primarily in furniture making.

Main vent: A vent header to which vent stacks are connected.

Main: The principal artery of the system of continuous piping to which branches may be connected.

Maintenance bond: A document given by the contractor to the owner, guaranteeing to rectify defects in workmanship or materials for a specified time following completion of the project. A one-year bond is normally included in the performance bond.

Maintenance factor (MF): A factor used in calculating illuminance after a given period of time and under given conditions. It considers temperature and voltage variations, dirt accumulation on luminaire and room surfaces, lamp depreciation, maintenance procedures and atmosphere conditions.

Maintenance period: The period of time after completion of a contract during which a contractor is required to make good at his own expense any work that needs repair. Also called warranty time.

Make good: To repair or correct a defect.

Malachite: Carbonate of copper of a green color, silky or velvety luster, and pronounced concretionary structure. A little harder then common marble, but it cuts to a sharp edge and acquires a good polish. To be had only in small pieces, and the table tops, vases, and other works of art constructed from it are invariably patchwork veneers. The principal source of the commercial article is the Ural Mountains.

Male thread: A thread on the outside of a pipe or fitting.

Malleability: A property that allows a material to be deformed when force is applied.

Malleable: Capable of being extended or shaped by beating with a hammer, or by the pressure of the rollers. Most metals are malleable. The term malleable iron has also the older meaning (still universal in Great Britain) of wrought iron, abbreviated mall.

Mallet, rubber: A mallet used for fitting parts. Made with a handle and a resilient rubber or plastic head.

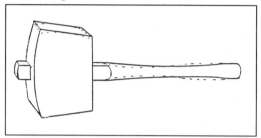

Mallet: A percussion tool used for driving wood chisels or light pieces of framing together. It consists of a rectangular head of beechwood from 5" to 8" long and from 3" to 5" thick, with a rectangular mortise slightly tapering in depth through which the handle passes. The handle should be of ash or other pliable wood and comparatively slender.

Mandatory and customary benefits: See benefits, mandatory and customary.

Manifest: A document having the gross weight, consignor, and consignee of a shipment.

Mantel: (A) A projecting hood or cover above a fireplace to collect the smoke and guide it into the chimney flue above. (B) A modern abbreviation for mantelpiece,

Mantelpiece: A structure forming a mantel, together with its supports. A similar structure built against a chimney around and above a fireplace, either as a decorative finish or to afford one or more shelves above the fireplace.

Manufactured building: A closed construction building assembly, or system of subassemblies, which may include structural, electrical, plumbing, heating, ventilating, or other service systems manufactured for installation or erection. It may include other specified components and encompass residential, commercial, institutional, storage, and industrial structures.

Manufactured package: Assembled by the manufacturer. (The unit may or may not be factory insulated.)

Manufacturer: Making, fabricating, constructing, forming, or assembling or reassembling, a product from raw, unfinished, semifinished, or finished materials.

Maple: A hard wood that is beige to reddish-brown in color and easy to work with.

Marble, bardiglio: Marble with a bluish-gray ground traversed by dark veins. Obtained from Mont' Alto in southern Tuscany. In the variety *bardiglio fiorito* the veining gives a fancied resemblance to flowers. The *bardiglio 'scuro* is gray or bluish and saccharoidal, inferior to the above.

Marble, Belgian black: A well-known black marble from the provinces of Golzines, near Dinant, and Namur, Belgium.

Marble, bird's-eye: Any marble whose uniformity of color is broken by lighter or darker spots, fancied to resemble a bird's eye. For example, the bird's-eye *griotte*, of France.

Marble, black and gold: A compact, brownish gray stone traversed by irregular veins and blotches of dull yellow. From the island of Palmaria in the Gulf of Spezia and Porto Venere.

Marble, bougard: A stone similar in general appearance to the formosa and from the same locality. Perhaps a trifle lighter in color.

Marble, breccia: Any stone composed of angular fragments imbedded in a finer ground or paste. Among the best known of breccia marbles are the Egyptian breccia, many of the Numidian marbles, and the breccias of Gragnuano and Serravezza, in Italy.

Marble, breche voilette: A coarse breccia of sharply angular white, pink, and red fragments in a dull red-brown paste.

Marble, bocatelle (Italian brocatello antico): A compact stone of dull yellowish and drab color traversed by irregular veins and blotches of dull terra cotta red. Often variegated by patches or spots of white crystalline calcite. Now brought from Catalonia in northern Spain.

Marble, campan: From the French Pyrenees, and of a variety of colors indicated by their trade names-*Campan, vert clair, vert fonce, isabelle, hortensia melange, melange* and *rouge*.

Marble, Carrara: A name given to the white and sometimes blue-gray veined and blotched saccharoidal marbles quarried at and near Carrara, in Italy.

Marble, cipollino: A white stone variegated with green and gray, called cipollino, from the Italian *cipolla*, (onion), owing to its fancied resemblance to a cross-section of an onion. Originally from the island of Euboea in the Aegean Sea. Name now commonly applied to any white crystalline marble containing greenish mica, especially the schitose varieties.

Marble, Egyptian breccia: A course breccia containing fragments of porphyry, basalt, quartz, and granite in a greenish or purplish ground. Said to be from quarries between Kossur and Kroft in Egypt.

Marble, fioto: A light chocolate and white mottled marble somewhat resembling the dark variegated varieties of Tennessee. From Italy. Also called *fiorto di Persico*.

Marble, forest: An impure limestone showing on a cut surface fanciful resemblances of forest landscapes. Also called landscape marble.

Marble, formosa: A dark gray and white mottled stone sometimes blotched with reddish; highly fossiliferous. From Nasseau, Germany.

Marble, griotte, French red: A brilliant red, sometimes white-spotted compact marble found in the valley of the Barouse and elsewhere in the French Pyrenees. One of the best of red marbles.

Marble, Hymettian: A blue-gray marble from Mt. Hymettus.

Marble, Irish black: A compact black marble occurring in counties Galway and Kilkenny in Ireland. One of the best of black marbles. Also called Kilkenny marble.

Marble, languedoc, French red: A compact marble of brilliant red color blotched with white which resembles the *griotte*. It is from the Montagne Noire and elsewhere in the Pyrenees.

Marble, Lepanto: A trade name given to a shell marble quarried near Plattsburg, New York.

Marble, Lisbon yellow: A compact yellow marble somewhat resembling that of Siena, but inferior. From Estremoz, Portugal.

Marble, Lucullan: A black marble from the island of Malos. It is named after Lucullus, a Roman Consul.

Marble, lumachelle, shell marble: Several varieties are recognized. The best known modern stone bearing this name is that from Bleiberg and Hall in the Tyrol. The ground is dark gray-brown interspersed with shells, which still retain the nacre or pearly lining.

Marble, lychnites: Probably the Parian marble.

Marble, lyonaise: A trade name for the coarsely mottled marble of Malletts Bay on Lake Champlain.

Marble, madrepore: A marble containing fossil madreporian corals.

Marble, mischio: A coarsely brecciated, very showy marble composed of whitish and pinkish fragments with a darker cement. From Serravezza, Italy.

Marble, nero antico: A deep black marble with occasional white spots or lines, said to be found on the promontory of Taenarum in Greece.

Marble, Numidian: This is found, not in Numidia proper, but in the Mountain of the Capes (Djebel-el-roos) in the provinces of Africa and Mauritania in Algeria. The colors range through shades of yellow, drab, and pink to deep red.

Marble, onyx: A compact form of travertine or stalagmite, of a white, green, brown, or red color, often beautifully clouded and banded; translucent. Erroneously called alabaster.

Marble, paonazzo: A variety of Numidian marble. The name is probably a corruption of *pavonazetta*, since the description of the stones correspond to the last name.

Marble, Parian, greco duro: A white, granular, saccharoidal marble used for statuary and for building. It is from the island of Paros in the Aegean Sea and called Lychnites by Pliny.

Marble, parmazo: White to Isabelle yellow with purplish veins. Also known as Phrygian marble, because obtained at Phrygia in Asia Minor. Said to have been a favorite with the Emperor Hadrian.

Marble, Pentelic, marmor pentalicum, greco fino: A white to grayish crystalline granular stone from Mt. Pentelicus, between Athens and Marathon in Greece. Used in the construction of the Parthenon at Athens.

Marble, phengites, marmor phengite, biance egiallo: A white, yellow-veined marble capable of receiving a very high polish, from Cappadocia.

Marble, Porta Santa, marmor iassence: A purplish red and white clouded stone from the island of Iasus or Caria or, according to some authorities, the island of Chios. Used in the door jambs of the Porta Santa of S. Peter's church in Rome, hence the name.

Also called Claudian stone, because a favorite with the Emperor Claudius.

Marble, Potomac breccia: A marble composed of rounded and angular fragments, of varying sizes up to several inches in diameter, of limestone imbedded in a fine calcareous ground. It is from the triassic formations near Point of Rocks in Maryland and used in columns of Old Hall of Representatives in the Capitol in Washington.

Marble, purbeck: A shell limestone found in the south of England. It has been used in building since the thirteenth century. When polished it is dark gray and much used for interior shafts, especially in Gothic churches. It is not very durable.

Marble, rosso de levanto: A chocolate-red, mottled stone much resembling the Tennessee variegated varieties, from Spezia, Italy.

Marble, rouge antique: Red antique marble. A red marble much used by the ancients and found at Cynopolis and Damarestica in Greece.

Marble, ruin: A compact yellowish or drab limestone which has been shattered almost like glass and the fragments recemented with comparatively little displacement. Cut and polished slabs give a mosaic-like effect, representing ruins of buildings. From the Val di Sieve, environs of Florence, Italy.

Marble, Saint Anne: A deep blue-black marble, variegated with short veins of white, from Saint Anne, Belgium.

Marble, Sarrancolin: A breccia marble quarried near Sarrancolin in the French Pyrenees. The colors are extremely variable, gray, yellow, and red predominating.

Marble, Siena: Yellow and drab marbles, often brecciated, from near Siena in Italy. A very compact stone of almost waxy luster, which has always been in great demand for interior work.

Marble, statuary: Any white, crystalline, granular, saccharoidal marble suitable for statuary. For example: Parian and Carrara.

Marble, tabrez: A travertine or onyx marble, from near Lake Oroomiah in Persia. Mainly of a white color.

Marble, verdantique: (Italian, *verde antico*; antique green.) A compact variety of serpentine used as a marble.

Marble, Winooski: A reddish and brownish, variegated with white dolomitic, marble quarried near Winooski, in Chittenden County, Vermont.

Marble chips: Graded aggregates of maximum hardness made from crushed marble to be thrown or blown onto a soft plaster bedding coat to produce marblecrete.

Marble: Any stone consisting essentially of carbonate of lime or the carbonates of lime and magnesia, of such color and texture as to make it desirable for the higher grades of building, monumental, or decorative work. The varying shades of gray and the black colors of marbles are due to the presence of carbonaceous matter; the yellow, brown and red colors to iron oxides, and the green to the presence of silicate minerals, such as mica and talc. The veined and clouded effects are due to an unequal distribution of the coloring constituents throughout the mass of the stone.

Marblecrete: See finish coat.

Marezzo: An imitation marble formed with Keene's cement to which colors have been added. Cast on smooth glass or marble beds.

Marking knife: A tool used for setting out dimensions with greater accuracy than can be obtained with a lead pencil. Also for cutting in or striking shoulders. The severance of the fibers of the wood by the knife gives a cleaner shoulder than can be obtained from the saw alone.

Marking: The reference letter or number marked on each component of a delivery, keyed to its position in the structure, used to facilitate installation. The same symbols are shown on master drawings and job specifications.

Masking: Method of affixing paper, plastic, or any flexible protective material or coating to protect adjacent work. Particularly used in plastering machine applications. The increase of sound intensity to over another sound.

Masonry, dry: That done without mortar.

Masonry, pise: A cheap masonry of compressed earth. The most suitable solid is a claylike, somewhat sand, loam, and vegetable earth. It is mixed with straw or hay to prevent it from cracking as it dries. After being screened, if necessary, it is moistened and thoroughly worked to mix in the straw. For very rough work the laborer puts it in place with an ordinary shovel, with which the face to lines are dressed. For careful work the wall is built sections by means of a movable frame about 3' high and 10' long. The two sides of the frame are boards kept apart the thickness of the wall. This frame is placed on the wall, and between the sides, the earth is rammed or beaten in 4" layers. When the box is full, it is taken apart and set up in another part of the wall. As the wall goes up, the keys in the cross pieces are driven in to make the box somewhat narrower and the wall thinner. The end of each block is sloped about 60°, and care is taken that these joints do not come over those below them. The wall is strengthened by bedding withes or rods in it. When used for enclosing walls pise is covered with thatch held in place by plastered earth which is renewed at intervals. The pise is much stronger when it is mixed with a milk of lime instead of water. When the walls are dry they are plastered with one part of lime mixed with four parts of clay, with plasterers' hair. The foundations of walls of pise should be of stone to a few inches above the ground.

Masonry, rubble: That made with stones smaller and less regular than ashlar and what is called cut stone.

Masonry wall clip: See wall furring base clip.

Masonry: The art and practice of building with stone, (natural or artificial) brick, and, by extension, molded earth (as in adobe and pise); also, the work so produced. Stones and bricks are generally lain in mortar but may be laid without it (dry masonry), care being taken so to superimpose the materials as to bind or bond together those below them.

Master plumber: An individual licensed and authorized to install and assume responsibility for contractual plumbing agreements and to secure any required permits. The journey plumber is allowed to install plumbing only under the responsibility of a master plumber.

Mastic: A general term usually referring to high viscosity solvent-based adhesives. A heavy pliable adhesive used to seal joints.

Mat: A piece of semiflexible insulation cut into easily handled sizes, usually square or rectangular in shape, and composed of random arrangement.

Match, set or drop: Pattern match designates the arrangement and dimensions of the repeating units comprising the design of patterned carpet, including woven patterns, prints, tufted high lows, and others. A typical pattern repeat might be 36" wide x 24" long. In set match, this rectangular pattern unit is arranged in parallel rows across the carpet width. In a half drop pattern, the start of each pattern repeat unit is transposed to the midpoint of the side of the adjacent unit. In quarter drop match, each unit would start 6" past the neighboring pattern unit's starting point. Thus, pattern repeat units in drop match repeat diagonally across the width, and in set match they repeat straight across the width perpendicularly to the length. Pattern repeat dimensions and match are significant to specifiers and purchasing agents because they influence the amount of excess carpet (over measured area) needed in multiple width installations.

Match: To bring to equality, uniformity, or similarity. Thus the planks of a floor are required to be matched as is customary in all floors of any elegance or finish, thickness, width, color, and surface, as for greater smoothness or a coarser or finer grain. By extension (as applied to floor plank, sheathing, and the like), the term includes the working of tongues and grooves upon the edges, so that flooring spoken of as matched is understood to be tongued and grooved.

Material only: See loose and long.

Material supplier: See supplier.

Material: Any of several kinds of building supplies such as timber, concrete, and insulation.

Materials deficiency: (A) A substantial deficiency in performance of a magnitude requiring correction to prevent a breach of contract. (B) Defective materials. (C) Shortages of specified materials furnished by others.

Materials storage: Provision for storage of materials before installation either onsite or offsite.

Matte surface: A nonglossy dull surface, rather than a shiny (specular) surface. Light reflected from a matte surface is diffuse.

Mean temperature: Operating temperature + ambient temperature / 2 (thermal conductivity charts are calculated to use mean temperatures).

Measurement and payment: A system of paying for work completed by measuring the work in place and applying a previously agreed unit cost to the measured amount to determine the total payment.

Mechanic's lien: A lien on privately owned real property created by state statute in favor of persons who have not received full payment for labor or materials furnished for structures on the property. In some jurisdictions, a mechanic's lien also exists for the value of professional services. Clear title to the property cannot be obtained until the claim is settled, and the claimant may be able to foreclose on the lien and take possession of the improved real estate. Advance notice to owners and general contractors of the possibilities that liens will be filed are generally required under state laws.

Mechanical application: Application of plaster mortar by mechanical means, generally pumping and spraying, as distinguished from hand placement.

Mechanical bond: The physical keying of one plaster coat to another or to the plaster base.

Mechanical couplings: Bolting devices used in assembly of piping such as victaulic couplings for grooved piping.

Mechanical trowel: A motor-driven tool with revolving blades used to produce a denser finish coat than by hand troweling.

Mechanics: The action of force on materials.

Media room: A room that has sound and screening equipment, and television all in one room.

Mediterranean style: A twentieth century style that uses heavy carvings and scales and uses wrought iron or leather as trim.

Medium density fiberboard: A dry formed panel product manufactured from lignocellulosic fibers combined with a synthetic resin or other suitable binder. The panels are compressed to a density of 31 pounds per cubic foot to 50 pounds per cubic foot in a hot press by a process in which substantially the entire interfiber bond is created by the added binder. Other materials may have been added during manufacture to improve certain properties. The product should meet the standards of National Particleboard Association NPA 4-73.

Medium pressure condensate: That condensate directly received from medium pressure steam.

Medium pressure steam: Steam under 75 pounds per square inch gauge, but above 15 pounds per square inch gauge.

Medium velocity duct: A duct with air flow designed at more than 2,000' per minute velocity with static pressure below 6".

Melting I2t: The minimum I2t required to melt the fuse element.

Member: An individual piece of solid stock or plywood that forms an item of millwork.

Membrane fireproofing: See fireproofing.

Membrane reinforcement: See glass fabric.

Membrane: A lath and plaster system that is separated from the structural steel members, in most cases by furring or suspension, to provide fireproofing.

Mercury lamp: A high intensity discharge (HID) lamp in which the major portion of the light is produced by radiation from mercury. Includes clear, phosphor-coated, and self-ballasted lamps.

Metal base clip: A formed wire section for fastening metal lath to flanges of steel joists.

Metal corner bead: Fabricated metal with flanges and nosings at the juncture of flanges, used to protect or form arrises.

Metal halide lamp: A high intensity discharge (HID) lamp in which the major portion of the light is produced by radiation from mercury. Includes clear, phosphor-coated, and self-ballasted lamps.

Metal jacketing: See jacketing.

Metal lath, expanded: Metal lath is of two types: diamond mesh (also called flat or self-furring expanded metal lath), or rib. Metal lath is slit and expanded, or slit, punched, or otherwise formed, with or without partial expansion, from plain or galvanized steel coils or sheets. Metal lath is coated with rust-inhibitive paint after fabrication, or is made from galvanized sheets. Diamond mesh or flat expanded metal lath is a metal lath slit and expanded from metal sheets or coils into such a form that there will be no rib in the lath; 2.5 lbs.

painted; 3.4 lbs. painted or galvanized. Self-furring metal lath is a metal so formed that portions of it extend from the face of the lath so that it is separated at least 1/4" from the background to which it is attaches; painted or galvanized. Flat rib metal lath is a combination of expanded metal lath and ribs in which the rib has a total depth of approximately 1/8", measured from top inside of the lath to the top side of the rib, painted. 3/8" rib metal lath is a combination of expanded metal lath and ribs of a total depth of approximately 3/8", measured from top inside to the lath to the top side of the rib; 3.4 lbs., painted or galvanized, 4.0 lbs. painted. 3/4" rib metal lath is a combination of expanded metal lath and ribs of a total depth of approximately 3/4", measured from the top inside of the lath to the top side of the rib, painted. Paper-backed metal lath is a factory-assembled combination of any of the preceding defined types of metal lath with paper or other backing, the assembly being used as a plaster base.

Metal partition base: A fabricated integral metal section which also may serve as a ground for the plaster (attached to framing member or masonry).

Metal work: (A) Work done by melting metal and molding or casting it in forms that can then be more or less finished by hand, as with cutting tools and files.

Metallic fiber: Synthetic fiber made of metal, metal coated plastic, or plastic-coated metal sometimes used in small amounts in carpet to dissipate static electricity, thus preventing shock.

Meter: A device to measure the amount of current consumed.

Metes and bounds: The boundaries, property lines, or limits of a parcel of land, defined by distances and compass directions.

Mezzanine: A small floor that is between two main floors.

Mil: A unit used in measuring thickness (0.001").

Mildew: A fungus growth occurring in insufficiently vented and damp surface areas.

Milestone level: The level of management at which a particular event is considered to be a key event or milestone.

Milestone report flag: A numeric code that may be entered on an activity or event name card to flag the successor event as a milestone.

Milestone report: An output report at a specified level showing the latest allowable date (TL), expected date (TE), scheduled completion date (TS), and slack for the successor event contained on each activity or event name card flagged as a milestone at the level specified.

Milestone: A key network event that is of major significance in achieving the program or project objectives.

Mill run: See loose and long.

Mill-mixed: See gypsum.

Miller act bond: For work on federal contracts, the government under 40 U.S.C. Section 270(a) requires that the general contractor post a bond for performance and payment. The payment bond recites certain conditions and limitations such as requiring suit within one year of the date after a party does the last work on a project. It also requires materials suppliers and subcontractors to give written notice in a certain form to the general contractor within 90 days after the date they last supplied the job to have a valid claim under the bond.

Milling machine: A single-disk machine used to cut slabs.

Millwork: Architectural woodwork and related items.

Mineral wool (fiber): Any inorganic fibrous insulation.

Minor change (in the work): A minor change in the work not involving an adjustment in the contract sum or contract time, which may be effected by field order or other written order issued by the architect.

Minus pressure: See negative pressure.

Miter, lock: A miter joint employing a tongue-and-groove working to further strengthen the joint.

Miter, shoulder: Any type of a miter joint that presents a shoulder, such as a lock miter or a splined miter.

Miter: The joining of two members at an angle that bisects the angle of junction

Model: The original from which a mold or copy is made.

Mixed air duct: A duct located at a point where air returned from a space inside the building and air from outside the building are mixed to be redistributed.

Mobile home: Any residential unit constructed to the Federal Mobile Home Construction and Safety Standards, 42 USC 4501 et seq, and rules and regulation promulgated by HUD and found in 24 CFR Parts 3280, 3282 and 3283.

Modification (to the contract documents): (A) A written amendment to the contract signed by both parties. (B) A change order. (C) A written or graphic interpretation issued by the architect. (D) A written order for a minor change in the work issued by the architect. See change order, field order.

Module: A repetitive dimensional or functional unit used in planning, recording, or constructing buildings or other structures. A distinct component forming part of an ordered system.

Modular design: A design based on fixed modules. Prefabricated or industrialized building or construction.

Module: A flexible unit of measure valued for prefabricated building components. The basic measurement usually is 4".

Modulus: (A) A unit of measure assumed in determining the strength of materials as against stretching, bending, or rupture. (B) Same as module.

Moist cure: See curing.

Moisture barrier: See condensate barrier.

Moisture content: The weight of the water in the wood expressed in percentage of the weight of the oven-dry wood.

Mold and mildew resistance: That property enabling a material to resist the formation of fungus growths.

Mold: (A) A form used to make a copy, whether a solid object requiring an exact reproduction by casting or a profile cut out of a board or piece of sheet metal, used for running plaster moldings and the like. (B) The hollow into which melted metal, liquid plaster, or the like is poured in casting. Such a mold is itself a direct case or impression of a mold in sense A. (C) Same as molding. A common abbreviation used by the trades in composition, as bed mold.

Molded edge: Edge of piece machined to any profile other than square or eased edge.

Molding, annular: Any molding, of whatever section, that forms a ring about a surface of revolution, as a shaft, base, or capital. The fillet, torus, etc., of a classic base, the astragal of the necking, the echinus and annuli of the capital, are all annular moldings.

Molding, anthemion: One decorated by anthemions.

Molding, back: Same as wall molding, especially as applied at the back of the trim around a window or the like.

Molding, balection, belection, bolection: In paneled work, a molding next to the stiles and rails and projecting beyond the plane of their face (rare in the United States).

Molding, band: In carpentry, any molding applied to a flat surface as a band.

Molding, base: Any horizontal molding forming a base or part of a base. In particular, the molding at the top of a baseboard or other similar member.

Molding, bed: The molding or group of moldings immediately beneath the projecting soffit of a cornice or similar projecting surface. In the Ionic and Corinthian cornices, in particular, the moldings below the dentil band.

Molding, billet: One composed of one or more series of billets; that is, of small cylindrical or prismatic members placed at regular intervals so that their axes and that of the entire series is parallel to the general direction of the molding.

Molding, bird's beak: A molding having a profile like a bird's beak, convex on the upper or outer face and concave on the lower or inner face.

Molding, bolection: Molding used to hide the joint between two surfaces with different levels.

Molding, brace: A molding composed of two ogees, each the reverse of the other, having the general outline of a printer's brace or bracket.

Molding, cable: A form of molding resembling a rope or cable, used occasionally in the Romanesque or round-arched period of medieval architecture.

Molding, calf's tongue: One formed by a series of pendant, pointed, tongue-like members relieved against a plane or, more usually, a curved surface. This decoration is commonly found in archivolts of early medieval British architecture, the tongues, radiating from a common center.

Molding, cant: A beveled molding. It may have a beveled back for nailing into a corner or angle, as between a wall and ceiling, or a face or profile with a cant or oblique surface.

Molding, chain: A molding in the form of a chain with links, occasionally met with in

Norman and Romanesque buildings (twelfth century).

Molding, chinbeak: A molding common in Renaissance and modern work, consisting of a convex followed below by a concave profile, with or without a fillet below or between, as an inverted ogee, or an ovolo, fillet, and cove.

Molding, crown: Any molding serving as a corona or otherwise forming the crowning or finishing member of a structure or of a decorative feature. Especially in the trades, a molding having the form of the cyma recta.

Molding, edge: A molding whose general form is rounded convexly, the curves being interrupted by a fillet or concave curve making a sharp edge at about its center line. Typically, it has a quarter round above, then a horizontal fillet, then a quarter round above, then a quarter round of smaller radius. Many modifications of this form are, however, designated by the term.

Molding, hood or head: Any molding having the form of a miniature hood; especially the molding that, in medieval architecture, is often carried in projection above the opening of a door or window and commonly follows and is parallel to the lines of the opening. This feature is very common in English domestic architecture, and the hood molding is either in the form of a pointed arch or straight bar terminating the lintel or flat arch at top and having vertical returns carried downward.

Molding, nebuly: An overhanging band whose lower, projecting edge is shaped to a continuous undulating curve. The term is evidently derived from the heraldic adjective nebulee or nebuly. Common in Romanesque architecture and perhaps derived from the so-called wave molding.

Molding, ox-eyed: A concave molding assumed to be less hollow than the scotia but deeper than the cavetto.

Molding, pellet: In Romanesque architecture, a fillet or small fascia ornamented with small hemispherical projections. Pellet ornamentation is the treatment of any surface with similar projections arranged geometrically or in patterns; especially used in pottery.

Molding, picture: A continuous molding of wood from 1-1/2" to 2-1/2" or 3" wide, nailed near the top of the wall of a room, serving as or sometimes forming the lower member of the cornice, or to separate the frieze from the wall field below, adapted to receive picture hooks from which pictures may be hung.

Molding, quirk: Any molding characterized or accentuated by one or more quirks, as the beads worked along the edges of common sheathing.

Molding, rised: Same as balection molding.

Molding, raking: (A) Any molding adjusted to a rake or ramp. (B) Any overhanging molding having a soffit that has a rake or slope downward and outward.

Molding, returned: A molding continued in a different direction from its main direction.

Molding, reverse ogee: A double curved molding, convex above and concave below.

Molding, roll: (A) Any convex, rounded molding approaching a cylindrical form. The term has no absolute meaning and may be applied to a simple round, as a torus or bowtell, or to a more elaborate form, as an edge molding. A common form is semicylindrical, interrupted at about its center line with a vertical projecting fillet. This and any other kindred form is frequently known as a roll and fillet molding. (B) A semi-circular section molding.

Molding, sprung: In carpentry, a molding or group of moldings, that is given a considerable projection with a minimum use of material by being worked along one face of a board whose width corresponds to the sloping dimension of the moldings from edge to edge. The board is then set at a slope following the general direction of the projection.

Molding, star: In Romanesque architecture, a molding whose surface is carved into a succession of projecting starlike shapes.

Molding, thumb: In carpentry, a molding having a cross section supposed to resemble the lateral profile of the end of a thumb.

Molding, wall: A molding used to conceal the joint between a trim and the wall behind by being closely fitted into the angle.

Molding, wave: A decoration for flat numbers, as a fascia, composed of a succession of similar undulations somewhat resembling curling waves, first used in Greek architecture and common in all derived styles.

Molding, weather: Any molding which is weathered so as to throw off water to protect the structure below, as a hood, drip, or water table.

Molding: (A) The plane, curved, broken, irregular, or compound surface formed at the face of any piece or member by casting, cutting, or otherwise shaping and modeling the material to produce modulations of light, shade, and shadow. Generally signifies such a surface when continued uniformly to a considerable extent, as a continuous band or a series of small parts. (B) By extension, a piece of material worked with a molding or group of moldings on one or more sides. The piece is usually just large enough to receive the molding and to afford one or two plane surfaces by which it is secured in place for decorative or other purpose. (C) From the common use of wooden moldings made separately and very cheaply in the molding mill, any slender strip of material planed and finished, used for covering joints, concealing wires, and the like. Note: Moldings having specific names descriptive of their particular forms are not defined here because the use of the attributive term is self-explanatory, as in cove molding, drip molding.

Moldings: Contours given to trimmings and projections.

Moment of inertia: A quantity in constant use in computing the strength and deflection of a beam or column. When a beam is bent, the fibers on the concave side are compressed, and on the convex side, extended, though all are not equally extended or compressed. If we suppose the section of a beam to be divided into infinitely small areas and each area multiplied by the square of its distance from a line passing through the center of gravity of the section, the sum of these products is the moment of inertia of the section and, when multiplied by the strength of the fibers, represents the sum of the resistance of the different fibres to stress. The square of the radius of gyration r^2 is the moment of inertia, divided by the area of the section. It is the sum of the squares of the distances of the small areas from the axis about which the moment is taken.

Monitoring: Following the progress of the project. This phase follows the preparation of the CPM plan and schedule.

Mop basin: A service sink set on the floor. Also called a mop receptor.

Mortise and tenon, slotted: A mortise and tenon right angle joint in which the tenon is visible on two edges once the joint is completed.

Mortar, brick dust: Mortar reddened with brick dust.

Mortar, cement: Mortar with a considerable proportion of cement. One advantage of building with this material is that it sets rapidly, and therefore walls can be carried up in freezing weather because the frost will not have time to affect the mortar before it hardens. Its resistance to moisture is, however, its most valuable quality. In ordinary building above ground, mortar is rarely made of cement and sand alone, but the mixture of half cement and half lime, or one-third cement and two-thirds lime is made, and this then is mixed with the amount of sand thought expedient.

Mortar bed: A mixture of concrete, sand, and water applied in layers and used in the traditional method of installing marble.

Mortar color, stain: Pigment intended for coloring mortar for the joints of masonry; sometimes ground coal or powdered brick, now more often a special preparation marketed in many tints.

Mortar: A mixture of lime, cement, or both, with sand and water or some other material, such as plaster of Paris. Ordinary mortar is made with lime and sand alone, that made with cement is generally called cement mortar, and that with plaster of Paris is called gauge mortar. By extension, bitumen, Nile mud, adobe clay, etc., are called by this name. The use of mortar in building is not primarily to adhere two masses together, but to interpose its soft and yielding, but soon hardening, mass between courses of stone or brick, and thus enable the uppermost one to take a more perfect bearing or bed upon the surface below. Its secondary purpose is to afford an artificial matrix, in which small materials may be so bedded that, when the whole mass of mortar is hardened, the wall, pier, or the like forms a solid homogeneous mass. This object is gained in one of two ways: first, by laying the mortar in quantity upon the upper surface of the masonry already completed and bedding the bricks or small stones upon it while it is still soft; second, by mingling the mortar with the small materials and throwing the whole mass together into the place to be filled by it.

Mortise, chase: (A) A mortise to contain a pulley in a cased frame. (B) Same as chase mortise.

Mortise, mortise: A hole or recess, rather long and narrow and usually with parallel sides, formed in one piece of a structure to receive and hold securely another corresponding part as a tenon in wood framing the lock of a door.

mortise, stub: A shallow mortice hole that does not pass through the entire thickness of the timber in which it is made.

Mortise, through: A mortise passing through the timber.

Mortise and tenon, blind: A mortise and tenon joint in which the tenon does not extend through the mortise and is not visible once the joint is completed, also blind tenoned.

Mortise and tenon, stub: A short tenon inserted in a plow or groove.

Mortise and tenon, through: A mortise and tenon joint in which the inserted tenon extends completely through the mortise and the end of the tenon remains visible once the joint is completed.

Mortise and tenon joint: A joint formed by a projecting piece fitting or tenon into a socket or mortise.

Mortise and tenon: Joining two pieces of wood by cutting a hole (mortise) that will receive a part that has been shaped to fit the hole (tenon).

Mortise: A slot cut into a board, plank, or timber, usually edgewise, to receive a tenon of another board, plank, or timber to form a joint.

Mosaic: Surface decoration or design made up of small pieces of glass, marble, or stone.

Most likely time estimate (m): The most realistic estimate of the time an activity might consume. When only one time estimate is given, this one is used.

Mounting height: When specifying or installing an item, unless noted otherwise, it is the distance from the floor to the top edge or surface of the object.

Mullion: A vertical division in a frame separating two or more sections.

Multidisk machine: A machine for cutting blocks used for mass-producing tiles.

Multiple finish network: A network that has more than one finish activity or finish event.

Multiple of direct personnel expense: A method of compensation for professional services based on the direct expense of profesional and technical personnel, including cost of salaries and mandatory and customary benefits, multiplied by an agreed factor.

Multiple start network: A network that has more than one activity/event as start.

Muntin: A small, slender mullion in light framing, as a sash bar, a middle stile of a door. The vertical part in a door or window frame that butts into the horizontal rails. A sash bar.

Mutual agreement: An offer by one party and its acceptance by another that it is essential to a contract.

N

Nadir: Directly below the luminaire or lamp; designated as 0°.

Nail, cut: Nail cut by a machine, rather than wrought and wire nails. The invention of the cut nail machine, and the increase of woodworking machinery, which produced cheap clapboards, shingles, etc., was largely instrumental in developing the wooden building of the United States. The metal of the cut nail is compressed by the machine so much that it is too brittle to be clinched, but it is practicable to soften it sufficiently by heating and allowing it to cool slowly. Same as trenail.

Nail, wire: Nail cut from a wire, having a cylindrical shank, sharp point, and a head made by flattening the metal. These are the nails of Europe. They have been much used in the United States for certain delicate kinds of cabinet work, as for planting separate moldings on to rails and stiles, etc., and they have recently been imported and manufactured in considerable quantities, even in the larger sizes. They are usually capable of clinching.

Nail, Wrought: Anciently, a nail worked by hand, each piece having been forged separately. Long after the introduction of the cut nail, wrought nails were still used where clinching was thought desirable. Now rare, except when it is desirable to complete decorative wrought-iron work by having the visible nailheads also finely de-

signed. There is then an infinite variety of simple and effective patterns into which the heads can be worked.

Nail heads: A decoration made of or resembling the head of a nail.

Nail popping: The protrusion of the nail usually attributed to the shrinkage of or use of improperly cured wood framing.

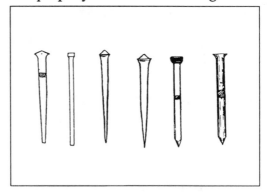

Nail: A slender and small piece of material, usually metal, intended to be driven into anything, especially a board, plank, joist, or other wooden member to hold fast, usually by the elastic force of the wood pressing against it. In composition (as in treenail or trenail) a different signification is implied, which does not generally concern the architect or builder.

Nailable studs: See studs.

Nailed: Members secured together with nails, including power driven nails or staples. On exposed surfaces, staples shall run parallel to the grain.

Nailing, blind, secret or tosh: In flooring, and the like, the securing of planks or boards to the beams or other supports by driving the nails diagonally into the edge, so that each plank, when put into place, conceals the heads of the nails in the adjoining plank. The object of this is partly the smoother appearance of the floor, but chiefly the avoidance of the risk of the nails drawing out as the planks tend to warp.

Nailing, skew: Securing by means of nails driven obliquely to the surface or joint either to conceal the nailhead, as in blind nailing, or where the nail cannot be driven perpendicularly through the first or outer piece, as where an upright is to be secured to a horizontal.

Nailing channel: Fabricated from not lighter than 25-gauge steel to form slots that permit attachment of lath by means of ratchet-type annular nails or other satisfactory attachments.

Nailing type: Fabricated from not lighter than 26-gauge steel to form slots that permit attachment of the lath by means of specially designed nails, staples or screws. Widths: 2", 2-1/2", 3-1/4", 3-5/8", 4", 6".

Nailing: The operation of securing by means of nails; the result of such operation.

National fire protection association (NFPA): Develops and publishes codes, standards, and other materials concerning fire safety.

National joint forms (AGC-ASA-ASC): Standard forms published jointly by the Associated Specialty Contractors, Inc., Associated Specialty Contractors of America, and American Subcontractors Association for use by contractors and subcontractors. These include a standard sub-bid proposal, a subcontractor's application for payment, and a work authorization form for non-contractual work ordered by one contractor from another.

National joint guidelines: Guidelines adopted by the Associate Specialty Contractors, Inc., jointly with the Associated General Contractors of America and/or American Subcontractors Association to advise members of the construction industry, including architects and engineers, and, in some cases, owners, of appropriate and efficient ways of administering construction projects.

National joint policy statements: Policy statements adopted nationally by Associated Specialty Contractors, Inc., in conjunction with the Associated General Contractors of American and/or American Subcontractors Association outlining recommended policies to be followed by owners, contractors, subcontractors, architects, engineers, suppliers, insurance carriers, and government agencies to effect efficient working relationships.

Natural finish: A transparent finish that does not seriously alter the original color or grain of the natural wood. Natural finishes are usually provided by sealers, oils, varnishes, water-repellent preservatives, and other similar materials.

Neat: Term used to denote plaster material requiring the addition of aggregate. See gypsum.

Negative pressure: Pressure within a pipe that is less that atmospheric pressure. Minus pressure.

Negligence: Failure to exercise that degree of care which a reasonable and prudent person would exercise under the same circumstances. Legal liability for the consequences of an act or omission frequently turns on whether there has been negligence.

Negotiation phase: See bidding and negotiation phase.

Netting: Interwoven wires of metal used as a reinforcement.

Network: A flow diagram consisting of the activities and events that must be accomplished to reach the program objectives, showing their planned sequence of accomplishments, interdependencies, and interrelationships.

Newel: A post to which the end of a stair railing or balustrade is fastened. Any post to which a railing or balustrade is fastened.

Niche: A curved or square recess in a wall used for housing statues, vases, telephones, or door chimes.

No-damage-for-delay clause: A clause in a construction contract permitting time extensions but no monetary damages for the contractor for delays of any nature not the fault of the contractor, including those caused by the actions or failures to act of the owner, architect, or other prime contractors.

Node: See event.

Nodule: A small, hard mass of chertlike or quartz material in soft rock.

Noise absorption: The noise level of a room can be greatly reduced by adding carpeting and drapes and other sound absorption materials.

Noise reduction coefficient (NRC): A single number rating that is the arithmetic average of the individual sound absorption coefficients at 250, 500, 1000, and 2000 Hz to the nearest .05.

Noise: Unwanted sound.

Non-contracted construction services: Services performed for another contractor on a job site that are not included in the scope of the construction contracts. These generally are for temporary site facilities.

Non-load bearing partition: A structurally non-essential interior wall assembly for compartmentalizing floor space. Also called nonbeaing wall.

Non-work unit: A calendar specified time unit during which work may not be performed.

Noncollusion affidavit: Notarized statement by a bidder that he has prepared his bid without collusion of any kind.

Noncombustible: A material that will not contribute fuel or heat to a fire to which it is exposed. Also called nonflammable.

Noncorfing work: Work that does not fulfill the requirements of the contract documents.

Nonglare glass: A nonreflecting glass used in picture frames.

Nosing: The projecting edge of a molding or drip. Usually applied to the projecting molding on the edge of a stair tread.

Notch: A chip, recess, depression, or slot.

Note: The means for identifying listed equipment may vary for each organization concerned with product evaluation, some of which do not recognize equipment as listed unless it is also labeled. The authority having jurisdiction should utilize the system employed by the listing organization.

Notice of award: Written notice to the contractor that his/her proposal has been accepted.

Notice to bidders: A notice in the bidding requirements informing prospective bidders of the opportunity to submit bids on a project and setting forth the procedures for doing so.

Notice to proceed: Written communication issued by the owner to the contractor authorizing him to proceed with the work and establishing the date of commencement of the work. This also applies to a notice from the prime contractor to a subcontractor to proceed, although such notices are often oral.

Nozzle: An attachment at the end of a plastering machine delivery hose, which regulates the fan or spray pattern. Devices used applications requiring special discharge patterns, directional spray, fine spray, or other unusual discharge characteristics.

NRC: Noise reduction coefficient is a standard of measurement of sound control in the design of acoustical materials.

Nuisance (unwanted) alarm: An alarm caused by everyday events such as cooking, cigarette smoke, dust, insects, etc.

Nummulitic limestone: A limestone composed largely of fossil nummulites. The pyramid of Cheops is largely of this stone.

O

O. C. (on center): The measurement of spacing for studs, rafters, joists, and the like from the center of one member to the center of the next.

Oak: A hard wood that is pale yellow-brown in color and mainly used for furniture because of its durability.

Objective event: An event that signifies the completion of a path through the network. A network may have more than one objective event.

Obscuration: A reduction in the atmospheric transparency caused by smoke usually expressed in percent per foot.

Observation of the work: The architect, by getting familiar with the progress and quality of the work ,determines if the work is proceeding in accordance with the contract documents.

Occupancy permit: See certificate of occupancy.

Occurrence (insurance): An accident or continuous exposure to conditions result in injury or damage, provided the injury or damage is neither expected nor intended.

Octave band: A frequency band with an upper frequency limit equal to twice the lower limit.

Off-set: The part of a wall that is horizontally exposed when the portion above is reduced in thickness.

Offer: A demonstration of willingness to enter into a bargain. The essential elements are an expression of intent to enter into a contract, definite and certain terms, and the communication of the offer.

Officer of the firm: An owner or employee of the construction firm who, by virtue of this position, is empowered to obligate the construction company.

Offices: Buildings only for professional use and not for any living purposes.

Offset: A combination of pipes and /or fittings that joins two approximately parallel sections of the line of pipe.

Ogee: (A) A double-curved line consisting of a convex and concave part. (B) A fourteenth century molding in the shape of an S.

On center (O.C.): The centerline spacing distance between framing members, fasteners or other points of reference.

One coat cement: A mixture of fibers and binders that results in a product that combines the insulating properties of an insulating cement and the aesthetic qualities of a finishing cement.

Opaque finish: A paint or pigmented stain finish that hides the natural characteristics and color of the grain of the wood surface and is not transparent.

Open account: An account, usually the interior designer's, to which things may be charged.

Open construction: Any building, building component, assembly, or system manufactured in such a manner that all parts or processes can be inspected at the installation site without disassembly, damage to, or destruction thereof.

Open joint: A visible junction between two adjacent slabs, having a 1mm (.04") gap.

Open web girder: Any girder of which the web is pierced or composed of parts having open spaces between them. Usually, a small truss.

Optimistic time estimate: The minimum time in which the activity can be completed if everything goes exceptionally well. It is generally held that an activity would have no more than one chance in 100 of being completed within this time.

Option (contractor's): See contractor's option.

Orientation: The siting of a building in relationship to the sun.

Orifice: Attachment to the nozzle on the hose of plastering machine, which may be changed to help establish the pattern of the plaster as it is projected onto the surface being plastered.

Original duration: The first estimate of an activity duration.

Out-of-sequence service: Service performed in other than the normal or natural order of succession.

Outfall sewers: Sewers receiving the sewage from the collection system and carrying it to the point of final discharge or treatment. It is usually the largest sewer of the entire system.

Outlet box: A box connecting the electrical outlet to the conduit.

Outrigger: An extension of a rafter beyond the wall line. Usually a smaller member nailed to a larger rafter to form a cornice or roof overhang.

Over (under) plan: The planned cost to date minus the latest revised estimate of cost to date. When planned cost exceeds latest revised estimate, a projected underplan condition exists. When latest revised estimate exceeds planned cost, a projected overplan condition exists.

Overcurrent: Any current in excess of conductor capacity or equipment continuous current rating.

Overhang: The protrusion of an element from the plane of a facade or other lower or adjacent elements. The portion of a roof that extends over the wall.

Overhead expense: Expenses of maintaining a company operation that continues whether a given project is under construction or not. Expenses not directly chargeable to a specific contract such as executive and clerical salaries, rent, home office utilities, advertising, bidding costs, etc. Sometimes referred to as indirect expense or general and administrative expense.

Overload: The operation of conductors or equipment at a current level that will cause damage if allowed to persist.

Overrun (underrun) (work performed to date): The value for the work performed to date minus the cost for that same work. When value exceeds cost, an underrun condition exists. When cost exceeds value, an overrun condition exists.

Oversailing courses: A series of masonry courses, each projecting beyond the one below.

Owner's inspector: A person employed by the owner to inspect construction in the owner's behalf.

Owner's liability insurance: Insurance to protect the owner.

Owner-architect agreement: Contract between architect and client for professional services.

Owner-contractor agreement: Contract between the owner and contractor for a construction project.

Owner-supplied materials: See furnished by others.

Owner: (A) Architect's client and party to the owner-architect agreement. (B) The owner of the project and party to the owner-contract agreement.

Oxidized sewage: Sewage in which the organic matter has been combined with oxygen and become stable.

P

P-trap: A P-shaped trap used on plumbing fixtures.

P.D.M.: Precedence diagramming method. A network planning technique.

Package dealer: A person or organization assuming responsibility under a single contract for the design and construction of a project to meet the specific requirements of another.

Paint: A liquid solution that has a pigment mixed into another solution such as water, oil, or an organic solvent.

Palisander: A French term for Brazilian rosewood. It is a hardwood, flesh pink to purplish in color.

Panel: A prefabricated unit of insulation and lagging. In house construction, a thin flat piece of wood, plywood, or similar material, framed by stiles and rails as in a door or fitted into grooves of thicker material with molded edges for decorative wall treatment.

Panelboard: Circuit breakers, fuses, and switches mounted on an insulated panel.

Paneling: Wooden boards used to cover a wall or ceiling.

Paper, building: Papers, felts, and similar sheet materials used in buildings regardless their properties or uses.

Paper, sheathing: A building material, generally paper or felt, used in wall and roof construction as a protection against the passage of air and sometimes moisture.

PAR lamps: Parabolic aluminized reflector lamps, which offer excellent beam control, come in beam patterns from very narrow spot to wide flood, and can be used outdoors unprotected because they are made of hard glass that can withstand adverse weather.

Parabolic louvers: A grid of baffles that redirect light downward and provide very low luminaire brightness.

Paragraph: In the AIA documents, the first subdivision of an article, identified by two numerals e.g., 2.2. A paragraph may be further subdivided into subparagraphs and clauses.

Parapet: A low wall around the roof of a building or a drop, intended for protection. A railing that acts as a firebreak to a roof or ceiling.

Pargeting: Applying cement to the face of backing material or the back of facing material.

Pargework: Decorative design applied to a ceiling or wall, usually plaster or stucco.

Parking area: A designated area in which motor vehicles may park.

Parlor: The primary room for entertaining guests and until the twentieth century considered a living room.

Parquet: Thin hardwood flooring laid in patterns. It is often inlaid and highly polished.

Parquetry: An inlay pattern of geometrical designs usually done with several colors in stone or wood.

Partial occupancy: Occupancy by the owner of a portion of a project before completion.

Partial payment: See progress payment.

Particleboard: A mat-formed flat panel consisting of particles of wood bonded together with a synthetic resin or other suitable binder. The particles are classified by size and dried to a uniform moisture content, after which they are mixed with a binder, mat-formed into a panel, compressed to proper density, and then cured under heat and pressure.

Particles of combustion: Substances (products that either remain at the site of burning, such as ash, or scatter as volatile products) resulting from the chemical process of a fire.

Parting stop or strip: A small wood piece used in the side and head jambs of double-hung windows to separate upper and lower sash.

Partition cap: A formed metal section used at the end of a freestanding solid partition to protect plaster, also used as a stairrail cap, mullion cover, light cover cap, etc.

Partition: A wall that subdivides spaces within any story of a building. Some types are known as bearing, dwarf partition, fire partition, nonbearing partition, hollow partition, or solid partition.

Party wall: A special-purpose wall system used to divide compartments for different occupancies. May have requirements for fire and sound. A wall that is shared between two buildings.

Passing braces: Long straight braces passing across other members of the truss.

Patch: A repair made by inserting and securely gluing a sound piece of wood of the same species in a place of a defect that has been removed. The edges shall be cut clean and sharp and fit tight with no voids. Boat patches are oval shaped with sides tapering in each direction to a point or a small rounded end; router patches have parallel sides and rounded ends; sled patches are rectangular with feathered ends.

Patching: See reinsulate.

Patina: The result of oxidation in copper and copper alloys. It can also refer to the sheen that furniture develops with age.

Patio: An inner courtyard open to the sky. An outdoor seating area attached to a house, often covered. Common in North and Latin American architecture.

Pattern control: A blade in the air passage of an air handling luminaire, which sets the direction of air flow from the luminaire.

Pattern: Artistic decorative design on the surface of carpet. It may be printed, woven with colored yarns, or sculptured in multiple pile heights.

Pay item: Any item of work designated on the contract or an item of work both parties agree will be paid for, if and when it should arise during the work on the project.

Pay-when-paid provisions: Clauses in some subcontracts that state that the subcontractor shall be paid for the work performed after the prime contractor has received payment from the owner. A clause that states that the subcontractor shall be paid when the prime contractor receives payment and is silent on what happens if the prime contractor does not receive payment is a pay-when-paid provision but is not a conditional or condition precedent clause in most states. Therefore, the prime contractor is considered obligated to pay promptly upon receiving payment, but is not relieved of an obligation to pay within a reasonable time if payment is not received from the owner for any reason that is not the subcontractor's

fault. However, a pay-when-paid provision that states that payment shall not be made to the subcontractor until and unless the contractor receives payment will often be considered a condition precedent clause and will foreclose payment to the subcontractor regardless of the reason the prime contractor does not receive payment. See conditional payment clause and condition precedent.

Payment bonds: See labor and material payment bond.

Payment claim denial: Refusal of a party to an agreement to pay a claim made by the other party on the grounds that the claiming party is not entitled to the payment under the contract. In some cases, an explicit denial is required to institute the dispute procedure of the contract or to undertake litigation for breach of contract.

Payment clause modification: Changes made by mutual consent in payment clauses in a proposed agreement to make the agreement acceptable to both parties. Normally, this applies to changes proposed by a subcontractor to make a subcontract agreement proposed by a general contractor acceptable.

Payment clauses: Clauses in a contract agreement, subcontract and related contract documents, such as general condition pertaining to billing of progress and final payments, review and certification of such billing by party's creditors, retainage from progress payments, reduction of retainage at a specified milestone, final release of retainage, affidavits of payment to subcontractors and suppliers, conditional lien waivers, and procedures for requisitioning and receiving payment for work performed.

Payment entitlement: A condition under which the contractor has complied with applicable terms of the contract documents and is due payment for work performed and material stored.

Payment for work certified: Payment by the owner to the prime contractor, prime contractor to subcontractor, or subcontractor to sub-subcontractor for work performed and material stored up to the date of the last billing for which the owner's authorized representative has certified the performing contractor is entitled to payment.

Payment request: See application for payment.

Peak let-through current (Ip): The maximum instantaneous current passed by a current-limiting fuse when clearing a fault current of specified magnitude.

Penal sum: The amount a contract signatory would have to pay if contractual obligations are not performed.

Penalty cause: A provision in the construction contract for a charge against the contractor for failure to complete the work by a stipulated date. Penalties are normally uncollectible for breach of contract, but provisions for actual damage or liquidated damages specified in the contract are enforceable if they are related in magnitude to actual damages incurred and not regarded as a penalty. Incentive contracts that reward the contractor with a bonus above the contract sum for performing below the agreed cost or time budget but penalize the contractor for being above the cost or time budget are enforceable when benefits and penalties are explicit.

Pencil rods: Mild steel rods of 3/16", 1/4", or 3/8" diameter.

Penny: Originally indicated the price per hundred nails. The term now is a measure of nail length and is abbreviated by the letter "d".

Penthouse: The top floor of an office or residential building, usually a living space. A subsidiary structure on top of another structure with a lean-to or other separate roof.

Percent complete: A comparison of the status to the projection. The percent complete of an activity is determined by inspection of quantities placed as hours expended compared with quantities planned or hours earned.

Percentage agreement: An agreement for professional services in which the compensation is based upon a percentage of the construction cost.

Percentage fee: Compensation based upon a percentage of construction cost. See fee.

Percolation: The flow or trickling of a liquid downward through a contact or filtering medium; the liquid may or may not fill the pores of the medium.

Performance bond: A bond of the contractor in which a surety guarantees to the owner that the work will be performed in accordance with the contract documents. Except where prohibited by statute, the performance bond is frequently combined with the labor and material payment bond. See surety bond.

Performance criteria: Criteria against which the performance of a party to a contract is measured to determine if that party's obligations are fulfilled.

Performance specifications: Specifications that delineate the results to be achieved rather than the specific methods or materials.

Performing organization: The contractor or government organization that will work on a work package.

Perimeter relief: construction detail that allows for building movement. Gasketing materials that relieve stresses at the intersections of wall and ceiling surfaces.

Perlite: A siliceous volcanic glass properly expanded by heat and weighing not less then 7-1/2 nor more than 15 lbs. per cu. ft. used as a lightweight aggregate in plaster.

Perm: A unit of measurement of water vapor permeance; metric unit, Nanograms per Pascal, second meter squared; U.S. unit 1 grain per hour/square foot/inch of mercury.

Permanent distribution cable: Cables placed to extend the building cable distribution system permanently, e.g., cables connecting different buildings on the same property.

Permeability: The property of a material that permits a fluid (or gas) to pass through it. In construction, commonly refers to water vapor permeability of a sheet material or assembly and is defined as water vapor permeance per unit thickness. Metric unit of measurement, metric perms per centimeter of thickness.

Permeance (water vapor): The ratio of the rate of water vapor transmission (WVT) through a material or assembly between its two parallel surfaces to the vapor pressure differential between the surfaces. Metric unit of measurement is the Nanograms per Pascal, second meter squared; U.S. unit, 1 grain per hour/square foot/inch of mercury.

Permit, building: See building permit.

Permit, occupancy: See certificate of occupancy.

Permit, zoning: See zoning permit.

Personal injury: Injury or damage to the character, reputation, or body of a person.

Personnel protection: Insulation installed to protect personnel from high or low temperature surfaces, high-frequency sound, etc.

PERT schedule: Charts the activities and events anticipated in a work process. See critical path method.

PERT: An acronym for project evaluation and review technique, which is a network scheduling scheme used in defense and industrial production. PERT is sometimes erroneously used as a synonym for another scheduling technique, the critical path method, which is much more common in construction. See critical path method.

Pessimistic time estimate : The maximum time required for an activity under adverse conditions. It is generally held that an activity would have no more than one chance in 100 of exceeding this amount of time.

Pewter: An alloy combination of lead and tin, antimony, or copper.

pH: A measure or the acidity of alkalinity of a solution, numerically equal to 7 for neutral solutions, increasing with increasing alkalinity and decreasing with increasing acidity; (potential of) (Hydrogen).

Phenolic foam: A foamed insulation made from resins of phenols condensed with aldehydes.

Phenolics: Plastics that can withstand heat up to 330° F and are very strong. They are resistant to fire, acids, and oils. Phenolics are poor heat conductors and will yellow due to light exposure. They are mainly used for appliance parts, handles for utensils, and electrical insulation.

Photoelectric smoke detector: In a photoelectric light scattering smoke detector, a light source and a photosensitive sensor are so arranged that the rays from the light source do not normally fall on the photosensitive sensor. When smoke particles enter the light path, some of the light is scattered by reflection and refraction onto the sensor, causing the detector to respond.

Pickled finish: The white finish that appears when old paint is removed.

Pier, compound: A pier with multiple shafts.

Pier: A column of masonry, usually rectangular in horizontal cross section, used to support other structural members.

Pigment: Highly colored insoluble powdered substance used to impart color to other materials. White pigments, e.g., titanium dioxide, are dispersed in fiber forming polymers to produce delustered (semidull and dull) fibers.

Pilaster: A shallow pier projecting from a wall. A column or pier with a capital and base.

Pin: A cylindrical metal fastener of variable diameter, used for reinforcing joints.

Pine: A softwood, white or pale yellow in color, which can either be clear or knotty.

Pinhole: A small hole appearing in a cast when the water-stucco ratio has not been accurately measured. Excess water causes pinholes.

Pipe: A cylindrical conduit or conductor, with a wall thickness sufficient to receive a standard pipe thread. May be installed threaded or plain ended.

Pise: Clay or soil mixed with gravel and used for building walls. It is compressed into formworks until it hardens. Common in the ancient Middle East.

Pitch pocket: A well defined opening between the annual growth rings, which contains pitch. (A) A very small pocket is a maximum of 1/16" in width x 3" in length, or 1/8" in width x 2" in length. (B) A small pocket is a maximum of 1/16" in width x 6" in length, or 1/8" in width x 4" in length. (C) A medium pocket is a maximum of 1/16" in width x 12" in length, or 1/8" in width x 8" in length.

Pitch streak: A well defined accumulation of pitch in the wood cells in a more or less regular streak. (A) A very small pitch

streak is a maximum of 1/16" in width x 12" in length, or 1/8" in width x 6" in length. (B) A small streak is a maximum of 1/8" in width x 12" in length, or 1/4" in width x 6" in length. (C) A medium streak is a maximum of 1/4" in width x 16" in length, or 3/8" in width x 12" in length.

Pitch: (A) An accumulation of resin that occurs in separations in the wood or in the wood cells themselves. (B) Indicates the closeness of the pile tufts along the width of a woven carpet as expressed in the number of warp or lengthwise lines contained in every 27" of width. The higher the pitch number, such as 180, 189, 216, etc., then the closer the pile tufts are to each other widthwise in the carpet. See Gauge. (C) The physical response given to frequency. (D) The slanting incline of a roof or horizontal pipe.

Pith: A small, soft core occurring in the center of the log.

Plain: A sheet or slab having an incombustible core, essentially gypsum, surfaced with paper suitable to receive gypsum plaster. One face may be treated, such as by mechanical pricking or indenting or impregnation with catalyst.

Plan deposit: See deposit for bidding documents.

Plan: A two-dimensional graphic representation of the design, location, and dimensions of the project, seen in a horizontal plane viewed from above. See drawings. The horizontal design or arrangement of building parts as well as the drawing that represents it.

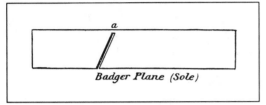

Badger Plane (Sole)

Plane, badger: A plane similar in size and appearance to the wood panel plane, but with a skew mouth with the cutter passing through the stock at an angle with the side. This brings the cutter up to the extreme right-hand edge of the sole, which enables the plane to be used for finishing sinkings, rebates, or rabbets. It is a double iron plane; i.e., the cutters have a back or cover iron to stiffen them.

Plane, block: Small planes of wood or metal, chiefly used for cleaning off small surfaces where the regular smoothing plane would be too cumbersome.

Plane, bullnose: A metal rebate plane used to finish off rebates and other narrow surfaces close to stops or abutments. It is very essential in all planes that have their cutters face down that the face of the cutter be ground to a true plane, and not have to be forced into that position by the wedge. All of these planes are comparatively weak in the neck, and if wedged too tightly the sole will spring hollow and the mouth choke. Planes of this type should have a

cheese-head screw at the back, to receive the release blows of the hammer.

Plane, chariot: A small metal smoothing plane for hardwood, 3.25" long made in widths from 1-1/8" to 1-1/2".

Plane, compass: A smoothing plane with a convex sole, used for cleaning up curved surfaces. It has a sliding boxwood nose-piece that may be moved downwards to make the sole fit the work to be planed. The American variety has a malleable iron stock and carries an adjustable cutter frame to which a spring steel face is attached. It will work either concave or convex surfaces.

Plane, grooving: Planes used for sinking trenches or grooves across the grain. It has a rebated sole, the cutters being in the tongue portion, which is usually made 1/2" deep and varies in width from 1/4" to 1-1/8". It has a screw-stop for adjusting the depth of cut and a double-toothed cutter for separating the fibers of the iron.

Jack Plane

Plane, jack: The first plane used in preparing material. It is used to remove irregularities left by the saw and produce a fairly smooth surface. It consists of a beechwood or steel stock 17" long x 2.75" x 3" with a 2.25" cutting iron and similar back iron. The cutter is better parallel or gauged, because once fitted, the wedge will then always sit properly, and the size of the mouth remain the same throughout. This applies to all planes whose cutters are fixed by wedges.

Plane, molding: Planes used to make molding shaped, seldom used today. They are usually made of wood and come in many molding shapes.

Plane, panel: A plane ranging in size from 9" with 2.25" irons to 15" with 2.5" irons. Longer planes in this type, up to 20" long with 2.75" cutters, are called jointers.

Panel Plane.

Plane, plough: An adjustable grooving plane of great utility. It will sink a groove of any width between 1/8" and 5/8" to any depth required up to the depth of the guide iron of about 1.5", and at any distance from the edge of the piece, within the length of the sliding stems. Some patterns have the front end of the guide turned up with a skate end. These pass over mortises easily. There are nine irons to a set. In adjusting these, care must be taken to set the

V groove in the iron accurately upon the fore end of the guide.

Planes, rebating or rabbeting: A plane used for forming rebates or rabbets, or sinkings on the edges of material. Wooden ones have a solid beech stock, 9" long, 3.75" high, and from 5/8" to 2" wide. It is made both with square and skew mouth.

Plane, sash fillister: A variety of rebate plane used to form rebates or rabbets on the off side of material. They are provided with vertical and horizontal adjustments. They have a tooth or cutting knife slightly in advance of the cutting iron, to sever cross grain or to cut through knots.

Plane, scraper: A tool used for giving a high finish to hardwoods. An ordinary steel scraper takes the place of the plane iron, which can be adjusted to any degree of fineness by the set screw. The pitch of the scraper can also be altered to suit the texture of the wood scraped. This tool may also be used as a toothing plane by substituting a toothing iron for the scraper.

Plane, shoulder: A special form of rebate plane in metal, used principally for smoothing and correcting hardwood shoulders after the saw. The casting is hollow and filled in with a hardwood core. The iron is set face down and at a low angle. The wedge projects to form a rest for the hand, and improved forms have a spur worked in the top core just over the mouth, which adds to the power of the grip. Square mouths are preferable in these planes, because they are required to work both right and left handed.

Plane, side fillister: A variety of rebate plane used to form rebates or rabbets on the near side of material. They are provided with vertical and horizontal adjustments. They have a tooth or cutting knife slightly in advance of the cutting iron, to sever cross grain or to cut through knots.

Plane, side rebate or rabbet: Planes used for enlarging grooves rather than rebates as their name suggest. They are made in pairs to work right and left handed. The American pattern is metal with reversible nose-pieces which enable them to be worked up to the end of stopped groove.

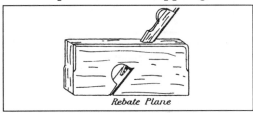
Rebate Plane

Plane, smoothing: A plane used chiefly for smoothing or finishing the surface after manipulation by other planes. The standard size of stock is 8" x 3" x 2.75", carrying 2.25" double irons.

Plane, trying: A plane with a stock 23" long x 3", with a 2.5" cutter. It follows the jack plane in reducing the wood to a truly plane surface, or in producing straight edges for joints.

Planned cost: The approved planned cost for a work package or summary item. This cost when totaled with the planned costs for all other work packages results in the total cost estimate committed under contract for the program or project.

Planning: The establishment of the project activities and events, their logical relations and interrelations to each other, and the sequence in which they are to be accomplished.

Plans: The official approved plans, profiles, typical cross sections, working drawing and supplemental drawings, or exact reproductions thereof, which show the location, character, dimensions, and details of the work to be performed.

Plaque: Flat, thin pieces of wood, metal, porcelain, etc. used for wall ornamentation.

Plaster bond: The state of adherence between plaster coats or between plaster and a plaster base, produced by adhesive or mechanical interlock of plaster with base or special supplementary materials.

Plaster grounds: Strips of wood used as guides or strike-off edges around window and door openings and at the base of walls.

Plaster: A cementitious material that, when mixed with of water, forms a plastic mass and, when applied to a surface, adheres to it and subsequently hardens, preserving the form or texture imposed during the period of plasticity. The term plaster is used with regard to the specific composition of the material and does not denote either interior or exterior use. See gypsum, Portland cement plaster, lime plaster.

Plastering machine: A mechanical device by which plaster mortar is conveyed through a flexible hose to deposit the plaster in place; also known as a plaster pump or plastering gun. Distinct from "Gunite" machines in which the plaster or concrete is conveyed, dry, through the flexible hose and hydrated at the nozzle.

Plastic backing sheet: A thin sheet, usually phenolic, applied under pressure to the back of a laminated plastic panel to achieve balance by equalizing the rate of moisture absorption or emission.

Plastic: A substance made from polymerized organic compounds that can be shaped into products.

Plasticity: Workability and water-retentive characteristics imparted to plaster mortars by such agents as natural cement, lime, asbestos, flour, clays, air-entraining agents or other approved lubricators or fatteners. The duration of mixing time may be a factor in the plasticity of some mortars.

Plasticizing agent: A product used to increase the flow or workability of plaster.

Plate, sill: A horizontal member anchored to a masonry wall.

Plate, sole: Bottom horizontal member of a frame wall.

Plate, top: Top horizontal member of a frame wall supporting ceiling joists, rafters, or other members.

Plate: The horizontal framing member at the top or base of wall framing. A covering for exterior nails and studs.

Plenum chamber: A distributing duct that connects to an air compartment.

Plenums: Enclosures for the collection of air at the termination or origin of duct systems. They may be a space below floors, above ceilings, a shaft, or a furred area. An enclosed chamber such as the space between a suspended finished ceiling and the floor above.

Plot plan: A scale drawing indicating the location of the construction in relation to the site.

Plotter: The hardcopy graphic output device used to prepare a plot. The method used varies from computer controlled moving pens to electrostatic processes similar to photocopy machines.

Plow: A rectangular groove or slot of three surfaces cut parallel with the grain of a wood member, in contrast to a dado, which is cut across the grain.

Plug date for scheduled date: A date externally assigned to an activity that establishes the earliest or later date in which the activity is allowed to start or finish.

Plug-in wiring: Electrical distribution system that has quick-connect wiring connectors.

Plumb: Exactly vertical.

Plumbing appliance: A plumbing fixture that is intended to perform a special plumbing function. Its operation or control may be dependent upon one or more energized components, such as motors, controls, heating elements, or pressure or temperature-sensing elements. Such fixtures may operate automatically through one or more of the following actions: a time cycle, temperature range, pressure range, measured volume or weight; or the fixture may be manually adjusted or controlled by the user or operator.

Plumbing appurtenances: A manufactured device, prefabricated assembly, or on-the-job assembly of component parts that is an adjunct to the basic piping system and plumbing fixtures. An appurtenance demands no additional water supply nor does it add any discharge load to a fixture or the drainage system. It is presumed that it performs some useful function in the operation, maintenance, servicing, economy, or safety of the plumbing system.

Plumbing engineering: The application of scientific principles to the design, installation, and operation of efficient, economical,

ecological, and energy-conserving systems for the transport and distribution of liquids and gases.

Plumbing fixtures: Installed receptacles, devices or appliances that are supplied with water or that receive liquid or liquid-born wastes and discharge such wastes into the drainage system to which they may be directly or indirectly connected. Industrial or commercial tanks, vats, and similar processing equipment are not plumbing fixtures but may be connected to or discharged into approved traps or plumbing fixtures.

Plumbing inspector: Any person who, under the supervision of the department having jurisdiction, is authorized to inspect plumbing and drainage systems as defined in the code for the municipality and complying with the laws of licensing or registration of the state, city, or county.

Plumbing system: All potable water supply and distribution pipes plumbing fixtures and traps; drainage, vent pipe and building (house) drains, including their respective joints and connections, devices, receptacles, and appurtenances within the property lines of the premises. This includes potable water piping, potable water treating or using equipment, fuel gas piping, water heaters and vents for same.

Plumbing wall: A building wall in which the plumbing pipes are installed. Usually directly behind bathroom plumbing fixtures.

Plumbing: The practice, materials, and fixtures used in the installation, maintenance, extension, and alteration of all piping, fixtures, appliances, and appurtenances in connection with any of the following: sanitary drainage or storm drainage facilities; the venting system; and the public or private water-supply systems within or adjacent to any building, structure or conveyance; water supply systems or the storm water, liquid waste, or sewage system of any premises to their connection with any point of public disposal or other acceptable terminal.

Plus pressure: A pressure within a sanitary drainage or vent piping system greater than atmospheric pressure.

Ply: Denotes the number of thicknesses or layers of roofing felt, veneer in plywood, or layers or built-up materials in any finished piece.

Plywood: A panel composed of a cross-banded assembly of layers or plies of veneer, or veneers in combination with a lumber or particleboard core, that are joined with an adhesive. Except for special constructions, the grain of alternate plies is always approximately at right angles, and the thickness and species on either side of the core are identical for balanced effect. An odd number of plies is always used.

Pneumatic: Operated by air pressure.

Podium: A speakers platform. The arena platform in an amphitheater. A continuous base supporting columns.

Point method lighting calculation: A lighting design procedure for predetermining the illuminance at various locations in lighting installations by use of luminaire photometric data.

Point-block housing: A high block that reserves the center for staircases and elevators. Suites or apartments radiate from the center.

Point: .001" (a thousandth of an inch). The thickness of some boards and papers is indicated by points.

Pointing: The exposed mortar finishing to masonry joints raked out with a trowel to receive it.

Poke through: A term used to describe an unlimited or random penetration through the fire resistive floor structure. Used to facilitate the installation of distribution wires for power and communications.

Polarization: The process by which the transverse vibrations of light waves are oriented in a specific plane. Polarization may be obtained by using either transmitting or reflecting media.

Polish: To make plaster finish coat smooth and glossy by troweling.

Polyester decorative paper edging: A two or more ply cured polyester saturated decorative paper a minimum of 12 mils in thickness. A high viscosity hot-melt adhesive may be pre-applied to the edging. The edging shall be applied to the panel with 375° to 450° heat and pressure. The surface shall withstand 500° without blistering. The surface shall meet the requirements of NEMA LD 3-80. The adhesive, whether pre-applied or not, shall be a pigment extended, resin modified, ethylene-vinyl acetate co-polymer base, hot-melted adhesive. Physical properties of this glue are as follows; (A) Viscosity at 200° 75M - 100 CPS (B) Ring and Ball melting point 97°-101° C (C) Penetrameter, 150 grs. at 25° C 6.0-8.0

Polyester: A fiber-forming thermoplastic synthetic polymer used in some carpet fiber. Essentially all polyester carpet fiber is staple and the yarns are spun yarns. Polyester for carpet is made from terephthalic acid and ethylene glycol and is known chemically as poly (ethylene terephthalate). Polyester fibers were introduced still later and became increasingly popular because of their soft, luxurious appearance close to that of wool as well as their bright lustrous shades. They possess a good resistance to abrasion, very good resilience and texture retention, and adequate cleanability.

Polyethylene: A chemical and stain resistant plastic. It is often used for toys, ice cube trays, and dishes. Polyethylene is flexible and can withstand heat up to 100°F.

Polymers: High molecular weight chemical compounds formed by repeated linking of smaller chemical units called monomers. Polymers from which fibers are made are long chain molecules in which the monomers are linked end to end linearly. Synthetic polymers used for carpet fiber include nylon-6, 6 and nylon-6 (polyamides), polyester, polypropylene, and polyacrylonitrile (acrylics). In popular terminology, polymers are also called plastics or resins.

Polystyrene: A resin made by polymerization of styrene as the sole monomer.

Polyurethane: A resin made by the condensation of organic isocynates with compounds or resins that contain hydroxol groups.

Polyvinyl fluoride (PVF): A polymerized vinyl compounding fluoride.

Polyvinyl chloride (PVC): A polymerized vinyl compound.

Polyvinyl edging: Application: vinyl (PVC) edging on seamless rolls to be applied on single/double side edge banding machines using hot-melt adhesives. Specifications, product to be calendared, of wood design, grained or smooth material, solid color. Product to be chip proof, flame resistant, and impervious to moisture. Thickness of 0.45 mm (0.0177"), 0.40 mm (0.0157"), 0.60 mm (0.0256") with tolerance of ±0.001" and tear strength of approximately 1,800 lbs. per sq. in. Product to be antistatic and equipped with an adhesive agent for bonding.

Pool: A water receptacle used for swimming or as a plunge or other bath, designed to accommodate more than one bather at a time.

Pops or pits: Ruptures in finished plaster or cement surfaces which may be caused by expansion of improperly slaked particles of lime or by foreign substances.

Porch: The covered entrance to a building.

Pores: Wood cells of comparatively large diameter that have open ends and are set one above the other to form continuous tubes. The openings of the vessels on the surface of a piece of wood are referred to as pores.

Porphyry: A rock that is found in igneous ground containing crystals.

Port control faucet: A noncompression, single-handled faucet that contains a port for both cold and hot water.

Portcullis: An iron gate that slides vertically in grooves made in the doorway jambs. Used in castles and forts.

Portico: A porch supported by columns. A roofed space forming the entrance of a building.

Portland cement plaster: Plaster made with Portland cement usually applied in three coats, except when direct to masonry or concrete surfaces.

Portland cement-lime plaster: Portland cement and lime (either type S hydrated lime or properly aged lime putty) combined in proportion as outlined in applicable building codes.

Portland cement: A hydraulic cement produced by pulverizing clinker consisting essentially of hydraulic calcium silicates, and usually containing one or more forms of calcium sulfate as an interground addition.

Post-and-beam: A construction system with horizontal beams and vertical posts.

Post-completion services: Additional services rendered after issuance of the final certificate for payment, such as consultation regarding maintenance, processes, systems, etc.

Posts: Vertical timbers that carry longitudinal roof members. Main vertical wall timbers. Small metal or wood columns.

Potable water supply system: All water service pipes, distributing pipes, and necessary connecting pipes, fittings, control valves, and appurtenances.

Potable water: Water that is satisfactory for drinking, culinary, and domestic purposes and meets the requirements of the health authority having jurisdiction.

Power driven fastener: A fastener attached to steel, concrete, or masonry by a power charge cartridge or by manual impact.

Power of attorney: An instrument authorizing another to act as one's agent. See attorney in fact.

Power stretcher: An installation tool used to stretch longer areas of carpet than can properly be done by the knee kicker. The back end is braced against an immovable object such as a wall, post, etc. Extended tubes are added on for the approximate distance of desired stretch. Then the head, containing rows of angle sharp steel pins adjustable in length to extend into the pile and a short distance into the carpet backing, is connected. The down movement of the handle attached to the head causes the head and the carpet to move forward several inches and thus stretch the carpet from the back end of the tool to the head.

Pretrimmed wallpaper: Wallpaper that has a selvage.

Preamble: A statement at the beginning of a law, act, or group of laws, explaining why the law being enacted and what it is hoped will accomplish.

Precast concrete: Factory manufactured concrete components.

Precedence diagram: (A) A scheduling diagram showing the sequence in which events are planned to occur. (B) A network on which the activities are represented by the nodes with connecting lines showing dependencies among activities. See critical path method.

Precipitation: The total measurable supply of water received directly from the clouds as snow, rain, hail, and sleet. It is expressed in inches (mm) per day, month, or year.

Preconstruction CPM: A plan and schedule for the concept and design phase preceding the award of contract.

Predecessor event: An event that signifies the beginning of an activity in a network.

Prefabrication (site): Components and systems assembled at the building site before installation.

Preheat fluorescent lamp: A fluorescent lamp designed for operation in a circuit requiring a manual or automatic starting switch to preheat the electrodes that start the arc.

Preheating: Heating air before the other processes begin.

Preinstallation test: A simulation of the on-site installation test, performed in the workshop to verify dimensions and the match of colors and patterns.

Preliminary CPM plan: CPM analysis of the construction phase made before the award of contracts to determine a reasonable construction period.

Preliminary drawings: Drawings prepared during the early stages of the design of a project. See schematic design phase, design development phase.

Preliminary estimate: Project costs prepared by the architect during the development phase for the guidance of the owner.

Prequalification of prospective bidders: Investigating the qualifications of prospective bidders on the basis of their competence, integrity, and responsibility relative to the contemplated project.

Preservative: A treating solution that prevents decay in wood by inhibiting the growth of decay fungi.

Pressure forming: Air pressure can also be sealed by pressing the top of a sheet and building pressure by compressed air. This is pressure forming.

Pressure maintenance (jockey) pump: Pump with controls and accessories used to maintain pressure in a fire protection system without the operation of the fire pump. Does not have to be a listed pump.

Pressure sensitive tape: A tape with adhesive preapplied.

Pressure-reducing valve: An automatic device that converts high, fluctuating inlet water pressure to a lower constant pressure. A pressure-regulating valve.

Pre-stressed concrete: Reinforced concrete which contains tensioned rods or cables that induce compression prior to loading. The result is a stronger member.

Primavera: A hardwood, light in color, with a stripe in the grain.

Prime contract: Contract between the owner and the general or specialty contractor for construction of a project.

Prime contractor: Any contractor on a project having a contract directly with the owner.

Prime professional: Any person or firm having a contract directly with the owner for professional services.

Primer: The first coat of paint in a paint job that consists of two or more coats; also the paint used for such a first coat.

Principals: A pair of vertically inclined timbers of a truss that carry common rafters.

Principal (in professional practice): Any person legally responsible for the activities of a professional practice.

Print: A design that is transferred from another medium.

Private line or private wire: A channel or circuit furnished to a subscriber for his exclusive use.

Private or private use: Fixtures used in residences, apartments, private bathrooms of hotels, or other buildings intended for use of one family.

Private sewage disposal system: A septic tank with the effluent discharging into a subsurface disposal field, one or more seepage pits or a combination of subsurface disposal field and seepage pit, or of such other facilities as may be permitted under the procedures set forth in a code.

Private sewer: A sewer that is privately owned and not directly operated by public authority.

Private use: Applies to plumbing fixtures in residences and apartments, private bathrooms in hotels and hospitals, rest rooms in commercial establishments containing restricted-use single fixtures or groups of single fixtures and similar installations, where the fixtures are intended for the use of a family or an individual.

Privity of contract: A legal principle limiting the effects of a contract to the parties to the contract unless those parties expressly agree to confer a contractual benefit on a third party. Normally, one cannot sue to enforce a contract to which one is not a party. This concept is widely used by government contracting agencies and other owners to disclaim any interests in claims of subcontractors against prime contractors.

Processed quicklime: See lime.

Producer: Manufacturer, processor, or assembler of building materials or equipment.

Professional engineer: Designation reserved usually by law for a person or organization professionally qualified and duly licensed to perform such engineering services as structural, mechanical, electrical, sanitary, civil, etc.

Professional liability insurance: Insurance designed to insure an architect, engineer, or any person or firm undertaking design responsibility, such as design-build contractor, against claim for damages resulting from alleged professional negligence.

Professional practice: The practice of one of the environmental design professions in which services are rendered within the framework of recognized professional ethics and standards and applicable legal requirements.

Profile: A charted line indicating grades and distances and usually depth of cut and height of fill for excavation and grading work; commonly taken along the centerline. A side view, as distinct from a plan or overhead view.

Program: A written statement setting forth the conditions and requirements for a project.

Progress payments: Partial payment made for work completed or materials suitably stored during progress of the work.

Progress schedule: A diagram, graph, or other pictorial or written schedule showing proposed and actual times of starting and completion of the elements of the work. See critical path method.

Progress trend: An indication of whether the progress of an activity or project is increasing, decreasing, or remaining the same over a given period of time.

Project control: The ability to determine project status as it relates to the selected time plan and schedule.

Project cost: Total cost of the project including professional compensation, land costs, furnishings, equipment, financing and other charges, construction cost.

Project finish date: The later schedule calculated date on the project.

Project manual: The manual prepared by the architect for a project, including the bidding requirements, conditions of the contract, and technical specifications.

Project network analysis (PNA): A group of techniques based on the network project representation to assist the managers in planning, scheduling, and controlling the project.

Project representative: The architect's representative at the project site who assists in the administration of the construction contract.

Project site: See site.

Project time: The time dimension in which the project is planned. It must be consistent and is a net value (less holidays).

Project-wide retainage: Retainage conditions, which are uniform for the prime contractor and all subcontractors on the project. Such uniformity also applies to provisions for reduction or elimination of retainage after accomplishment of a certain level of completion and release of retainage upon final completion.

Project: The overall work being planned. It must have one start point and one finish. The total construction designed by the architect, of which the work performed under the contract documents may be the whole or a part.

Projected beam (smoke) detector: In a projected beam detector, the amount of light transmitted between a light source and a photosensitive sensor is monitored. When smoke particles are introduced in the light path, some of the light is scattered and some absorbed, thereby reducing the light reaching the receiver, causing the detector to respond.

Projected (overrun) underrun: The planned cost minus the latest revised estimate for a work package or summary item. When planned cost exceeds latest revised estimate, a projected underrun condition exists. When latest revised estimate exceeds planned cost, a projected overrun condition exists.

Prompt payment: Payment for work performed, after the owner's representative has certified entitlement, with no delays except those necessary to receive invoices and write and transmit checks.

Property damage insurance: Part of a general liability insurance covering injury to or destruction of tangible property, including loss of use resulting therefrom, but usually not including property which is in the care, custody and control of the insured. See, care, custody, and control.

Property insurance: Insurance on the work at the site against loss or damage caused by perils of fire, lightning, extended coverage (wind, hail, explosion commotion, aircraft, land vehicles, and smoke), vandalism and malicious, mischief and additional perils. See special hazards insurance.

Proposal (contractor's): See bid.

Proposal schedule: The first schedule issued on a project that accompanies either the client's request or the proposal.

Public conveniences: Rest rooms, telephones, and drinking fountains and other facilities intended for public use.

Public liability insurance: Insurance covering liability of the insured for negligent acts resulting in bodily injury, disease, or death of others than employees of the insured, or property damage.

Public use: Plumbing fixtures in general toilet rooms of schools, gymnasiums, hotels, bars, public comfort stations, and other unrestricted installations.

Public sewer: A common sewer directly operated by public authority.

Puddling: A condition of mechanical dash textures resulting in glazing, texture deviation, or discoloration caused by holding the plastering machine nozzle too long in one area.

Pumice: A lightweight volcanic rock, which when crushed and graded, may be used as a plaster aggregate.

Pump: See plastering machine.

Pumped condensate (discharge): Condensate in liquid state from receivers to feed water heaters, aerators, or boilers.

Pumping agent: A product used to increase the flow of plaster through hoses during machine applications.

Punch, center: A punch with its end turned to an obtuse conical point, used for making a slight depression in metal from which to start a drill.

Punch list procedures: Procedures set forth in contract documents and guidelines to effect prompt and orderly final inspections. See inspection list.

Punch list: Use inspection list.

Punches: Short lengths of steel rod tapered to a blunt point. They are used for driving the heads of brads or nails below the surface, so that the hole made by the nail may be filled in with putty or composition. The point of the punch used should always be smaller than the head of the nail, so that the hole may not be unnecessarily enlarged, and squared points are better than round ones.

Puncture resistance: (A) That property of a material that enables it to resist punctures or perforation under blows or pressure from sharp objects. See mechanical properties of insulation.

Purity: The percentage of $CaSO_4 + 2H_2O$ in the calcined gypsum portion of a gypsum plaster or gypsum concrete, as defined by Specifications C28 for gypsum plasters. The percentage of $CaSO_4 + 2H_2O$ in the gypsum portion of fully hydrated, dry, set, gypsum plaster (C 471, C 28).

Purlin, collar: A single timber that carries collarbeams and is supported by crown-posts.

Purlin, side: Timber pairs occurring up the slope of the roof that carry common rafters.

Purlin: A horizontal longitudinal timber. A piece of timber that rests between a joist and a rafter.

Purple heart: See amaranth.

Putlock: Holes in a wall used to support scaffolding during construction.

Putrefaction: Biological decomposition of organic matter with the production of ill-smelling products which usually takes place when there is a deficiency of oxygen.

Putty coat: A troweled finish coat composed of lime putty or type S hydrated lime gauged with gypsum gauging plaster or Keene's cement. Fine aggregate may be added.

Putty: A type of cement usually made of whiting and boiled linseed oil, beaten or kneaded to the consistency of dough, and used in sealing glass in sash, filling small holes and crevices in wood, and for similar purposes. Product resulting from slaking, soaking, or mixing lime and water together.

Pylon: A high, isolated structure used to mark a boundary or for decoration. A pyramidal tower that flanks an ancient Egyptian temple gateway.

Q

Quadrangle: A rectangular courtyard or mall surrounded by buildings.

Quality assurance: (A) The system for insuring that the contract's technical requirements are met. (B) The planning, training, management, and other technical actions performed by the owner before the construction phase to ensure the control of quality by the contractor at the jobsite during construction.

Quality control: Tests and sampling techniques to see that required quality is provided.

Quality level: The specific degree of excellence, basis, nature, character, or kind of performance of a particular item or group of items established by the designer and included in the plans and specifications.

Quantity overrun/underrun: The difference between the original estimated contract quantities and the quantities in the completed work.

Quantity survey: Detailed analysis and listing of all items of material and equipment necessary to construct a project.

Quantity: Term used to indicate the amount of work to be performed under a variety of items and measurements; e.g., lineal feet, cubic yard, square yard, per each, etc.

Quarry deposit: The volume of available material to be quarried.

Quarry faced: Squared off ashlar left with the finish as it comes from the quarry.

Quarrying: The extraction of stone from an excavation.

Quarter match: A pattern used for very decorative floors or facings, so named because the pattern is formed by four tiles or slabs. Also called quarter round.

Quartering: A log sawed into four parts.

Queen-post: A pair of vertical timbers placed symmetrically on a tiebeam and supporting side purlings.

Quicklime: See lime.

Quirk: A sharp v-shaped cut in or between moldings.

Quoin: (A) One stone helping to form the corner of a wall of masonry, especially when accentuated by a difference in the surface treatment of the stones forming the corner from that of the rest of the wall mass; one of the stones forming such a corner. (B) A wedge to support and steady a stone; a pinner. (C) The keystone or voussoir of an arch.

Quotation: A price quoted by a contractor, subcontractor, material supplier, or vendor to furnish materials, labor, or both.

R

Rabbet: A continuous small recess, generally understood as having a right angle included between its sides, especially one whose sides enclose a relatively restricted area; one formed by two planes very narrow compared with their length, such as the small recess on a door frame, into which the edge of a door is made to fit, the recess of a brick jamb to receive a window fr ame, and the like. A joint formed by the rabbet(s) on one or both members; also rabbeted edge joint, rabbeted right angle joint.

Raceway: Any channel for holding wires, cables, or busbars, that is designed expressly for this purpose. The term includes conduit (rigid and flexible, metallic and nonmetallic), electrical metallic tubing, underfloor raceways, cellular floor raceways, surface raceways, wireways, cablethroughs, busways, auxiliary gutters, and ventilated flexible cableway.

Racking: Lateral stresses exerted on an assembly.

Radiant heat: A heat source that transmits thermal energy by radiation rather than convection. An example is electric resistance wires concealed in a finished ceiling surface. A method of heating, usually consisting of a forced hot water system with pipes placed in the floor, wall, or ceiling; or with electrically heated panels.

Radiation: Direct electromagnetic waves in the heat or infrared range. The passage of heat from one object to another without warming the space between.

Rafter, angle: In English usage, strictly the principal rafter under the hip rafter. It carries the purlins, on which rest the jack rafters and hips. More commonly, in the United States, any rafter at the angle of a roof, whether principal or secondary.

Rafter, auxiliary: In a truss, a rafter used to stiffen the principal rafter by doubling it, or, as in a queen post truss, to go from the tie beam to the queen post, thus doubling the sloping chord of the truss in that place. Also called cushion rafter.

Rafter, binding: A timber to support rafters at a point between the plate and the ridge. It may be a purlin.

Rafter, common: A rafter to which the roof sheathing is nailed, as distinguished from the main or truss rafters and from hip, valley, and other special rafters. In trussed roofs they are ordinarily carried by the purlins, and spaced 16", 20", or 24" on centers; their scantling varies greatly according to the character of the roof.

Rafter, compass: In an ornamental roof truss or the framing of a gable, a rafter cut to a curve, either at both edges (inner and outer) or on the inside only.

Rafter, hip: A rafter that forms the intersection of an external roof angle.

Rafter, jack: One reaching from the angle rafter to the ridge, and therefore short.

Rafter, knee: One taking the place of a knee, i.e., of a brace fitted into the angle between a principal rafter and the tie beam or collar beam. Also called crook and kneeling rafter.

Rafter, principal: The diagonal member of a roof truss or principal.

Rafter, valley: A rafter that forms the intersection of an internal roof angle. The valley rafter is normally made of double 2"-thick members.

Rafter: A roof beam. One of those which are set sloping, the lower end bearing on the wall plate, the upper end on the ridge piece or its equivalent.

Rafters, common: Rafters of equal scantling found along the length of a roof.

Rafters, principal: Rafters that serve as both common rafters and principals.

Rafters: Inclined lateral timbers sloping from wall-top to apex and supporting the roof covering.

Raggle: A masonry groove cut in masonry to receive a roof edge.

Rail, frieze: In a framed door or the like, that next below a frieze panel.

Rail, hanging: That rail in a door, window sash, or shutter, hung with hinges at the top or bottom, to which the hinges are attached.

Rail clamp: In carpentry work, a piece receiving the ends of several boards in part of the ceiling; a platform, trapdoor, or the like. The clamp usually has a groove run along the edge into which the ends of the boards fit with tongues or tenons. In the United States, called more often cleat or batten.

Rail lock: In a framed door, that rail which comes nearest to the place for the lock, therefore, about three feet from the ground.

Rail: A horizontal member in a door or window frame or panel. In carpentry, any horizontal member mortised or otherwise secured between or upon two posts, forming a frame or panel as, first, in fencing, whether the closure is made by several parallel rails or by only two to give nailing to palings; second, as a coping to a balustrade when it is called a hand rail; third, in paneling, doors, and the like, being the horizontal member of the frame in which the panels are set, the vertical members being the stiles.

Railing: Any structure or member composed mainly of rails. In common use, a small parapet, enclosure, or the like made with slender bars. Such a parapet, whether consisting of balusters (see baluster), a trellis of wire or laths, or iron bars equal or nearly so in thickness, parallel or nearly so, is called a railing, but the term does not commonly include balustrades or the like of stone.

Rainwater head: A metal structure used to collect water from a gutter and discharge it into a downpipe.

Rainwater leader: A pipe that conveys storm water from a roof to a storm drain. A conductor or downspout.

Raised grain: Roughened condition of surface of dressed lumber on which hard summerwood is raised above the softer springwood but not torn loose from it.

Rake: Inclination or slope, as of a roof or of a flight of steps in a staircase. Trim members that run parallel to the roof slope and form the finish between the wall and a gable roof extension.

Ram, hydraulic: An automatic mechanical device that raises a small quantity of water by utilizing the force obtained by the fall of a large body of water. The height to which the water is raised is often many times greater than the fall. The water lifted may be from the same source that furnishes the power operating the machine or from a different source, and the ram is called either single- or double-acting. The raising power is given by the elastic reaction of a confined volume of air, which is compressed by the falling water.

Ram: (A) A large weight for driving piles and the like. (B) A machine for raising water.

Ramp: An inclined plane, as of a floor rising from a lower to a higher level, taking the place of steps. Specifically, a concave connecting sweep in a vertical plane, as on a coping or hand rail, where it turns from a sloping to a horizontal direction or rises from one level to a higher level. The part of a staircase handrail that rises at a steeper angle than normal.

Ramping device: An inclined plane effecting a small level change.

Ranch house: A one-story house found originally in the western United Sates.

Random ashlar: Masonry made of rectangular stones set without continuous joints.

Rapid start fluorescent lamp: A fluorescent lamp designed for operation with a ballast that provides a low-voltage winding for preheating the electrodes and initiating the arc without a starting switch or the application of high voltage.

Rate of rise heat detector: A device that will respond when the temperature rises at a rate exceeding a predetermined amount.

Raw footcandles: Same as footcandles. This term is sometimes used to differentiate between ordinary footcandles and ESI footcandles. (Footcandles or raw footcandles refers only to the quantity of illumination. ESI footcandles refers to task visibility by considering both the quantity and quality of illumination.)

Raw linseed oil: The crude product processed from flaxseed.

Ready-mixed plaster: A calcined gypsum plaster with aggregate added during manufacture.

Reasonable care and skill: See due care.

Reasonable time: A period of time that is in line with the provisions of an agreement or contract or not accompanied by an unreasonable delay.

Receptor: A plumbing fixture that receives the discharge from indirect waste pipes. Constructed and located so that it can be readily cleaned.

Recess: A depression in a surface.

Record drawings: Drawings revised to show significant and final changes made during construction, usually based on marked-up prints, drawings, and other data furnished by the contractors.

Reduced measure: A commercial measure obtained by deducting the allowance from the overall dimensions of a block or slab.

Reduced size vent: Dry vents smaller than those allowed by model plumbing codes.

Reducer: (A) A pipe fitting with inside threads, larger at one end than at the other. (B) A fitting so shaped at one end that it receives a larger pipe size in the direction of flow.

Redwood: A softwood used for paneling and outdoor furniture. It is extremely durable and grown almost exclusively in northern California.

Reed: (A) A type of molding. (B) Part of a carpet weaving loom consisting of thin strips of metal with spaces between them through which warp yarns pass. The motion of the reed pushes fill yarn tightly into the fabric.

Reflectance (reflectance factor): The ratio of reflected light to incident light (light falling on a surface). Generally expressed in percent.

Reflected glare: Glare resulting from specular reflections of high luminances in polished or glossy surfaces in the field of view. It usually is associated with reflections from within a visual task or areas in close proximity to the region being viewed.

Reflecting pool: A water receptacle used for decorative purposes.

Reflecting surface: A surface within a room that reflects sound.

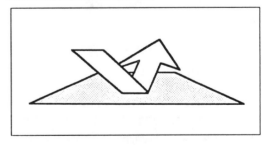

Reflection: Light striking a surface is either absorbed, transmitted, or reflected. Reflected light bounces off the surface, and it can be classified as specular or diffuse reflection. Specular reflection is characterized by light rays that strike and leave a surface at equal angles. Diffuse reflection leaves a surface in all directions.

Reflective insulation: Sheet material with one or both surfaces of comparatively low heat emissivity, such as aluminum foil. When used in building construction, the surfaces face air spaces, reducing the radiation across the air space.

Refraction: When the direction of a ray of light changes because its speed changes as it passes from one medium to another.

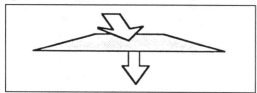

Refractory insulation: See insulation.

Refractory materials: Materials, usually fibers, that do not significantly deform or change chemically at high temperatures. Manufactured in blanket, block, brick, or cement form.

Refrigerant: Something that produces the effect of refrigeration.

Register: (A) A contrivance connected with a duct, arranged either to control the inward passage of warmed or fresh air or to allow foul air to escape. It is usually a pierced screen, behind which rotating or

sliding slats are arranged that are controlled by a handle in front of the screen. (B) Same as meter.

Regular seal trap: See common seal trap.

Reimbursable costs or expenses: Amounts expended because of the project which, in accordance with the terms of the appropriate agreement, are to be reimbursed by the owner.

Reinforced brick masonry: Masonry that has steel inside the brick to reinforce it.

Reinforced concrete: Concrete that has been reinforced by insertion of steel mesh or rods. This increases the tensile strength of the material, which is inherently strong in compression and weak in tension.

Reinforcing cloth or fabric: A woven cloth of glass or resilient fibers used as reinforcement to a mastic vapor/weather barrier.

Reinforcing: Steel rods or metal fabric placed in concrete slabs, beams, or columns to increase their strength.

Reinsulate: To repair insulation to its former condition. (If insulation is to be removed and replaced, it should be so stated.)

Rejection fuse: A current-limiting fuse with high interrupting rating and with unique dimensions or mounting provisions.

244

Rejection of offer: An offer may be rejected by a stated refusal to accept it; counteroffer, which rejects the offer by implications; or conditional acceptance, which is really a counteroffer and thus a rejections by implication.

Relative humidity: The ratio expressed as a percentage of actual water vapor pressure to the saturation water vapor pressure at a given temperature.

Relay: An electromagnetic device operated by changing conditions in an electrical circuit which in turn operates other devices, such switches, in the same or different circuit.

Release of Lien: Instrument executed by person supplying labor, materials, or professional services on a project that releases the mechanic's lien against it. See mechanic's lien.

Relief valve: A safety device that provides automatic protection against excessive temperatures or pressures.

Relief vent: A vent designed to provide air circulation between drainage and vent systems or to act as an auxiliary vent.

Relief: Ornamented prominence of parts of figures above a plane surface.

Relieve: To assist any overloaded member by any construction device. For example, a lintel can be relieved by building over it a discharging or relieving arch to transfer the burden to the beams of iron or steel to receive the imposed weight, or by placing between the lintel and supporting pier a bolster or brace. A pier or section of wall can be relieved by spreading the weight of a girder bearing upon it over a larger surface by interposing a plate of metal or wood. In the case of a girder in wood construction that bears a partition or portion of the frame, a truss with suspension rods can be built in the partition or frame to transfer the weight to the piers or walls. A foundation pier can be eased from the burden by broad levelers of stone or concrete by inverted arches connected with other piers.

Remaining available resources: The difference between the resource available and resource required level in any given project day (time unit).

Remaining duration: The estimated number of work time units needed to complete an activity beyond the data date.

Remodeling: A construction project of revising the existing structure.

Render: (A) In building, to apply plaster directly to brickwork, stonework, tiles, or slate. Render applies especially to the first coat. The application of the final coat is described by the term to set, and an intermediate, when used, by to float. Two-coat work is hence often called render and set, or render set, work; three-coat is known as render, float, and set. (B) To give to a mechanical drawing a more or less complete indication of shades and shadows, whether in ink, color, or other medium.

Renewable element: The field-replaceable element of a renewable fuse. Also referred to as a renewal link.

Renewable fuse: A fuse that can be restored for service by the replacement of its element.

Repousse work: Relief work in thin metal wrought by being beaten with hammers on the reverse side. The art of modeling and decorating the surface of plaques or vessels of gold, silver, copper, or other thin malleable metals by hammering the metal on the underside with special tools to bulge it in ornamental patterns, forming reliefs on the upper side. In fine work the pattern thus raised is modified, dressed, and finished by placing the metal face uppermost upon a yielding bed and beating it back so as more clearly to define the subject and correct its outlines, and by chasing and engraving it.

Required accessible areas: Areas that must be functionally usable and physically accessible by physically disabled people.

Required completion date: The required date of completion assigned to a specific activity or project.

Resident engineer: A person representing the owner's interests at the project site during the construction phase; term frequently used on projects in which a governmental agency is involved.

Residential building: Structure in which families or households live, or sleeping and accessory accommodations are provided, including dwellings, multiple-family dwellings, hotels, motels, dormitories, and lodging houses.

Residual Pressure: Pressure remaining in a system while water is discharged from outlets.

Resiliency: That property of a material which enables it to recover its original thickness after compression.

Resin: A transparent organic substance applied to brecciated or fissured marble for reinforcement.

Resistance (R): A measure of the ability to retard heat flow rather than the ability to transmit heat. R is the numerical reciprocal of U or C, thus R=11/U or 1/C. Thermal resistance R, is used in combination with numerals to designate thermal.

Resistance to acids, caustics, and solvents: The property of a material that resists decomposition by acids, caustics, and solvents to which it may be subjected.

Resistance values: R-11 equals 11 resistance units. The higher the R, the higher the insulating value. All insulation products, regardless of material, can have the equivalent resistance (R) factor, provided the proper insulation thickness based on the materials conductivity (K) is used.

Resistance: (A) The power of any substance, such as building material, to resist forces, such as compression, cross breaking, shear, tension, torsion. (B) In HVAC, thermal conduction reciprocal.

Resonance: The phenomenon that occurs when a periodic force, applied to an elastic body, has a frequency agreeing with the natural rate of vibration of the body. In architectural acoustics, the increased loudness of a note whose vibration frequently agrees with one of the natural rates of vibration of the air contained in the room.

Resorcinol glue: A glue that is high in both wet and dry strength and resistant to high temperatures. It is used for gluing lumber or assembly joints that must withstand severe service conditions.

Resource allocation process: The scheduling of activities in a network with the knowledge of certain constraints imposed on resource availability.

Resource availability date: The calendar date when a resource level becomes available to be allocated to a project activity.

Resource code: The code for a particular skill, material, or equipment type; the code used to identify a given resource type.

Resource description: A short description, including the unit of measure for a given resource code.

Resource histogram or resource plot: A graphic display of the amount of resources required as a function of time on a graph. Individual, summary, incremental, and cumulative resource curve levels can be shown.

Resource Limited Scheduling: A schedule of activities so that a preimposed resource availability level (constant or variable) is not exceeded in any given project time unit.

Resource: Any consumable, except time, required to accomplish an activity.

Respond: A half-pier that carries one end of an arch and is bonded into a wall.

Responsible bidder: See lowest responsible bidder.

Responsible organization: The organization responsible for management of a work package.

Restricted list of bidders: See invited bidders.

Retainage or retained funds: A sum withheld from progress payments to contractors and subcontractors in accordance with the terms of owner-contractor and subcontractor agreements. See retention.

Retainers and deposits: A designer will charge a retainer or flat consulting fee before the job is started. The client will pay a deposit before the work is started and the remaining sum on completion of the work.

Retaining wall: A wall erected at a place where a difference of level occurs in the soil, to retain the higher soil and prevent it from sliding. A wall that supports or retains earth or water.

Retarder: Any material added to gypsum plaster that slows up its natural set.

Retemper: Addition of water to Portland cement plaster after mixing but before setting process has started. Gypsum plaster must not be retempered.

Retrofit: The application of additional insulation over existing insulation, new insulation after old insulation has been removed, or new insulation over existing, previously uninsulated surfaces.

Return air: Air returned from conditioned spaces to an air handling unit.

Return offset: A double offset installed to return the pipe to its original alignment.

Return (recirculating) duct: A duct carrying air from a conditioned space to an air handling unit.

Return: The turn and continuation of a molding, cornice, wall, or projection in an opposite or different direction of the face of a building, or any member. The side of a structure that falls away at right angles from the front.

Reveal: That portion of the jamb of an opening which is visible from the face of the wall back to the frame or other structure which may be placed between the jambs. Thus, the windows of an ordinary brick building usually have 4" reveals because that is the width of each brick jamb visible outside of the window frames. The vertical face of a door or window opening between the face of the interior wall and that of the window or door frame, or the like.

Revent pipe: That part of a vent pipe line which connects directly with an individual waste or group of wastes, underneath or at the back of the fixture, and extends either to the main or branch vent pipe. Also known as individual vent.

Reverberation: The time it takes sound to decay, in seconds. The reflection of sound by the walls whereby it is returned into the room, as distinguished from transmission or absorption. This results in a prolongation of the sound or, if the source continues to act, in cumulative intensity. It is to be carefully distinguished from resonance.

Revision: Change in the network logic, activity denotion, or availability or resources demand that requires network recalculation and redrawing.

RFP: Request for proposal.

Rib, diagonal: In a ribbed vault, one of the two intersecting ribs extending from one corner of the compartment to that diagonally opposite.

Rib, ridge: A longitudinal rib sometimes used at the apex of medieval vaulting.

Rib, wall: That one of the two *formerets* which is closely attached to the exterior wall of the vaulting square in question; therefore, parallel with and opposite the other which is a part of the nave arch or the arch leading into some other, vaulted compartment.

Rib lath: See metal lath.

Rib: A molding on an arched or flat ceiling. Specifically and more properly, in medieval vaulting, an arch, generally molded, forming part of the skeleton upon which rest the intermediate concave surfaces that constitute the shell or closure of the vault.

Ribbon (girt): Normally a 1" x 4" board let into the studs horizontally to support ceiling or second-floor joists.

Ribbon-back chair: A rococo style chair back that has a carved splat resembling ribbons and bows.

Ribbon: (A) A narrow belt of decoration in any material or in color alone. (B) In carpentry, a thin strip of bent wood, such as is used in shaping convex or concave surfaces. In ship carpentry, where it is more frequently used, it is called rib band.

(C) A thin, grooved strip of lead used in glazing stained glass windows, or in setting the quarrels or panes in leaded sashes. (D) In the balloon frame construction of the United States, a light girt or similar piece secured to the faces of the studs, forming a continuous tie around the building and supporting the ends of the beams.

Ridge, ridge-piece: A longitudinal, horizontal timber at the apex of a roof supporting the rafter ends.

Ridge board: The board placed on edge at the ridge of the roof into which the upper ends of the rafters are fastened.

Ridge: The horizontal line at the junction of the top edges of two sloping roof surfaces.

Rights and remedies: Something that is legally fair and just or to which a person is entitled and the method by which the court will enforce the legal demand or claim for damages or injury.

Rigid wrap-around insulation: Segments of insulation material that have been adhered to a facing, gives rigid insulation materials flexibility of application.

Rigidity: That property of a material which opposes any tendency for it to bend (flex) under load.

Rim: An unobstructed open edge of a fixture.

Rimmers: Bits for enlarging holes.

Ring, annual growth: The growth layer put on in a growth year.

Rise: (A) The vertical distance between two consecutive treads in a stair; sometimes, the entire height of a flight of stairs from landing to landing. (B) The vertical height of the curved part of an arch; that is, the distance measured vertically from the springing line to the highest point of the curved intrados.

Riser, open: The space between two adjoining treads in a stair when such space is not filled with a solid riser.

Riser closet: A location where riser cables terminate for further distribution through the floor. May also serve as an apparatus closet or satellite closet, depending upon the size of the building and the telephone facilities involved.

Riser: (A) The upright of one step, whether the step is in one piece as a block of stone or built up. In the former case, the riser is the surface alone. In the latter case, the riser is the board, plate of cast iron, or similar thin piece that is set upright between two treads. (B) By extension, the same as rise. A stair in which the treads are separate planks, slabs or slate, plates or iron, or the like, is sometimes built without risers. In this case, an incorrect extension of the term is used, and such a stair is said to have open risers. (C) A water supply pipe that extends vertically one full story or more to convey water to branches or fixtures. A

vertical pipe used to carry water for fire protection to elevations above or below grade as a standpipe riser, sprinkler riser, etc.

Riveting: Rivet heads that are placed on either side of a hole by a hot rivet.

Rivets: Soft metal bolts that fasten a metal plate to either another metal plate or a piece of wood.

Rock gun: A device for throwing aggregate onto a soft bedding coat in applying marblecrete.

Rock wool: See mineral wool.

Rocklath: A plastering base made from perforated gypsum board.

Rod, picture: A rod serving the same purpose as a picture molding

Rod: A strip of wood about 2" square, such as could be cut out of a plank, used by carpenters for setting out their work. The strip is marked with feet and half feet, and sometimes with inches and half inches for a part of its length. It is generally cut 10' long and is then called ten-foot rod.

Rodding: Cement reinforcement put into structurally unsound marble.

Roll roofing: Roofing material composed of fiber and saturated with asphalt that is supplied in 36" wide rolls with 108 square feet of material. Weights are generally 45 - 90 pounds per roll.

Roll: (A) A small, nearly cylindrical member; especially a rounded strip of wood fastened to and continuous with a ridge or hip of a roof; a false ridge pole. (B) In a roof of lead or other metal, one of a series of rounded strips of wood secured at regular intervals along the slope, extending from the ridge to the eaves, over which the ends of the roofing plates are turned and lapped, preventing the crawling of the metal by alternate expansion and contraction. (C) A rounded piece made by the metal sheathing alone or with the support of a wooden batten.

Romex: A cable comprised of flexible plastic sheathing that contains two or more insulated wires for carrying electricity.

Roof, bowstring: A roof constructed with curved timber truss and horizontal tie beams connected by diagonal wood latices.

Roof, common rafter: A roof in which pairs of rafters are not connected by a collar beam.

Roof, compass: See roof, cradle.

Roof, coupled: A ridged or double pitched roof of the simplest construction, often without tie beam or collar beam, depending upon the stiffness of the walls for its permanence and, therefore, of small span.

Roof, coupled rafter: A roof in which the rafters are connected by collar beams.

Roof, curb: One in which the slope is broken on two or four sides; so called because a horizontal curb is built at the plane where the slope changes.

Roof, double-framed: A roof constructed with longitudinal members such as purlins.

Roof, flat: (A) One whose surface is horizontal or with no perceptible slope. The mud, earth, or cement roofs of tropical countries and the roofs of brick or terra cotta supported by iron beams and covered with water-tight material characteristic of modern fireproof buildings are examples. (B) A roof having a slope so slight that one can walk or sit upon it as upon a floor. Of this kind are the metal-covered roofs of Europe and America in which the slope is often 1\2" to a foot or 1 in 24". The plates of metal in these cases must be soldered together with care.

Roof, French: A curb roof with sides set so steep they sometimes approach verticality; the top above the curb may be nearly flat or have a visible slope, though much less steep than the lower slope. The term is of U. S. origin and applies especially to a form of roof that beginning about 1865, became very common all over the country.

Roof, gable; gabled: A ridge roof that terminates at each end in a gable, as distinguished from a hipped roof. A gambrel roof is a form of gable roof.

Roof, gambrel: A curb roof with only the two opposite sides sloping; it is therefore a gabled curb roof.

Roof, helm: A roof with four inclined faces joined at the top, with a gable at each foot.

Roof, hip; hipped: Roof having hips by which the projecting angles between two adjacent slopes are squared. Thus, a pyramidal roof is one that has four hips. In some cases a roof may have more hips than four, which often alternates with valleys.

Roof, homogeneous: One in which the same mass of material furnished the outer pitch and the surface exposed within; that is, a roof forming a solid shell either of compact masonry, as often in Byzantine art, or slabs of stone, as in Syria and in a few churches of Europe.

Roof, hyperbolic paraboloid: A roof structure in the shape of a geometrical form made of double curved shell generated by straight lines.

Roof, jerkin head: A ridge roof in which the ridge is shorter than the eaves and has two gables, which are truncated about half-way up so that the roof is hipped above. It may be otherwise explained as a hipped roof, of which the hips starting from the ridge are too short to reach the eaves, so that the roof below becomes a gabled roof of which the gables are truncated.

Roof, lean-to: One with a single slope; as where the aisle of a church is usually roofed with a single slope from the wall of the clerestory outward.

Roof, M: One in which two ridges parallel or nearly so are separated by a receding or dropping valley, gutter, or the like. This device was used to diminish the height of the roof, as in supposed necessities of the architectural style, and sometimes resulting from the building of an addition without disturbing the earlier roof.

Roof, mansard: A curbed roof with dormer windows of some size; that is, a roof that will best provide for habitable rooms within it. This is the roof common in neoclassic and modern *chateaux* and public buildings in France. The deck or upper slope is usually small in proportion to the lower slopes, whereas in the French roof the reverse may be the case.

Roof, pavilion: A roof hipped on all sides giving it pyramidal or nearly pyramidal form.

Roof, penthouse: A roof with one pitch, like that of a shed or of the aisle of a church in the ordinary distribution.

Roof, pitched: A sloped roof with gable ends.

Roof, pyramidal: One in the form of a pyramid or, by extension, a hipped roof in which the ridge is relatively short so that the sloping sides end nearly in a point.

Roof, ridge; ridged: A double pitched roof, the two slopes of which meet at a horizontal ridge.

Roof, saddleback: A gable roof in some peculiar position, as when a tower is roofed in this way instead of terminating in a flat terrace.

Roof, shed: Same as penthouse roof.

Roof, single-framed: A roof framed without trusses. The opposite rafters are tied together by the upper floor frame or boards nailed across horizontally to serve as ties or collars.

Roof, slab slate: A roof covered with slabs or flags of slate, as in cottages built in the neighborhood of slate quarries.

Roof, span: A roof composed of two equal slopes, as a nave roof, rather than one slope, as an aisle roof or penthouse roof.

Roof, terrace: A flat roof, especially when the roofing is of masonry and the surface allows the roof to be used for walking.

Roof, trough: Same as M roof.

Roof, truss: A roof whose rafters are supported on a truss or series of trusses by purlins.

Roof, valley: Roof that covers a building so arranged with projecting wings or pavilions, nearly on the same level as the main roof, that there are valleys at the junction of the two parts of the roof. The term is hardly applied to roofs that have merely the valleys of dormers and small gables.

Roof covering: The closure laid upon a roof frame, including the wood sheathing or boarding and the outside protection by metal, slate, tiles, shingles, painted canvas, tarred paper, thatch, any composition of tar, bitumen, asphaltum, etc., with gravel, or any other form of protection against the weather. In the few cases of incombustible construction, the slates or tiles are tied by lead wire to iron laths; or, the roof being filled up with brick, terra cotta, or cement blocks, large sheets of copper, zinc, or lead may be nailed upon it, lapping over one another like slates, and left free at the lower end to allow for expansion and contraction. In flat roofs, large slaps of slate or stone are bedded in cement. In the more usual cases, roofs of any pitch may be covered with metal, which is nearly always of tin plates in the United States, though term or copper plates are used and, much more rarely, zinc (France) or lead, (Great Britain). The term leads, applied in England to a nearly flat roof that may be used as a floor, is unknown in the United States, where such a roof would be covered with tin plates or tar and gravel. Steep roofs alone may be covered with tiles, slate, or shingles, laid in the usual way, without any filling or cementing of the joints; rain and snow may beat in through the crevices to a slight degree without serious damage.

Roof drain: A drain installed to remove water collecting on the surface of a roof and discharge it into the leader (downspout).

Roof jacket or flange: A flange or jacket installed on vent stack roof terminals and stack vents to prevent rainwater from entering into the building around the vent pipe.

Roof sheathing: The boards or sheet material fastened to the roof rafters on which the shingle or other roof covering is laid.

Roof: That part of the closure of a building which covers it in from the sky. Upon this part of a building depends in large measure the character of its design as a work of architecture. Roofs are distinguished in two ways. First, by their form and method of construction: the flat roof, characteristic of dry, tropical countries and modern commercial buildings in the United States, and the sloping roof, including gables, hipped, penthouse, mansard, and gambrel roofs with their varieties. Second, by the character of their covering, thatched, shingled, battened, slated, tiled, metal-covered, tarred, asphalted, gravelled, etc. (A) In carpentry, the timber framework that supports the external surface. In sloping roofs this consists usually of a series of pairs of opposite rafters or couples, of which the lower ends are tied together to prevent spreading. Where the span is too great for such simple construction and there are no intermediate upright supports, the frame-

work is a series of rafters supported by longitudinal horizontal purlins, which are generally carried on a system of transverse timber frames or trusses spaced 8' - 20' apart.

Room cavity ratio (RCR): A numerical relationship of the vertical distance between work plane height and luminaire mounting height to room width and length. It is used with the zonal cavity method of calculating average illumination levels.

Room: An enclosure or division of a house or other structure, separated from other divisions by partitions. An apartment, a chamber; as a chamber in a house, a stateroom in a ship or railroad car, a harness room in a stable.

Rough cast, hard cast: Plaster made with strong lime mortar and sand mixed with clean gravel until it resembles a concrete, used for the exterior faces of rough masonry walls, as of small country houses. In different parts of Great Britain and the United States different processes are used. Sometimes the mortar is very hot when the gravel is mixed with it. The surface is often colored by a wash while still wet.

Rough material: Rough blocks from quarries; specifically, products without surface finishing.

Rough service lamps: Incandescent lamps designed with extra filament supports to withstand bumps, shocks, and vibrations with some loss in lumen output.

Roughing-in: (A) Any coarse, mechanical process preparatory to finished work, as the rough coat of mortar forming a foundation for one or more coats of fine plaster, or, in a scheme of decoration, the necessary mechanical groundwork of colors or modeling. (B) In plumbing, the establishment of the system of pipes for supply and waste, done while the house is prepared for plastering and before the pipes are connected with the fixtures.

Round edge: A rounded, paper-bound edge on gypsum board, commonly used for gypsum lath.

Router, electric: A power woodworking tool used to plough, gouge, or rout material. They can be hand-held or mounted on a router bench or stand. Also used for edging and other high-speed and fine finishing processes.

Router, groove: A router used for increasing the depth and leveling the bottom of grooves formed by some other tool. It consists of a hardwood block about 5" x 3" x 3.5" wide (the grain running the width) with a wedge. Plough irons are used for cutters. The American variety is metal. It is provided with two cutters only, 1/4" and 1/2". It is easier to adjust than the English form.

Router, quirk: A tool for sinking narrow grooves in curved surfaces, chiefly in connection with moldings. It has three knives or cutters of different thicknesses, which are adjustable in both directions.

Router bits: Cutting bits used in routers. They come in many shapes for gouging, molding, and edging material.

Routine: Programs or program modules that provide edit or maintenance functions to files.

Routing: The process of cutting out material with a router.

Rubber-emulsion paint: Paint that consists of rubber or synthetic rubber dispersed in fine droplets in water.

Rubble masonry: Rough, irregular courses of building stones.

Run: A length of straight or nearly straight piping.

Running trap: A trap in which the inlet and outlet are in a straight horizontal line and the water way is depressed to below the bottom of both.

Rust spot: Tiny, natural stain of iron hydroxide.

Rustication: (A) Masonry blocks with deep separation joints used to give texture. Often left in rough state. (B) The beveling or rabbeting of the edges of a veneer slab to make the joints conspicuous.

S

S clip: A support device for banding or jacketing.

S curve: (A) A chart showing when and how much money must be paid by the owner to the contractor for the anticipated job progress on the contractor's requisitions. The base data from this is taken from the C.P.M. chart which shows anticipated rates of progress on the job and is translated into the dollars needed by the owner to pay for job progress. (A) A financial tool showing the cash flow to the job.

S-trap: An S-shaped, water seal trap.

S-trap (3/4): A trap shaped like three-fourths of the letter s.

Sabin: An audible vibration.

Saddle bars: Small iron bars into which leaded glazed panes are fastened. Used in casement glazing.

Saddle tie: A specific method of wrapping hanger wire around main runners; also of wrapping tie wire around the juncture of main runner and cross furring.

Saddle: (A) The cap of a doorsill or the bottom piece of a door frame forming a slightly raised ridge upon which the door, when shut, fits rather closely. The object is to give the underside of the door such height above the floor as to prevent its striking or binding when thrown open. Saddles are made of wood, cast-iron, brass,

marble, etc. (B) Anything used to interpose a vertical support and the foundation or the load upon the support; especially in temporary work, as in shoring.

Safing: A noncombustible product used at the perimeter of floors and around other penetrations as a fire barrier.

Samples: Physical examples furnished by the contractor for the architect's review and approval, which illustrate materials, equipment, or workmanship, and establish standards by which the work will be judged.

Sand filter: A water treatment device for removing solid or colloidal material with sand as the filter media.

Sand float finish: Lime mixed with sand, resulting in a textured finish.

Sand: Small particles of stone, formed sometimes by the trituration of stones or rocks when carried by water, sometimes by the decomposition of the cementing substance of crystalline rocks. Sand for building purposes is generally found in the beds of streams, pits in the earth, and on the seashore. It should be silicious, gritty, not too fine, and clean and free from loam. Sand formed by the trituration of finely grained or amorphous rocks, or really fine pebbles may be used for mortar, if of hard material, and no other can be obtained. Silicious material is preferred.

Sanded, cross: Sanded across, rather than parallel to, the grain of a wood surface.

Sanded, machine: Sanded by drum or equivalent sander to remove knife or machine marks. Handling marks or grain raising due to moisture shall not be considered a defect.

Sanded, smoothly: Sanded sufficiently smooth so that sander marks will be concealed by painter's applied finish.

Sanitary drainage pipe: Pipes to remove the waste water and waterborne wastes from plumbing fixtures.

Sanitary sewer: The conduit or pipe carrying sanitary sewage. It may include storm water and the infiltration of ground water.

Sapwood: The outer zone of wood, next to the bark. In the living tree it contains some living cells (the heartwood contains none), as well as dead and dying cells. In most species, it is lighter colored than the heartwood. In all species, it lacks decay resistance.

Sash balance: A device, usually operated by a spring or tensioned weatherstripping, designed to counterbalance a double-hung window sash.

Sash: A single assembly of stiles and rails into a frame for holding glass, with or without dividing.

Satinwood: A hardwood light in color and used on fine furniture. It is very smooth and found in southern Asia.

Satter-dash: A cement mixture that hardens to provide a coat of plaster. Also a finish produced by throwing the mixture of cement, sand, and mortar.

Saturated felt: A felt impregnated with tar or asphalt.

Sauna: A steam bath created by pouring hot water over hot rocks.

Saw, band: A power woodworking or metalworking saw with a continuous blade traveling over two or more wheels. Used for cutting curving lines or contours. Also used in large scale for ripping lumber.

Saw, bow: A saw used in cutting quicker sweeps than can be accomplished by a compass saw. It consists of a beechwood frame, with a ribbon saw secured to two revolving handles passing through its lower ends. A light stretcher across its middle keeps the arms of the frame apart, and the saw-blade is sprung tight by twisting a short bar in the loop of a cord wound around the upper end of the frame. The stretcher acts as a fulcrum and prevents the winding bar from flying back. The handles should work rather stiffly in the arms. Better are furnished with brass bushes and set screws, to prevent the accidental turning of the frame. The blade is capable of complete a revolution as the cut requires, but care must be taken that the whole length of the blade is in one plane (not twisted), or the saw will run from its course and be liable to snap. The saw blades of these vary in length from 6" to 24" and in width from 1/8" to 1/2". The larger frames have wood sleeves.

Saw, chain: A gasoline or electric powered saw used for rough sawing. Its name derives from the chain containing teeth that revolve on a track or guidebar.

Saw, circular: A power woodworking saw with a circular blade. It is usually hand held and serves many of the crosscutting and ripping functions formerly required of the carpenter's hand saw.

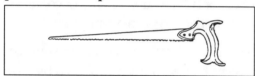

Saw, compass: A thin, pointed saw with 12 teeth to the inch, shaped like rip-saw teeth. It is used for cutting to curved lines.

Saw, cross-cut: A class of saws that attack the wood in the direction of its greatest resistance. Its teeth are small and spaced closely, and the angle of the cutting edge is more acute than in ripping saws. The thinner a saw blade is, the better, if it possesses sufficient stiffness to withstand the necessary thrust without bending. If the blade is ground properly-that is, thinner at the back edge than at the teeth-little or no set will be required in cutting dry material; likewise, circular saws are ground thinner at the periphery than at the center. In cutting wet material, considerable set is sometimes necessary, because the fibers, being softened

by the water, are dragged out rather than cut, and the ragged ends spring up and bind the saw blade so firmly that it cannot be driven through them.

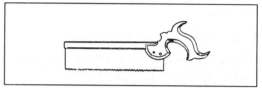

Saw, dovetail: A smaller back saw, used for fine and light cutting either way of the grain. It is much used for dovetails in small work, hence its name. The side of the blade varies from 1.5" to 2.25" wide, by 7" to 10" long, with 15 teeth per inch. It has peg teeth and an open handle.

Saw, hack: A fine-toothed metal cutting saw. It has an adjustable frame and handle that tautly hold replaceable blades. They range in size from 8" to 12" in length and have 14 to 32 teeth per inch.

Saw, hand: A cross-cutting saw with a blade from 20" to 26" long. The teeth are spaced 6.5 to the inch and 1/8" deep. The angle of the cutting face with line of the points is 75°. This is the saw generally used for cross-cutting in conversion. For finer work on the bench, a panel saw is used.

Saw, jig: A power woodworking tool with a reciprocating thin blade suspended in a frame. It is used to cut fine, curved, and thin material. Smaller version of a fret saw.

Saw, keyhole: A small saw from 9" to 12" long, tapering in width from 3/8" to 1/8". It is fixed in the handle by two set screws in the brass ferrule, which is slotted to receive the heel of the saw in such a manner that it will not pass down into the pad, but when out of use, the blade may be slipped into the handle, point first, as indicated by the dotted lines. This saw is used for cutting, keyholes, and starting interior cuts for the larger saws after a hole has been bored for its insertion.

Saw, panel: A cross-cutting saw that is smaller and lighter than a Hand saw. It has teeth spaced from 8 to 10 to the inch. The length of the blade is 16" to 24".

Saw, radial or Radial arm: A bench or shop saw with a movable arm holding a circular saw. The blade can be tilted to different and compound angles. It is used for cross-cutting, ripping, ploughing, and other machining functions.

Saw, reciprocating: A handheld power woodworking tool with a reciprocating thin blade clamped on one end into the chuch of the saw. It is used to cut fine, curved, and thin material. Similar in function to the saber saw but for larger, rougher work.

Saw, ripping: A class of saws whose teeth are spaced widely apart with considerable depth or throat; the cutting edges are very obtuse, with little spread or set. These saws are used parallel to the fibers, and act by scraping or tearing a strip out equal to the thickness or set of the teeth; the sides of the fibers are sheared off at the same time. The particle of wood removed by each tooth in a longitudinal direction is long and if the teeth were not widely spaced and relatively deep the spaces between them would quickly get packed up with the shreds, and the teeth would cease to cut. In machine ripping-saws, where the material is fed rapidly to the saw, a large throat or gullet has to be made at the root of each tooth to receive the sawdust while the saw is passing through the material.

Saw, saber: A handheld power woodworking tool with a reciprocating thin blade clamped on one end into the chuch of the saw. It is used to cut fine, curved, and thin material. Similar in function to the fret saw or keyhole saw.

Saw, tenon: Also called a back saw, which is used for cross-cutting of a finer grade than the panel saw. One of its chief uses is the cutting of shoulders to tenons, and it would be more accurately named a shoulder saw, because its teeth are too fine for the dipping down required for tenoning.

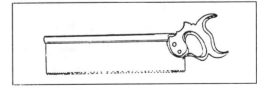

To obtain fineness of cut, the blade has to be made so thin that it is necessary to stiffen it with a solid back or bar of iron or brass, which is pinched tightly on the tip edge. The blade is about 3.5" wide, from 12" to 18" long. Saws more than 14" long are called sash saws. The teeth average 12 to the inch and should be of equilateral triangle shape. These are sometimes called peg teeth.

Saw arbor: Shaft on which a circular saw is mounted.

Saw blade: Flat metal part of the saw with cutting teeth.

Saw kerf: A shallow groove or cut made by a saw blade.

Saw nest: A set of saw blades used with a common interchangeable handle.

Saw points: The number of points per inch. A crosscut saw usually has 7, 8, or 9 points per inch; a ripsaw has 6 or 7; a hacksaws has 14 to 32 points per inch.

Saw set: Setting is the bending of each tooth (or group of teeth) alternately to the right and left of the blade, thus causing the teeth to cut a path slightly wider than the thickness of the blade, allowing it to pass through the material with less friction. A saw with much set is more difficult to keep in line, however, than one with less, as the former drifts from side to side of the cut.

Saw set: The angle of saw teeth. The tool used to set the angle of saw teeth.

Saw teeth: The points on a saw that perform the cutting.

Saw-finished slab: A slab with an exposed face that has not been finished after sawing (as by polishing or bush hammering).

Sawbuck: A sawhorse.

Sawhorse: A portable support frame to hold material being sawed or fitted. Usually used in pairs.

Sawing: Cutting blocks with a frame saw.

Scab: A short piece of lumber used to give support, usually temporary.

Scaffold: A temporary framework put together with nails or ropes to afford a footing for erecting the walls of a building or access to ceilings and other parts that cannot be reached from the floors.

Scaffold, French: (A) A double row of poles or squared timbers is set up along the whole frontage to be built. It is stiffened by X-bracing. Continuous girts are lashed or bolted to the uprights and support cross sleepers, on which planks are placed at convenient levels. A species of tower with a pulley hoists material, which is trundled over the scaffold to its destined position. (B) A term applied in England to scaffolds built of squared timbers framed together by bolts, collars, fish-joints, etc., which can be taken down and re-erected without injury; Also called jenny scaffold.

Scagliola: An imitation marble. Scagliola is usually precast, using Keene's cement.

Scale: (A) A straight line divided into feet and inches, meters and centimeters, or the like, according to a stated proportion to reality, as one forty-eighth (4' to 1"), one one-thousandth, etc. Drawings of all kinds when made by mathematical instruments are made to scale; the scale may be laid down on the drawing or may be on a separate piece of paper or wood (see definition B). (B) A rule, generally of metal, plastic, or wood, marked with one or several scales, to facilitate the making of drawings and diagrams to any convenient scale. (C) In architectural drawings, the size of the drawings as compared with the actual size of the object delineated, as one-quarter of an inch to the foot. (D) In architectural design, the proportions of a building or its parts, with reference to a definite module or unit of measurement. (E) A system of proportions to measure the size of a piece of furniture relative to the sizes of the other pieces of furniture in the room.

Scarf: The oblique joint that unites the ends of two pieces of timber. The long ends usually cut with projections and recesses that fit one another, and these are sometimes forced together and tightened by keys or wedges and secured by iron straps and bolts. Also, the part cut away and wasted from each timber in shaping it to form this joint.

Schedule of values: A statement furnished by the contractor to the architect reflecting the portions of the contract sum allotted for the various parts of the work, used as the basis for reviewing the contractor's applications for progress payments.

Schedule: The plan for completion of a project based on a logical arrangement of activities.

Scheduled completion date (Ts): A date assigned for completion of an activity or accomplishment of an event to meet specified schedule requirements.

Scheduled event time: In PERT, an arbitrary schedule time that can be introduced at any event but is usually only used at a certain milestone or the last event.

Scheduling: The assignment of early/late start and early/late finish to all or a group of activities that belong to a project.

Schematic design phase: The first phase of a construction project in which the architect consults with the owner to ascertain the requirements of the project and prepares schematic design studies for approval by the owner. The architect also submits a statement of probable construction cost.

Schematic: A plan, diagram, or arrangement.

Scissor braces: A pair of braces that cross diagonally between pairs of rafters.

Scope bidding: Bidding based on a description of the general scope of a project in terms of architectural design, dimensions, major parts, and the type of structural, mechanical, and electrical systems. The contractor is required to furnish all items required for the proper execution and completion of the work to accomplish the intent described, and the decision of the architect as to the work included under the scope document is final and binding. See performance specifications.

Scope criteria: General descriptions of performance requirements used to define the scope of the project when scope bidding is practiced. See performance specifications.

Scope document: Any document among the bidding or contracting documents setting forth the intent that the contract documents indicate only the general scope of the project with performance criteria, and that the contractor shall be required to perform all work and furnish all materials necessary to accomplish construction to the general scope standards to the satisfaction of the architect.

Scope: (A) The extent or intention of the construction activity. Thus, change orders issued under a construction contract must be within the scope of the contract. (B) The portions of the plans, specifications, and addenda on which a subcontractor has based its bid.

Scorched finish: A means of surface processing suitable for igneous and silicious rocks, achieved by heating the rock crystals with an acetylene blowtorch. Extreme temperature changes cause a cratering of the stone, conferring a distinctive appearance.

Scoring: Grooving, usually horizontal, of Portland cement plaster scratch coat to provide mechanical bond for the brown coat. Also a decorative grooving of the finish coat.

Scratch coat: First coat of plaster in three-coat plastering work.

Scratching: The roughening of the first coat of plaster, when fresh, by scratching or scoring its surface with a point so that the next coat may adhere to it more firmly. Also called scoring.

Screed: (A) A narrow strip of plastering brought to a true surface and edge, or a strip or bar of wood, to guide workers in plastering the adjoining section of the wall surface. (B) A layer of mortar applied to concrete for the purpose of laying tiles. (C) Long narrow strips of mortar applied horizontally or perpendicularly along a wall or ceiling surface and faced out straight and true to serve as guides for plastering the intervals between them.

Screen: Any structure of any material having no essential support function and serving merely to separate, protect, seclude, or conceal. In church architecture, specifically, a decorated pattern of wood, metal, or stone, closed or open, that separates a chapel from the church, an aisle from the nave or choir, the chancel from the nave, etc.

Screw-drivers: Tools designed to drive in or extract screws. They can be flat with slanted sides (standard) or with straight sides (cabinet), phillips (with an X-shaped tip) and other shapes. They come in many sizes and styles.

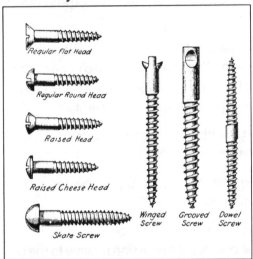

Regular Flat Head
Regular Round Head
Raised Head
Raised Cheese Head
Skate Screw
Winged Screw
Grooved Screw
Dowel Screw

Screw: A solid cylinder having a ridge wound around it evenly in a spiral direction, though sometimes the piece has rather the look of a thread being cut into the solid cylinder. In building, this is used in the form of a bolt and in the form of a wood screw. A wood screw or screw replaces a nail and is driven by a screwdriver, for which purpose it has a slot in the head, which may be flat or rounded. Gimlet

screws are wood screws that have a sharp pointed end so that they can be driven, at least into a softwood, without the preparatory boring of a hole.

Screwable type: Studs fabricated from not lighter than 26 gauge metal with knurled flanges to facilitate easier penetration of self-tapping screws or divergent point staples.

Scribe cutting: Cutting the exact irregularities in one carpet edge to fit the contours of another carpet edge.

Scribe: To mark with an incised line, as by an awl; hence, to fit one piece to another of irregular or uneven form, as a plain piece against a molded piece, or as in shaping the lower edge of a baseboard to fit the irregularities of the floor.

Scribing: Method of transferring the exact irregularities of a wall, floor, or other surface onto a piece of carpet or other material by a tracing technique.

Seal: (A) A device usually consisting of a wafer or an impression upon wax or paper, that is used in the execution of a formal legal document such as a deed or contract. The statute of limitations applicable to a contract under seal is ordinarily substantially longer than to a contract not under a seal. (B) An embossing device or stamp used by a design professional on his drawings and specifications as evidence of registration in the state where the work is to be performed. (C) To make water tight.

Sealer: A paint or varnish used to prevent excessive absorption of finish coats by a substratum; also used to prevent bleeding or bonding of chalked masonry surface when painting.

Sealing: The securing of anchors into a stone component. In open-jointed installations, it is done with a compatible filler or adhesive; in closed-joint installations (as for flooring), with cement.

Seasoning: Removing moisture from green wood to improve its serviceability.

Secondary cut: A cut made with the grain that is not as easy as a smooth cut.

Section (drawing): A drawing of a surface revealed by an imaginary plane cut through the project, or portion thereof, in such a manner as to show the composition of the surface as it would appear if the part intervening between the cut plane and the eye of the observer were removed.

Section (of specification): A subdivision of a division of the specifications which should cover the work of no more than one trade.

Section: (A) The surface or portion obtained by a cut made through a structure or any part of one, to reveal its structure and interior detail when the part intervening between the cut and the eye of the observer

is removed. (B) The delineation of such a section. In general scale drawings, sections usually represent cuts made through a structure on vertical planes, which are plans.

Securely attached: Attached by nails, screws, or a groove or plow joint securely glued, forming a rigid assembly.

Securements (insulation): Any device, wire, strap, or adhesive used to fasten insulation into its service position and hold it there.

Seepage pit: A lined excavation in the ground that receives the discharge of a septic tank and permits the septic tank effluent to seep through its bottom and sides.

Segment: Section of a circle smaller than a semicircle.

Segmental: A curved member less than a full circle.

Selected bidder: The bidder selected by the owner for discussion relative to the possible award of the construction contract.

Selected list of bidders: See invited bidders.

Selective calling: The ability of a transmitting station to select which of several stations on the same line is to receive a message.

Selectivity: A main fuse and a branch fuse are selective if the branch fuse will clear all potential overcurrent conditions before the main fuse opens. Selectivity is desirable because it limits outage to the portion of the circuit that has been overloaded or faulted.

Self-ballasted mercury lamps: Any mercury lamp of which the current-limiting device is an integral part.

Self-edge: Application to the edge of plywood or particleboard of a plastic laminate of the same pattern as the face surface.

Self-extinguishing: That property of a material which enables it to stop its own ignition after external ignition sources are removed.

Self-syphonage: The loss of seal caused by the discharge of the fixture to which the trap is connected.

Semiconductor fuse: An extremely fast-acting fuse intended for the protection of power semiconductors. Sometimes referred to as a rectifier fuse.

Semigloss paint or enamel: A paint or enamel made with a slight insufficiency of nonvolatile vehicle so that its coating, when dry, has some luster but is not very glossy.

Semigloss: Surface glossiness of a paint or finish that falls between eggshell and a high or full gloss.

Separate contract: One of the prime contracts on a construction project.

Septic tank: A watertight receptacle that receives the discharge of a drainage system, and is designed and constructed to separate solids from the liquid and digest organic matter through a period of detention.

Service entrance: Point at which power utility wires enter a building.

Service fitting: A box mounted on the finished floor that houses the connecting device for communication and power circuits.

Service sink: A deep basin sink that accommodates a scrub pail. A slop sink.

Set: The change in mortar from a plastic, workable state to a solid, rigid state.

Setting space: The space between the back-up wall and the marble.

Setting time: The elapsed time required for a gypsum plaster to attain a specified hardness and strength after mixing with water.

Sewage ejector: A mechanical device or pump for lifting sewage.

Sewage: Any liquid waste containing animal, vegetable, or chemical wastes in suspension or solution.

Sewer: A conduit of brickwork, or a vitrified cement or iron pipe channel, intended for the removal of the liquid or semiliquid wastes from habitations, including in some cases rain waste. Street sewers are laid in public streets and intended for all the houses and lots composing a city block or blocks, and house sewers, the lateral branches for each building.

Sgraffito: A procedure for decorative purposes generally consisting of two or more layers of differently colored plaster. While still soft, part of the top layer is removed by scratching, exposing part of the base or underlying layer.

Shaft: (A) An upright object, high and comparatively small in horizontal dimensions. The term is applied to a building, as when a tower is said to be a plain shaft; to an architectural member, as when a high building is said to present a more elaborate basement and a less adorned shaft above; or to a single stone, an obelisk, menhir, cathstone, or the like.

Shake: (A) A separation of the wood, normally between growth rings. (B) A thick hand-split shingle, resawed to form two shakes; usually edge-grained.

Shapeless block: A rough block that has not been cut into a regular geometric shape.

Shear (strengths, values): The resistance of an assembly to lateral movement.

Shear strength: The property of a material that indicates its ability to resist cleavage.

Shearing weight: Breaking weight or force that acts by shearing; i.e., by pushing one portion of a member or material past the adjoining part, as by a pair of shears.

Shearing: Carpet manufacturing process for producing a smooth carpet face, removing fuzz, or creating random sheared textures. Carpet shears have many steel blades mounted on rotating cylinders which cut fibers on carpet surfaces in a manner analogous to a lawn mower cutting grass. Depth of shearing may be indicated by a modifier word, e.g., defuzz and tipshear suggest a shallow cut of the shear, whereas a full shear would imply a deep cut as used for producing mirror-finished plush.

Sheathing board: A board prepared for sheathing, often with tongue and groove for jointing.

Sheathing paper: A coarse paper specially prepared in various grades and laid with a lap under clapboards, shingles, slates, etc., to exclude weather, or between the upper and under flooring, for deafening. When made with asbestos or with magnesocalcite it is used for fireproofing.

Sheathing: A covering of boards, plywood or paneling, etc., applied to the exterior rafters, joists, or studs to strengthen the structure. In carpentry, a covering or lining to conceal a rough surface or to cover a timber frame. In general, any material, such as tin, copper, slate, tiles, etc., prepared for application to a structure as covering.

Sheet lath: See metal lath.

Sheet metal work: All components of a house employing sheet metal, such as flashing, gutters, and downspouts.

Sheetrock: Gypsum plasterboard placed between paper.

Shelf life: The period of time during which a packaged adhesive, coating, or sealant can be stored under specified temperature conditions and remain suitable for use.

Shellac: A wood finisher and resin used in varnish. A transparent coating made by dissolving lac, a resinous secretion of the lac bug (a scale insect that thrives in tropical countries, especially India), in alcohol.

Shielding: An arrangement of light-controlling material to prevent direct view of the light source. Method of protecting adjacent work by positioning temporary protective sheets of rigid material; particularly used for machine applications.

Shim: To build up low areas; to level or adjust height.

Shingle: (A) Originally, a thin parallelogram of wood (in the United States generally 6" x 18" x 24" inches), split and shaved (more recently sawn), thicker at one end than the other; used for covering sides or roofs of houses. About 4" or 5" of its length is exposed. Shingles are now sometimes made of metal in the form of tiles. Roof covering of asphalt, asbestos, wood, tile, slate, or other material cut to stock lengths, widths, and thicknesses. (B) Various kinds of shingles, such as wood shingles or shakes and nonwood shingles, that are used over sheathing for exterior sidewall covering of a structure.

Shiplap: A joint that overlaps and joins two boards.

Shoe: A piece of stone, timber, or, more commonly, iron, shaped to receive the lower end of any member, either to protect the end, as in the case of a pile that is to be driven into hard ground, or to secure the member at its junction with another. In this case, commonly adapted to prevent the penetration or rupture of one member by the other, as in the case of a plate under the end of a post or under the nut of a tie rod. A formed metal section used in attaching metal studs to floor and ceiling tracks. The end section of a channel turned to an angle (usually 90°) to permit attachment, generally to other channels.

Shooting board: (A) A slab of wood or metal used by carpenters and provided with a device for holding an object while it is being shaped for use. (B) An inclined board fitted to slide material from one level to another.

Shooting or sprouting: Emergence of long pile tufts above the normal pile surface. The condition is often correctable by cutting the sprouted tufts even with the pile before or after installation.

Shooting the bank or sectioning the work: In a unit price contract, a surveyor's final mathematical determination as to how much material was removed or placed within the pay lines.

Shop drawings: Drawings, diagrams, illustrations, schedules, performance charts, brochures, and other data prepared by the contractor or any subcontractor, manufacturer, supplier or distributor, that illustrate how specific portions of the work shall be fabricated or installed.

Short circuit: Excessive current flow caused by insulation breakdown or wiring error.

Should: Wording used in a design specification when an instruction is advised but not required.

Shoulder: The projection or break made on a piece of shaped wood, metal, or stone where its width or thickness is suddenly changed, as at a tenon or rebate The break is usually at right angles.

Shrink: The natural contraction of wood that hasn't been correctly dried.

Shrinkage: A decrease in dimensions occurring when a wallcovering is exposed to moisture. The property of a material that indicates it proportionate loss in dimensions or volume when its temperature is changed.

Shutter, box: An inside folding shutter, so contrived that when not in use it can be folded back into a recess provided for it in the deep window jamb. Usually the upper and lower sections are separate for independent opening and closing.

Shutter, louver: Shutter fitted with louver boards; i.e., slats set diagonally and immovable, as distinguished from adjustable slats.

Shutter, rolling: A shutter made of thin, slender strips secured edge to edge by hinge-like joints, so that the combination results in a flexible structure that can be rolled and unrolled, usually at the top of the opening. The strips may be of wood but are most often of iron or steel and used to protect openings from fire, burglars, etc. Rolling shutters, an invention of the second half of the nineteenth century, are wholly distinct from shutters with rolling slats.

Shutter bar: A bar for locking a pair of window shutters on the inside, generally pivoted on one leaf and dropping into a socket on the other.

Shutter lift: A small shutter bar with a handle for convenience in opening or closing and locking shutters.

Shutter: A movable screen, cover, or similar contrivance to close an opening, especially a window. In the United States the term commonly includes all varieties of hinged and swinging blinds, as well as any solid or nearly solid structure to close an opening tightly at the outside.

Shuttering: See formwork.

Shutters, Venetian: Shutter with slats; either rolling slats held together by a strip that causes them all to move or to roll simultaneously, or a louver shutter.

Siamese: A hose fitting for combining the flow from two or more lines into a single stream. See fire department connection.

Side vent: A vent connected to the drain pipe through a fitting at an angle not greater than 45° to the vertical.

Siding, bevel (lap siding): Wedge-shaped boards used as horizontal siding in a lapped pattern. This siding varies in butt thickness from 1/2" to 3/4" and in widths up to 12". Normally used over some type of sheathing.

Siding, dolly, varden: Beveled wood siding that is rabbeted on the bottom edge.

Siding, drop: Usually 3/4" thick and 6"- 8" wide with tongued-and-grooved or shiplap edges. Often used as siding without sheathing in secondary buildings.

Siding, novelty: In the United States, wooden siding boards with rabbets or grooves at the lower edges to lap over corresponding tongues along the upper edges. Thus all the boards can be nailed flat against the frame.

Siding: The covering or covering material for the exterior walls of a frame building. It forms the final finished surface, as distinguished from the sheathing, on which the siding is nailed.

Sill cock: A lawn faucet to which a garden hose may be attached. A hose bib.

Sill: A horizontal member at the base of a framed wall or the bottom of a door frame or window opening. The lowest member of the frame of a structure, resting on the foundation and supporting the floor joists or wall uprights .

Silvered bowl lamps: Incandescent A lamps with a silver finish inside the bowl portion of the bulb. Used for indirect lighting and glare reduction.

Single contract: Contract for construction of project under which a single prime contractor is responsible for all of the work.

Single hung: Secured to one side or at one point only, as a sash that is hung by one card, pulley, and weight. This plan is followed where a window is divided by a mullion that for any reason is to be made as slender as possible. When solid mullion is put in place, the two sliding sashes are each hung on the outer edge; the single weight being heavy enough to counterbalance the sash. It is usually necessary to insert rollers of some kind in the other stile of each sash to prevent their binding or sticking.

Sisal: See fiber.

Site conditions or site facilities: The facilities on a construction site utilized by the contractors during construction and usually dismantled upon project completion. These include access roads, storage, contractors' offices, lighting, electrical power, heating, water, manlifts, material hoists, and sanitary facilities.

Site: Geographical location of the project, usually defined by legal boundary lines. The location on which a building is or will be installed.

Size, sizing: A wall sealer used before applying wall paper.

Size: (A) Any glutinous covering matter applied to the surface of plaster and sometimes to wood as a preparation for painting or, more especially, gilding with gold leaf. It provides a uniform surface with little porosity. (B) To apply size or sizing, as in preparation for painting and gilding.

Skeleton construction: Framework construction with a non-loadbearing outer covering. Depending for its strength upon a skeleton; especially, beginning about 1885, a manner of building in which, while the exterior is of masonry, the whole structure is of iron or steel which supports the exterior walls and roof. It is common to carry these exterior walls by means of cantilevers, upon which one or two stories are built up at a time so that the structure may be completed and the roof put on before any part of the walls are in place. The

walls may even be built in the tenth story before those of the eighth and ninth stories are completed, and so on.

Skew: Any member cut or set to present a sloping surface; especially for other necessary parts of a structure to butt against, as in a gable or the abutment of an arch.

Skewback: The portion of an abutment that supports an arch.

Skim coat: Last and final coat.

Skirt: An apron-piece or border, as the molded piece under a window stool or the plinth board or mopboard of a room or passage, which in the United States is called base or baseboard.

Skirting: An edging attached to the base of an interior wall.

Skylight, double: Skylight in which a lower and usually horizontal glazed frame completes the ceiling of a room or gallery, while the space between this and the skylight proper serves for ventilation.

Skylight: A glazed aperture in a roof. It could be a simple glazed frame set in the plane of a roof or a structure surmounting a roof with upright or sloping sides and perhaps an independent roof; the entire structure consists wholly, or in large part, of glazed frames. In its more elaborate forms, a skylight may be constructed as a lantern or have the semblance of a dormer window, from which it is sometimes hardly to be distinguished. The term is, however, only applicable to such lights when located decidedly above, rather than at the sides of, the space immediately covered by the roof, although, perhaps, extending considerably down the lateral slopes of the roof. The frame is of wood or, preferably, metal, braced or tied with iron rods. If it is large, the metal sash bars are shaped with gutters to carry off the water of condensation and glazed with sheets of fluted or rough plate glass, varying from 12" x 48" and 3/16" thick to 20" x 100" and 6/16 of an inch thick; if ordinary double thick glass is used, the sheets are from 9" to 15" wide, and from 16" to 30" long. In metal sash bars or mountings these sheets are set without putty. Skylights are often provided with ventilators that open or close by cords from below, and a flat decorated inner skylight is frequently placed beneath the outer skylight in a ceiling panel when it is desired to make this feature an element in an architectural composition as seen from beneath. Sometimes, as in the covering of interior courts, winter gardens, exposition buildings, conservatories, marquises or canopies, and horticultural buildings, the entire roof is a skylight and emphasized as an especial architectural feature. Occasionally smaller skylights are in the form of glazed scuttles arranged to be opened for access to the roof.

Slab end: The lateral end face of a slab, as wide and thick as the slab itself.

Slab face: The surface of a slab, as long and wide as the slab itself.

Slack paths: The sequences of activities and events that do not lie on the critical path or paths.

Slack: See float.

Slaking: The act of hydrating quicklime into a putty by adding water.

Slat: A flat, thin board or strip, especially if relatively narrow, usually of wood.

Slate: In building, roofing slate; that is, a fossil variety of argillite used mainly for roofing and, in more solid masses, for sinks, floor tiles, mantels, and the like. Roofing slate is obtained by splitting the larger masses into thin slabs, which are then trimmed to standard dimensions. The varieties of slate are very great, and the preference for this or that quarry has varied from time to time, partly according to the color in vogue or specified and partly by the favor shown to a particular surface with or without glass and the like. Purple, green, and red are the common colors, and each of these colors is often very agreeable; moreover, it is easy to make somewhat effective patterns of their combination. The very darkest slate, that which approaches black, is preferred by many architects, and some of the best qualities of slate are of this color.

Slatehanging: Overlapping shingles made from slate. Used as exterior wall covering.

Slating: Applying roofing slate to the sheathing boards or battens of strips that are nailed to the rafters. Because the slating must overlap for a definite proportion of its length, the distance apart of the places for nailing can be determined beforehand. Thus, if slates 24" long are used and if it is required that each slate overlap the one below it for 14" (leaving 10" "to the weather" in each course), then the rows of nails will be 10" apart. Nails may be driven near the center of each slate or near the head. It is rare that both methods are used, since two nails to a slate of ordinary size is considered sufficient. Nails should be of copper or in some way protected by a noncorrosive metal composition, and the holes through which they are driven must be made in advance, which is done usually by the sharp point of the slater's hammer.

Sleeper wall: An underground wall supporting sleepers or piers.

Sleeper: A horizontal piece of timber that concrete flooring is attached to.

Sleeve or pipe sleeve: A circular opening through the floor structure to allow passage of cables and wires.

Sliding bevel: A tool that takes the place of the square when any angle other than 45° or 90° is to be obtained, the blade being adjustable. There are four sizes, commonly ranging from 6" to 12".

Slot: An opening through the floor structure, usually rectangular, to allow the passage of cables and wires.

Sludge: The accumulated suspended solids of sewage deposited in tanks, beds, or basins, mixed with water to form a semiliquid mass (sludge).

Slush: In masonry, to throw mortar on top of a course to form a bed for the next course. Slushed work permits bricks to be laid dry on such a bed in the interior of a wall and makes inferior work. Shoved work requires each brick in the interior of a wall to be surrounded with mortar to avoid any dry or open joints.

Smoke density: The amount of smoke given off by the burning material compared to the amount of smoke given off by the burning of a standard material.

Smoke detector: A device that detects the visible or invisible particles of combustion.

Smolder resistance: Materials in which nonflaming combustion is inhibited or prevented.

Smoldering: Combustion without flame. It may burn for a long time and generate smoke, toxic gases, and heat.

Smooth cut: A cut with the grain of a rock.

Socket: A depression or cavity, shaped to receive and hold in place the foot of a column or beam, the end of a bolt; or, in the case of heavy doors or the like, a revolving pivot.

Sod: The thin layer of soil matted together by the roots of grass and other small herbs that forms the surface of a lawn or grassy field; also, with the article, a small piece of this layer. "Turning the first sod" is a ceremony akin to laying the cornerstone.

Soffit: The underside of an archway, cornice, bead, etc.

Soil cover (ground cover): A light covering of plastic film, roll roofing, or similar material used over the soil in crawl spaces of buildings to minimize moisture permeation of the area.

Soil mechanics: The study of the composition soils, their classifications, strength, water flow through them, and active and passive earth pressure in relation to them.

Soil pipe: Any pipe which conveys the discharge of water closets, urinals or fixtures having similar functions, with or without the discharge from other fixtures, to the building (house) drain or building (house) sewer.

Soil sampler (Sampling spoon): A tube driven into the ground to obtain an undisturbed sample. Used primarily for clays, since the technique of getting undisturbed

samples of clean sand is much more complicated.

Soil stack: A vertical line of piping extending one or more floors that receives discharge water from closets, urinals, etc.

Soil survey: Use subsurface investigation.

Soil test: A test to ascertain whether soil is suitable for leaching and determine the size of the tile field.

Soil: Generic term for fine earth material produced by the decomposition of various

rocks, mixed organic matter and decomposed vegetable matter above bedrock.

Solar resistance: The property of material to resist decomposition by ultraviolet rays or the passage of radiant heat from the sun.

Solder: An alloy of varying composition, but always easily fusible, employed in joining pipes or surfaces. Solder for making wiped joints in lead pipe consists of three parts lead and two parts tin.

Soldering: To unite metallic substances, as in tinware, by solder, dropped when molten on the parts to be joined and then run together with a hot iron that keeps it fused.

Sole or sole plate: See plate.

Solid bridging: A solid member placed between adjacent floor joists near the center of the span to prevent joists from twisting.

Solid stock: (A) A mold that is worked on the article itself, rather than an applied mold. (B) Solid, sound lumber (rather than plywood), which may be more than one piece of the same species, securely glued for width or thickness.

Solids content: The percentage of the non-volatile matter in adhesives, coatings, or sealants.

Solvent: Any substance, usually a liquid, which dissolves another substance.

Sound absorption coefficient (SAC): The percentage of sound energy incident on the surface of a material that is absorbed by the material.

Sound board, boarding: Pieces of board put between floor joists to form a horizontal surface to receive deafening.

Sound transmission (room to room): Sound passing from one room to another, normally through an air return plenum. Also called crosstalk.

Sound transmission class (STC): A single number rating of the sound insulation value of a partition or wall. It is derived from a curve of its insulation value as a function of frequency; the higher the number, the more effective the sound insulation.

Sound transmission clip: A flexible, resilient metal clip used to decrease sound transmission through partition and floor assemblies. Also used to lessen plaster

cracking resulting from structural movement.

Sound: (A) Absence of decay. (B) Audible vibration communicated to the air or other surrounding media by the sounding body. Sound consists of a train of waves, alternately of condensation and refraction, propagated with a velocity of the medium. Any portion of the air moves to and fro over a very minute path in the direction to which the sound is propagated; its motion is, therefore, what is known as longitudinal vibration.

Sounding board: A reflector placed behind and above the speaker or orchestra to strengthen the sound to the audience. It is unfortunate that the term sounding board has also been applied to this, for the action of a reflector is very different from that of a true sounding board: in so far as it does vibrate, it is inefficient.

Sound transmission loss (STL): The reduction in level measured in decibels as sound energy passes through a material or composite construction.

Space planning: The functional planning of interior space. A design specialty practiced by interior designers and architects which concentrates on establishing space needs and utilization in the early or preliminary stages of design.

Spacing ratio: The ratio of the distance between luminaire centers to the height above the work plane. The maximum spacing ratio for a particular luminaire is determined from the candlepower distribution curve for that luminaire and, when multiplied by the mounting height above the work plane, gives the maximum spacing of luminaries at which even illumination will be provided.

Spackle: A plastic paste used to cover cracks and joints before painting.

Span: The distance between structural supports such as wall, columns, piers, beams, girders, and trusses.

Spandrel: The space between two adjacent arches. The triangular space between the sides of an arch. The horizontal drawn from the level of its apex and the vertical of its springing.

Spar varnish: A varnish that is resistant to salt, sun, and water.

Special conditions: A section of the conditions of the contract, other than general and supplementary conditions, prepared for a particular project. See conditions of the contract.

Special detail drawings: Larger-scaled and sometimes full-size detailed drawings of specific areas made to insure the builder full information.

Special hazards insurance: Additional perils insurance to be included in property insurance (as provided in contract documents or requested by contractor or at option of owner) such as sprinkler leakage, collapse, water damage, all physical loss, or insurance on materials and supplies at other locations or in transit to the site. See property insurance.

Special wastes: Wastes that require some special method of handling, such as the use of indirect waste piping and receptors, corrosion resistant piping; sand, oil, or grease interceptors; condensers or other pretreatment facilities.

Specialty contractor: A contractor who performs the work of a single construction trade either as a prime contractor or subcontractor of any tier, or who performs some of the work and subcontracts the rest.

Species: A distinct kind of wood.

Specific gravity: Ratio of the density (weight per unit volume) of a material to the density of water under standard conditions. Arithmetically, densities and specific gravities expressed in metric units are approximately equal. Carpet fiber specific gravities range from 0.91 for polypropylene (lighter than water) to 1.38 for polyester (about 38% denser than water).

Specific heat: The ratio of the amount of heat required to raise a unit mass of a material 1° to that required to raise a unit mass of water 1° at some specific temperature.

Specific quality control: The tests, control, performance, or certifications specifically required in each technical section of the specification to ensure the specified quality level of a particular item or group of items.

Specification: A detailed description of what is wanted.

Specifications: A part of the contract documents contained in the project manual, consisting of technical descriptions of material, equipment, construction systems, standards, and workmanship. Under the Uniform System, the specifications comprise 16 divisions.

Spectral energy distribution (SED) curves: A plot of the level of energy at each wavelength of a light source.

Speculative builder: One who develops and constructs building projects for subsequent sale or lease.

Speech privacy: The extent to which people in public areas can speak without being overheard by others or disturbing others.

Sphere illumination: The illumination on a task from a source providing equal luminance in all directions about that task, such as an illuminated sphere with the task located at the center.

Spike roll: Part of a tufting machine that pulls the primary backing and tufted carpet through the working area of the machine. It consists of a pinned, driven roll that grips the cloth. The relationship of spike roll rotational speed and strokes per minute of the needle bar determines the number of stitches per inch in the tufted product.

Spindle: A member that is round in one direction, as if revolved upon one axis. The term fusiform, which means spindle-shaped, implies a form larger in the middle and approaching a point at each end. Spindle is applied more loosely to the turned part of a post, baluster, or other piece fashioned in the lathe.

Splash block: A small masonry block laid with the top close to the ground surface to receive roof drainage from downspouts and carry it away from the building.

Splay angle: Where two surfaces come together forming an angle of more than 90°.

Splay: Any surface larger than a chamfer or bevel making an oblique angle with another surface; specifically said of the oblique jamb of an opening, as in a window or doorway.

Spline, feather tongue: A spline cut to a bevel.

Spline: (A) A thin, narrow board, corresponding generally to boards used for ceilings, and the like. (B) Same as loose tongue. (C) A joint formed by the use of a spline.

Split pin: A pin, as a spike, split at the point, so as to spread when it is driven in, giving somewhat the form of a dovetail and making it difficult to extract.

Split: A separation of the wood due to the tearing apart of the wood cells. A very short split is approximately as long as one-half the width of the piece. A short split is approximately as long as the width of the piece.

Spokeshave: A variety of compass plane that is adapted to quicker curves. They are made in several sizes with cutters from 1.5" to 4" wide.

Spot detector: A device whose detecting element is concentrated at a particular location. Typical examples are bimetallic detectors, fusible alloy detectors, certain pneumatic rate of rise detectors, certain smoke detectors, and thermoelectric detectors.

Spot ground: See dot.

Spray texture: A surface finish achieved by application of finish coat material with a plastering machine or gun.

Sprayed-in-place insulation: See insulation.

Spring: (A) The line of plane at which the curve of an arch or vault leaves the upright or impost. (B) Resilience, as of a floor; its elasticity when compressed.

Springing line: The horizontal line from which an arch rises.

Sprinkler system classification: Automatic sprinkler system types; wet-pipe systems, dry-pipe systems, pre-action systems, deluge systems, combined dry-pipe and pre-action systems. Occupancy classification: relates to sprinkler installations and their water supplies only. They are not intended to be a general classification of occupancy hazards. Extra hazard occupancies: occupancies or portions of other occupancies where quantity and combustibility of contents are very high and flammable and combustible liquids, dust, lint, or other materials are present, introducing the probability of rapidly developing fires with high rates of heat release. Extra hazard occupancies involve many variables that may produce severe fires. The following shall be used to evaluate the severity of extra hazard occupancies: Extra hazard (group 1) includes occupancies with little or no flammable or combustible liquids. Extra hazard (group 2) includes occupancies with moderate to substantial amounts of flammable or combustible liquids or where shielding of combustibles is extensive. Light hazard are those occupancies where the quantity or combustibility of contents is low and fires with relatively low rates of heat release are expected. Ordinary occupancies hazard (group 1) includes occupancies where combustibility is low, quantity of combustibles does not exceed 8' (2.4 m) and fires with moderate rates of heat release are expected. Ordinary hazard (group 2) includes occupancies where quantity and combustibility of contents are moderate, stock piles do not exceed 12' (3.7 m) and fires with moderate rate of heat release are expected. Ordinary hazard (group 3) includes occupancies where quantity or combustibility of contents is high, and fires of high rate of heat release are expected.

Sprinkler system: An integrated system of underground and overhead piping designed in accordance with fire protection engineering standards. The installation includes one or more automatic water supplies. The portion of the sprinkler system above ground is a network of specially sized or hydraulically designed piping installed in a building, structure, or area, generally overhead, to which sprinklers are attached in a systematic pattern. The valve controlling each system riser is located in the system riser or its supply piping. Each sprinkler system riser includes a device for actuating an alarm when the system is in operation. The system is activated by heat from a fire and discharges water over the fire area.

Sprinkler: A system of perforated pipes extending through a building, which at frequent points is connected with a water supply controlled by fusible plugs. When melted by an accidental fire near by, the plugs automatically turn on the water and start the sprinklers to extinguish the flames.

Sprinklers, concealed: Recessed sprinklers with cover plates.

Sprinklers, corrosion-resistant: Sprinklers with special coatings or platings to be used in an atmosphere that would corrode an uncoated sprinkler.

Sprinklers, dry pendent: Sprinklers for use in a pendent position in a dry-pipe or wet-pipe system with the seal in a heated area.

Sprinklers, dry upright: Sprinklers designed to be installed in an upright position on a wetpipe system, to extend into an unheated area with a seal in a heated area.

Sprinklers, extended coverage sidewall: Sprinklers with special extended, directional, discharge patterns.

Sprinklers, flush: Sprinklers in which all or part of the body, including the shank thread, is mounted above the lower plane of the ceiling.

Sprinklers, intermediate level: Sprinklers equipped with integral shields to protect their operating elements from the discharge of sprinklers installed at high elevations.

Sprinklers, large-drop: A listed sprinkler is characterized by a K factor between 11.0 and 11.5 and proven ability to meet prescribed penetration, cooling, and distribution criteria prescribed in the large-drop sprinkler examination requirements. The deflector/discharge characteristics of the large-drop sprinkler generate large drops of such size and velocity as to enable effective penetration of the high-velocity fire plume.

Sprinklers, open: Sprinklers from which the actuating elements (fusible-links) have been removed.

Sprinklers, ornamental: Sprinklers that have been painted or plated by the manufacturer.

Sprinklers, pendent: Sprinklers designed to be installed so that the water stream is directed downward against the deflector.

Sprinklers, recessed: Sprinklers in which all or part of the body, other than the shank thread, is mounted within a recessed housing.

Sprinklers, residential: Sprinklers that have been specifically listed for use in residential occupancies.

Sprinklers, sidewall: Sprinklers having special deflectors that are designed to discharge most of the water away from the nearby wall in a pattern resembling one quarter of a sphere, with a small portion of the discharge directed at the wall behind the sprinkler.

Sprinklers, special: Sprinklers that have been tested and listed as prescribed in special limitations.

Sprinklers, upright: Sprinklers designed to be installed so that the water spray is directed upwards against the deflector.

Sprocket: A timber placed on the back and foot of a rafter to form projecting eaves.

Spur stone: A stone projecting from the angle of a corner to prevent traffic damage.

Spur: A decoration placed at the transition of a square plinth to a circular pier.

Square, carpenter's: A steel implement forming a right angle with a shorter and a longer area, each divided into feet and inches or other measurements.

Square, joiner's: A tool used in the production of right angles, either in the drawing of lines or in the planing up of materials. In the latter operation smaller sizes are used e.g. 3", 4", or 6". These are called trying squares. The larger ones, 9", 12", or 18" are simply called squares. As the ultimate accuracy of the setting out of framing depends greatly on the truthfulness of the square edges, care should be taken to select a square that is true.

Square, miter: A square with its blade set at an angle of 45° with the edge of the stock. It is used similarly to the try square, but for producing lines and edges at angles of 45°.

Square, set: A square with two of its edges at right angles. It is used for ascertaining the squareness of internal angles and in fitting work together. It can be made of a piece of dry hardwood but is most often made of aluminum or plastic.

Square, steel: An L-shaped piece of steel, with the edges of its blades divided into inches and parts. This is a universal carpenter's tool that can be used for everything from ordinary squaring operations to calculating stair rises and rafter pitches.

Square: (A) An open space, generally more or less rectangular, in a town, formed at the junction of two or more streets or by the enlargement of one for a short distance; especially, such a place provided with a park or parks. (B) Same as block (C) An instrument intended primarily for laying out right angles, consisting usually of two arms fixed, or capable of being accurately adjusted, perpendicularly to each other. (C) A unit of measure-100 square feet-usually applied to roofing material. Sidewall coverings are sometimes packed to cover 100 square feet and are sold on that basis.

Stability: As applied to structures, the property of remaining in equilibrium without change of position, although the externally applied force may deviate to a certain extent its mean amount of position. The conditions of equilibrium of a structure are these: (A) That the forces exerted on the structure by external bodies shall balance each other. The external forces are the force of gravity, causing the weight of the structure, the pressures exerted against it by bo-

dies not forming part of it, and the supporting forces, or resistances of the foundations. (B) That the forces exerted on each piece of a structure shall balance each other. These forces are the weight, the external load, and the resistances, or stresses, exerted at the joints of the piece. (C) That the forces exerted upon each of the parts into which the pieces of a structure can be conceived to be divided shall balance each other. That is the stress exerted at the ideal surface of division between the part in question and the other parts of the piece. (D) Stability consists in the fulfillment of the first and second conditions of equilibrium under all variations of load within given limits. Strength consists in the fulfillment of the third.

Stack cleanout: A plugged fitting located at the base of soil or waste stacks.

Stack group: The location of fixtures in relation to the stack so that proper fittings, vents may be reduced to a minimum.

Stack vent: The extension of a soil waste stack above the highest horizontal drain connected to the stack. Also known as waste or soil vent.

Stack venting: A method of venting a fixture or fixtures through the soil or waste stack.

Stack: The vertical main of a system of soil, waste, or vent piping extending through one or more stories.

Stacking of trades: Congestion caused when crews of several contractors or subcontractors are trying to perform work in the same physical area at the same time.

Staff: Plaster casts made in molds and reinforced with fiber. Usually wired or nailed into place.

Stain, shingle: A form of oil paint, very thin in consistency, intended for coloring wood with rough surfaces, such as shingles, without forming a coating of significant thickness or gloss.

Stain: (A) A coloring liquid or dye for application to any material, most often wood. It differs from paint as being thinner and readily absorbed by the pores of the material, instead of forming a coating on the surface, so that the texture and grain of the material are not concealed. In America stain has been used for exteriors of frame houses; the shingles and clapboards take on a rougher and far more picturesque look than if painted. (B) Any ingredient used to change the color of a material by chemical action, such as glass, in which a deep blue is obtained by protoxide of cobalt and a green by copper and by iron, as in the production of pot metal. Silver stain is more properly an enamel applied to the surface without changing the color of the mass. (C) A variation (normally blue or brown) from the natural color of the wood. It should not be confused with natural red heart. Slight stain is a light color, barely perceptible. Medium stain is pronounced discoloration. Heavy stain is the darkest color that develops in lumber. (D) Foreign material (soil, liquids, etc.) on carpet that is not removable by standard cleaning methods.

Stair, back: Any stair situated at the rear, or back, of a building, as for domestic service or other subordinate purpose. Hence, any retired and unimportant stair for a similar use, wherever situated.

Stair, box: One made with two closed strings, so that it has a boxlike form of construction, and may be more or less completely finished before being set up on the site.

Stair, carriage: Supporting member for stair treads. Usually a 2" plank notched to receive the treads; sometimes called a rough horse.

Stair, cockle: From cochlea; a helical or corkscrew stair.

Stair, dog-leg, dog-legged: A half-turn stair consisting of two parallel flights, with their strings and hand rails in the same vertical plane. The hand rail of the lower flight commonly butts against the underside of the string of the upper flight, there being no well hole.

Stair, geometrical: Stair constructed without newels at the angles or turning points. The intersecting strings and hand rails are, therefore, usually joined by means of short, curved portions called wreaths.

Stair, newel, neweled: One constructed with newels at the angles to receive the ends of the strings, as distinguished from a geometrical stair. The term is sometimes, with no apparent reason, limited to a dog-legged stair.

Stair, open neweled: A neweled stair built around a well; apparently, a term adapted to distinguish such a stair, which is open as regards the existence of a well, from a dog-legged stair, which has no well. Each is neweled.

Stair, open riser: Stair with no riser in the sense of a solid board, metal casting, or the like; the whole rise between treads is left open. When this arrangement is followed in costly staircases of elaborate buildings, it is usually to allow light to pass, as from a window.

Stair, screw: A circular stair; especially, one in which the steps radiate from a vertical post or newel.

Stair, straight: Stair that rises without turns in one direction only.

Stair, water: Stairs or steps communicating between any water level, as of a river, lake, or harbor, and the land, for convenience of embarkation or debarkation.

Stair, winding: Any stair constructed wholly or chiefly with winders.

Staircase: (A) Properly, the structure containing a stair; a stair together with its enclosing walls. (B) Improperly, but in common usage, a stair or series of stairs; i.e., the complete mechanical structure of a stair or set of stairs with its supports, hand rails, and other parts.

Stairway: Three or more risers constitute a stairway.

Stale sewage: Sewage that contains little or no oxygen and is free from putrefaction.

Stanchion: A vertical supporting member.

Standard block for frame-saw cutting: A squared block of optimum dimensions that can be cut with a frame saw.

Standard design: Any buildings, system, model, series, or component intended for duplication or repetitive construction or manufacture.

Standard deviation of activity: A measure of uncertainty about the event expected date. It is calculated by computing the square root of the sum of the squares of the activity standard deviations on the longest path leading to the event under consideration.

Standard fabric: Fabrics that conform to the minimum performance characteristics of their respective class.

Standard forms: Preprinted contract document forms used by the construction industry.

Standard network diagram: A predefined network used in the past or intended to be used more than once in any given project in the future.

Standard roll: The standard unit of measure for wall covering, 36 sq. ft.

Standards of professional practice: Statements of principles promulgated by professional societies to guide members in the conduct of professional practice.

Standpipe, dry: A system having no permanent water supply may be so arranged through the use of approved devices as to admit water to the system automatically by opening a hose valve.

Standpipe, wet: A system having a supply valve open and water pressure maintained in the system at all times.

Standpipe system: An arrangement of piping, valves, hose connections and allied equipment installed in a building with the hose connections located so that water can be discharged in streams or spray patterns through attached hose and nozzles, to extinguish a fire and protect a building, its contents, and the occupants. This is accomplished by connections to water supply systems or by pumps, tanks, and other equipment necessary to provide an adequate supply of water to the hose connections.

Standpipe: (A) A pipe, usually vertical, intended to facilitate the supply of water to elevated points. Thus, at certain points along an aqueduct, a standpipe may be used into which water is forced by mechanical means, thus providing a pressure sufficient to raise the water supply higher than the normal level. (B) In architectural practice, chiefly, a pipe intended to extinguish fires. It is sometimes on the exterior of a building and sometimes within, with branches in the different stories; but always with a mouth near the street and outside and a coupling to which the hose of the fire engine can be attached.

Staple: A U-shaped metal fastener used to attach building paper, expanded metal, wire, gypsum lath, and accessories to framing.

Starling: A pointing projection on the pier of a bridge used to break wave action.

Starter clip: A metal section used at the floor, or initial, course of gypsum lath.

Starting event (beginning event): An event that signifies the beginning of one or more activities on a network.

Static shock: Discharge of electrostatic potential from carpet to person to conductive ground e.g., a doorknob. Shoe friction against carpet fiber produces an electrostatic charge. Static control systems and finishes are used in contract carpet to dissipate static charge before it builds to the human sensitivity threshold.

Status line: A vertical line on a time scaled schedule indicating updating or reporting date.

Status: The condition of the project at a specified point in time.

Statutes of limitations: A statute specifying the period of time within which legal actions must be brought for alleged damage or injury. The lengths of the periods vary from state to state and depend upon the type of legal action. Ordinarily the period commences with the discovery of the act resulting in the alleged damage or injury, although in construction industry cases some jurisdictions define the period as commencing with completion of the work or services performed.

Statutory bond: A bond, the form or content of which is prescribed by statute.

Stay: Anything that stiffens or helps to maintain a frame or other structure, as a piece of timber or iron acting as a strut or brace; or a tie of any material.

Steam boiler and machinery insurance: Special insurance covering steam boilers, other pressure vessels, and related equipment and machinery. This insurance covers damage or injury to property resulting from the explosion of steam boilers not covered by extended coverage perils.

Steeple: (A) A tall, ornamental construction surmounting a tower and composed usually of a series of features superimposed and diminishing upward, as the steeples of Sir Christopher Wren's churches. In contrast a spire is a tall pyramid uninterrupted by stories or stages. (B) A tower terminated by a steeple or spire, the term covering the whole structure from the ground up.

Stenciling: A process of color application onto another material through a heavy waterproof template.

Step-shaped wainscoting: Wainscoting cut to align and ascend with a staircase.

Steps: One to three consecutive risers or treads.

Stereobate: A mass of masonry used as a base of a wall or series of columns.

Stick: To run, strike, or shape with a molding plane; by extension, to shape, as longitudinal moldings, splays and the like, by the molding mill.

Sticker: A piece of metal channel inserted in concrete or masonry walls for the attachment or support of wall furring channels.

Stiffener: A horizontal metal shape tied to vertical members (studs or channels) of partitions or walls to brace them.

Stiffness: A property that allows a material to resist deformation.

Stile, diminished, diminishing: In a glazed door, a stile whose upper part above the middle rail is narrower than the lower part to admit a sash wider than the panelling below.

Stile, gunstock: A diminished stile in which the reduction in width is made by a long slope, usually of the whole width of the lock rail.

Stile, hanging: (A) In the framing of a door, hinged casement window, or the like, that stile to which the hinges are secured, and by which the door, etc., is hung to the jamb or doorpost. (B) Same as pulley stile.

Stile, pulley: That surface of the box frame of a window against which the sashes slide up and down. It receives its name from the sash pulleys which are set into it near the top and through which the sash cords or chains are passed.

Stile, shutting: In a hinged door, the stile opposite the hanging stile which strikes the rebate of the jamb when the door is shut.

Stile: Any plane surface forming a border. Specifically, in carpentry work and joinery, one of the plane members of a piece of framing into which the secondary members or rails are fitted by mortise and tenon, as in paneling. In framed doors and the like, it is nearly always a vertical member.

Stilted: Raised higher than normal, or seeming to be so raised. The term is almost wholly limited to the arch, which is said to be stilted when the curve does not spring at or close to the top of the capital or

the molded or otherwise strongly marked impost. The term is extremely vague, since many arches have no architecturally marked impost, and as it is considered an error to start the curve immediately upon such an impost in any case; but those arches are called stilted that have a vertical jamb or intrados below the curve more than about one quarter of their total rise.

Stipulated sum agreement: Contract in which a specific amount is set forth as the total payment for performance of the contract.

Stone: (A) The material of which rocks are composed. (B) A fragment of a rock. (C) Any aggregate of mineral matter, natural or artificial, as in precious stone, "artificial stone." The kinds of stone used for construction or general interior decorative, monumental, or art work may be roughly grouped under five general heads: granites, sandstones, marbles, limestones, and slates.

Stonecutter's chisel: A toothed, impact-processing tool.

Stoop: A small residential entrance platform.

Stop valve: A valve used for the control of water supply, usually to a single fixture.

Stop work order: An order issued by the owner's representative to stop project work for failure to perform according to contract specifications, unsatisfied liens, labor disputes, inclement weather, etc.

Stop-chamfer: The decorative termination of a chamfer.

Stops: Projections at the ends of masonry courses or molding used to butt terminate the course or molding.

Stored materials and equipment: Materials and equipment stored on the job site or in an offsite location approved by the owner, such as a bonded warehouse, for future installation under a contract. In many cases, the contractor may bill for such materials at the time of their purchase and delivery, and receives progress payments including such stored materials before their installation.

Storm sash or storm window: An extra window usually placed on the outside of an existing one as additional protection against cold weather.

Storm sewer: A sewer used for conveying rain water, surface water, condensate, cooling water or similar liquid wastes, exclusive of sewage and industrial waste.

Storm water drainage system: A piping system used for conveying rainwater to the storm sewer.

Story: The space between the upper surface of one floor and the upper surface of the floor above, or between the floor and roof of a building.

Strain diagram, polygon: A geometrical diagram used in the graphical method of determining the strains in a framed structure, such as a truss. The given loads or other outer forces are represented in amount and direction by a series of lines; other lines are plotted to the same scale corresponding in direction to the respective members of the structure. On completion of the polygon, these latter may be directly measured by scale on the drawing. The process is similar to that employed in the polygon, and the parallelogram of forces.

Strain: The deformation or change of shape of a body as the result of a stress.

Strainer: A filter or sieve used in fluid piping to trap scale and other intrained particles.

Stratification: An effect that occurs when air containing smoke particles or gaseous combustion products is heated by smoldering or burning material and, becoming less dense than the surrounding cooler air, rises until it reaches a level at which there is no longer a difference in temperature between it and the surrounding air. Stratification can also be caused by forced ventilation.

Stratum: The layer of rock to be quarried.

Streamlined specifications: Specifications containing adequate technical information for the construction of the work but written in an abbreviated manner.

Stress: The resistance to a change in shape or size that is caused by an external force.

Stressed-skin construction: Construction in which the outer skin or shell acts with the frame members for a structurally strong unit.

Stressed-skin panel: A panel of outer materials such as plywood fastened over a frame or core, forming a unified structural member.

Stretcher: (A) A brick laid flat so that the horizontal dimension is greatest and parallel to the wall. (B) An H- or X-shaped crossbar that connects chair legs. (C) In masonry, a solid, as a brick or stone laid lengthwise in the wall.

Strike clauses: Clauses setting forth obligations and relief from obligations of the contractor in the event of strikes by employees or the employees of other companies upon whose performance the contractor depends. These include provisions for notices, security of the job site, and time extensions.

Strike-off: A sample of a paper or fabric design.

Striker: A slightly beveled metal plate set in the jamb of a door to receive and guide the door latch to its socket in closing.

String, stringer: A timber or other support for cross members in floors or ceilings. In stairs, the support on which the stair treads rest; also stringboard.

Stringboard: Any board, plank, or facing of thin pieces glued together, that covers the ends of steps in a stair, as when hiding the true string, or cover the edge of a floor where a wellhole is cut through it. Often called a bridge board.

String course: A continuous molded horizontal band on the surface of an exterior wall.

String wire: Wire used on open stud construction, placed horizontally around the building to support weatherproofing paper.

String: One of the sloping members of a stair, usually a thick plank, which supports the steps and landings. By extension, the ramp or side piece of a stone or other solid-built stair, if not so high as to be a parapet.

Stringer: A heavy horizontal timber that acts as a support for a staircase.

Strings: Two sloping members that carry the ends of treads and risers of a staircase.

Strip (base): A straight or barlike section of molding.

Strip development: A continuous string of houses or buildings along a road or street.

Strip flooring: Wood flooring consisting of narrow, matched strips.

Strip lath: Metal or wire fabric used over joints of gypsum lath. Sometimes used to obtain fire rating.

Strip reinforcement: See strip lath.

Structural clay tile: A masonry structure constructed with clay or fire clay that has been burned.

Structure (of the rock): All geological characteristics of a rock: crystallization, grain size, shape and dimension of crystallized minerals, etc. It can be seen only with a microscope.

Structure-borne sound: Sound transmitted through a structure.

Strut: A vertical or oblique timber that runs between two members of a roof truss but does not directly support longitudinal timbers.

Stucco: A finish for walls made from sand, lime, and cement mixed with water. It can be smooth or textured. Any material used as a covering for walls and the like, put on wet, that dries hard and durable. Plaster when applied to walls in the usual way is a kind of stucco, and the hard finish is almost exactly like fine Roman stucco except that it is applied in only one thin coat instead of many. The term is used commonly for rough finish of outer walls. The practical value of stucco is very great, because it is nearly impervious to water. Thus, an excellent wall three stories high, or even higher, may be built with 8" of brick on the inner side, 4" of brick on the outer side, an air space of 2" or 4" across which the outer and the inner walls are well tied, and two coats of well-mixed and well-laid stucco on the exterior, this being finally painted with oil paint.

Stud: (A) A relatively small projecting member as a boss, small knob, or salient nailhead, for ornamental or mechanical purpose. (B) Vertical framing members for interior and exterior wall construction. Often 2 x 4's of wood or metal. (C) Used to hold heavy insulation or panels in place. Applied with arc welder, studs differ from pins in that studs are generally 1/4" or greater in diameter.

Studio: (A) The working room of an artist, preferably arranged in north latitude and especially free from cross lights. (B) Any large apartment fitted as a working room, especially for more or less artistic employments, as photography and designing of all sorts.

Studs (metal, load-bearing): Formed from minimum 20-gauge, structural grade strip steel, with punched webs. Widths: 2-1/2", 3-1/4", 3-5/8", 4", 6". Also available in double form in 2-1/2" and 3-5/8" widths to permit attachment of lath by nailing or by other means.

Studs (metal, nonload-bearing): (A) 18-gauge channel shapes with perforated webs. (B) Double 7-gauge cold drawing rods welded to a 7-gauge rod bent in diagonal truss design between them (No longer manufactured). (C) Two 16-gauge angle shapes welded to a 7-gauge rod bent in diagonal truss design between them.

Study: Preliminary sketch or drawing to facilitate design development .

Sub-bidder: One who tenders to a bidder on a prime contract a proposal to provide materials or labor.

Sub-main sewer: A sewer into which the sewage from two or more lateral sewers is discharged. Also known as branch sewer.

Sub-subcontractor: A person or organization who has a direct or indirect contact with a subcontractor to perform a portion of the work at the site.

Subcontract: Agreement between a prime contractor and a subcontractor to perform some of the work at the site or to supply labor and materials.

Subcontractor bonds: A document given to the prime contractor by the subcontractor, guaranteeing performance of his contract and payment of all labor and materials bills in connection with that contract.

Subflooring: A rough base floor which rests on joists.

Subnetwork: A portion of a larger network, generally for a unique area of a project or given responsibility.

Subparagraph: In the AIA documents, the first subdivision of a paragraph, identified by three numerals, e.g., 2.2.2. A subparagraph may be subdivided into clauses.

Subrogation: The substitution of one person for another with respect to legal rights such as a right to recovery. Subrogation occurs when a third person, such as an insurance company, has paid a debt of another or claim against another and succeeds to all legal rights that the debtor may have against other persons.

Subsoil drain: A drain that receives only subsurface or seepage water and conveys it to an approved place of disposal.

Substantial completion: See date of substantial completion.

Substantial inequity: An unreasonable and harmful result incurred by one of the parties to a contract, which exceeds the effect that could be contemplated by the parties at the time the contract was formed, for which relief is sought.

Substitution: A material or process offered in lieu of and as being equivalent to specified material or process.

Subsurface investigation: The soil boring and sampling program associated laboratory tests necessary to establish subsurface profiles and the relative strengths, compressibility, and other characteristics of the strata encountered within the depths likely to have an influence on the design of the project.

Subsystems: Definable portions of a construction project including all of the materials, equipment, and labor necessary for a functional assembly; e.g., air conditioning, lighting, electrical power distribution, heating, foundation, integrated ceiling-floor sandwich.

Successful bidder: Use selected bidder.

Successor activity: Any activity that exists on a common path with the activity in question and occurs just after its start or finish.

Successor and assigns: Legal entities that assume the obligations, rights, or property of a party to a contract as a result of inheritance, title transfer, or trusteeship for the benefit of creditors.

Successor event: The event that signifies the completion of an activity. Also called ending event.

Suction: The power of absorption possessed by a plastered surface. For example, the basecoat must have suction to absorb the water out of the finish coat.

Summary item: An item appearing in the work breakdown structure.

Summary network: A summarization of the CPM network for presentation purposes.

Summary number: A number that identifies an item in the work breakdown structure.

Sump pump: A mechanical device for removing liquid waste from a sump.

Sump: A tank or pit, located below the normal grade of the gravity system, that receives sewage or liquid waste, and must be emptied by mechanical means.

Sunk: Having the surface lowered or cut away. A sunk square is usually an ornamental feature. Sunk work is usually decoration in relief upon a sunken panel but may be incised or impressed.

Superintendent: Contractor's representative at the site who is responsible for continuous field supervision, coordination, completion of the work, and, unless another person is designated in writing by the contractor to the owner and the architect, accident prevention.

Superstructure: A structure raised upon another structure, as a building upon a foundation, basement, or substructure.

Supervision: (A) Direction of the work by contractor's personnel. Supervision is neither a duty nor a responsibility of the architect as part of basic professional services. (B) The ability to detect a fault condition in the installation wiring which would prevent normal operation of the fire alarm system.

Supervisory (tamper) switch: A device attached to the handle of a valve, that, when the valve is closed, will annunciate a trouble signal at a remote location.

Supplementary conditions: A part of the contract documents that supplements and may modify provisions of the general conditions. See conditions of the contract.

Supplier: A person or organization who supplies materials or equipment for the work, including that fabricated to a special design, but who does not perform labor at the site. See vendor.

Supply air duct: A duct that carries conditioned air from air supply units to room diffusers or grilles.

Supply bond: A document given by the manufacturer or supply distributor to the owner guaranteeing that materials contracted for will be delivered as specified in the contract.

Supply mains: The pipes in a piping system from the source to the runouts and risers.

Support (insulation): A device that carries the weight of insulation.

Supports: Devices for supporting and securing pipe and fixtures to walls, ceilings, floors or structural members.

Surcharge: An extra charge added to the purchase price when less than the minimum is bought.

Surety bond: A legal instrument under which one party agrees to answer to another party for the debt, default, or failure to perform of a third party.

Surety: A person or organization who, for a consideration, promises in writing to make good the debt or default of another.

Surface check: The separation of a wood, normally occurring across the rings of annual growth, usually as a result of seasoning, and occurring only on one surface of the piece. A fine surface check is not longer than 4". A small surface check is more than 4" and not longer than 6". A medium surface check is more than 6" but not longer than 8", without any gaps.

Surface location: The area designated for placement of the ignition source in mockup furniture flammability testing.

Surface Temperature (Ta): The surface temperature of finished insulation.

Surveillance: A close watch or observation kept over a contractor's inspection system to insure that it is functioning properly, performed concurrently with the construction representation inspections.

Survey: (A) Boundary or topographic mapping of a site. (B) Measuring an existing building. (C) Analyzing a building for use of space. (D) Determining owner's requirement for a project. (E) Investigating and reporting of required data for a project.

Suspended ceiling: A ceiling system supported by hanging from the overhead structural framing.

Suspended ceilings: See ceilings.

Swag: A festoon formed like a draped cloth over supports.

Swatch: A small carpet sample. Carpet specifiers should retain swatches to verify color, texture, weight, and other quality factors when carpet is delivered.

Sweat out: Soft, damp wall area caused by poor drying conditions.

Swell front: See bow front.

Swimming pool: A structure, basin or tank containing water for swimming, diving or recreation.

Swing Joint: A joint in a threaded pipe line permitting motion in the line.

Switching Equipment: In-building circuitry and supporting hardware required for the operation of tenant-operated station apparatus.

Synthetic gypsum: A chemical product, consisting primarily of calcium sulfate dihydrate ($CaSO_4 + 2H_2O$) resulting in primarily from an industrial process.

Syphonage: Suction created by the flow of liquid in pipes.

System actuator: Same as security device.

System: The structural, plumbing, electrical, mechanical, thermal efficiency and life safety elements, materials, or components of a building.

Systems building programs: A program for installing systems made up of subsystems, utilizing unconventional bidding and contracting procedures and performance specifications.

Systems: Combining prefabricated assemblies, components and parts into single integrated units utilizing industrialized production, assembly and methods.

T

T & G: Tongue-and-groove joint.

T-branch: A branch having an arm at right angles with the main part, giving three openings.

Table, earth: The lowest course or courses of a stone wall visible above the ground, especially when forming a projecting member for a water table.

Table, ledgement: A band or belt course, usually molded, especially one carried along the lower portion of a building, which projects to form an earth table.

Table, skew: A stone set at right angles to the coping of a gable wall at its foot and built into the masonry to prevent the coping stones from sliding and serve as a stop for the eaves, gutter, etc., of the side wall. When it projects, as a corbel beyond the angle of the building, it is called a skew corbel.

Table, water: A string course or other projecting member with a weathering and otherwise so devised as to guide water away from the face of the wall.

Tablet: (A) A small slab or panel, usually a separate piece, set into or attached to a wall or other larger mass, usually intended to receive an inscription. (B) A horizontal coping or capping of a wall, sometimes called tabling.

Tack: The property of an adhesive that enables it to form a measurable bond immediately after adhesive and adherent are brought into contact under pressure.

Tail beam: A relatively short beam or joist supported in a wall on one end and by a header at the other.

Tamp: To ram an earth surface to harden it and form a floor, or the bottom of a trench to make it fit to receive foundations.

Tapered edge: An edge formation of gypsum board that provides a shallow depression on the paper-bound edge to receive joint reinforcement.

Target date: The date an activity is desired to be started or completed, imposed or requested by client or project management.

Task lighting: Lighting directed to a specific surface or area that provides illumination for visual tasks.

Task: That which is to be seen. The visual function to be performed.

Teak: A hardwood medium brown in color found in Asia. It resists moisture and is used mainly for furniture making.

Tear strength: Resistance to the propagation of an existing tear. That property of a material which enables it to resist being pulled apart by opposing forces.

Temper: (A) To mix, moisten, and knead clay, so as to bring it to proper consistency to form bricks, pottery, terra cotta, etc., preliminary to hardening by fire. (B) To bring a metal, as steel, to a proper degree of hardness and elasticity by alternately heating and suddenly cooling the metal. Its color, by those processes, gradually changes from light yellow to dark blue, and the metal becomes harder at each stage. (C) To toughen and harden glass by plunging it at a high temperature into an oleaginous bath under the process invented by M. de la Bastie, or by heating and suddenly cooling it, according to the Siemen process. (D) To mix and knead lime, sand, and water proportionately to make mortar for masonry or plastering.

Temperature and pressure relief valve: A safety valve designed to protect against excessively high temperature pressure.

Temperature limits: The upper and lower temperatures at which a material will experience no change in its properties.

Temperature: Used to distinguish differences in heat levels.

Tempered water: Water ranging in temperature from 85° F (29° C) up to 11° F (43° C).

Template: (A) A paper or cardboard pattern used by installers as a guide for cutting carpet for areas having complicated or unusual shapes. (B) A stone block set on top of a brick wall to carry the weight of joists or trusses. (C) A gauge, pattern, or mold used as a guide to produce arches, curves, and other work. Texture: see finish coats.

Temporary facilities: See site facilities.

Temporary heat: See site facilities.

Tenon, teaze: A double tenon, one tenon above another, with a double shoulder, wrought on the top of a post, to receive two horizontal timbers at right angles to each other.

Tenon: Projecting tongue-like part of a wood member to be inserted into a slot (mortise) of another member to form a mortise and tenon joint. The cutting of the end of a rail, mullion, sill, or beam to form a projection of smaller transverse section than the piece, with a shoulder, so that it may be fitted into a corresponding hold or mortise in another piece.

Tensile strength: The breaking strain of yarns or fabrics. A high tensile strength indicates strong yarns or fabrics.

Tension bar: A bar or rod to which a strain of tension is applied or by which it is resisted.

Tension member piece: In a framework, truss, or the like, a piece calculated to resist strains of tension; as a tie.

Tension: A force that stretches or pulls apart a body.

Terminal expenses: Expenses incurred in connection with the termination of a contract.

Terminal: (A) A point at which information can enter or leave a communications network. (B) The input-output equipment associated therewith.

Termination clauses: Clauses in a contract providing the conditions under which the contract may be terminated and steps to be taken to protect the interests of the parties.

Termination: The end, a cancellation; the act of concluding something.

Termite shield: A shield, usually of non-corroding metal, placed in or on a foundation wall, other mass of masonry, or around pipes to prevent passage of termites.

Termites: Insects that superficially resemble ants in size, general appearance, and habit of living in colonies; hence, they are frequently called white ants. Subterranean termites establish themselves in buildings by entering from ground nests after the building has been constructed. If unmolested, they eat out the woodwork, leaving a shell of sound wood to conceal their activities. Damage may proceed so far as to cause collapse of parts of a structure before discovery. About 56 species of termites are known in the United States; but the two major ones, classified by the manner they attack wood, are ground-inhabiting or subterranean termites (the most common) and dry-wood termites, which are found almost exclusively along the extreme southern border and the Gulf of Mexico in the United States.

Terneplate: Sheet iron or steel coated with an alloy of lead and tin.

Terra cotta: Hard-baked pottery, especially that used in architecture or large-scale decorative art. It may be left with its natural brown surface unglazed and uncolored, painted as was customary among the Greeks, or it may be covered with a solid enamel of grave or brilliant colors.

Terrazzo: Marble or stone chips set into cement for a flooring substance.

Texture (of a rock): A petrographic term that defines the characteristics of a rock that are visible to the naked eye, caused by the disposition of its mineralogical components.

Thermal conductivity: Ability of a material to transmit heat. It is the reciprocal of resistivity. Good insulators, including some carpets, have high resistivity (R-value) and low thermal conductivity.

Thermal lag: When a fixed temperature device operates, the temperature of the surrounding air will always be higher than the operating temperature of the device itself. This difference is commonly called thermal lag and is proportional to the rate at which the temperature is rising.

Thermal shock resistance: The ability of a material to be subjected to rapid temperature changes without physical failure.

Thermal shock: A stress created by an extreme change in temperature that may result in cracking of the plaster that has not yet attained its ultimate strength.

Thermoforming: Thermoplastic sheets are heated to a formable state and shaped to a mold. Air pressure is evacuated between the sheet and the mold.

Thermometer: A temperature measuring instrument.

Thermoplastic fabrics: Materials such as vinyl, olefin, polyester, and nylon that become soft or moldable when heat is applied.

Thermostat: A device that controls heat temperature and responds to temperature change.

Thick slab: A slab with a thickness exceeding 80 mm (about 3-1/4").

Thin slab: A slab with a thickness of less than 20 mm (about 3/4").

Three-coat work: Plastering put on in three coats; superior to two-coat work. Ordinarily, in three-coat work the first coat is rough mortar, the second is scratched, that is, scored with the trowel to enable the finishing coat to hold to it more firmly, and the third is the finishing coat, which may be of sand finish or white finish.

Three-quarter bath: A bathroom containing a water closet, lavatory, and shower bath.

Three-way lamps: Incandescent lamps that have two separately switched filaments permitting a choice of three levels of light such as 30/75/100, 50/100/150 or 100/200/300 watts. They can only be used in the base down position.

Threshold current: The minimum available fault current at which a fuse is current limiting.

Threshold: A strip fastened to a floor beside a door.

Through: Any receptacle for fluids in the nature of an open channel or gutter with or without an outlet.

Thrust: A force that pushes and tends to compress, crush, displace, or overturn a body. The thrust of an arch is the force tending to push back or overturn the pier or abutment. It may also be defined as the horizontal component of the reaction of the abutment, and, therefore, uniform throughout the arch.

Tie, chain: An iron tie to connect and hold securely the columns and piers in arched construction or other parts of masonry buildings. The tie bars, or rods, have an eye at each end set upon the hooked ends, or pins, of other bars set in the masonry. Chain ties of many-linked bars were used to excess in French buildings of the last century and are still used in Paris to tie the walls together through the floors, even where iron beams are used for the latter. Chain ties are also employed as belts about the bases of domes and in consolidating defective masonry.

Tie, land: A tie rod or chain tie used to hold a retaining wall, outdoor flight of stairs, or the like, against the pressure of the earth, as after rain. It is built into the wall and may be secured to a massive pier or simply held to the earth by timbers or stone beams set crosswise.

Tie beam: In common wooden-framed construction, especially in roofing, the large horizontal piece that crosses from wall to wall or between any points of support and forms the lowest member of a truss into which the rafters are framed. Its center is often kept from sagging by a king-post. The main horizontal transverse timber that carries the feet of the principals at wall-plate level.

Tie rod: A rod, usually of iron, used as a tie to prevent the spreading of an arch or piece of wood or iron framing. In the commonest form it replaces the tie beam, king post, or other simple member intended to resist tension.

Tie wire: Soft annealed steel wire used to join lath supports, attach lath to supports, attach accessories, etc.

Tie: Anything used to resist a pull and prevent the spreading of the two sides of a roof, the separating of the two solid parts of a hollow wall, the collapsing of a trussed beam, and the like. Much used in composition.

Tied activity: An activity that must start within a specified time or immediately after its predecessor's completion.

Ties: There are two types used for the attachment of lath: (A) the butterfly tie, which is formed by twisting wire and cutting so that the two ends extend outward oppositely and (B) the stub tie, which is twisted and cut at the twist. See saddle ties.

Tile, book: In the United States, a hollow terra-cotta tile for light fireproof roofs and ceilings, so called because it has the form of a closed book. When laid, the convex edge of one fits into the concave edge of the next. The plane edges are supported by light T irons or the like.

Tile, crest: Tile made to form part of a cresting or ridge covering, as of a roof. It may form part of a very elaborate cresting.

Tile, crown: A flat roofing tile, called also in England plain, thack, or roof tile. They are laid like slates with two nailings upon laths or battens, with or without mortar. The term is also applied to a ridge tile.

Tile, Dutch: A wall tile of enamelled and painted earthenware. The term was applied originally to tiles made at Delft and elsewhere in the Netherlands and used for the facing of chimney pieces and the like. They are generally painted in dark blue on a white ground.

Tile, encaustic: In English ceramic work, a tile decorated with a painted pattern, rather than one of a uniform color, which is called a mosaic tile. The term encaustic is inaccurate as used in the United States, and is to be considered a trade name.

Tile, foot: A paving tile 12 inches square.

Tile, hip: A ridge tile that covers a hip; each tile laps over the one next below.

Tile, hollow: Same as hollow brick.

Tile, pan: (A) A roofing tile having a concave surface, distinguished as an imbrex or gutter tile, alternating with one having a convex surface, distinguished as a tegula or covering tile. The joint between two of the former is covered by one of the latter, so that when laid, the surface of the roof presents a series of ridges and furrows running continuously from the ridge to the eaves; hence, this species of tiling is sometimes called ridge and furrow tiling. (B) A roofing tile made with a ridge and furrow or a double curvature in each piece, or so that, when laid, the upturned edge of the concave part of one tile is fitted to the downward-turned edge of the adjoining tile, making a water-tight joint.

Tile, plane: A flat roofing tile, usually about the size of a small slate.

Tile, ridge: A tile of arched form made to fit over a ridge and correspond with the pan tiles or flat tiles of the roof. Somewhat similar tiles are laid over the hips. Otherwise called crown tiles. In some cases the raised arched ridge is a part of the same tile with the flat covering part. The whole is then called a ridge tile.

Tile, roll roofing: Tile whose joints are covered by overlap, or of separate gutter-shaped pieces inverted. When laid such tiles form a series of continuous ridges alternating with furrows running at right angles or diagonally to the ridge pole.

Tile, wall: Tile, thinner than floor tile, especially adapted to the facing of a wall, as in the lining of a passage or in a bathroom.

Tile, weather: A tile used as a substitute for shingles, slates, or weatherboards in covering the walls or roof of a frame building. Such tiles are thin, pierced with holes for nailing, arranged to overlap, and often cut with round or polygonal-shaped tails.

Tile or flag: A mass-produced slab of preset dimensions.

Tile: (A) A piece of solid material used for covering a roof. Roof tiles may be either flat or of different sections to produce ridges and valleys, and so that one form covers the joints between tiles of another form. (B) Any slab of hard material, large or small, but especially one of many rather small pieces, used together to form roofing, flooring, wall facing, or the like. Most tiles have always been made of baked clay, but marble, stone, and other materials are used. (C) By extension, and because of the application of the name to all pieces of baked clay used for accessories to building, a piece of drain pipe; one section of a continuous tube. Often called draining tile or drain tile.

Timber: Growing or cut wood suitable for building because of its quality and size, fit for use in building, excluding that which has been cut up into planks or boards and, in the United States, that cut smaller than about 6" X 6".

Time and material (T & M): Work agreed to between the owner and the contractor with payment based on the contractor's cost for labor, equipment, material, and an add-on factor to cover overhead and profit, or based on material costs plus a specified amount per hour of labor which includes direct labor and overhead profit.

Time and material change orders: Change orders under which the contractor is reimbursed under the time and material method.

Time clauses: Clauses providing times for commencement and completion of work and, sometimes, for completion of portions of the work within specified milestones. Also, provisions for time extensions.

Time delay fuse: A fuse that will carry an overcurrent of a specified magnitude for a minimum specified time without opening. The current and time requirements are defined in the UL 198 fuse standards.

Time extension: See extension of time.

Time is of the essence: A contract provision requiring one or both of the parties to fulfill their obligations within a specified time. Failure to do so is a substantial breach of contract.

Time now line: See status line.

Time of completion: Date established in the contract, by name or number of days, for substantial completion of the work. See completion date, contract time.

Time: Time limits or periods stated in the contract. A provision in a construction contract that time is of the essence of the contract signifies that the parties consider that punctual performance within the time limits or periods in the contract is a vital part of the performance and that failure to perform on time is a breach for which the injured party is entitled to damages in the amount of loss sustained.

Timely completion: Completion of the work or designated portion thereof on or before the date required.

Timely manner: Performance of contractual obligations, including notices, submittals, and responses in time to prevent interference with the other party's performance.

Timely payment: Payment within the time prescribed by the contract documents. See prompt payment.

Toenailing: To drive a nail at a slant with the initial surface to permit it to penetrate into a second member.

Tolerance: An allowance given to a member because exact measurements are impossible.

Tongue, cross: A piece similar to a dowel, used to strengthen a tenoned frame. On either side of the tenon a strip of hardwood is let in to the shoulder of the piece upon which the tenon is worked. These strips fit into slots cut on either side of the mortise in the other piece, thus giving great additional stiffness.

Tongue, loose: A slender strip for securing the joint between two abutting parts by being driven into two corresponding grooves formed on their adjoining faces or edges.

Tongue and groove: Finished with tongues and grooves, as the planks intended for flooring. Usually, each plank has one edge tongued and the other grooved.

Tongue: A projecting member, as a tenon; a continuous ridge left on the edge of a board or plank, intended to fit into a groove worked in the edge of another board plank. This joint is in constant use in flooring and occasionally in the siding of houses. Some object to tongued-and-groove flooring because, when heavy pressure comes at a point near the edge of a plank, one side of the groove may break away and the floor be permanently injured.

Tool: To finish or dress a surface, especially of stone, so as to leave the marks of the tool; said especially of work with the drove chisel and the toothed chisel.

Tooth chiseling: Processing with a stone-cutter's chisel that produces parallel stripes.

Toothing: Leaving projections or tenons on the end of a wall, so that when required, another or the same material may be bonded into it and make a continuous surface. The jamb stones of an aperture are made long and short so as to tooth in with the general wall surface, whether of stone or brick.

Top flat surface: The flat surface that can be sanded with a drum sander.

Topographic survey: The configuration of a surface, including its relief and the locations of its natural and manmade features. Usually recorded on a drawing showing surface variations of contour lines indicating height above or below a fixed datum.

Torn grain: A roughed area caused by machine work in processing.

Torsion: The act or result of twisting, as of a timber so distorted in drying or under some especial strain.

Torsional strength: The strength of a member or material to resist a torsional force; i.e., a force tending to separate or break by twisting; an abbreviated and erroneous term.

Torus molding: A rounded or convex edge manufactured at an end of a slab or other stone product.

Total float: The difference between the amount of time available to accomplish an activity and the time necessary. The difference between an activity's late start and its early start. The amount of extra time available to an activity, assuming that all activities preceding have started as early as they can and that all activities following will start as late as they can. See critical path method.

Total flooding system: Supply of Halon 1301 arranged to discharge into and fill to the proper concentration, an enclosed space or enclosure about the hazard.

Traced: Supplying auxiliary heat to a pipe or piece of equipment by a comparison line containing a hot fluid or electric resistance. It can be thermally or mechanically bounded to the pipe or equipment.

Tracery: Decoration made of lines, narrow bands and fillets, or of more elaborately molded strips, but always without, or but little, representation of natural objects.

Tracings: In times past, architects paid people to make tracings of their original drawings to give to the contractors. This process was supplanted by blueprinting and left us with the term tracing which is still used to describe that original drawing on translucent paper. The blueprinting process itself has since been largely replaced by a much more inexpensive process called *diazo*.

Trade (craft): (A) Occupation requiring manual skill. (B) Members of a trade organized into a collective body. (C) Contractors whose employees perform the work of the trade.

Trailer park sewer: That part of the horizontal piping of a drainage system that begins 2' (0.6m) downstream from the last trailer site connection, receives the discharge of the trailer site and conveys it to a public sewer, private sewer, individual sewage disposal system, or other approved point of disposal.

Trammel: A light-braced frame with two arms at right angles, containing shallow grooves in which two of the pointers move while the third describes the curve. The points are usually driven into a soft slip of wood, easily fitting the grooves, but even with this assistance it is difficult to draw the lines evenly, and it may be better accomplished with the aid of a square.

Transfer molding: Similar to compression molding but the plastic is heated to flexibility before it reaches the mold. It is forced into the mold by a hydraulic plunger.

Transition: In architectural style, the passing from one style to another. This process is always slow and is marked by the designing of buildings, or parts of buildings, in which the new style is not yet fully in control. This will be more visible in buildings of secondary importance, though occasionally a monument of great size and cost will show the changing style.

Transmittance (U): The combined thermal value of all the materials in a building section, air spaces, and surface air films. It is the time rate of heat flow and usually expressed as Btu/(h).

Transparent finish: A stain or clear finish that allows the natural characteristics and color of the grain of the wood surface to show through the finish.

Trap, bell: A trap consisting of a bell, or cup, inverted over the mouth of the pipe, which rises under it from the bottom of a basin or cistern. It is so adjusted that the edge of the bell is submerged by the liquid that drains into the basin. Thus, the liquid can pass under the bell to the pipe, while the gas is prevented from rising by the bell.

Trap, D: A trap having the general shape of the letter D or, at least, one nearly semi-circular bend, as a boxlike receptacle into which a soil pipe empties and another leads out. This form is not used in good modern work.

Trap, grease: A device for preventing the accumulation of kitchen grease in waste pipes, whereby they become stopped up. Grease traps retain the grease and permit it to solidify. Some are forms made in iron or brass are attached directly under the kitchen or pantry sink. Sometimes iron or stoneware grease traps are placed outside of the building, on the line of the kitchen drain. They are useful for kitchens of large institutions.

Trap arm: That section of a plumbing fixture drain between the trap weir and the vent pipe connection.

Trap primer: A device or system of piping to maintain a water seal in a trap.

Trap seal: The maximum vertical depth of liquid that a trap will retain, measured between the crown weir and the top of the dip of the trap.

Trap: A device attached to a plumbing fixture, consisting essentially of a bent or U-shaped part of a pipe (with or without enlargement). Although it permits the discharge of water when the fixture is used, it is intended to retain enough to form a water seal against the passage of air or gases from soil, sewer, or waste pipes. There are many kinds of traps, including drain and sewer traps, waste-pipe traps, non-siphoning traps, and traps with anti-siphon vent attachments.

Traverse: Any member, or structure, set or built across an interior or an opening, especially (A) a screen, railing, or other barrier, used to keep away intruders, to allow passage from one place to another by an official or dignitary, or to conceal anything. (B) A transom, or the horizontal member of a chambranle.

Tread: (A) That part of a step in a stairway, of a doorsill, or the like, upon which the foot rests, as distinguished from the riser. The term applies equally to the upper surface alone, and to the plank, slab of marble or slate, or thin casting of iron, in those staircases that each step is not a solid mass. (B) The horizontal distance from one riser to the next. Thus, a stair is said to have 12-1/2" tread, that being the whole distance which a person moves horizontally in ascending one step. This distance is measured without regard to the nosing, which, where is exists, projects beyond the riser in each case.

Triangulation: The achievement of stability in an assembly of triangular struts and ties.

Trim: (A) The framing of a wall, door, window opening, or around an architectural element. (B) Water supply and drainage fittings installed on a fixture to control the flow of water into the fixture and the flow of waste water from the fixture.

Trimmed slab: A slablike building element cut to the shape and size required for installation; also called a tile or flag.

Trimmer: A beam or joist to which a header is nailed in framing for a chimney, stairway, or other opening.

Trimming: Cutting slabs or semifinished products to size with a disk machine.

Trowel finish: See finish coat.

Trowel: (A) A mason's tool made of a thin plate of metal, approximately lozenge-shaped, always pointed at the end, and fitted with a handle; used for spreading and otherwise manipulating mortar in laying up masonry and for breaking and trimming bricks. (B) A plasterer's tool, generally a small parallelogram of thin wood with a handle underneath; used either like a pallet to hold putty or mortar or to spread or float the last coat upon walls or ceilings. Masons use a tool of the same sort for kneading and mixing putty in pointing joints.

Truss, howe: A bridge truss in which the struts are diagonal, crossing one another, and the chords are held together by vertical ties.

Truss, pratt: A bridge truss in which the struts are vertical and the ties diagonal.

Truss, scissor beam: A roof truss in which the feet of the principal rafters are connected, each with a point on the upper half of the opposite rafter, by ties that cross at the middle like the two halves of a pair of scissors. It is a weak truss, fit for small spans only.

Truss, warren: One with parallel chords between which the braces and ties are set at the same angle, to form a series of isosceles triangles.

Truss: A frame or jointed structure designed to act as a beam of long span, while each member is usually subjected to longitudinal stress only, either tension or compression.

Tube: A conduit or conductor of cylindrical shape, with walls too thin to receive a standard pipe thread.

Turbulence: Any deviation from parallel flow in a pipe due to rough inner wall surfaces, obstructions, or directional changes.

Turnkey operation: Performance by a single company or joint venture of all phases necessary to design and build a construction project, including land acquisition, financing, design, and construction. Sometimes used to describe design and construction by one company, excluding land acquisition and financing.

Turpentine: A volatile oil used as a thinner in paints and as a solvent in varnishes. Chemically it is a mixture of terpenes.

Turtle back: (A) Same as blistering. (B) Denotes a small localized area of windcrazing. See blister.

Two-coat plastering: The application of plaster in two successive coats. In two-coat plastering the basecoat is applied in one operation.

Two-wire smoke detector: A smoke detector that initiates an alarm condition on the same two wires that also supply power to the detector.

Type S hydrated lime: See lime.

U

Underlayment: A material placed under finish coverings, such as flooring or shingles, to provide a smooth, even surface for applying the finish.

Underabsorbed overhead or unabsorbed overhead: An accounting term referring to the inability of overhead recovery based on a percentage of contract billings to cover fixed overhead costs during periods in which contract billings are substantially reduced because of project delays.

Undercoat: A coating applied before the finishing or top coats of a paint job. It may be the first of two or the second of three coats. In some usage, same as priming coat.

Undercroft: An underground vaulted room.

Undercut: In carving, as in high reliefs, cut away behind; said of the background or of the whole carving, the figures standing clear, or nearly clear, from the background.

Underfloor raceway: Any facility provided to hold wires, cables, or bus bars. Raceways may be of metal or insulating material. The term includes right metal, nonmetallic, flexible conduit, cellular metal, or concrete raceways and underfloor duct.

Underground piping: Piping in contact with the earth below grade.

Uniform system: Coordination of specification sections, filing of technical data and product literature, and construction cost accounting organized in 16 divisions based on an interrelationship of place, trade, function, or material.

Unilateral mistake: An error in a bid or contract formation caused by one party to the contract without knowledge of the other.

Unions: A coupling device for connecting pipes.

Unit prices: Amounts stated in a contract as prices per unit of measurement for materials or services as described in the contract documents.

Unknown conditions: Conditions concealed underground (or in existing facilities to which new construction will be attached) which are not observable by either designers or contractor at the time of bidding and that increase costs or time for performance beyond what a prudent bidder would anticipate.

Unqualified bidders: Bidders whose experience, expertise, financial capacity, or past performance may render them unqualified to perform adequately the work being bid. See lowest responsible bidder.

Unreasonable delay: Delays of a type and duration that both parties could not reasonably have contemplated at the time of entering into the contract.

Unwritten warranties: Implied warranties under law or custom not explicitly set forth in contract documents or written certificates.

Updating: The regular review, analysis, evaluation, and recomputation of the CPM schedule.

Upset price: See guaranteed maximum cost.

Upstream: Location in the direction of flow before reaching a referenced point.

Urea and melamine: Plastics that are resistant to acids and chemicals. Urea's temperature performance is from -70° F to 170° F and Melamine's temperature performance is from -70° F to 210° F. These plastics are hard and strong but can be broken. They will not burn, but flames will cause discoloration. They are mainly used for laminated surfaces, electrical devices, tableware and buttons.

Urinal: A toilet room or plumbing fixture intended for men's use, consisting of a trapped bowl, trough, or gutter, connected with a waste or drain pipe and arranged with a flushing device similar to that for water-closets. The room in which this fixture is placed or fitted up.

Utilities: Services provided by public utilities, or substitutes thereof, such as electric power, natural gas, water, and telephone service. See site facilities.

Utility column: Post placed between the ceiling and floor in conjunction with ceiling distribution systems. It is used to conceal communications and electrical wiring from the ceiling space to the desk.

Utility lawn building: Any detached accessory structure used exclusively for the light storage of lawn and garden equipment, materials, and other similar items. Such buildings are incidental to residential and commercial facilities and shall not be used for the storage of major appliances, heavy equipment, shop machinery, vehicles, etc.

Utility: A program to maintain or edit files or perform other needed functions.

V

Vacuum breaker: See backflow preventer.

Vacuum relief valve: A device to prevent excessive vacuum in a pressure vessel.

Vacuum: Any pressure less than that exerted by the atmosphere and may be termed a negative pressure.

Valley: The internal angle formed by the junction of two sloping sides of a roof.

Valuation: Estimate; appraisement. As applied to the cost of a structure, the valuation is approximated either by comparing it, according to its relative cubical area, with the known cost of another similar building, or, more accurately, by estimating it in detail, according to the quantity, character, and cost of material and labor involved in its erection.

Value (work performed to date): The planned cost for completed work, including that part of work in process that has been finished.

Valve: (A) In a double door, French window, or the like, one of the two folds, or leaves. (B) Any device that regulates liquid or gas flow by opening, closing, or obstructing its passage. They may be of the screwed, sweated, body only, or welded types.

Vanity: A bathroom lavatory set into a cabinet.

Vapor barrier: A material or materials that, when installed on the high vapor pressure side of a material, retard the passage of the moisture vapor to the lower vapor pressure side. Any material that has a water vapor permeance (perm) rating of one or less.

Variable-length slab: A slab with a fixed width and length that varies within certain limits.

Variance of activity: The square of the activity standard deviation. Used in determining the standard deviation of an activity successor event. A variance can be a difference between intended and actual dollars, time, materials or configuration.

Variance: Any actual or potential deviation from an intended or budgeted figure or plan.

Varnish: A substance made from a resinous material dissolved in linseed oil.

Vehicle: The liquid portion of a finishing material; it consists of the binder (nonvolatile) and volatile thinners. The liquid portion of a paint.

Veiling reflections: The reflections of light sources in the task that reduce the contrast between detail and background (e.g. between print and paper), thus imposing a "veil" and decreasing task visibility. Veiling reflections are sometimes referred to as reflected glare but this is properly used only when specular reflections of the light source in the task and background are so bright as to be disturbing, whereas veiling reflections are often much less obvious. Their subtle effect in reducing contrast and thus visibility is nonetheless present.

Velocity: The time it takes to move an object in a straight line from point to point.

Vendor: A person or organization who furnishes materials or equipment not fabricated to a special design for the work. See supplier.

Veneer, quartered: Veneer in which a log is sliced or sawed to bring out a certain figure produced by the medullary or pith rays, which are especially conspicuous in oak. The log is flitched in several ways to allow the cutting of the veneer in a radial direction.

Veneer, rift cut: Veneer in which the rift or comb grain effect is obtained by cutting at an angle of about 15° off of the quartered position. Twenty-five percent (25%) of the exposed surface area of each piece of veneer may contain medullary ray flake.

Veneer, rotary cut: Veneer in which the entire log is centered in a lathe and turned against a broad cutting knife which is set into the log at a slight angle.

Veneer, sliced: Veneer in which a log or sawn flitch is held securely in a slicing machine and thrust downward into a large knife which shears off the veneer in sheets.

Veneer plaster base: A gypsum board used as the base for application of a gypsum veneer plaster.

Veneer plaster lath: A large-size base for veneer plasters, having an incombustible core, essentially gypsum, surfaced with a special face paper suitable to receive veneer plaster.

Veneer plaster: A specially formulated high-strength plaster for third coat application to large-size veneer plaster lath.

Veneer: A thin sheet or layer of wood, usually rotary cut, sliced or sawn from a log or flitch. Thickness may vary from 1/100" to 1/4".

Vent, loop: Any vent connecting a horizontal branch or fixture drain with the stack vent of the originating waste or soil stack.

Vent pipe or system: Pipe or pipes installed to provide a flow of air to or from a drainage system or to provide air circulation to protect trap seals from back pressure and syphonage.

Vent stack: A vertical vent pipe installed primarily for the purpose of providing circulation of air to and from any part of the drainage system.

Vent: A pipe or duct that allows flow of air as an inlet or outlet.

Ventilating air: Air supplied to or removed from a source by natural or mechanical means.

Ventilating duct: General duct work involved with the process of supplying or removing air by natural or mechanical means, to or from any space.

Ventilation: To remove or give air naturally or mechanically.

Vermiculation: Masonry block decoration, consisting of shallow channels resembling worm tracks.

Vermiculite: A mineral that can expand when heated into a lightweight, porous material, used as aggregate with various gypsum plasters.

Vertical access: Stairs, ramps, elevators, or other means of traveling from one floor level to another. In designing access for physically handicapped people, escalators are usually not considered as an acceptable means of vertical access.

Vertical pipe: Any pipe or fitting that is installed in a vertical position or makes an angle of not more than 45° with the vertical.

Vertical shaft turbine pump: A centrifugal pump with one or more impellers discharging into one or more bowls and a vertical educator or column pipe used to connect the bowls to the discharge head on which the pump driver is mounted.

Vestibule: A small waiting room ancillary to a larger room. An entrance hall.

Vibration resistance: The ability of a material to resist mechanical vibration without wearing away, settling, or dusting off.

Vibration service lamps: See rough service lamps.

Vibration: The alternation of direction or pressure of motion.

Vinyl: Plastic that can withstand heat up to 130° F and is resistant to most foods, oil, water and cleaning products. Vinyl is mainly used for raincoats, insulation, plugs, and wall and floor coverings. It is recommended for use indoor only.

Visual comfort probability: (VCP) A discomfort glare calculation that predicts the percent of observers positioned at a specific location (usually four feet in front of the center of the rear wall) who would be expected to judge a lighting condition comfortable. VCP rates the luminaire in its environment, considering such factors as illumination level, room dimensions and reflectances, luminaire type, size and light distribution, number and location of luminaries, and observer location and location and line of sight. The higher the VCP, the more comfortable the lighting environment. IES has established a value of 70 as the minimum acceptable VCP.

Visual edge: The line on an isolux chart that has a value equal to 10% of the maximum illumination.

Visual field: The field of view that can be perceived when the head and eyes are kept fixed.

Vitrified sewer pipe: Conduit made of fired and glazed earthenware installed to receive waste, sewage, or sewerage.

Volatile thinner: A liquid that evaporates readily and is used to thin or reduce the consistency of finishes without altering the relative volumes of pigments and nonvolatile vehicles.

Volt: The unit for measuring electric potential. It defines the force or pressure of electricity.

Voltage rating: The maximum voltage at which a fuse is designed to operate. Voltage ratings are assumed to be AC unless specifically labelled DC.

Volume method (of estimating cost): Method of estimating probable total construction cost by multiplying the adjusted gross building volume by a predetermined cost per unit of volume.

W

Wadding: Hanging staff by fastening wads made of plaster of Paris and excelsior or fiber to the casts and winding them around the framing.

Wainscot: The lower 3' or 4' of an interior wall when it is finished differently from the remainder of the wall.

Waiver of lien: An instrument by which a person or organization who has or may have a right of mechanic's lien against the property of another relinquishes such right. See mechanic's lien.

Waiver of subrogation rights: Relinquishment of the right to subrogate against another party. Sometimes required to avoid unnecessary duplication of legal expense. See subrogation.

Wall covering: Any type of paper, plastic, fabric, or other material fastened to a wall as a finish surface.

Wall wash lighting: A smooth, even distribution of light over a wall.

Wallplate: a longitudinal timber laid on top of a wall to receive the ends of the rafters.

Wall-hung: A plumbing fixture supported by a wall.

Walls: Vertical partitions dividing one space from another or enclosing a space.

They may or may not bear a load from above.

Walnut: A hardwood, dark brown in color, used almost exclusively in furniture making because it receives polish well and is easy to work with.

Wane: Bark or lack of wood from any cause, except eased edges, on the edge or corner of a piece of lumber.

Warp: (A) Weaving term for yarns in woven fabrics and carpets that run lengthwise. Warp yarns are usually delivered to the loom from a beam, a large spool with hundreds of ends wound on it, mounted behind the loom. Woven carpets usually have three sets of warp yarns, which may be wound on three loom beams. These include stiffer warp for lengthwise strength and stiffness, pile warp which forms the carpet surface tufts, and chain warp which interlaces with fill yarn to lock the structure together. (B) Any deviation from a true or plane surface, including crook, bow, cup, twist, or any combination thereof.

Warpage: The change in the flatness of a material caused by differences in the temperatures or humidities on the opposite surfaces of the material.

Warranty: (A) An obligation of a manufacturer or seller for quality and satisfaction performance of a product. (B) A statement that certain facts are true by one party to a contract and accepted by the other party.

Wash-out: Lack of proper coverage and texture buildup in machine-dash textured plaster caused by the mortar being too soupy.

Wash: A thin coat of plaster, cement, or paint applied to a surface or material.

Washability: The ability to withstand occasional cleaning with an appropriate detergent solution.

Washer (insulation): Used with weld pins to hold insulation in place.

Waste and overflow fitting: A bathtub drain fitting that provides both bathtub drain outlet and an overflow to drain excess water.

Waste material: Portions of a block or slab, usually along the perimeter, that are removed during manufacturing.

Waste mold: A precast plaster mold made to form a decorative monolithic or cast-in-place concrete. Mold cannot be removed without being destroyed.

Waste pipe: The discharge pipe from any fixture, appliance, or appurtenance in connection with the plumbing system that does not contain fecal matter.

Waste stack: A vertical line of piping extending one or more floors that receives the discharge of fixtures other than water closets and urinals.

Waste: The discharge from any fixture, appliance, area or appurtenance, that does not contain fecal matter.

Water absorption: The increase in weight of a test specimen expressed as a percentage of its dry weight after immersion in water for a specified time.

Water closet: A waterflushed plumbing fixture designed to receive human excrement directly from the user of the fixture.

Water conditioning or treating device: A device that conditions or treats a water supply to change its chemical content or remove suspended solids by filtration.

Water cooler: An electric appliance combining a water cooling unit and a drinking fountain.

Water hammer arrester: A device, other than an air chamber, designed to provide protection against excessive surge pressure.

Water hammer: the forces, pounding noises, and vibration that develop in a piping system when a column of noncompressible liquid flowing through a pipe line at a given pressure and velocity is stopped abruptly.

Water heater: An appliance for heating water for purposes other than space heating.

Water main: The water supply pipe for public or community use. Normally under the jurisdiction of the municipality or water company.

Water meter: A device used to measure the amount of water that passes through a water service.

Water repellent: A wood-treating solution that deposits waterproof or water-resistant solids on the walls of wood fibers and ray cells, thereby retarding their absorption of water. Having the quality of retarding the absorption of water by wood fibers and ray cells.

Water resistant gypsum backing board: A gypsum board designed for use on walls primarily as a base for the application of ceramic or plastic tile.

Water resistant: Capable of withstanding limited exposure to water.

Water riser: A water supply pipe that extends vertically one full story or more to convey water to branches or fixtures.

Water service: The pipe from the water main to the water distributing system of the building.

Water softener: An appliance that removes dissolved calcium and magnesium and other water hardness minerals from water by ion exchange.

Water supply fixture unit (WSFU): A measure of the probable hydraulic demand. The supply fixture-unit valve for a particular fixture depends on its volume

rate of supply operation and the average time between successive operations.

Water supply system: The building supply pipe, the water distributing pipes and the necessary connecting pipes, fittings, control valves, and all appurtenances carrying or supplying potable water in or adjacent to the building or premises.

Water vapor permeability: The property of a substance that permits passage of water vapor and is equal to the permeance of a 1" thickness of the substance. Permeability is measured in perm inches.

Water vapor transmission (WVT): The rate of water vapor flow, under steady specified conditions, through a unit area of a material between its two parallel surfaces and normal to the surfaces. Metric unit of measurement is $1 \text{ g}/24 \text{ h} * \text{m2}$. See permeability, permeance, perm.

Water-distributing pipe: A pipe that conveys potable water from the building supply pipe to the plumbing fixtures and other water outlets in the building.

Water-repellent paper: Gypsum board paper surfacing that has been formulated or treated to resist water penetration.

Water-repellent preservative: A liquid designed to penetrate into wood and impart water repellency and a moderate preservative protection. It is used for millwork, such as sash and frames, and is usually applied by dipping.

Water-resistant core: A gypsum board specially formulated to resist water penetration.

Water-service pipe: The pipe from the water main or other source of water supply to the building served.

Waterproof cement: Portland cement to which waterproofing agents, such as surface repellents, have been added at time of blending materials at the mill.

Waterproof: Impervious to prolonged exposure to water.

Watt (W): The unit for measuring electric power. It defines the power or energy consumed by an electrical device. The cost of operating an electrical device is determined by the watts it consumes times the hours of use. It is related to volts and amps by the following formula: watts = volts x amps.

Wave molding: A molding consisting of a convex curve between two concave curves.

Weather barrier: A material that when installed on the outer surface of thermal insulation, protects the insulation from weather damage incurred by rain, snow, sleet, wind, solar radiation, and atmospheric contamination.

Weather/vapor barrier: A material that combines the properties of a weather barrier and a vapor barrier.

Weatherboarding: Horizontal, overlapping board siding used in wood frame or timber construction.

Weatherstrip, narrow: Narrow or jamb-width sections of thin metal or other material to prevent infiltration of air and moisture around windows and doors. Compression weather stripping prevents air infiltration, provides tension, and acts as a counterbalance.

Weld pin: Made of carbon steel, stainless steel or aluminum in various lengths for attaching insulation to metal surfaces. Applied by welding. Manufactured in 10, 12, and 14 gauges.

Weld stud: See stud.

Welded wire fabric (interior or exterior lath): A plaster reinforcement of copper-bearing, soft annealed wire not lighter than 16 gauge, zinc coated, electrically welded at all intersections, forming openings not to exceed 2" x 2", may have an absorptive paper separator and an additional paper backing or foil backing for waterproofing or insulation; flat or self-furring.

Welding: Two pieces of metal that are fused by heat and another metal. Welding equipment is run by gas or electricity.

Well matched for color and grain: Members shall be selected so that the color of adjacent members is similar and nearly uniform in appearance. The grain figure or other natural markings shall be similar in character and appearance. Members with only flat grain shall not be permitted adjacent to members with only vertical grain. Members with mixed grain are only permitted adjacent to members with similar grain at the adjacent edge.

Wet vent: A vent that also serves as a drain.

Whitecoat: See putty coat.

Wicking: Action of absorbing by capillary action.

Width: The cross-direction wall covering measurement after trimming for hanging.

Wind pressure: The force exerted by wind upon any part of a building. This is generally a matter of inquiry and precaution only in the matter of high roofs or spires since the walls of an ordinary building, when built in the common way, are not affected by any winds but tornadoes or tropical hurricanes. The force of wind upon a roof is generally considered as a horizontal force, tending to push the roof over; but it really acts along a line normal to the sloping surface.

Windbraces: Short curved braces connecting side purlins with principals.

Winder: A step, more or less wedge-shaped in plan, adjusted to the angle or curve of a turn in a stair. Since a winder cannot conform in width to the size assumed for the fliers, this regular spacing is usually measured on the curve naturally followed by a person ascending with his hand on the rail along the well or newel side. This is usually taken as a curve parallel to the rail, and from 15" to 18" from it. The risers of such steps should not radiate from a common center except in a winding stair. It is more convenient, and safer, to cause them to converge somewhat before the turning place is reached, so that the fliers pass almost insensibly into the winders. The common plan in an ordinary stair, and one to be generally condemned, is to permit three or even four steps to occupy a quarter-pace, with risers radiating from a common point.

Window, compass: In England, a bay window of a semicircular or otherwise curved plan; rare or obsolete in the United States.

Window, dormer: Originally a window of a dormer. In modern times, a window in the vertical face of a relatively small structure projecting from a sloping roof. The vertical face may be a continuation of the wall carried up above the eaves. In common speech the term is applied to the whole structure, including the vertical side walls, which are usually triangular, and the roof, which may be gabled, hipped, or of penthouse form. See bay window.

Window, hit and miss: A window used in stables. The upper sash is fixed and glazed; the lower half of the window is filled in with two wood gratings, the outer one being stationary, the inner one moving in a groove. The bars of the movable grating are made wider than the openings of the stationary one, so that these openings are completely covered when the inner sash is closed down.

Window, lowside: A window, usually very small, set much below the level of the larger windows, especially in a church, principally English.

Window, pede: A window so positioned with another larger window above as to be supposed to symbolize one of the feet of Christ.

Window, rose: A circular window divided into compartments by mullions, forming tracery radiating from, or having more or less geometrical relations with, the center.

Window, transom: (A) A window divided by a transom into an upper and lower part. (B) A window above a transom, as in a doorway.

Window, Venetian: A window characteristic of the neoclassic styles, having an arched aperture flanked by a narrow, square-headed aperture on either side, separated by columns of pilasters.

Window, wheel: A large, circular window on which the radiation of tracery from the center is more or less distinctly suggested. It may be considered a variety of

the rose window, in which the tracery is more distinctly committed to a spokelike arrangement. Also called Catherine wheel window.

Window, wyatt: In Ireland, a square-headed Venetian window, or a wide window divided into three openings by two mullions.

Window: An opening for the admission of light and sometimes air into the interior of a building; by extension, the filling of this opening with glass, as usual in modern times, with the frame and sash, or casement, and their accessories. The term is usually confined to openings in vertical or nearly vertical surfaces, as walls. It is impracticable to distinguish between the opening and the filling, as can be done between doorway and door.

Wire cloth lath: A plaster reinforcement of wire not lighter than No. 19 gauge, 2 1/2 meshes per inch and coated with zinc or rust-inhibitive paint. (Not to be used as reinforcement of exterior portland cement plaster.)

Wire fabric lath: See welded wire fabric.

Wire housing facilities: The facilities provided, as part of the building, to conceal wires, cables, and the associated terminations.

Wire: Assembly of conductors within a common protective sheath.

Wireless radio linker: A device that receives, verifies and retransmits binary coded low power radio frequency alarm and supervisory signals generated by smoke detectors and initiating devices.

Wireless smoke detector: A smoke detector that contains an internal battery or batteries that supply power to both the smoke detector and integral radio frequency transmitter. The internal power source is supervised and degradation of the power source is communicated to the control panel.

Withholding payments: Delaying payment of moneys that would otherwise be due under a contract for reasons generally specified in the contract, such as inadequate performance or failure to pay subcontractors or suppliers, thus creating lien liabilities for the owner. May also be used to describe delays in payment that constitute breaches of the contract.

Witness: See expert witness.

Wood failure: The area of wood fiber remaining at the glue line following completion of a shear test, expressed as a percentage of the test area.

Wood fiber plaster: See gypsum plaster.

Wood fiber: See fiber.

Wood filler: An aggregate of resin and strands, shreds, or flour of wood, used to fill openings in wood and provide a smooth durable surface.

Wood rays: Strips of cells extending radially within a tree and varying in height from a few cells in some species to 4" or more in oak. The rays serve primarily to store food and transport it horizontally in the tree.

Wood stain: A dye used to color wood. Different types of stain includes water stain, varnish stain, alcohol stain, and chemical stain.

Work breakdown structure (WBS): A subdivision of a project into logical phases, functions or areas similar to an organizational chart.

Work item: See activity.

Work order: (A) A field order interpreting the contract documents. (B) A change order, particularly when issued by a prime contractor to a subcontractor and not related to a change order issued by the owner. (C) An order for work not within the scope of the contract documents by a subcontractor or contractor to another subcontractor or contractor.

Work pace inertia: A description of the rhythm of work crews or breaks in the rhythm caused by interference, deviations from schedules, or delays.

Work plane: The plane at which work is done and illumination is specified and measured. Unless otherwise indicated, this is assumed to be a horizontal plane 30" above the floor.

Work unit: A calendar time unit when work may be performed on an activity

Work: (A) All labor necessary to produce the construction required by the contract documents, and all materials and equipment to be incorporated in such construction. (B) Handling marks and/or grain raising due to moisture, not considered a defect.

Workability: See fat.

Worked: Machined or formed in any manner except surfaced on four sides.

Working conditions: (A) Conditions on the job site reflecting on productivity of labor, including safety, housekeeping, congestion, accessibility, and availability of lifts and material hoists. (B) Conditions in labor agreement other than wages, monetary benefits, and administrative clauses.

Working drawing: Any drawing showing sufficient detail so that whatever is shown can be built without other drawings or instruction; a detail. See drawings.

Workmanship, first class: The finest or highest class or grade of workmanship. All joints shall be tight and true. Cabinet parts shall be square, plumb, and in alignment and securely glued. The exposed surface shall be free of splits, torn or chipped surfaces, tool marks, cross sanding, gouges, dents, sand through, and other similar defects.

Workstation: Furniture and space used by employees for longer than one-half hour at a time.

Workers compensation insurance: Insurance covering liability of an employer to his employees for compensation and other benefit required by workers compensation laws with respect to injury, sickness, disease, or death arising from their employment.

Woven wire fabric: A plaster reinforcement of zinc-coated wire, not lighter than no. 18 gauge when woven into 1-inch openings, or not lighter than No. 17 gauge when woven into 1-1/2" openings. Lath may be paper-backed, flat or self-furring.

Wrought iron: A hard iron that softens when heated enough to be molded into desired shape. It contains less than .02% of carbon. This is peculiarly important, beyond that of any other hammered metal work, partly because of the abundance and the hardness of iron, but more especially because of its ability be welded and forged.

X,Y,Z

XCU: Letters that refer to exclusions from coverage for property damage liability arising out of (A) explosion or blasting, (B) collapse of, or structural damage to, any building or structure, or (C) underground damage caused by and occurring during the use of mechanical equipment.

Y branch: One having an arm at an oblique angle with the main part, giving three openings.

Yankee screwdriver: A screwdriver that when the handle is pushed down the screw turns quickly.

Yew: A softwood, pale red in color, that receives a polish well and is close grained.

Yoke vent: A pipe connecting upward from a soil or waste stack to a vent stack to prevent pressure changes in the stacks.

Z bar metal: The colloquial name given to a soft aluminum metal manufactured in Z-shaped lengths and used in wall-to-wall carpet installation to hold and protect ends of carpet in nontraffic areas.

Z beam: A beam whose section is nearly that of the letter Z of the Roman alphabet, having a web perpendicular to two flanges which it connects by their opposite edges. Those of the smaller dimensions are commonly called Z bars.

Z clip: See S clip.

Zebrawood: A hardwood extremely colorful and difficult to work with. It is straight grained and strangely striped

Zonal cavity method lighting calculation: A lighting design procedure used for predetermining the relation between the number and types of lamps or luminaries, the room characteristics, and the average illuminance on the work-plane. It considers both direct and reflected flux.

Zoning permit: A permit issued by the appropriate governmental authority authorizing land to be used for a specific purpose.

Permissions

Additional material in this book was used with the following permissions:

Includes material from ASPE Data Book, Ch. 21: Formulas, Symbols & Terminology, published by the American Society of Plumbing Engineers. Used with permission.

Carpet and Rug Institute

Contract Document Terminology, reprinted with permission by Associated Specialty Contractors, Inc.

National Insulation and Abatement Contractors Association, 99 Canal Center Plaza, Suite 222, Alexandria, VA 22314

Project management terms used with permission of Calin M. Popescu, PE, Ph.D

The Illumination Engineering Society

Western Institute of Cabinetmakers